BEYOND BROADWAY

The Quest for Permanent Theatres

BEYOND

* * * * * * *

BROADWAY

THE QUEST FOR
PERMANENT THEATRES

By Julius Novick

A Dramabook

 HILL AND WANG · NEW YORK

PREFACE
TO THE
1969 EDITION

In the eighteen months since I finished this book, most of the resident theatres, most of the time, have been continuing to grind out *The Three Sisters* and *Six Characters* and *Twelfth Night*, more or less as they had been doing. There is a widespread feeling among the actors, directors, and managers I've been talking to that it's very difficult to do good work and lead a decent life, under the conditions that prevail in most resident theatres: lack of money, lack of time, lack of talent, an abundance of in-fighting and jockeying for position. Personnel turnover continues to be high; several artistic directors have left their theatres,* and so have innumerable actors; the permanent, close-knit ensemble with a style of its own still seems, at most theatres, to be a not-quite-attainable, or not-yet-attainable, or totally unrealistic, ideal.

All this is not yet cause for despair. I have argued throughout this book that mediocre work is not always, from the point of view of an audience, a total loss, and that nearly (though not quite)

---

* Douglas Seale has departed from Center Stage in Baltimore and Michael Flanagan from the Loretto-Hilton Center in St. Louis; Richard Block is out and Jon Jory is in at the Actors Theatre of Louisville; and K. Elmo Lowe, at the age of seventy, has retired as head of the Cleveland Play House, and has been succeeded by William Greene, formerly head of the workshop program at the Tyrone Guthrie Theatre. It seems, however, that artistic directors, when they depart, are doing so more amicably than they used to; they no longer hurl accusations at their boards of directors, and consequently the businessmen on those boards no longer seem to be such a menace to free expression. Perhaps the businessmen have become more flexible, or perhaps the more rebellious artistic directors have all been forced out. Of course, the war between the artists and the businessmen could break out again at any moment.

any professional theatre is better than none; every once in a while, in the theatre—in almost any theatre—things do have a way of falling miraculously right. All the same, mediocrity punctuated by an occasional miracle isn't what anybody has been hoping for.

Not everything, of course, has stood still. The new programs to provide professional training for the theatre, recently instituted at a number of campuses, have begun to turn out graduates; there has not yet been time for these young artists to exert much influence, but I continue to believe that they will. And, in the past year or two, certain widespread and significant developments have begun to make themselves felt in the resident theatres. One of these new tendencies is economic, and for the worse; one primarily artistic, and for the better.

Our country, it seems, has fallen upon peculiar times. We have money for guns *and* for butter. We pour billions into Vietnam and prepare to lavish billions on playing the anti-missile-missile game, yet there seems to be plenty of money left for the private sector of our domestic economy. The suburbs pullulate with bungalows and split-levels, and every middle-class kitchen and living room and family room and rumpus room is chockablock with appliances and gadgets; the big-car builders and the mink-breeders are both doing very well. But suddenly there seems to be a desperate shortage of money for communal, public, civilian concerns. Welfare programs, hospitals, colleges, schools, and libraries all face shortages and cutbacks.

These cutbacks reflect a limitation in government funds, and where the arts have been dependent upon government subsidies, they have also suffered. The National Endowment for the Arts, which makes grants of federal money to arts institutions, has cut back sharply on its disbursements, jeopardizing a number of resident theatres.

Some people have been saying that sooner or later the government would have to take over the major responsibility for subsidizing the performing arts, but most of the money to meet the inevitable and ever-growing deficits of performing-arts organizations has traditionally been raised not from government but from private sources. Nowadays, however, private money for the arts, like government money, is becoming increasingly difficult to find. (The money, it is said, is going instead for "urban" or "ghetto" projects—

the sort of projects for which there is less and less government money available, as the need for them grows more and more obvious and imperative.) It is well known that Lincoln Center, with all its prestige and all its connections, is having difficulty raising funds. The symphony orchestras have a traditional claim on society money (as the resident theatres do not), and they have recently been recipients of a dazzling burst of Ford Foundation munificence which far eclipses anything that Ford or anybody else has done for the theatre; yet symphony orchestras in several cities are currently talking merger, as a drastic way of cutting costs. When money for all the arts is so tight, it is not to be expected that the resident professional theatre, a relatively new and ill-endowed kind of institution, could escape feeling the pinch.

It is true that new professional theatres continue to be founded. In January, 1968, Theatre Toronto made its debut, the result of a merger between two smaller Canadian companies. The new organization was housed amid the Edwardian splendors of the Royal Alexandra Theatre, a 1,500-seat house in downtown Toronto; its artistic director was Clifford Williams of the Royal Shakespeare Theatre. In October of the same year, the Atlanta Municipal Theatre, a tripartite organization comprising the Atlanta Repertory Theatre, the Atlanta Ballet Company, and the Atlanta Opera Company, began its career as a tenant of the new $13,500,000 Atlanta Memorial Arts Center. Its first production was *King Arthur*, a masque by John Dryden and Henry Purcell, which employed all three of the AMT's component troupes and cost $250,000. For the moment, Atlanta had two resident professional theatres: the Atlanta Repertory Theatre, and the older, somewhat less lavish Theatre Atlanta. And beginning in October, 1969, the Goodman School of Drama in Chicago, which has previously offered student productions with imported professional stars in leading roles, will sponsor a fully professional resident company.

Yet it seems these days as if more theatres are dying than being born. The Pittsburgh Playhouse folded at the end of its 1967–68 season. The Front Street Theatre in Memphis probably will not open in the fall of 1969. The National Repertory Theatre lasted only one season at Ford's Theatre in Washington; there was a dispute between the NRT and the committee of Washingtonians in charge of Ford's, and the NRT has not been heard of since the dispute subsided. Even the APA, which had begun to seem like a fixture on Broadway, has been forced to leave New York. It had hoped that its usual $250,000 grant from the National Endowment for the Arts would be raised to $500,000; instead, because of a cut in congressional appropriations, there was no grant at all. On top of that, the only popular success of the 1968–69 season was Molière's *Misanthrope*; the failure of the season's last production, an unfortunate *Hamlet* starring Ellis Rabb himself, was the last straw. Even the tremendous profits of a tour of *The Show-Off*, starring Helen Hayes, were not enough to save the situation. The APA and the Phoenix Theatre, which sponsored it, dissolved their ties. The Phoenix will continue to produce in New York; the APA will take to the road again.

The new companies have also been vulnerable. At Theatre Toronto, Clifford Williams resigned as artistic director after opening his second season with an unhappy production of Marlowe's *Edward II*; a company called Theatre Toronto will take up residence late in 1969 at Toronto's new St. Lawrence Center, but it will be essentially a new organization. The Atlanta Municipal Theatre folded ignominiously after only two months of existence, having run up over $300,000 in debts. It appears as if the AMT's former ballet company will survive on its own; the opera company is defunct; the Alliance Resident Theatre, formed to replace the Repertory Theatre, finished out the season on a more modest basis, and is to be continued for another season at least. At around the same time that the Atlanta Municipal Theatre went broke, Theatre Atlanta, the other local company, was evicted from its splendid theatre; it owed the landlady a lot of money, and furthermore she is widely reported to have been displeased by Theatre Atlanta's production of *Red, White, and Maddox*, a satirical musical about Georgia's governor. At this writing the company is not functioning, and its future is doubtful.

Eighteen months ago I wrote, "In spite of setbacks, the trend is still up." That seems to be no longer true. The retrenchment period has begun; nobody knows how long it will last. Now we will see which theatres (if any) will survive.

As things get worse on the economic front, however, they seem—in one way at least—to be getting better on the artistic front. The resident theatre has been traditionally uneasy about doing new plays, although a few groups have specialized in them: the Theatre Company of Boston, for instance, and the Firehouse Theatre (lately of Minneapolis, now planning to move elsewhere). Recently, these new-play theatres have been joined by the Public Theatre of the New York Shakespeare Festival, the Forum of the Repertory Theatre of Lincoln Center, and the Negro Ensemble Company, all in New York, and each of these newer groups has had at least one outstanding critical and popular success. Furthermore, even the companies not explicitly committed to experimentation have increasingly tended to include new plays—either world premières of American works, or American premières of foreign works—in their regular subscription seasons. People have begun to realize that simply "doing the classics" will not bring the millennium; the new catch phrase is "contemporary relevance," and this is often taken to mean new plays. Unfortunately, it turns out that new plays will not bring about the millennium either; many of them are pretty bad.

But one or two of these new plays have been quite formidably good—so much so that the resident theatre has very suddenly become an important source—perhaps the most important source—of new American plays. The resident theatre has traditionally spent much of its time redoing the plays that Broadway and Off-Broadway have done already; now, at last, with the spectacular success of *The Great White Hope* leading the procession, there is some traffic in the other direction. This season (1968–69), for the first time, Broadway and Off-Broadway have been significantly affected—one might almost say dominated—by work which originated in the resident theatre.

The transfer from resident theatre to Broadway is handled in various ways. The Broadway production of *The Great White Hope* is essentially the production that was originally done at the Arena Stage in Washington, redirected for the proscenium stage by the original director, and presented by a commercial management. The Broadway production of *We Bombed in New Haven* by Joseph Heller, on the other hand, was essentially a new production, with a new director; only a couple of cast members were retained from the original production at Yale.

This by no means exhausts the roster of regional theatre scripts produced on Broadway during the same season. There were two that had been first done by the professional company at Brandeis University, one from the Milwaukee Repertory Theatre, and one from the Washington Theatre Club. Theatre Atlanta brought its entire production of *Red, White, and Maddox* to Broadway. (A huge success in Atlanta, it was a failure in New York.) In the fall of 1969, Broadway will see *Indians* by Arthur Kopit, which was mounted this spring at the Arena Stage; Gene Frankel will once again direct, and several cast members will be retained.

In the case of both *The Great White Hope* and *We Bombed in New Haven*, the script had been significantly tightened and improved for the Broadway production, presumably because the author had had a chance to ponder the lessons of the earlier mounting. (Mr. Heller improved his script more than I would have thought possible.) Clearly, a regional theatre production affords an author a much better chance to tinker with his script than he would have amid the frenzies of the conventional pre-Broadway road tour or Broadway preview period. This state of affairs has not escaped notice; the production of Edward Albee's *Box-Mao-Box* at the Studio Arena Theatre in Buffalo seems to have been specifically intended as a Broadway tryout, and the Washington production of *Indians* has something of the same aspect.

This means that tremendous new resources of talent, and perhaps even money, are now open to the resident theatre—but, perhaps, tremendous new opportunities for corruption as well. What will it do to a theatre's integrity if it gets into the habit of mounting productions with one eye on New York? If too many members of the permanent company get transferred to New York, who will be left at home to mind the store? (This is what ruined Joan Littlewood's Theatre Workshop company.) Yet there is something encouraging about these foreboding questions; it is no small triumph that the resident professional theatre, so often merely a repository of genteel stodge, should have become alluring enough to be in danger of this kind of seduction. It suggests that these theatres are becoming what they have never yet been: an important creative force. This may help them to survive in these difficult times; and it may enable them to deserve to survive.

JULIUS NOVICK

July 2, 1969

PREFACE

This is not primarily a book about plays or actors or productions; it is a book about theatres, professional theatres in the United States, with a few from Canada thrown in—some fifty of them in all. Ten years ago such a book would not have been possible because most of these theatres did not then exist. It is only lately that communities all over the country have been rediscovering that a theatre can be an institution, not merely a piece of real estate. This book is about that rediscovery.

Not every professional theatre aspiring to permanence is included, for several reasons. Theatres are constantly emerging (and sometimes disappearing) in all directions; there is no telling where one will break out next, or where one has just broken out, unbeknownst to the wider world. Futhermore, there is the problem of definition: how professional does a theatre have to be in order to be a professional theatre? Every authority has a different list. A contract with Actors' Equity, the performers' union, is the most common criterion, but many theatres that have "gone Equity" use amateurs in small roles; on the other hand, there are several important theatres that do use professional actors, but that for one reason or another have not signed up with Equity.

I finally decided that as far as I was concerned, any theatre that paid salaries to a significant proportion of its acting company was a professional theatre, and that, with certain exceptions, I would write about as many of these as possible. I left out all crassly commercial ventures (Barn Dinner Theatres and so forth), for obvious reasons. I also left out the New York Off-Broadway and Off-Off-

Broadway theatres, because they are different kettles of fish altogether and deserve books of their own. But I think I may claim, with these exceptions, that theatres of all kinds are included, and that no individual theatre of any particular significance is omitted.

This book offers no final judgments; it is an eyewitness report on the present state of a highly volatile phenomenon. It is a personal book, a book about what I have seen and heard during some two hundred and fifty evenings, afternoons, and mornings spent watching plays at theatres which hope they are permanent institutions. Theatres change from season to season, and from production to production; I may have been unfair to certain theatres through the ill-luck of having visited them when less than their best work was on view. I have tried to guard against this, however, by seeing at least two productions (and sometimes many more) at nearly every theatre discussed in this book, and by being careful how I generalized.

There are some facts in the book, but also a great deal about my own reactions and opinions. The judgments offered are subjective ones, because I believe that in talking about any kind of art, these are the judgments that matter most. This is a book about organizations, buildings, budgets, programs, policies, and personalities, but ultimately, I hope, it is a book about art. And art cannot be measured; it can only be felt.

JULIUS NOVICK
January 2, 1968

ACKNOWLEDGMENTS

In the summer of 1965, the Ford Foundation's Program for Reporters, Editors, and Critics of the Visual and the Performing Arts gave me a grant to enable me to take a year off and devote myself full-time to becoming a better critic. One of the means by which I pursued this laudable end was a transcontinental tour of the resident professional theatres, which I undertook in the spring of 1966. Out of that journey grew this book. The foundation gave me the grant, however, as its contribution to my general development as a critic, and not with the expectation that any particular piece of writing would result from it. The foundation did not sponsor this book, and indeed I have traveled many thousands of miles in the book's interest since the grant expired. I am grateful to the foundation, but I have not written as if I were beholden to it.

Robert Hatch, the managing editor of *The Nation,* asked me for a series of articles on resident professional theatres, and I spent that first, Ford-financed trip gathering material for this series, which duly appeared in *The Nation* during the summer of 1966. These articles were the basis of this book. It was Mr. Hatch, also, who first suggested that the articles might warrant expansion into a book; I am particularly grateful to him for his encouragement.

In writing the book, I have drawn not only on my resident-theatre series in *The Nation,* but on a number of other articles of mine that appeared in *The Nation, The Village Voice,** *Harper's Magazine, The Educational Theatre Journal, The New York*

* Reprinted by permission of *The Village Voice.* Copyrighted by The Village Voice, Inc. 1958, 1960, 1963, 1964, 1965, 1966, 1967.

Times,* and *The National Observer*. I am grateful to all of these publications for permission to reprint this material.

The book's title comes from a headline that *The Nation* supplied for one of my articles; it probably owes something also to Norris Houghton, whose book *Advance from Broadway* (New York, 1941) had a chapter entitled "Broadway and Beyond," in which Mr. Houghton urged the establishment of the kind of theatres that my book deals with.

In the course of my researches, I spoke and corresponded with nearly two hundred people, most of them connected with various theatres. I am grateful to them for sharing their time, their knowledge, and their ideas with me; this book could not have been written without their help.

* © 1967/1968 by The New York Times Company.

CONTENTS

FOREWORDS
FOR THE RESIDENT
PROFESSIONAL THEATRE

"I'm scared that the regional theatre, by the time it is mature, will have bored the shit out of millions of people all over the country."

> —Andre Gregory, former artistic director of the Theatre of the Living Arts, Philadelphia, and the Inner City Repertory Company, Los Angeles*

"We need money, but as much as we need money we need—individually—to find, heighten and explore the informing idea of our theatres. We need to find our own faces. And not by looking at each other but by looking within ourselves. We already look too much alike. It has become a bore.

"And when we know what we are about, that is when we will have real acting companies instead of merely collections of actors. Then, and not before. . . .

"If we seek the Negro audience, America's new proletariat, we should integrate our acting companies and seek out plays that speak to Negro concerns. If we want high school and college-age

---

* Speech delivered at the Tulane Drama Review Theatre Conference, New York, November, 1965, reprinted in "The New Establishment," *Tulane Drama Review*, T32 (Summer, 1966), p. 115.

audiences, we must compete with films in terms of the vividness and size of our work, its tempo and color, its immediacy of themes. If we wish to attract what Herbert Marcuse, the professor of philosophy at the University of California, calls "the new working class"—engineers, technicians, researchers and teachers— who are not economically depressed but sensorially dead, then we must attract them with the directness of our work, its abrasion, its physical energy, its source within life itself. . . ."

—Zelda Fichandler, producing director
of the Arena Stage, Washington, D.C.*

"A play is not a document; it is an *address*; the first considera- tion must be the relevance to the audience for which it is performed."

—Harold Clurman†

* Speech delivered at the American Educational Theatre Association Con- vention, New York, August, 1967.
† "Reflections on True Theatre," *The Nation*, May 16, 1966, p. 587.

BEYOND BROADWAY

The Quest for Permanent Theatres

1 INTRODUCTORY

The Rise of the Hinterland Legits

The American theatre is currently in the midst of a profound redeployment. Broadway is not dying, and it is not going to die, but it can no longer perform all its old functions. It used to be that Broadway *was* the professional theatre in America. It supplied us with all kinds of plays: serious and light, domestic and foreign, new works and revivals. Through its provincial extension, "the road," it served the entire country. Today Broadway has virtually abandoned its old function of reviving the classics, and year by year it comes closer and closer to the abandonment of serious new plays as well. Broadway is becoming an institution devoted more and more to the purveying of light entertainment. (So what else is new?)

This is a legitimate function, and, on occasion, Broadway performs it very well indeed. If only we had a theatre in this country that could do Shakespeare and Sophocles as well as Broadway does Neil Simon and Abe Burrows! (Of course, Shakespeare and Sophocles are harder to do.) It seems to me beside the point (though it is lots of fun for those who have the temperament for it) to attack Broadway for the functions it has abandoned. What we have to do is find and foster theatrical institutions capable of taking up these functions and performing them well. Off-Broadway and, latterly,

Off-Off-Broadway have helped to fill the vacuum, but they have severely limited resources and a severely limited audience. (Readers in Atlanta, Baltimore, Syracuse, St. Louis, Milwaukee, and Seattle are invited to compose essays on the subject, "What Off-Broadway and Off-Off-Broadway Mean to Me.") Something more is needed—something, in particular, that can reach audiences outside of New York. And this something more is finally being supplied.

On March 9, 1966, a historic headline appeared above the lead article in *Variety*, the theatrical trade paper. "Hinterland Legits Top Broadway," it proclaimed. The article announced that "For the first time since the heyday of stock, there are more professional actors working in regional theatre than in Broadway and touring productions . . . it appears that the numerical focus of legit has shifted from Broadway, with all the ramifications that fact may suggest." Evidently, as *Variety* put it, "something big in legit is happening outside New York, with attendant grist for touters of an American culture boom." (Of course, this "something big" is happening inside New York too, at Lincoln Center, in Central Park, and elsewhere.) All over the country there are professional theatres where for many decades there were none.

But what kind of theatres are they? Not the familiar "little theatres" and "community theatres" that have for so long provided the hinterland with amateur theatricals. The new companies do not rely on part-timers and hobbyists for talent, except sometimes in minor capacities; they employ professionals and pay them a living wage (more or less). Usually they have contracts with Actors' Equity and sometimes with other theatrical unions. Professional theatres they are, but not commercial theatres. They do not compete with the road-company houses, where those exist; for the most part, they do not bother much with Broadway commercial comedies; they are interested in art, not money (although they try not to be self-righteous about it). They are all incorporated as nonprofit institutions, and most of them operate on deficits. They survive by going to the public as Good Causes; they enroll ladies' auxiliaries to help out in annual subscription campaigns; they solicit funds from foundations, from government, and from private donors. Because of our tax laws governing contributions and donations, this means that they are in effect partly supported by the general public; this, it seems to me, ought to obligate them to serve the general public.

These theatres aim to become permanent institutions. Most of them have permanent premises. Usually they try to assemble a resident company of actors who remain together from play to play throughout part or all of a season of thirty or forty weeks, with guest performers to play roles that cannot be cast from the company. A core of actors is usually retained from one season to the next, in the hope of developing a genuine ensemble. Always there is some continuity of management and policy, some attempt to create something more than a lot of single, separate, unrelated productions, some effort, however timid and tentative, to stand for something.

To cite once again the inevitable analogy, these theatres exist to provide a public service for their communities, like the local library, art gallery, and symphony orchestra. Some of them offer a wide variety of theatrical resources: experimental productions (on Monday nights or in a second, smaller auditorium); special performances for children and teen-agers; courses in acting and other theatrical subjects; advice to amateur drama groups; speakers who will talk about theatre wherever two or three are gathered together; free open-air productions in the parks; tours of the surrounding areas; and so on. But in almost every case the primary offering remains a subscription series of major productions mounted by and at the theatre itself.

There are a number of generic names for these theatres, none entirely satisfactory. They are sometimes called repertory theatres, as similar institutions are in England. But "repertory" has another meaning: in a strict sense it denotes a theatre in which two or more plays are constantly being presented in alternation, so that the bill changes several times a week, as at the Comédie Française, the Moscow Art Theatre—or the Metropolitan Opera. We have a few such theatres: the Seattle Repertory, for instance, and the Tyrone Guthrie Theatre in Minneapolis. But by this definition such theatres as the Milwaukee Repertory Theatre, the Repertory Theatre, New Orleans, and the Repertory Theatre of Lincoln Center are not repertory theatres at all, since they operate, like most of our theatres, on the stock system, whereby a production has an uninterrupted run of several weeks and then makes way for another.

Why not call them stock companies then? Because the word is redolent of the worst kind of old-fashioned, routine professionalism. These theatres have their faults, but they are not merely the cold-weather equivalent of summer stock.

They are often called regional theatres, but this too is a half-misnomer. To many people it suggests folk plays being performed somewhere in Appalachia by genuine hillbillies. The new professional theatres are in regions, I suppose—everyplace is in a region, just as everyone is a native. But these theatres draw very little except their audiences from their regions. They are not parochial; they do not perform "regional drama"; their plays come from the international repertoire of classics and "serious" plays, with special attention to what Broadway and Off-Broadway have been doing lately. Their actors, with few exceptions, come not from the neighborhood but from the New York talent pool. Their function, so far, has been not to create new locally originated drama but to import and disseminate metropolitan and international drama through productions that have been made on the spot but betray few local signs. The nature, the identity of each theatre depends far more upon its artistic director than upon any other factor, and most artistic directors would do the same sort of work wherever they found themselves.

The most common designation is resident professional theatre, cumbersome as that is. I will use "resident theatre" and sometimes "regional theatre" more or less interchangeably.

The ancestors of these theatres are the amateur "little theatres" which sprang up in various parts of the country during the twenties, full of high hopes and ringing manifestoes, to present the avant-garde drama of the day. The hopes and the manifestoes were never justified; with the Depression, another theatrical renaissance bit the dust. A number of little theatres survived, however, with their ideals somewhat impaired, by turning to conventional Broadway material. One such theatre—the Cleveland Play House—turned professional, but almost nobody followed its example.

Then in 1947 the late Margo Jones founded her famous professional theatre (now defunct) in Dallas. In the same year Nina

Vance, who had worked with Miss Jones, founded a new amateur group, the Alley Theatre, in a rented dance studio in Houston; seven years later Miss Vance (who had moved her enterprise into a converted fan factory) signed up with Actors' Equity, and turned the Alley into a professional theatre. Meanwhile in 1950 Zelda Fichandler, a housewife in Washington, D.C., took over an old movie house and started the Arena Stage, which "went Equity" in its second season. And in 1952 Herbert Blau and Jules Irving, two teachers at San Francisco State College, began the Actor's Workshop of San Francisco in a loft behind a judo academy. (Both Blau and Irving had originally come from New York; they later went back there, with results that were not altogether happy. But that is another story.)

The Alley and the Workshop remained amateur houses for several years; they and the Arena were all born in poverty and struggled for a long time, with survival a vividly immediate problem, before they took hold and began to grow. Slowly these theatres began to attract attention; slowly it became clear that resident professional theatre was a conceivable, a possible, even a practical thing. In 1959 the Ford Foundation began to spend money on it, allotting $479,000 for three-year matching grants to the Alley, the Workshop, and the Arena to enable them to import established professional actors on full-season contracts at $200 a week. Since 1962, the Ford Foundation has granted over ten million dollars directly to various resident theatres; other foundations have followed suit on a more modest scale; recently the National Endowment for the Arts, an arm of the U.S. Government, has begun making grants to resident theatres.

A major breakthrough came when Sir Tyrone Guthrie turned his tremendous talents and tremendous prestige toward the founding of such a theatre in Minneapolis. Because Guthrie was Guthrie, his theatre did not need to start small, in makeshift quarters, with a company of unknown actors and an infinitesimal budget. A committee of Minneapolis businessmen raised money for a new $2,250,000 theatre and a $715,000 operating budget, and Dr. Guthrie recruited a company headed by Jessica Tandy, Hume Cronyn, George Grizzard, and Rita Gam. The opening of the Tyrone Guthrie Theatre attracted national attention; in its first season, the new company played to 193,344 people. Thanks to

Guthrie, moreover, it immediately became not only one of the biggest but possibly the best of the resident professional theatres in this country.

By this time, many businessmen and civic leaders were becoming aware that resident professional theatre was a Good Thing. As the mayor of Milwaukee said, in proclaiming Milwaukee Repertory Theatre Week, "The Milwaukee Repertory Theatre increases Milwaukee's prestige and competitive stature among other cities which recognize theatre as an important community asset not only for its own citizens but for attracting industry . . ." Even if an executive never goes to the theatre himself, he may well be glad to be reassured that he is not establishing his new plant in a cultural desert and he can use the existence of the theatre as an inducement to attract new personnel to work for him. A theatre lends "class" to a city; class is pleasant for its own sake and is likely in the long run to be profitable. And so something new began to happen: groups of sober, nonartistic citizens began to band together—in Seattle, in Philadelphia, in Providence—of their own accord, without prodding from theatre people, to raise money and hire a director from New York to come out and start a theatre.

Meanwhile, the Ford Foundation allotted another million dollars to set up an organization called the Theatre Communications Group, with headquarters in New York City, to act as a liaison and service agency for the resident theatres. TCG sponsors exchange visits among directors and staffs of various companies; holds semiannual auditions to help theatres and actors find each other; keeps files on actors and other personnel so that if a theatre needs someone it can put in a phone call and get a list of recommendations; provides transportation money to get directors and designers out to the provinces; provides expert consultants to advise on subscription sales and other matters. Above all, it gives people who run theatres a chance to talk to other people who run theatres. Thanks largely to TCG, resident-theatre people began to develop the sense that they were part of a "movement."

For some time now, the trend has been up. Audiences are increasing, sometimes rapidly. Theatres are moving from makeshift premises in the suburbs to splendid custom-built theatres downtown, often in civic arts centers on the order of Lincoln Center in New York. Some of these arts centers have been criticized by architects, city planners, and journalists, but the theatrical facilities they supply are desperately needed by the resident companies. The new houses usually have twice as many seats as the old, and in several of them, provision will be made for a small, flexible second stage for experimental work. Government money—from the Federal Aid to Education Act and the National Endowment for the Arts—is becoming available. The men who run the resident theatres are young men, most of them in their twenties and thirties, and they are full of plans.

But they are no longer so full of confidence as they once were. Disquieting things have been happening lately. In the summer of 1966 the Actor's Workshop folded in San Francisco after fourteen years of struggle. That same summer saw the opening of the Ypsilanti Greek Theatre in Ypsilanti, Michigan: an attempt to found a major festival devoted to ancient Greek drama. Attendance was so low, and losses were so high, that the new venture barely got through its first season and was unable to mount a second; its revival is unlikely. For the 1966 season, attendance at the Tyrone Guthrie Theatre in Minneapolis was down by 25,000, and the theatre lost $170,000 on the season, a sum more than twice as large as the previous season's deficit, which had been the first in its brief history. During the year after the demise of the Workshop, there were life-or-death financial crises at theatres in Pittsburgh, New Haven, and Memphis, in which the theatres announced that unless they could raise a certain sum by a certain date, they would be forced to close their doors. These crises were reminiscent of the one at the Actor's Workshop the previous year, which the Workshop had survived—temporarily. The result was a widespread sense of turmoil and disquiet; one theatre director described 1967 as "the 1929 of the Regional Theatre."

I do not think the situation is quite so critical as that. The Pittsburgh Playhouse, the Long Wharf Theatre in New Haven, and the Front Street Theatre in Memphis all managed to raise the money they needed; at the moment of writing at least, all three survive. Moreover, during this same season of crisis, new theatres began operations in Atlanta, New Orleans, Syracuse, Detroit, and Oakland, Michigan. The APA Repertory Company established itself in New York, and the American Conservatory Theatre did likewise in San Francisco. The Guthrie Theatre decided to expand into the neighboring city of St. Paul with a three-play winter season. And the Arena Stage in Washington, the Playhouse in the Park in Cincinnati, the Mummers Theatre in Oklahoma City, and the Alley Theatre in Houston are all going ahead with plans for new buildings. In spite of setbacks, the trend is still up.

But the setbacks are real, and the atmosphere of crisis is not entirely unjustified. Nobody knows how many theatres are only slightly less shaky than those that were forced to make their difficulties public, or how many will die in the next few years.

What seems to be the trouble?

In each case, of course, local factors apply. But in general, the immediate problem is that many theatres are reaching the awkward age. They are no longer brand-new. This means, for one thing, that they have had a chance to make mistakes, and their mistakes have had a chance to catch up with them. One theatre, for instance, mounted a summer season of new plays, three world premières plus one American première of an English play, and lost $60,000 on it. Another had been economizing by not paying its taxes; there is a limit to how long you can do that.

Another problem is that by the time a theatre has been around for a few years, its honeymoon with its financial backers is over. The fact that there is enough money in a town to start a theatre does not necessarily mean that there is enough to maintain it. Virtually all resident professional theatres run on deficits, must run on deficits, will always run on deficits.* It takes a while for this realization to sink in. It is not so difficult to raise money once to get a theatre started, but it must be a terrible moment when the board of directors finally realize that they and their friends will be expected to kick in forever. It stands to reason that not all theatres will long survive that moment.

At just about this time the honeymoon with the audience is also over. People will no longer come to the theatre because it is an intriguing novelty; they will only come if they really like it. And

---

* Just about everyone professionally connected with resident professional theatres acknowledges this as a fact; for statistical confirmation by two professors of economics, see William J. Baumol and William G. Bowen, *Performing Arts—The Economic Dilemma* (New York, 1966): the standard source on the economics of the performing arts. Baumol and Bowen add that the deficits will inevitably grow larger and larger as the years pass.

yet student programs and other long-term efforts to develop new audiences will have had no chance to bear fruit.

The real importance of the crises is that they may serve to remind us that the resident professional theatres are still in a very precarious position. They were started as acts of faith: nobody knew, until they tried, whether the major cities of this country contained large enough potential audiences to support theatres. And nobody knows yet. It stands to reason that in some places the answer will be no. Some weeding out must take place. The arts in general have failed to secure an important place in our national life, and the theatre is no exception. If our prosperity holds, many of the resident professional theatres may well prosper also; but if there is a depression, these costly institutions are likely to be found expendable. (A portent may be found in a recent action of New York's culture-loving Mayor Lindsay, who, faced with a budget crisis, cut by $100,000 the city's contribution to Joseph Papp's free-admission Shakespeare Festival.)

If the resident theatres die, not many people, statistically speaking, will miss them. Professional theatre of any kind reaches only an infinitesimal percentage of the people of the United States and Canada. And most of the people who do go to the theatre are uninterested in anything more demanding than *Hello, Dolly!* The resident professional theatres are very small organizations. The auditoriums that they are trying so desperately to fill are seldom large enough to hold even a thousand people; many can accommodate fewer than five hundred. Even those splendid new theatres that are going up in so many places tend to have only about eight hundred seats. Yet in these same cities there are usually concert halls or municipal auditoriums that seat 2,000 to 3,000, and often ball parks that seat upward of 40,000. A theatre of eight hundred seats in a metropolitan area of, say, two million, will have a hard time making much of a dent in the life of the community.

The audience for resident professional theatre, moreover, is almost exclusively a bourgeois audience. All the statistical surveys make this clear, and standing around in a few dozen lobbies makes it clearer. A survey made at the Arena Stage in Washington showed that more than 70 per cent of the audience earned over $10,000 a year, and in this respect the Arena is probably not too far from typical. Now, it represents real progress, no doubt of it, that doctors and lawyers and college professors and perhaps even a few accountants can see serious plays professionally done in Baltimore and Winnipeg and Memphis as well as in New York, but what about the truck drivers and the plumbers and the steelworkers, much less the typists and the ribbon clerks, much less the farmers, much less the poor?

When this question was raised by Richard Schechner of *The Drama Review* (then the *Tulane Drama Review*), Zelda Fichandler of the Arena Stage replied,* "Where were the poor? Mr. Schechner, you ask. Where were the well-to-do? I ask you. The well-to-do have the money and the habit by now and the education and supposedly are in the midst of replacing 'quantitative' issues with 'qualitative' ones? Where are they?"

Mrs. Fichandler runs one of the oldest, most stable, and best of the residential theatres. She is located in Washington, D.C., where, in spite of the strong evidence to the contrary that appears every day in the newspapers, the incidence of intelligent, well-educated people is very high. If any theatre has finally developed a dependable and enlightened audience, it is hers. And yet even the Arena Stage audience has not been fully secured. When Mrs. Fichandler "finally decided the theatre had an audience and could begin to close in on the kind of repertory that really interested it," and planned a couple of seasons accordingly, the theatre lost half its old subscribers (twice as many as usual), and had to pull in its horns.

The point is that the development of an audience that will not function as a drag and a clog on a theatre's artistic efforts is a painfully slow and delicate process that has not yet been completed anywhere. In Washington and elsewhere, progress—substantial progress—has been made; "the people who only came to see Helen Hayes in *Mrs. McThing* now come to see nobody they know in *Major Barbara*," says Mrs. Fichandler.† Already, in Washington, in Philadelphia, and in other cities, the audiences at the resident theatres are far livelier than the Broadway audience.

---

* In a speech delivered at a convention of the American Educational Theatre Association, New York, August 1967.
† *Ibid.*

The task of developing a responsive audience is far from hopeless.

Still, if this is how conditions are after so many years, in a city such as Washington, it can be imagined that to run a newer theatre in a less sophisticated city must be a delicate balancing act, a constant agony of compromise and gamble. On the whole, the audience that comes to the resident theatres—when it comes —likes to see plays it has heard of; it likes to laugh; it is wary of anything too "unusual." A theatre has an obligation to survive; it can only survive by pleasing these people. Yet survival can be purchased at too high a price. The great and difficult secret of success in running a theatre is to devise a program that will challenge the audience without alienating it entirely.

If even the bourgeois audience "who have the money and the habit by now and the education" are so hard to win, it can be imagined that most resident-theatre directors lack the time, energy, and money to do much toward the development of new audiences from among the culturally disenfranchised. I am not the sort of bourgeois radical who gets sentimental about the workers; I see no reason to believe that their presence in the audience would suddenly transform the resident theatres into vigorous, challenging, ballsy, gutsy, independent-minded agencies for the regeneration of our society, as some people seem to think. But this is a democracy, which means that we are committed to the belief that the good things in life should be available to all. The resident theatres have already broken through the geographical barriers that isolated most Americans from the professional theatre. As non-commercial institutions pledged to the public good, and as permanent institutions (so they hope) expecting to be around long enough to be able to wage long fights and enjoy slow-coming victories, the resident theatres, and they only, are in a position to break down social barriers as well. Slowly, I think it is beginning to bother some of the people who run theatres that they have not yet done so. After all, for a theatre to become part of the community at large, and not just the avocation of a tiny minority, is the best way of assuring that it will survive.

Some efforts are being made. By dint of arduous sacrifice, ticket prices are being kept low; in many cases a seat at the theatre— sometimes even a good seat, even on a weekend—is as cheap as a seat at the movies. Even the ribbon clerks could afford it, if they wanted to. But the problem is not fundamentally a financial one; it has simply never occurred to most Americans that going to the theatre is something that *they* could do, and might enjoy doing.

Perhaps it is too late to do much about the mass of adults who don't go to the theatre, but nearly all the theatres are earnestly going after their children. Cut-rate tickets for students are almost universal, but the attempt does not stop there. Many resident theatres give special children's plays on Saturday afternoons. They hold acting classes for children and teen-agers. They send individual actors around to the schools to talk to the students; they send troupes of actors to present programs of scenes in the high schools. They give special performances, at special rates, to which students are bussed in from the schools. More than 100,000 high school students in Providence, New Orleans, and Los Angeles— 35,000 to 40,000 in each city—now get to see three or four productions annually, free of charge, as a result of grants from the federal government. At the American Shakespeare Festival in Stratford, Connecticut, more than a quarter of a million teen-agers attend the student performances annually. Now that funds from the Federal Aid to Education Act are available to school boards for "cultural enrichment programs," such student performances are certain to increase.

There are various dangers inherent in these student programs. Enough thought is not always given to the needs of young audiences; one director wonders very cogently why students are so frequently confronted with *Twelfth Night*, a very sophisticated work very far removed from their ordinary experience. (One of the great attributes of theatre is that it can show you things very far removed form ordinary experience, but it takes time and sophistication to realize this.) There may be very good reasons for showing *Twelfth Night* to students, but do the many directors who do so always know what these reasons are? (At one theatre they told me that of course they put in a lot of horseplay for the kids.) And sometimes the work is simply mediocre or bad, serving to confirm the assumption that theatre is either clumsy and shabby, or else chichi and precious, and in either case of no interest or relevance to the students who have been brought to it. I attended one performance that had been sold out to school groups, but it was half empty; you can lead a horse to water, but you can't always make him drink, especially if the water is tasteless and uninteresting.

Yet these programs are almost our only hope of putting the theatre in touch with a significantly wider audience than the tiny in-group that attends it now. I do not think this hope is entirely unfounded. At Hartford I watched *The Importance of Being Earnest* in the company of a group of high school boys and girls brought there by state funds: academically retarded Negro slum children enrolled in the "Higher Horizons" program. They were attentive and seemed interested; they seemed to be enjoying the occasion more than the play itself (I couldn't blame them; it was not a good production), but most of them now have at least a reasonably pleasant memory to associate with the idea of theatre. After the first act one girl asked, "Where everybody goin'?" At least now she knows what an intermission is. And perhaps some of them will want to return. After a student matinée at another theatre, a boy asked, "Can we come back in the evening by ourselves?" Many people are immune to the theatre virus; but if the entire high school population of a community is exposed to it, the susceptibles will at least be able to discover themselves. If there are enough of them, the survival of the resident professional theatres is assured. If not, perhaps these theatres do not deserve to survive.

Are They Any Good?

Resident professional theatres exist, then, in goodly and increasing numbers; they have become a movement; and they have made some progress in developing audiences. One fundamental question remains (a question that tends to be overlooked by those who go on about "cultural explosions"): is their work any good? I greatly regret, from the point of view of journalistic excitement, that I am in no position either to proclaim a renaissance or to expose a fraud. The work I saw varied in quality, of course; a little was brilliant, and some was bad. But most of the productions I saw tended to be uneven, averaging out to mediocre.

In most resident theatres there are no dependable standards. Clumsy, ill-trained actors labor alongside very fine ones; sometimes a brilliant director will all but camouflage poor acting; sometimes good acting will be wasted on a mixed-up production concept. Widely varying levels of achievement are all mixed up together. In all my travels I never saw a production without some redeeming feature; on the other hand, I seldom saw a production that I could really admire as a whole. The theatrical profession in general is not really ready for the demands that the resident theatres make on it. Many—most perhaps—of the productions I saw were earnest attempts at excellent plays, brought off just well enough to make the whole thing worthwhile for an audience that has no chance of seeing these plays done better.

The resident theatres are young, and certain to improve; even their present level of achievement is by no means contemptible. Nevertheless we may ask how it happens that so much energy, so much devotion, so much ardor, and even a good deal of intelligence and talent, have produced so much work that is barely adequate. It is easy to say that in an imperfect world, what is commonplace will always be more abundant than what is excellent. (So much is implied in the words themselves.) More relevantly, it appears to me that many resident theatres suffer at the same time from the disabilities of youth and the sins of age.

Being young, most of these theatres are still poor. Most people —even most people with money—simply do not understand how much first-rate theatre costs. I asked the artistic director of one theatre why his city had a great orchestra, internationally renowned, while the theatre was merely stable and workmanlike. He told me about a local civic leader, active in cultural affairs, who had recently died, leaving a million dollars to the symphony and $25,000 to the theatre. That is not the only reason of course, but it is by no means irrelevant. About many resident theatres there lingers a subtle atmosphere of makeshift, of cheese-paring, of we-would-do-it-differently-if-we-could-afford-it. Plays written for three settings are performed in two; musicals are done to piano accompaniment; crowd scenes are underpopulated; stages are too small. Compromises of this kind, even when the audience is unaware of them, can have a subliminal effect.

The result can be a vicious cycle: not much money to finance the productions tends to mean shabby productions which tend to mean small audiences which mean not much money at the box office which exacerbates the lack of money to finance the productions, and so on.

Partly because the resident theatres are poor, they have tremendous difficulty in finding and keeping good actors. Many actors, particularly mature actors, are reluctant to leave New York, for several reasons. First, New York is still the heart of the American theatre, and the actor's agent will probably do his best to persuade him to stick around and wait for something better. Second, the actor, especially the mature actor, will generally have settled down to raising his family in New York; bringing them along is difficult, and so is leaving them behind. In either case, maintaining two residences is expensive. Moreover, New York is generally believed to be a better place for an artist to live than Pittsburgh or Memphis. Few resident theatres can afford to pay an actor much more than $250 a week, which does not go very far toward overcoming all this reluctance. And so the resident-theatre directors must choose among the actors they can get, and thus have younger companies than they would like, so that their actors are often called upon to play parts for which they are too young by several decades. Furthermore, Equity contracts allow the use of a certain percentage of non-Equity performers, and the resident theatres are often forced to take broad advantage of this concession in casting smaller roles. This leads to raggedness around the edges: "Wait till you see the village girls in the second act," as one theatre official gloomily remarked.

But the basic problem with actors is that there are just not enough of them around who can meet the demands imposed by the variegated repertories of the resident companies. I saw very little patently phony emotional acting—the Stanislavskyite influence may be thanked for that at least—but a good deal else is wrong. American actors speak abominably, for one thing; it has sometimes seemed to me that the one absolutely indispensable qualification for employment in the resident theatre is a speech defect. A related fault is that "American actors," to quote Jacques Cartier of the Hartford Stage Company, "have in the main not been taught to characterize. American actors tend to want to be themselves in the author's situation. They don't change the way they walk, they don't change the way they speak." This does not matter so much on Broadway or in Hollywood, where an actor is cast for only one role at a time, and there are enough actors around to make it possible to find someone who is the right type by nature. In a resident company, on the other hand, versatility is important.

Many American actors, whatever role they are playing, are incapable of coming across as anything but young Americans of the twentieth century. This again is fine for certain kinds of drama; American actors are unexcelled at playing sensitive juvenile delinquents or neurotic cowboys. But the demands of resident theatres, with their international repertoires, are more extensive than this.

The inability to characterize, the lack of proficiency in the use of voice and movement, are notorious deficiencies of American acting, and their causes have been much discussed. Super-Stanis-lavskyite fanaticism and the absence of a tradition of classical acting in this country are the most common explanations. Stanis-lavsky himself insisted on the vital importance of good speech and technical training for the actor, but many of his American disciples give only the merest lip service to this aspect of the Master's teaching. And until very lately, the universal lack of resident theatres meant that there was virtually no place for the American professional actor to play anything but modern realistic plays; and so our actors are inexperienced. And, naturally, actors did not bother to learn skills for which there was no demand, and schools tended to neglect the teaching of such skills.

The actor situation is bound to get better. As the resident theatre expands, the demand for the well-trained actor increases, and professional training can be expected to improve in response. The actor on his own in New York now has more incentive to take classes in speech and in classical scene study; for the more organizationally inclined, there are new or revitalized programs to train professional actors at Yale, NYU, Columbia, Oakland University (Rochester, Michigan), and the University of Washington (Seattle); another such program is in the works at the Juilliard School of Music. The theatres themselves often have teachers of voice, speech, and movement on the payroll for the benefit of the actors. Directors report, moreover, that actors are more easily enticed from New York than they used to be, now that the idea of regional theatre has become familiar and the removal to Milwaukee or Louisville will no longer be read as a confession of failure in the Big Town. Salaries are looking up. And a group of actors who have spent several years, often their whole professional lives, in the resident theatre is developing; they at least will not be inexperienced.

But what about the directors? The men who stage most of the productions are the "artistic directors," who run the theatres, and their subordinates. They all complain incessantly about the difficulty of finding good actors; perhaps, however, some of the blame for the low standard of resident-theatre acting belongs to these same directors, who after all are responsible for choosing the actors and for coaching them. If American actors are so profoundly inexperienced in the more articulate kinds of theatre, it stands to reason that American directors must also be inexperienced; if American actors have been misled by Method fanatics, how have the directors escaped? One actor—a good one—wrote to *The New York Times* complaining that he found it hard to get work because directors thought his speech was too good; he might be willing to leave New York. The resident-theatre directors insist that they are looking for "the inner thing *and* the outer thing," but are they? And if so, how hard do they look? These are questions that only they and the actors can answer, but they are questions that a critic must ask.

It stands to reason that the young men who run the theatres must suffer from the unfamiliarity, in this country, of the very idea that they are trying to implement, from the lack of a tradition for what they are doing. Where did they learn to run a theatre? Many have never even worked in any theatre but their own. Many got to be artistic directors simply by going out and founding theatres. The only qualification really necessary in beginning a resident theatre is the ability to sweet-talk local plutocrats out of a hundred thousand dollars or more. And this does not necessarily imply creative directorial talent as well.

The final great weakness of the American resident professional theatres can be blamed on no one but the men who run them. These gentlemen are intelligent, articulate, and earnest. They have the most exalted ideas as to the function of their institutions: to "make a connection" with the audience, to "force the community into facing itself," to help people "understand our common humanity better," "to give people's lives a little more perspective, a little more fullness." Herbert Blau, a founder of the San Francisco Actor's Workshop, makes a majestic statement of the resident-theatre ideal:

> Who wouldn't want the theatre that is implied in the Panathenaic procession at the end of the *Oresteia*, where the life of the drama flows right into the life of the community, clarifying its laws, and the audience were to go home to carry it on.*

But between the idea and the reality falls the shadow. In practice, many directors are committed merely to running a theatre, with no particular idea of what effect they want to have on their audiences, of what, really, they want to do. An artistic director is likely to be so preoccupied with hiring actors, directors, and designers, propagandizing for his theatre at social functions, being nice to visiting philanthropoids from the foundations, talking to journalists, planning budgets, and generally holding together the institution he is building, that he may well be tempted unconsciously to take it easy in regard to what he is actually putting on his stage, and why.

According to Zelda Fichandler, this is the sort of conversation that ensues when resident-theatre directors get together:

> Got any good grants lately?
> What's really on Mac Lowry's mind? [He is the Ford Foundation's commissar in charge of giving money to theatres.]
> How's the subscription drive going? Three hundred per cent over last year! Well, good!
> Attendance 89 per cent! Deficit for the year? $100,000 over last year! Well, good! Trouble with the Board? That's bad!
> X Company took three of your actors this year? Listen, that guy you hired away from me has gone to *him* now. They doubled his salary, what are you going to do?
> Know any good T.D.'s [technical directors: the men who take charge of getting sets built]? Voice teachers? Promotion men? Prop

---

* Herbert Blau, *The Impossible Theatre* (New York, The Macmillan Company, 1965), p. 167. Copyright © 1965 by Herbert Blau. This quotation and other quotations from the book are reprinted by permission of the publisher.

girls? Directors? Business managers? Actors who will play supporting roles for $175 a week?

Hear *The Balcony* was too pale for Boston. Funny, it did well in Baltimore and Hartford. What do you think of it for Poughkeepsie?

Liked your brochure. Looked just like ours. And his. And theirs and theirs.*

And so on.

This would tend to indicate that the resident-theatre movement is united by a common concern for means unconnected to ends, and dozens of productions would tend to indicate the same thing. There is a lack of urgency behind many resident-theatre productions, as if the director had had no personal involvement with the play, no strong feeling as to what *this* play had to say to *this* audience at *this* time, no clear idea as to just how *this* play was going to make a connection, help people understand their common humanity, and the rest of it.

I doubt if many resident-theatre managers are really familiar with our heritage of dramatic literature; they stick pretty closely to the plays everyone has read in college. Shakespeare and Molière are popular; otherwise, drama is often assumed to have begun with Shaw and Chekhov. Yet, with all the emphasis on modern drama, very little thought is given to the question of what plays we really need to see *now*. I never heard of any resident theatre producing the *Philoctetes* of Sophocles, although its theme—the conflict between morality and *realpolitik*—is extremely pertinent to our current involvement in Vietnam. And if a play is chosen (as seldom happens) from eighteenth-century England, it will almost certainly be *The Rivals* (New Haven, New Orleans) or *She Stoops to Conquer* (Seattle, St. Paul), jolly, harmless pieces both, although Farquhar's *The Recruiting Officer* is just as funny, offers more opportunity for directorial whizz-bangery, and deals with the very interesting question of how the army induces young men from the poorer classes to go and die in foreign wars. My own political bias is now, I suppose, apparent; but surely an intelligent reactionary director, if there is one, could find a classic with a pertinent right-wing message for our times. (*The Clouds? Coriolanus?*)

* Fichandler, AETA convention speech.

The problem is not that bad plays are being done. I surveyed the schedules of thirty-three theatres for the 1967–68 season; Shakespeare is the most popular playwright, with seventeen productions (and my survey did not include Shakespeare festivals), followed by Shaw with thirteen, Molière with eleven, Albee with ten, Anouilh with seven, and Brecht, Pirandello, and Chekhov with six apiece. The previous season, in thirty-six theatres, it had been Shakespeare in the lead with twenty productions, followed by Shaw with ten, Arthur Miller with nine, Brecht and Molière with eight apiece and Anouilh, Chekhov, O'Neill, and Tennessee Williams with seven each.

It is true that the resident theatres have been slow to produce new plays. Out of 221 productions at the thirty-three theatres I surveyed, only twenty-one were of original scripts. Often a theatre will announce that its schedule will include "the world première of an exciting new American play," and then, at the designated time, produce something like *The Fantasticks* instead. Many artistic directors feel guilty about this. But I have never heard anybody except playwrights seriously allege that really good new scripts are going unproduced. And imagine an artistic director, faced with new plays that he knows his audience won't want to see (audiences resist unfamiliar works on principle) and that aren't really much good. Can you blame him for abjuring the Brownie points issued to directors who do new scripts, and mounting instead something that he has every reason to believe will be both more popular and *better*? Sooner or later the resident theatres, if they are to realize their potential, will have to start bringing forth good new plays. But right now I find it understandable, though far from heroic, that they are hanging back. And certainly the plays they are producing have something to say to us. These plays comprise a limited list, but they are our classics.

The problem is not even that too many theatres are doing the *same* plays; a wider variety would be pleasant for the traveling critic, but the resident theatres are not conducted for his edification. To the man who lives in Seattle and goes to the Repertory Theatre there to see Brecht's *Galileo*, it is immaterial that Boston, Philadelphia, Washington, Cleveland, and San Francisco have already seen it in other productions.

The problem is that good plays are being done, in too many

cases, merely *because* everybody else is doing them, and they come readily to mind when a season is to be planned. Consider, for instance, *The Importance of Being Earnest*. It is an exquisite play, but it is also exquisitely difficult to perform; it demands just those skills that American actors are likely to lack. On the other hand, the movie with Sir Michael Redgrave and the records with Sir John Gielgud both convey it brilliantly, vividly, and faithfully. Finally, although it is a true classic and always welcome for its own sweet sake, few people would argue that it is particularly pertinent to civilization as we know it in Hartford, Louisville, Winnipeg, and Seattle in our time. And yet the resident theatres in all four cities did the play during the course of one recent season.

It has been discovered that audiences respond particularly keenly to plays about their own localities: to New England plays like *The Crucible* and *Long Day's Journey* in Providence, to *Ballad of the Sad Café* in Memphis. This being the case, why do so few theatres ever reflect—in new plays, adaptations, revue sketches, even in the choice of works from the standard repertory—the particularities of their region? Nobody wants an entirely regional theatre that turns its back on the world and preoccupies itself with local color; in the long run the most valuable thing a resident theatre can do is to bring the outside world into its community. But these theatres are becoming "supermarketized"; they are too much alike; they tend to peddle standard merchandise in which they have no personal stake.

There is no reason to demand that all or each of these theatres should speak for one thing only; eclecticism can be a virtue, particularly when a theatre is the only one in town. But many theatres often do not speak for, or about, anything at all, and that is a deficiency that prosperity will not cure. It is a paradox that such young, ardent, dedicated, hard-working men as those who run our resident theatres should allow their attention to be deflected from ends to means, and so be liable to a subtle form of the old man's sin of sloth.

THREE
OLDER
THEATRES

*

The Cleveland Play House

Only a very few resident theatres are survivals from the days before World War II, and the oldest of all is the Cleveland Play House, which sedately celebrated its fiftieth anniversary in 1966. It was founded by a high-minded group of Cleveland amateurs; in its first five years it produced plays by Molière, Goldoni, Beaumarchais, Synge, Claudel, Maeterlinck, and Andreyev, plus a mysterious work called *Snow* by one Przybyszewski. (Names like Maeterlinck and Andreyev, who were among the leading "serious" playwrights of their time, may give us pause. How will our modern repertory of "serious" plays look, fifty years hence?)

In 1921, the Play House hired Frederic McConnell as its first professional executive director; by the time he retired thirty-seven years later, the Play House had evolved from a loosely organized, amateur avant-garde group to a large, stable, and prosperous professional theatre that did a little bit of everything, but specialized in recent Broadway hits and other safe scripts. When Mr. McConnell retired in 1958, he was succeeded by K. Elmo Lowe, whom he had brought with him to the Play House in 1921.

Today Mr. Lowe presides smilingly over one of the busiest of the resident professional theatres. During the 1966–67 season, between September and May, the Play House mounted no fewer than sixteen productions in its three theatres, for an audience of some 130,000 people. The Play House's annual Shakespeare Festival offered *The Tempest* at special matinées for 25,000 teen-agers. Children's theatre classes during the regular season involved 400 kids, and children's theatre performances had an attendance of 9,600. During the summer of 1967, a Play House company gave its annual series of performances at Chautauqua, before about 16,000 spectators. That same summer, a Play House company appeared for the first time in Cleveland's public parks, out of doors and free of charge, giving twenty performances of *The Tempest* before 15,000 people. And a special program of free summer theatre workshops involved 800 children from the nearby ghetto. The approximate grand total for the year, then, was an audience-plus-enrollment of 196,800 people. Clearly the Cleveland Play House is reaching the public.

The Play House is solid. Its annual budget is around $400,000; it owns some two million dollars worth of real property, including a flourishing restaurant that is run as a private club. It is true that over the years its neighborhood has become run-down and predominantly Negro, but something is being done about that: the area is scheduled for urban renewal, and the Play House will flee to a new site. Even the acting company (about twenty-seven Equity actors: one of the largest permanent Equity companies in America) is solid: performers come to Cleveland not just for a play or two, or even a year or two, but, in many cases, for a decade or two. (Of course, hardly any other theatres have been in existence for a decade or two.) The actress who played Penny in the Play House's production of *You Can't Take It With You* during the 1940–41 season did the role again in a Play House revival of the same play twenty-five years later. Many actors, over the years, have moved on to other theatres, to New York or Hollywood: Margaret Hamilton, Thomas Gomez, Russell Collins, Howard Da Silva, Ray Walston, George Voskovec. But even some of these keep coming back for old times' sake. The Play House is an American success story.

The problem with American success stories, however (and perhaps with success stories in general), is that though much may be accomplished, there is a tendency on the part of the successful to forget, from time to time, what it's all *for*. "I went into the theatre," says Mr. Lowe, "because of Mr. Stanislavsky and Gordon Craig. . . . I wanted the Moscow Art Theatre." He didn't get it.

It is not that the Play House devotes itself exclusively to Broadway commercial comedy. The Play House authorities claim, with some justification, that they put on the same plays as all the other resident theatres, and just as many of them—plus five or six light comedies as well. (They even do original plays now and then, which few theatres have the courage to undertake.) In 1966–67, for instance, the schedule included (among other offerings) *The Miser, The Subject Was Roses, The Skin of Our Teeth, U.S.A., Brecht on Brecht, The Hostage,* and *The Tempest,* as well as *Absence of a Cello, Life with Father, Blithe Spirit, Any Wednesday,* and *Barefoot in the Park.*

I do not condemn the Play House for putting on *Barefoot in the Park;* the provision of innocent merriment is a historic function of the theatre, and by no means a dishonorable one if the merriment provided is of good quality. (It does seem, though, that someone can always be found to produce *Barefoot in the Park;* finding someone to produce *Oedipus Rex* is harder.) But I make a distinction between *Barefoot in the Park,* a beautifully crafted piece of light entertainment, and *Any Wednesday* and *Take Her, She's Mine* (a Play House offering of the 1964–65 season), which are badly made and ugly. Worse, the Play House is often taken in by gussied-up hackwork that has pretensions to "significance." Recently, for instance, it produced Sidney Michaels' *Dylan,* which merchandises the life of Dylan Thomas for people more interested in gossip than in poetry, and Ira Wallach's *The Absence of a Cello,* which might have been tolerable trivia had it not been decked out with a maddeningly simple-minded hard sell for Integrity. (Why will popular playwrights never learn that the integrity of trivia is triviality?) And even its selections from the standard "serious" repertory are, in the aggregate, unadventurous and bland.

My own first visit to Cleveland, in March of 1966, coincided with the Play House's production of *The Amorous Flea,* a peculiarly tinny and vacuous musical-comedy debasement of Molière's *School for Wives* which had an Off-Broadway run some time ago. It is a coy, arch, twaddling, trifling, affected, graceless little show, and Cleveland gave it a performance to match, full of strutting, mincing, simpering, giggling, and pouting, with singing that ranged from tolerable down. It was a horrible triumph of pseudo-"style."

But there is a certain amount of Jekyll and Hyde about the Play House. While *The Amorous Flea* held forth in one of its theatres, another was occupied by an excellent production of *Who's Afraid of Virginia Woolf*. Incredibly enough, both productions were directed by the same man (the late Kirk Willis, who came to the Play House in 1929).

Mr. Lowe obviously had qualms about *Virginia Woolf*: ". . . we must caution our audience," he wrote, "that this enormously successful prize-winning play is brittle, brash, and frankly outspoken . . . We can say categorically that it is a play for adults who are shockproof and we urge you to consider this seriously before making plans to attend." A columnist in the Cleveland *Plain Dealer* called it "a sacrilege that this kind of slime should be flowing across the stage of the Play House . . ." The night I was there, however, the audience seemed to be taking the slime in their stride. They laughed loudly at the funny parts, but they also seemed absorbed in most of the emotional climaxes, and they spent the intermissions talking earnestly about what it all meant. ". . . so she created this myth," said one student-type to another, after the show. "And he went along with it. He needed it too; it was all he had," said the other. "I would like to see it again," said a respectable-looking gray-haired matron.

The women in the cast—Jo Ann Finnell as Martha and Catherine Heiser as Honey—were admirable, but the men were particularly interesting. Larry Tarrant, who played Nick (the ambitious young biologist), is either a clever good actor or a very lucky bad one. Nearly everything he did was halfhearted, hollow, unspontaneous, hackneyed, fake, yet all these characteristics seemed to belong to the character, not the actor. It was a clear and vivid portrait of a total opportunist, a man who lives every moment for what he can get away with. Better, I kept thinking, to be George or Martha, red in tooth and claw, than to be such a mechanical homunculus—which is surely the point Albee is trying to make.

George was played by William Paterson, a Play House stalwart since 1947 and a superb actor. In appearance and manner he was very much the man-of-distinction type, yet there was defeat and futility in the very set of his shoulders. His irony was relaxed, delicate, and sharp; he showed himself a master of understatement for both comic and pathetic effect. His other roles that season were in *Never Too Late, Poor Richard,* and *The Absence of a Cello.*

When I returned to Cleveland a year later, Mr. Paterson was appearing in A *Profile of Benjamin Franklin* and A *Profile of Holmes,* two one-man shows he had compiled from the works of Franklin and Holmes, whom he impersonates in full make-up and costume. (On occasional leaves of absence from the Play House, he tours throughout the country in these vehicles.) I saw the Franklin program and enjoyed it. The selection of material was somewhat superficial, giving a fairly vague idea of where Franklin stood on the great political and social questions. (The Play House in general shows no great eagerness to deal with the great political and social questions; that is the essence of my complaint against it.) The first half, in consequence, was a bit thin and held my attention insecurely. All through the evening, moreover, the transitions from one block of material to the next tended to be a bit jerky, and the staging, a matter of standing up for a while and then sitting down for a while, was unimaginative. The second part of the program, however, which dealt with Franklin's adventures among the ladies, was very funny. And Mr. Paterson's performance was impeccable throughout: a triumph of technique leavened by charm. (As a member of the audience remarked, "If you had seen this guy in any of his other performances, you wouldn't believe it. He doesn't look anything like that.") I was left with a sense of having been privileged to make the acquaintance of so rare and lovable a spirit as Mr. Paterson's Franklin.

On this visit to Cleveland, I found all three of the Play House's theatres occupied at once. Across the lobby from the small auditorium in which Mr. Paterson held forth, *Barefoot in the Park* was playing before a large and enthusiastic audience. And I was struck once again by the sheer *efficaciousness* of Neil Simon's play. How it *works!* How the Clevelanders laughed! How they enjoyed themselves! And I found myself laughing happily right along with them. The performance was marred by an effortful and overcute ingénue but was otherwise quite good. The ingénue—or anyone else interested in comic acting—might have learned some lessons from Dorothy Paxton, who played the mother. Miss Paxton (who is Mr. Lowe's wife, incidentally) did not strain or push; she made her character soft-spoken, shrewd, even meditative—and absolutely charming and hilarious.

Barefoot in the Park did not disturb me, but the Play House's production of *The Tempest* did. This offering was designated as the Play House's "Twenty-Eighth Annual Shakespeare Festival," and they should have stopped at twenty-seven. The performance, under Robert Snook's direction, was not bad, exactly—Robert Allman made quite a competent Prospero—but utterly without imagination or insight. Ferdinand resembled Little Lord Fauntleroy; Miranda and Ariel reminded me of the typical Hollywood combination of insipid ingénue and hoydenish sidekick. The whole thing looked as if someone had said, "All right, fellows, we've got to do *The Tempest*; there's no help for it, so let's get on with it." It is depressing to think that this production was shown to 25,000 high school students, and then, somewhat recast, given eighteen free performances in the parks, since it gave virtually no indication that Shakespearean drama can speak to modern audiences about matters that concern them. Had I been a student, I should not have had any great desire to come back next year and see another such exercise in empty cultural piety. If the Play House authorities cannot find better reasons for doing a play than the availability of outside money to finance it, they ought to leave it alone. If this is typical of their approach to the serious side of their repertory—I have no way of knowing, but I would guess that this is an extreme example of a recurrent condition—then they are better off with *Barefoot*.

The Play House is now a somewhat geriatric institution; it is the only resident theatre faced with the problem of a staff that is slowly dying off. Mr. Lowe himself, active and alert though he is, was born in 1899. The Play House has the advantages that often come with an advanced state of maturity: wealth, experience, a certain kind of solid proficiency, an intuitive knowledge of what can safely be done. But it also has the great disability that comes with age: timidity, conservatism, a tendency to continue in the same groove.

I believe that the highest function of a theatre is to challenge and stimulate its audience, but I do not believe that this is the *only* worthy function a theatre can have. If I did, I should have to declare the Play House an egregious failure. But it has found its audience; it gives them what they like; what they like is sometimes good. (The most popular plays in 1966–67 were *The Miser*, *The Skin of Our Teeth*, and *Barefoot in the Park*; in 1965–66, *Who's Afraid of Virginia Woolf*, *Tartuffe*, and *You Can't Take It with You*.) It has achieved stability on terms that are not too dishonorable; and that, in the American theatre, is a considerable accomplishment.

The Pittsburgh Playhouse

The Pittsburgh Playhouse is looking for stability on any terms.

Like its namesake in Cleveland, the Pittsburgh institution is long-established (founded in 1934) and possessed of certain substantial material assets (some 2.5 million dollars in real property). Like the Cleveland Play House, it has three theatres and a private-club restaurant; like the Cleveland Play House, it has numerous auxiliary activities (a children's theatre, a touring company that visits high schools as far away as Punxsutawney, West Virginia, and a theatre school for children and adults). It also began as an amateur group; unlike the Cleveland Play House, however, the Pittsburgh Playhouse remained essentially an amateur group until 1965. Among its performers, along with a few professional actors, were a truck dispatcher, a barber, a sheet-metal worker, a salesman, and a minister. Its plays, as former general manager Richard Hoover later admitted, were "stock pap"; when it did attempt a classic, business was terrible. In comparison, the Cleveland Play House *was* the Moscow Art Theatre.

For many years, the Pittsburgh Playhouse jogged along quite comfortably in this fashion, but in 1959 it began losing money and has continued to do so ever since. At the same time, word gradually began filtering into Pittsburgh from the outside world that other cities were setting up *professional* theatres, and discovering that there was an audience for plays more demanding than *Mary, Mary*. It was true that these theatres were also losing money, but they found it easier, because of the quality of the plays they produced, to raise funds; foundations, in particular, could often be induced to look kindly on them.

And so, in 1965, the Playhouse board fired its artistic director after twenty-eight years of service. The amateurs were cleared out; the board turned to William Ball, a highly admired young director (aged thirty-four) who had worked mostly off Broadway and at the New York City Opera, and invited him to make the Playhouse the first home of his American Conservatory Theatre. The ACT was sponsored by the Playhouse and the Carnegie Institute of Technology (a Pittsburgh institution which sent its advanced drama students to intern with the ACT); it was financed with the help of a $115,000 Rockefeller Foundation grant; but it was and is Bill Ball's company.

It opened in Pittsburgh on July 15, 1965. In the next six months it mounted a dozen plays in repertory in two theatres. In one single week it performed *Tiny Alice, The Apollo of Bellac, Antigone* (Anouilh's), *The Servant of Two Masters, King Lear, Tartuffe, Six Characters in Search of an Author, The Devil's Disciple,* and *Death of a Salesman.* Reviews were favorable. "In Pittsburgh," said the Pittsburgh *Post-Gazette,* "the theatre never had it so good. Mr. Ball and his American Conservatory Theatre have restored it to an eminence nobody hereabouts ever hoped for or dreamed of."

Some of the natives were restless. One man wrote to the *Post-Gazette,* saying that he and his wife had "been devoted members of the Pittsburgh Playhouse since 1947," but that *Tiny Alice* "is a sick play about mentally sick people by a sick author, Edward Albee. After hearing Mr. Ball's analysis, I am forced to the reluctant conclusion that the sickest of all was Director Ball . . . Candor forces me to say that I yearn" for the old Playhouse regime—and he was not the only one. Publicly, the Playhouse was undismayed. "Our audience not only multiplied, they changed," asserted a Playhouse official. "They became younger and more knowledgeable and eager for the finest things these professionals could do."

Yet at the end of the first six months, the ACT left the Playhouse forever. The reasons are not quite clear; some say that Mr. Ball was irresponsible and impossible to work with, others suggest that he was too audacious, too odd, too talented even, for the stodgy Playhouse management. The truth probably lies somewhere in between. At any rate, the ACT, still under Mr. Ball's direction, is now ensconced in San Francisco—permanently, it hopes. It will be discussed at greater length in Chapter Ten.

After the ACT left in January, 1966, the Playhouse slipped part way back into amateurism and "summer-stock material done in the winter"—but only part way. To fill his theatre for the winter and spring, Richard Hoover (still general manager, as before and during the ACT irruption) scheduled a "season of distinguished great plays" : *Rhinoceros, Who's Afraid of Virginia Woolf, The Complaisant Lover,* and *The Knack.* The Playhouse had a contract with Actors' Equity, but the locals got back into the act: "2 Squirrel-Hillers Star in Rhinoceros," said a headline in the *Squirrel Hill News.*

The Complaisant Lover gave me some idea of what the old regime must have been like. Although Graham Greene is the author, the play is a glossy, vacuous, French-windows-on-the-garden British comedy, and it was performed in Pittsburgh with a sort of cellophane-packaged urbanity by a cast of six professionals and three local people. The audience was sparse and unenthusiastic; even the young people in it had a settled, middle-aged look (a phenomenon I have also noticed at the Cleveland Play House). ". . . light, entertaining," I heard someone say. "I don't want anything that makes me think. I think all day."

Virginia Woolf was another matter. This is the kind of play that American actors are good at, and it was played very well in Pittsburgh by a cast of New York professionals. And of all the plays of the 1960's, none has so much to say to so many of us in this country as Mr. Albee's demonstration that people who need people aren't necessarily the luckiest people in the world. They flocked to it in Pittsburgh. "Not since last season's *Mary, Mary,*" said Mr. Hoover, "have we enjoyed such a box-office deluge." The audience had a tendency toward half-embarrassed giggling at all the sex talk; when Martha made as if to exhibit the "blue circles around her things," they fairly squealed with hilarity. But they paid attention; they applauded more than politely; and they left the theatre discussing the play. It had quite clearly not been wasted on them.

While this interim season was in progress, Mr. Hoover was hunting for a new artistic director who would form a resident company at the Playhouse. The choice fell on twenty-seven-year-old John Hancock, a stocky *wunderkind* from Harvard who had taken over as artistic director of the San Francisco Actor's Workshop after its founders departed for New York. In the Playhouse's brochure for the 1966–67 season, "A Message from the New Artistic Director" announced, "With this season, we renew our commitment to a radical departure from the presentation of 'warmed-over' Broadway hits." The projected schedule included a play by Samuel Beckett and two by Brecht.

In order to lure Mr. Hancock away from San Francisco, the Playhouse authorities promised him a large salary and an operating budget in the neighborhood of $712,000. Expecting about $300,000 to come from the box office, the Playhouse board set out to raise the rest. The A. W. Mellon Educational and Charitable Trust started the ball rolling with a grant of $150,000 a year for three years. The Sarah Mellon Scaife Foundation added another $50,000. After that, however, the ball stopped rolling. Nobody else wanted to give the Playhouse any significant amount of money.

Meanwhile Mr. Hancock's season began, in October of 1966, with *A Man's a Man*, one of Brecht's minor works, which the new artistic director had previously staged off Broadway. This was followed by *A Streetcar Named Desire* and then by Mr. Hancock's bitter, perversely brilliant version of *A Midsummer Night's Dream*, which he had previously done in San Francisco (where I had seen and greatly admired it). The day *Midsummer* opened, the Playhouse announced that it needed to raise $300,000 to finish the season, and would have to close its doors permanently unless a good proportion of that sum could be raised within two weeks. Amid tremendous local brouhaha, the money was raised and the theatre saved, with the help of an emergency grant of $25,000 from the federal government's National Endowment for the Arts.

Then on February 11, 1967, the Playhouse's board of trustees voted not to renew Mr. Hancock's contract. According to the chairman of the board, "Hancock cannot produce something that we can sell. . . . I don't think he tried to be accepted by the 'establishment' in Pittsburgh. Somebody has to teach an artist that you can't defy the public." Richard Hoover, the old general manager, who had hired William Ball, fought with him, brought in Hancock, and then announced his own resignation in the aftermath of the financial crisis, said, "Good theatre must appeal to everyone and not to a select group. Hancock was trying to draw the young intellectuals, but there just weren't enough of them." Eight board members resigned as a result of the decision to fire Mr. Hancock, charging that the board majority had "demonstrated either unwillingness or inability to make a commitment to professional resident theatre of quality." It was the old dilemma: a theatre has an obligation to stay ahead of its audience, but not so far ahead as to lose the audience altogether. It is the job of the artistic director to strike a balance between the two obligations. Whether the Pittsburgh audience—or *a* Pittsburgh audience—would eventually have come within hailing distance of Mr. Hancock's productions, or whether the theatre would have gone bankrupt first, is hard to say.

Other issues may be involved. Were there failures in management and promotion on the part of old-timers in the Playhouse management? Was Mr. Hancock made to suffer for the board's failure to raise the money they promised him for operating expenses? On the other hand, what about Mr. Hancock's productions: were they any good? I have seen enough of his work elsewhere to vouch for his talent; I admired his previous productions of two plays that he restaged in Pittsburgh. I did not see any of the productions that he personally directed in Pittsburgh. On my only visit there during 1966–67, I saw *The Three Sisters*, which was part of Mr. Hancock's original schedule, but for which he had engaged a guest director. I was not, however, greatly impressed by the actors Mr. Hancock had hired. But it was not the quality of Mr. Hancock's work that the board of directors took exception to, only its lack of popularity, which they obviously blamed on its far-outness.

In any case, it seems pretty clear that Mr. Hancock offered Pittsburgh a fairly adventurous program of theatre, and Pittsburgh was too conservative to take it. It is evident that the civic leaders of Pittsburgh have vague yearnings for culture (after clean air it is the obvious next step), but they scare easily. The board knew what they were getting; Mr. Hancock had been doing adventurous, far-out work in San Francisco, and he was hired to come to Pittsburgh and do more of it. According to Mr. Hancock, "I said I was going to lose you one-half of your audience, and it would take you three years to build a new one—and they agreed." Then when this began to happen, and the board discovered at the same time their inability to raise the money they had counted on, they panicked.

Evidently Mr. Hancock overplayed his hand. Two plays by Brecht in a single ten-play season, maybe. But two *minor* works by Brecht? Plus a play by Beckett about a woman buried up to her shoulders, then up to her neck, in sand? Plus *Maeterlinck?* That would appear to be asking for trouble; there are better plays, plays with *more* relevance to the lives of modern Americans, that would at the same time have attracted a larger audience, even in Pittsburgh. But having made his mistake, if that's what it was, Mr. Hancock showed a highly flexible willingness to amend it by substituting an Arthur Miller double bill for *Happy Days* (the Beckett play), and *Two for the Seesaw* for Brecht's *St. Joan of the Stockyards*. But even this did not save him: the board had repented of its courage and wanted a man with smaller dreams. A few weeks after deciding not to renew his contract for the next season, the board dismissed him outright and immediately, to prevent him from staging a new "Theatre of Fact" script about the "Hollywood Ten" hearings before the House Un-American Activities Committee. The season finished up with productions of *The Fantasticks* and *Barefoot in the Park*.

Perhaps Mr. Hancock was temperamentally unsuited for the job. If so, it is more of a reflection on Pittsburgh than on him. It may be that no really creative director could work at the Playhouse under the conditions imposed by the Pittsburgh cultural climate. In *A Man's a Man*, Mr. Hancock's first Pittsburgh production, there was a scene in which a character was represented as urinating onstage. It is said that this scene caused an important Pittsburgh citizen—*the* important Pittsburgh citizen—to change his mind about a $10,000 donation to the Playhouse, although he had not seen the production but only heard about it, and that the resentments created by "The Ten-Thousand-Dollar Piss," as the incident became known, helped to cause Mr. Hancock's downfall. When the firing was announced, Mr. Hancock received a telegram from his predecessor, William Ball:

Shakespeare had a word for every occasion. "You are not the first nor shall you be the last to suffer such calamities as this." Have patience, they know not what they do.

But when we speak of "Pittsburgh" and "the Pittsburgh cultural climate," it is not altogether clear whether the fault is ultimately that of the community in general, or the Playhouse board and the cultural power-structure in particular. Perhaps, considering the tastes of the Pittsburgh public and the financial situation of the Playhouse, the board had no alternative. But does there exist anywhere an artist-administrator-diplomat who would be capable of doing creative work while keeping on the good side of both the audience and the board? It will be interesting to see how Mr. Hancock's successor works out.

This successor is a twenty-nine-year-old New Yorker named Ronald Satlof, who has knocked around for several years as a director-stage manager. "I'm hired," he says, "for one year with the understanding—very clear—that it's a temporary appointment. . . . [But] presumably if I do a fabulous job of making this thing work, I will stay for about five years. . . . My job is to increase attendance by a minimum of 30 per cent to succeed in the goals that have been set for me." Mr. Satlof has cast himself as a sort of anti-Hancock: modest, level-headed, pragmatic. "The company was thought of as Ball's company or Hancock's company," he says, "not the Playhouse company. . . . My only policy is to build a Pittsburgh Playhouse company, where the name Ron Satlof doesn't become what the Pittsburgh Playhouse is about."

His administration began with the last production of the 1966–67 season: *Barefoot in the Park*. "We need to make money right now if we're going to exist at all," he explained. "We just can't afford a chancy script right now. . . . I'm not especially proud of that, nor am I especially ashamed of it. It's funny how theatre intellectuals, myself among them, cannot get over that nagging guilt about doing plays like *Barefoot*. . . . It's the kind of play I would not think of doing if I did not consider that I had a larger responsibility than to my own taste.

"What I'm trying to do next year is to keep the doors open. I've never seen a theatre do much good that didn't operate." To implement this goal, Mr. Satlof will be "trying to do *both* Broadway sex comedies and at the same time the best of classical drama." He proposes, for 1967–68, a season of Shakespeare, Shaw, Brecht, Miller, and other worthies, performed in repertory by a resident company, at the Playhouse's 540-seat Craft Avenue

Theatre, and a "Broadway-oriented" season—*Once upon a Mattress, Born Yesterday, The Subject Was Roses, A Delicate Balance*, and another musical—in the adjoining 340-seat Hamlet Street Theatre, with each production performed for a continuous run by a fresh cast, jobbed in for the occasion. All this is to be done on a budget of only $400,000 (compared to the $700,000-plus offered to Mr. Hancock).

Perhaps it will work. Perhaps Mr. Satlof is just what Pittsburgh needs. In any case, it is interesting to note that the Playhouse was doing fine as long as cozy Philistinism was financially viable, but was very nearly torn apart by the cultural explosion. Having been a happy theatrical backwater for so many years (while the Cleveland Play House was evolving, however slowly and timidly, to meet new necessities), it is having a terrible time trying to join the modern world of the resident professional theatres.

The Barter Theatre (*Abingdon, Virginia*)

Another ancient institution that was happier in the past than it is in the present is the Barter Theatre, the oldest resident professional theatre in the South. But partly because it began as a professional theatre, and partly because of its small-town isolation and its drawing power as a tourist attraction, the Barter has managed to survive without revolutionary changes.

A somewhat anomalous product of the Great Depression, the Barter began in 1932, when a young actor named Robert Porterfield was on tour with Walter Hampden in *Cyrano*. It occurred to young Porterfield that while there were plenty of hungry actors in New York, there were plenty of farmers in the southern highlands, his own native territory, who had plenty of food but no culture. "I said," he says, " 'Why don't you have people bring beans and potatoes and chickens and ham to see you act?' " And so he brought twenty-two actors to Abingdon, Virginia, in the mountains near the Tennessee border, set up shop in the town hall, and announced that produce would be accepted at the box office in lieu of cash. Thus the name of the new enterprise: the Barter Theatre.

There are plenty of wonderful stories about the old times at the Barter, but I do not propose to tell any; the reader is at liberty to imagine them for himself. Let us instead contemplate the theatre as it exists at the present day. It is a charming place, located on a quiet stretch of Abingdon's main street. The main theatre has a conventional proscenium stage and is fitted out with the interior furnishings that formerly graced the Empire Theatre in New York: chandeliers, rugs, plush seats, brocade for the walls, a portrait of Katharine Cornell. Across the street is a tiny second theatre, pleasantly rustic, with a thrust stage, which is used in the afternoon for children's shows and in the evening for productions that are, by Barter's standards, experimental.

The season at the Barter runs from March to October. It relies heavily on tourists for its audience, and these are to be found mostly in the summer. "We try to give 'em a cross-section of what I call good theatre," says Mr. Porterfield, who is still the theatre's managing director. "A good comedy, a good drama, a good mystery, and one or two good classics." There is even an occasional new play: "We've done more new plays than any theatre in the United States," says Mr. P. (Of course, the Barter has been around longer than any American theatre except the Cleveland Play House.) The 1966 season included *Hamlet, Charley's Aunt,* a new American play called *Five in the Afternoon, Luv, Barefoot in the Park, The Odd Couple, Romeo and Juliet, Arms and the Man,* and half a dozen others of similar ilk.

It is a pretty safe list; the Barter is careful not to give its audiences more than they can take. In a small town in the Bible Belt this is probably wise, perhaps necessary, but it does impose limits. In the early days the rule was "no hells, no damns, no cocktails," until the profanity barrier was finally broken by a production of Irwin Shaw's *Bury the Dead.* Today, the following notice appears at the bottom of the theatre's schedule cards:

GUIDE TO PLAY SUITABILITY:
fam—family, age 10 and older
adt—adult, age 18 and over
com—comedy
dra—drama

Thus *Who's Afraid of Virginia Woolf* is designated as "adt/dra," and *Luv* as "adt/com," and families with children are suitably warned.

It is natural for Mr. Porterfield to be sensitive to the feelings of the community, because he is a member of it: a genuine southern gentleman. (I had never met one before, and was much impressed.) With his gracious wife Mary Dudley, he dispenses lavish southern hospitality at his farm, Twin Oaks, thirteen miles from Abingdon; according to Mr. Porterfield, Twin Oaks "was never owned by anybody but the Porterfields and the Indians."

Mr. Porterfield has been named the "First Citizen of Abingdon." In what time he can spare from running the theatre and raising dairy cattle on his farm, he is involved in running the Martha Washington Inn (the area's leading hostelry, located right across the street from the theatre) and is a sponsor of Abingdon's Virginia Highlands Festival. Yet he still finds time to appear regularly before the curtain at the Barter to welcome the audience. He offers a free pair of Mary Gray nylon stockings, "made right here in Bristol" (the local metropolis), to the spectator who comes from farthest away; the night I was there, the stockings were won by a gentleman from San Francisco. Mr. P. goes on to tell us about the days when he worked for David Belasco, "my favorite showman of all time," and about how he once understudied Clark Gable. "If you like us," he says finally, "please talk about us; if you don't like us, just keep your mouth shut." (Big warm smile, and exit.)

It is a charming little speech: the material a bit thin, but masterfully put over. Nothing in the Barter's production of *Barefoot in the Park* was quite able to match it. The juvenile lead (a young man named Jack Cowles, who spends his winters in Hollywood) was generally effective, though he mistimed a line every now and then. But the ingénue had almost everything to learn about comic technique, and ought to have lost a little weight before appearing in those tight pants. The staging stuck pretty closely to Mike Nichols' Broadway promptbook, which is a sound but not very creative way to go about it. Still, I found the play amusing, as I always do, and all the deficiencies of the production were compensated for, as far as I was concerned, by the firefly I found right outside the theatre during the intermission.

While *Barefoot in the Park* occupied the main theatre, the little one across the street was taken up with a production of *Who's Afraid of Virginia Woolf?* In his speech before *Barefoot*, Mr. Porterfield asked for a show of hands from people who had seen

Virginia Woolf. A number of hands went up. "I'm glad to see so many far-out people here tonight," said Mr. P. As it happened, the far-out people got quite a good production of Mr. Albee's adt/dra. The set was poor; the juvenile was somewhat miscast (not enough of a charm-peddler); Max Jacobs and Margo McElroy, as George and Martha, were each twenty years too young. But Mr. Jacobs and Miss McElroy were admirable anyway, Mr. Jacobs being particularly notable for his sick malice, and Miss McElroy (a pretty girl with long dark hair, a patrician bearing, and a husky Bette Davis voice) for proud wrath. Dawn Nelson as Honey was very good too.

Through the years, the Barter Theatre has collected various laurels. In 1941 it was declared the State Theatre of Virginia. In 1948 it presented *Hamlet* at Kronberg Castle in Elsinore, Denmark. In 1949 the Civilian Branch of the U.S. Army (whatever that is) made a documentary film about it; an article on the Barter also appeared in *Amerika,* the magazine which our State Department publishes for distribution in the Soviet Union. In 1957, Mr. Porterfield was presented to the Queen of England.

Nowadays things are quieter. "At one time," says Mr. Porterfield, "I had three companies on tour, playing somewhere every night throughout the year." Barter companies appeared "in every city, every town in the state of Virginia. We played in every state of the union," up in the mountains at Aspen, Colorado, and down in the depths of Luray Caverns, Virginia. But about three years ago the tours were abandoned: the theatre could no longer afford it. According to Mr. Porterfield, "Right now is tougher on us than it was during the Depression. . . . Equity was awfully happy in 1932 when I took all these hungry actors and brought them down here. They got room and board and what I called snuff money." Today things are different, and Mr. Porterfield's toughest problem is "trying to meet the demands of the rising cost of labor. In the last three years, Actors' Equity minimum has gone up 70 per cent." This is no doubt true, but it exemplifies a tendency on Mr. Porterfield's part to look backward—not, perhaps, an entirely healthy tendency in a man who is running a going concern.

"The glamour, the magic—that's what we try to keep," says Mr. Porterfield, but cozy charm would be more like it. A plaque on the theatre's outer wall says:

The Barter Theatre pledges itself to combat the evils that would destroy the culture and enlightenment of the world by giving the best of its strength and devotion to the cause of truth, beauty, and spiritual nourishment of the human soul.

I didn't notice very much of all that while I was in Abingdon. I did notice, in my conversation with Mr. Porterfield, that he was much more disposed to provide me with colorful copy than to speak cogently about current theatrical realities—and the Barter is very much Mr. Porterfield's personal creation.

Mr. P's establishment strikes me as an easygoing, slightly somnolent sort of place that does provide live professional theatre where otherwise there would be none, and does occasionally turn up some good work. Clearly it is better than no theatre at all. And could any other kind of theatre survive in Abingdon, Virginia? Since the Barter is evidently the kind of theatre that Mr. Porterfield wants to run and knows how to run, he would seem to be the right man in the right place—if not quite, any more, at the right time.

3

WASHINGTON TO PHILADELPHIA

The Arena Stage (Washington, D.C.)

A theatre is traditionally an urban phenomenon, flourishing where people are most concentrated, and so it is not surprising that in this country, resident theatres are clustered most thickly in the Washington-to-Boston megalopolis. Washington itself has two of them; one of these, the Arena Stage, is materially and artistically one of the most successful theatres in America.

Mrs. Zelda Fichandler, the Arena's founder, "producing director," and guiding spirit, is (along with Nina Vance of the Alley Theatre in Houston) one of the matriarchs of the resident theatre movement. With her thick, dark hair, net stockings, and brown boots, she doesn't look like a matriarch, but then Zelda (as she is generally known) has only been at it for about seventeen years. In the resident theatre even the matriarchs are young; the Arena, which began in 1950 (when Zelda was twenty-five), is the oldest of the dozen or so such theatres on the eastern seaboard.

It opened in an old movie house with 247 seats, and was received, says Mrs. Fichandler, "with instant apathy." But she knew that in Washington, as in every major city, there was an audience that was not being served by the road companies. "I knew because I was one of them, and my friends were six others." And, after years of "staying at it, surviving, on Monday trying to get to Tuesday," it turned out that she was right. From the movie house the Arena moved to an abandoned brewery thenceforth known as the Old Vat, and from there it moved to its present home, a custom-built, 833-seat, million-dollar theatre (paid for mostly by the Ford Foundation). The new theatre is located in an urban-renewal wasteland far from downtown, with nothing around it but expensive new upper-middle-class housing and the Potomac; nevertheless it was filled in 1966–67 to 93 per cent of capacity, which amounts to a total attendance of some 185,000 people.

But even today, the relationship between the Arena and its audience is not quite the love feast that these statistics imply, as becomes clear from Mrs. Fichandler's own description of her theatre's recent history. After the season of 1965–66, she said:

> . . . after sixteen years and the production of about 150 plays we had lost half our subscribers—that is some 8,000 of them. (Twice as many as normally.) The loss was accompanied by much verbalization—letters, calls, conversations. Our work had become too "special," too "in-group" was the gist of it. Not as much "fun" as it used to be.
>
> Complaints were centered not only on the season just past but on the one before it as well—the year when I had finally decided the theatre had an audience and could begin to close in on the kind of repertory that really interested it. There had already been the long, patient years—hopefully unpatronizing—of spice and variety in between the pieces of meat: the Program for the Education, Pacification, and Diversification of the Audience. And it seemed time for something beyond eclecticism. Brecht's *Galileo* (before it did the resident-theatre circuit); Anouilh's *The Rehearsal*, the first production outside of New York; *Billy Budd*; *Heartbreak House*; Andreyev's *He Who Gets Slapped* in a surrealist production of a new acting version that emphasized the alienation of the artist from society; O'Neill's *Long Day's Journey into Night*; and a work commissioned from Millard Lampell, *Hard Travelin'*, a musical satire on the Depression period with contemporary parallels, to go with *The Lonesome Train*, Lampell's eulogy of Abraham Lincoln with music by Earl Robinson. . . .
>
> The second season under attack went like this: *St. Joan, Skin of Our Teeth*; a new play by Loring Mandel about the survival of human values in a computerized age; *The Three Sisters*; *Serjeant*

Musgrave's Dance, John Arden's obscure but compelling play; a bill of one-acts—*The Lesson* of Ionesco, *The Collection* of Pinter, and a new play by Howard Sackler—a bill centering around the use of language as an instrument of destruction. Then Joan Littlewood's *Oh What a Lovely War*.

Not terribly heady, any of that fare, in the last analysis. A beginning of inquiry. A beginning. . . . [But] what we did—to survive!—what we *had to do* was to acknowledge that the audience was our Master . . .

What we did was to plan a season that would please our Masters—no trick, actually, after so many years of experience. *Macbeth, The Magistrate, The Crucible, The Inspector General, Look Back in Anger, Andersonville Trial* replacing a new script not yet ready. No terrible compromises. Just ones of "quiet desperation." The result? Subscriptions up, audience happy, seats filled, no strain, another day, another dollar.*

In enlightened Washington, as in provincial Pittsburgh, the necessity for compromise remains. But it is compromise on a very different level: no *Barefoots* here. In 1967–68, the Arena Stage offered—in repertory, for the first time—*Major Barbara*, Anouilh's *Poor Bitos*, a new play by Howard Sackler called *The Great White Hope, The Tenth Man* (how did that get in there?), *Room Service*, and *The Iceman Cometh*. It is not, nowadays, an unusual program (except that it includes a new play); Mrs. Fichandler has never been as audacious in this regard as the hotheads at the Actor's Workshop in San Francisco. But she points out that though many theatres are doing these plays today, the Arena was doing them when hardly any other professional theatre dared. "We select our plays," she says, "with a view to the insights they provide into contemporary questions. We are a theatre of themes, with an emphasis on the variety of the statements, both as to content and style." For the most part, the record substantiates her claim.

My own first encounter with the Arena, in March of 1966, was a somewhat depressing experience: a flat and superficial *Three Sisters*, directed by Zelda herself. Chekhov is the most evanescent

* Speech delivered at a convention of the American Educational Theatre Association, New York, August, 1967.

of playwrights; everything depends on how sensitively the director and actor can seize his hints. "Men dine, just dine," he wrote, "and in that moment their fate is decided and their lives are destroyed." In this production the dining was there right enough (I could literally smell the soup in the first act), but the decisions and destructions were less clear. Naturalistic detail is important in Chekhov, but only as a means of revealing character; here there was plenty of "behavior," but psychology was not much in evidence. Most of the individual performances were quite creditable, as far as they went, but they did not go far enough to interact and kindle one another. And alas, there are only two kinds of Chekhov productions: exquisite and tedious.

Serjeant Musgrave's Dance, John Arden's murky, beautiful play, is a very difficult work to bring off, but the Arena did nobly by it. The Washington production opened just a few days after the Off-Broadway production of the same play in New York, and was by a good margin the better of the two. The Arena's arena, a big rectangular stage surrounded by the audience on all four sides, had made *The Three Sisters* seem unfocused (it is not a good stage for living-room drama), but it suited *Musgrave,* which is not only the story of four Victorian soldiers on a mysterious recruiting mission in the north of England but also a parable, didactic in intent and unrealistic in form, about the futility of violence.

Edwin Sherin, the Arena's associate producing director, staged it frankly, but not self-indulgently, as a piece of theatre. He began and ended by bringing on the whole cast in a circle dance; he had the simple scenery changed by the actors; important speeches were spoken directly to the audience; actors came up the aisles amid the spectators. All these devices have been used many times before, but seldom with such control and to such purpose. Usually, in the theatre, we are overhearing and peeping at an action confined to the stage; we can take it or leave it. In this production, what happened onstage was explicitly for us, to us, at us in the audience. We were never quite allowed to forget that we were watching something contrived for our benefit. Perhaps this is Brecht's famous "alienation effect," yet it did not alienate (not me, at any rate). The central characters never dwindled into mere metaphors or mouthpieces; things were happening to these people, and happening with conviction and intensity; emotional involvement with them was by no means excluded by the production—though it was made difficult by the diffuseness of the play.

What Arden offers for the emotions, in place of a cumulative involvement with one or more of the characters, is a poetry of atmosphere, cold and stark, punctuated with lines and dramatic moments that stab like a winter wind. *Serjeant Musgrave's Dance*, for all its meandering obscurity, is like a ballad of the Scottish border. This quality too was captured in Mr. Sherin's production, which created a world where soldiers and poor people spoke their minds in snatches of song as spontaneously as in ordinary talk, and where heel-beats and drumbeats sounded in a deserted land.

At the Arena as elsewhere, directors sometimes come through and sometimes do not; the actors do, almost always. They are sometimes miscast; they sometimes show the effects of too little help from the directors; but their work is almost always at least highly professional, and often something more than that. Jane Alexander in *Musgrave*, for instance, played a coarse, dirty, half-mad slut without stridency, but with passion, with desperation, and with a tragic dignity. As Masha, in *The Three Sisters*, Janet Sarno created in the first act, clearly and incisively, an intelligent, sophisticated young woman who rather despised her sisters with their vaporings and carryings-on. In the third act, when she broke down and confessed to them that she was in love with Vershinin, she seemed a different woman altogether; but her two inconsistent Mashas were both very well executed. Robert Prosky was excellent as Masha's husband, the stupid but kindhearted pedant Kulygin, and he was equally good as a glib, flashy second-rate swindler in a new one-act play. George Reinholt played two widely contrasting young men—the shy, earnest Baron Tusenbach in *Three Sisters* and the joke-telling, song-singing, card-tricking Private Sparky in *Musgrave*—most appealingly; too appealingly, perhaps, since both characters are supposed to be homely and awkward. In *The Collection* (one of Harold Pinter's one-act exercises in elegant ambiguity), Mr. Reinholt played a homosexual dress designer without quite enough attention to the character's origin in an English slum, but under Dana Elcar's taut and lucid direction he and Robert Foxworth (as another ambiguous young man) had the air crackling with innuendo.

What the company seemed most notably to lack was a heroic actor, a deficiency that was apparent in *Serjeant Musgrave's Dance*. Ted D'Arms, who had been very good as Andrey in *The Three Sisters*, played Musgrave as simply a sergeant, with a brisk manner and a good throaty bellow. The deeper authority and strength, the grandeur and mystery, the fanaticism, the madness, were missing. But then, who could have provided them? Olivier? Scofield? O'Toole? Burton? Brando? Actors of that sort are in short supply everywhere.

Since *Musgrave*, I have seen nothing at the Arena that imperatively required such an actor. In December of 1966 I returned for a look at *The Magistrate*, Arthur Wing Pinero's farce (vintage 1885). As far as I know, this was the first professional production of the play in America for several decades; it turned out to be quite a stageworthy piece of Victoriana. The eponymous magistrate is one Aeneas Posket, who is unaware that the lady who pinched him under the table in the dark in a private dining room at the disreputable Hotel des Princes is his wife Agatha. Since *The Magistrate* is an English farce and not a French one, none of the characters is bent on adultery, or even fornication; the fun arises rather from the incongruity between the profound respectability of the characters and the compromising circumstances in which they find themselves. This means that it takes a great deal of manipulation to get them all into that private dining room while keeping their motives reasonably pure; *The Magistrate* is thus somewhat contrived, somewhat mechanical; and the machinery creaks. But it has a very funny second act, and it is on the whole a nice little old play, with mysterious period-piece lines such as, "Don't you know that in a four-wheeled cab, the fewer knees there are, the better?" and nice old farcical lines such as, "You are in the presence of ladies, sir. Take off my hat."

A really brilliant revival of *The Magistrate*, such as H. M. Tennent might perhaps put on in London, could be a treasurable memory; the Arena's in-and-out production was pretty good Christmas fun. The stage was somewhat of an impediment, as it usually is when scene-changes are necessary without an intermission; Mrs. Fichandler is devoted to arena staging, but it is sometimes difficult to see why. The director was David William, an Englishman who has done good work at Stratford, Ontario; his staging of *The Magistrate* was affectionate and brisk, though not notably inventive. James Kenny was a pleasant, harrumphing, bumbling old magistrate, but Phyllida Law, a guest actress from England, sang her lines somewhat too insistently as his wife. One actor—quite a good actor—was miscast, and made a rather sedentary and slightly effeminate retired colonel; as he went on about his soldierly career, you wondered why the British hadn't lost India fifty years earlier, and the incongruity marred the otherwise splendid second act.

One pivotal character hitherto unmentioned is Mrs. Posket's son by a former marriage, a sporty nineteen-year-old who is greatly given to gambling, champagne, late suppers, and girls; this behavior, natural under the circumstances, is made to seem peculiar by the fact that Mrs. Posket has convinced everyone, including the boy himself, that he is only fourteen. (When he discovers the truth, he says, "Oh, I say, Mater, this is a frightful sell for a fellow," which is the kind of dialogue seldom heard any more in the Age of Osborne.) This ambiguous stripling was brilliantly played by Robert Foxworth, who looked, in his sublimely foolish flaxen wig, like a superannuated David Copperfield; Mr. Foxworth's performance was at once a witty parody of the delicate and ardent sort of British child star, and a hilarious piece of farcical acting.

When I got back to the Arena in the spring of 1967, the Age of Osborne had returned with a production of *Look Back in Anger*. I have heard Englishmen speak of this play as a period piece of the fifties, but I found it blazingly immediate: a cry of agony at a world empty of feeling. And the nervous giggles that came from the audience at certain places tended to indicate that the play has not, in ten years, lost its power of making people uncomfortable.

The leading roles were played by Douglas Rain and Martha Henry, two stalwarts of the Shakespearean Festival at Stratford, Ontario. Mr. Rain is a fuzzy, chubby, rounded personage, whereas Jimmy Porter should be played by an angular, nervous type; the part can use a keener edge of agony than Mr. Rain provided. Furthermore, the actor is just a bit old for Jimmy's adolescent ragings. Robert Foxworth, on the other hand, who played Jimmy's buddy Cliff, is slim, sensitive-looking, almost exquisite, and he used an impeccable King's-English accent. He seemed less like the stocky, earthy, unpretentious proletarian he was supposed to be than like an Old Etonian who had deserted to the enemy (though his delicate kindness made an effective contrast with Jimmy's fury). Perhaps they should have traded parts; certainly Mr. Rain would have been ideal as Cliff.

But this Mr. Rain is so good an actor that he can play a part he is not temperamentally suited for, and play it beautifully. He knows how to handle Jimmy's educated-working-class accent and the famous iron-shod rhetoric, and he was always in it emotionally. As for Miss Henry, she was perfect: a frail, beautiful girl with a husky voice, able to convey suffering just by the way she ironed Jimmy's pants. These actors from Stratford, Ontario, are an ornament to any company they visit; I only wish we could get more of them to come south.

Look Back was directed by Hy Kalus, who occasionally allowed the awkward stage to defeat him: several times, from where I sat, actors were obscured while saying important things. In other respects his work was admirable. He made no attempt to update the play into "swinging England": no rock 'n' roll, no vinyl. His staging had the proper amount of adolescent bouncing about, and he kept the stage alive with real, complex, intense relationships. The production's success indicated that the naturalistic tradition, which we all claim to be so tired of, has plenty of vitality yet.

The last production of the 1967 spring season was *The Andersonville Trial* by Saul Levitt. Mr. Levitt's play, which was produced on television in 1957 and on Broadway in 1959, deals with an actual historical occurrence: the trial of Captain Henry Wirz, the commandant of the notorious Confederate prison camp at Andersonville, where 14,000 Union soldiers died of exposure, starvation, and disease. The play is intrinsically a moderately interesting courtroom drama which raises, sometimes vividly, some important issues. But its dramaturgy is often repetitive, its ideology somewhat simple-minded, its style sometimes ponderous. Still, it was a good choice for Washington, D.C. in 1967, first because the play is set in Washington, and second, because it raises the question of what a man ought to do when his responsibility is to execute immoral, inhuman, or murderous orders. This is a question that needs to be raised, especially at the headquarters of the Vietnam war. Captain Wirz' defense was, in effect, "I was only doing my job." When he shouts out, "Ask them in this room if they would have done different. Ask them!" the question hangs in the air. (And because the Arena is an arena, "this room" was the room in which we too were sitting.)

While *The Andersonville Trial* was running in Washington, Captain Howard Levy was being tried, convicted, and sentenced to three years at hard labor for the opposite offense: refusing to obey orders to train medics for service in Vietnam. To present this play at this time was to fulfill the theatre's obligation to talk to the community about matters that vitally concern it—an obligation which, for the most part, the resident theatres are neglecting.

As for the performance, it was excellent the day I saw it. The qualification is necessary because, as an experiment, thirteen members of the company each rehearsed in two roles, and the "A" cast and the "B" cast performed alternately. The performance I attended was dominated by Robert Foxworth, who, as the prosecutor, manifested a rare ability to make everything he said seem important. But I was greatly impressed by the strength of the company as a whole. The play requires a large cast to provide for a long parade of witnesses; at the Arena, one fine character-cameo followed another, long after many theatres would have been reduced to sending on the assistant prop-man. Like all "permanent" companies in this country, the one at the Arena undergoes a substantial turnover every year; but judging from what I have seen, the Arena has, in general, one of the best acting companies in the United States. And for the most part, those in charge seem to know what to do with it.

My latest visit to the Arena, in December 1967, was to see the world première production of *The Great White Hope*, a remarkable play by Howard Sackler based on the life of Jack Johnson, the first Negro heavyweight champion, who was hounded out of the country (or so Mr. Sackler has it) by the white power structure. Mr. Sackler has written a great sprawling chronicle in twenty scenes, laid between San Francisco and Budapest, as "Jack Jefferson" wanders the earth looking for a place where he can live in peace with his heavyweight title and his white mistress. Aristotle named "spectacle" as one of the parts of tragedy, and *The Great White Hope* is spectacular: it features a cakewalk, a prayer meeting, a voodoo ceremony, a funeral, and crowd scenes of all sorts; among the characters are "Reporters," "Photographers," "Crap Players," "Rangers," "Men at Fight," "Civic Marchers," "Deputies," "German Officers," "Stage Hands," "Mexicans," "Fight Fans," and "Pinkerton Men." What a movie it would make!

As a play, it demands a large stage and an enormous cast; very few theatres in this country could begin to muster the resources for it. The Arena Stage recruited a company of more than sixty actors, augmenting its regular company with a number of well-known New York actors, and with some thirty local amateurs to fill out the crowds; Edwin Sherin, who directed, managed to bring this huge, heterogeneous mob to the point where it functioned like a genuine professional ensemble. Some of the actors were now and then defeated by the Arena's difficult acoustics, and some of them occasionally pushed a little too hard, but not a single performance was less than competent, and the major ones were admirable. James Earl Jones had the heavyweight physique, the heavyweight emotional power, and the mischievous but pointed irony needed to play Mr. Sackler's formidable hero, and Jane Alexander of the permanent company played his mistress with conviction and grace.

The Arena's stage is well suited (insofar as it is well suited to anything) to big, extroverted, fast-moving productions that do not require an elaborately detailed physical environment. Mr. Sherin had the action hurtling boldly across it, yet there was no flash and dazzle for its own sake; the staging served the play. The last scene especially, after Jack has lost his title, when the new champion, the triumphant "white hope," is carried off enthroned as Jack stands humiliated—both men bloody and dazed like sacrificial victims—this scene was corrosively moving, not as a spectacle merely, but as the resolution of the conflict that the play records, and the image of its hero's destiny.

Mr. Sackler's play is by no means one entire and perfect chrysolite. For one thing, it is far, far too long; I do not object to three-and-a-half-hour plays on principle, but this one repeats itself too many times. Furthermore, some of the important characters are unrealized in the writing; the champion's mistress, especially, is far too gracious, too faithful, and generally too perfect to be altogether convincing. Even Jack Jefferson himself, until he is undermined by the persecutions he suffers, is somewhat too good to be true. For a wide array of additional reasons, a number of scenes fail to come off; the script "needs," as they say, "work."

But *The Great White Hope* matters very much all the same, just as it stands, because Mr. Sackler has gotten hold of a vitally significant piece of history, has realized just why it is significant, and has put that significance, in vivid human terms, on the stage. Jack Johnson/Jefferson, as Mr. Sackler depicts him, is not a well-behaved, serious-minded Negro like Booker T. Washington or Sidney Poitier; he mocks at white society, and he sleeps with a white woman. And this, in the land of the free and the home of the brave, is unendurable; America, Mr. Sackler suggests, absolutely cannot stand a "bad nigger."

For a while I sat watching the play and fighting its implications. I had it in mind to accuse Mr. Sackler of catering to the absurd, ugly, and dangerous kind of Negro paranoia that considers family planning a genocidal plot against the colored races. But then I thought of Adam Clayton Powell, and, even more, of Cassius Clay, who had recently been sentenced to a $10,000 fine and five years in prison for refusing induction into the army. The play is by no means a calm and balanced assessment of the situation, but it seems clear to me that what Mr. Sackler implies is at least basically true: ours is still a racist society. (This view has since received confirmation from the President's Commission on Racial Disorders.) But whatever conclusion we come to, the play demands of us, in urgently dramatic terms, that we examine the whole question, and our stake in it. I wish it could have been shown in the schools, in the House of Representatives, and in other places where immature minds seek to cope with the pressing problems of our day.

More and more, the Arena is expanding beyond its old preoccupation with producing familiar plays for its contented middle-class audience. It has undertaken a program to teach improvisational techniques to teachers in the Washington public school system for use in the classroom, with special emphasis on reaching children from "nonverbal" homes. A special professional company has been organized to play for children, at the theatre and in schools throughout Washington and its suburbs. In another direction, a European tour is being contemplated. And a new, 1.5-million-dollar building is planned, adjoining the present one; it will contain a 450-seat, open-stage auditorium for American plays, especially new ones. It will be interesting to see what kind of scripts Mrs. Fichandler will be able to find for it, and whether Washingtonians will come.

The Washington Theatre Club

The Washington Theatre Club is not a club at all, but an ordinary, open-to-the-public professional theatre. With only 145 seats, however, it is one of the smallest Equity houses in the country. It exists on a shoestring budget. Its artistic director, Davey Marlin-Jones, was formerly head of the Equity Library Theatre in New York, where he put on forty-three productions for less than a thousand dollars; he believes that he has learned to cut costs without lowering standards (although at ELT, which was sponsored by Equity as a showcase, he had the advantage of not having to pay his actors). Since the Club can break even on a very small attendance, it is able, as Mr. Marlin-Jones says, to take chances "that a General Motors operation can't take." Yet its program is actually not very unconventional, tending toward lesser-known plays by big-name authors (Pinter's *The Lover*, O'Neill's *Hughie*, Albee's *Tiny Alice*, Ionesco's *The Killer*), and occasional small-scale musicals.

Although spectacle and glamour are impossible on the Club's small stage and small budget, and although I noticed nothing much in the way of imagination and flair that might have made up for this lack, the work I saw there was in general not bad. In *The Birthday Party* (which closed, in April of 1966, just a few days before the Arena put on another Pinter play), each actor seemed to have his own ideas about what kind of accent was required, and none of these ideas was correct; otherwise the acting, under Marlin-Jones' direction, was satisfactory. As Stanley, who takes refuge in a not-quite-boardinghouse at a seaside resort until two mysterious strangers come to get him, John Hillerman was highly impressive in his before-our-very-eyes nervous breakdown, all the way to homicidal mania and hysterical laughter.

The Eccentricities of a Nightingale, which followed *The Birthday Party* on the Club's schedule, was advertised as "a new play by Tennessee Williams," but it turned out to be only a rewritten

version of *Summer and Smoke* (which the Arena had presented in
its original form some years back). It seemed like a preliminary
draft rather than a revised version; John Buchanan, the young
doctor whom poor Miss Alma loves so unsuccessfully, is reduced to
a dim, mother-ridden zombie, and the perennial Williams message—it's always Be Kind to Misfits Week in Williams country—
becomes naggingly insistent. Moreover, the new version retains the
two great drawbacks of the old: first, since the author sets his
heroine jiggling with sexual hysteria at the beginning of the play,
he is invariably led to a certain amount of repetition in order to
get her through three acts, and second, we have already met this
lady, more subtly depicted in more interesting circumstances, in *A
Streetcar Named Desire*. And yet, there is no getting around it:
poor Miss Alma and her palpitations may be annoying, but they
are affecting too. Marlin-Jones' production was somewhat prosaic,
but Melinda Miller was good as Miss Alma, the pathetic "Nightingale of the Delta," and Raymond Thorne played John Buchanan
with pleasant professionalism.

In the spring of 1967, the Club put on *The Waters of Babylon*
by John Arden, whose later, better work, *Serjeant Musgrave's
Dance*, had been done by the Arena the year before. *The Waters
of Babylon* is an odd sort of farce-parable-extravaganza, with songs,
about a Polish refugee in London who leads a double life as a
seedy slumlord-brothel-keeper and a respectable, dignified assistant
in an architect's office. It seemed that Mr. Arden must have had a
point to make—nobody brings references to Buchenwald and
Auschwitz into a play just for the fun of it—but what that point is
I have not the faintest idea. The staging was unimaginative and
undisciplined, but Haig Chobanian as the hero had an amusing air
of ironic disgruntlement. The whole thing was pleasantly accept-
able as an evening of zany, good-natured high jinks, rather like
The Hostage, only not so good. (But I wonder what on earth Mr.
Arden really had in mind?)

For two years now, the Club has ended its season with "an
original, topical satirical revue." I caught the 1967 edition, entitled
Son of Spread Eagle. God knows there is a need in our country—
and especially in Washington—for all the political satire we can
get; but *Son of Spread Eagle* stuck firmly to a sub-Bob-Hope level
of cogency.

The Washington Theatre Club is not much of an experimental theatre; what it really is, it seems to me, is a *small* theatre. But even this is enough to give it more of a personality than some theatres have. And since it ran at 99 per cent of capacity for the 1966–67 season, it would appear to be making a go of it on that basis.

Center Stage (Baltimore)

Like so many resident theatres, Center Stage is now in the intermediate stage between small beginnings in the recent past and large hopes for the future. It began in January, 1963, in a cramped and ill-equipped former gymnasium. In 1965 it moved into a former Oriole Cafeteria which had been converted into a comfortable, well-equipped 350-seat theatre. In five years, subscriptions increased from 600 to 7,000; attendance increased from 17,000 to 70,000 for the season; the budget increased from $40,000 to $425,000; and the operating deficit increased from $4,000 to about $150,000. That's progress. (Statistics like these are by no means atypical in the resident theatre movement.)

The theatre runs an extensive program of auxiliary activities: a high school tour, financed by the state government, which in 1967–68 will visit all but two of Maryland's 159 high schools; a smaller tour of elementary schools in Baltimore; plays and theatre classes for children; a summer film festival; miscellaneous lectures and symposia; experimental productions on Monday nights.

Meanwhile, a competent but somewhat unexciting group of actors, under the artistic directorship of Douglas Seale (an Englishman who has directed at all three Stratfords: rather a biggish name for a resident theatre), works its way through a carefully balanced schedule. Mr. Seale has programed a number of works that are not on the resident-theatre beaten track: Shakespeare's *Titus Andronicus,* for instance, and *A Penny for a Song* by John Whiting. In the spring of 1967, he even planned to do, as a major production, a play that came out of the Monday-night experimental series, written by the theatre's resident playwright, C. Lester Franklin. This play was based on the Hattie Carroll case, the famous Maryland scandal that arose when a rich farmer caned a Negro maid to death, and which also inspired a Bob Dylan song.

But the production was canceled in favor of *Noah* by André Obey, which Baltimoreans were less likely to regard as cutting too close to home. According to the theatre, its lawyers had declared the play was probably libelous; according to the author, the theatre simply finked out.

I first made the acquaintance of the Baltimore company during the Year of *The Birthday Party*; of the three productions I saw of Harold Pinter's "comedy of menace" during the spring of 1966, the one at Center Stage seemed to me the best. It was directed for maximum nerve-wracking effect by Brooks Jones (who is producer-director of the Cincinnati Playhouse in the Park). Kate Wilkinson, a guest actress for this production, used a singsong, floating-off-into-space delivery to give an amusing and endearing performance, at once portrait and parody, of a vague, vacuous old lady. William McKereghan of the resident company provided an almost Dickensian performance, ebulliently oily, as Goldberg, one of the mysterious men who come to take away the obscurely fugitive Stanley.

The Days Between by Robert Anderson (the author of *Tea and Sympathy*) was offered to Center Stage through the American Playwrights Theatre, which Mr. Anderson describes as "a group of college and community theatres which has come together to get a chance to produce the plays of 'established' playwrights *before* not after Broadway." About fifty such theatres are supposed to have mounted *The Days Between*, but very few professional theatres would touch it. Its theme is the perennial, almost obsessional theme of the American drama since O'Neill: the self-deluder forced in the end to face himself for what he really is. Anderson's hero is a writer, the author of a good novel in his youth, who has been struggling ever since to write his second novel. Five minutes after the play begins we know he never will, and all we can do for the rest of the evening is wait for the characters to realize it.

This fatal disability aside, the play is competently—somewhat too competently—constructed in the old-fashioned way: everything is smooth and neatly dovetailed; you can see where every line is going. The dialogue is high-falutin' and hollow ("I became sick with this indescribable longing." "How can you say that?" "Because it's the truth."), and the characters are gracious, grammatical puppets. There was a certain amount of entertainment to be derived from watching them glide neatly through their carefully arranged paces (or perhaps I thought so because no play about "writer's block" can ever be entirely without interest to a writer). But *The Days Between* is dead. Douglas Seale's production, on an impressive multi-level set by Mark Rodgers, was decent enough, but unavailing; the leading actors looked about ten years too young for their roles, but it did not matter.

The Chinese Wall by Max Frisch, which succeeded *The Days Between* at Center Stage, is a very different kind of bad play: shapeless, whereas *The Days Between* is all too carefully shaped. Buried in *The Chinese Wall* is an unsubtle but effective one-act parable about an ancient emperor of China, "Tsin She Hwang Ti, called the Son of Heaven, he who is always in the right," who presides at the trial of a mute child on the charge of being a revolutionary called The Voice of the People, and who is provoked by the mute's impassiveness into screaming out the truth about his own tyrannical crimes. (This emperor was strongly played in Baltimore by John Schuck.) But Herr Frisch has added a character called the Contemporary, a twentieth-century intellectual (or so the playwright says) who gets involved in the action and spouts yards and yards of platitude. The point seems to be something about the impotence of well-meaning intellectuals in the face of tyranny, but it is not made very economically. And then Frisch has filled out his cast with Romeo and Juliet, Napoleon, Columbus, Pontius Pilate, Don Juan, Brutus, Philip of Spain, and Cleopatra, who carry on and for no good reason that was evident to me; perhaps it all has something to do with the Teutonic sense of humor.

In this meandering free-for-all, Seale saw the opportunity for a directorial tour de force. Influenced perhaps by Peter Brook and *Marat/Sade*, he set the play (not in a madhouse but) in a circus. The Contemporary became the ringmaster, Romeo and Juliet the acrobats, Napoleon a clown, Cleopatra a gum-chewing stripper, and so on. In the Emperor's speech about "the Great Order, which we call the True Order and the Only Order and the Final Order!" (according to the published translation), the word "Order" was changed to "Society." The Mandarins were dressed like the Ku Klux Klan; Brutus wore a big "Make Love Not War" button pinned onto his leotards. A big emotional scene was set to pounding rock 'n' roll music; the first act ended with a mass frug by the cast. The Contemporary made his long speech (not a very good speech) about the Bomb from a lectern that rose from the floor in the middle of the auditorium; the speech was punctuated by cheers, heckling, and miscellaneous ad-libbing from actors in their wildly glitzy circus costumes circulating up and down the aisles. In the first act, it seemed to me, Mr. Seale's inventiveness was not quite sufficient to offset the innate dullness of the script; but the second (which contains, along with some more dull stuff, most of the action in the play) was a splendid piece of theatre.

At any rate, the production showed a laudable intention on the part of Center Stage to stir things up in Baltimore. Interestingly enough, *The Days Between,* which is pseudo-realistic and easy to follow, was not popular; people seemed to prefer an absurdist comedy-melodrama like *The Birthday Party,* or a didactic extrava-ganza like *The Chinese Wall.*

When I returned to Baltimore in December of 1966, another side of Mr. Seale's eclecticism was in evidence: as a Christmas *bonne bouche,* he was presenting a musical-comedy version of the famous Victorian melodrama, *Lady Audley's Secret,* adapted and directed by himself, with music by a pop songwriter and lyrics by the theatre's business manager. It had songs entitled "A Mother's Wish Is a Daughter's Duty," "The English Country Life," "The Audley Family Honor," and (the finale) "Forgive Her Forgive Her." The show in general was reprehensibly vapid and arch, like Gilbert and Sullivan without Sullivan's melodies or Gilbert's wit. The only acting of any note was provided by William McKere-ghan, the company's most interesting performer, as a coarse, leering, low-class villain who kept saying, "I knows what I knows"; Mr. McKereghan made him less of a cliché than my description would suggest. But there were some funny moments, a few good numbers, and the whole thing was not too hard to take. The Baltimoreans loved it.

This cozy little musical was followed by, of all things, a lucid, bold, and disciplined production of *The Balcony.* "Lucid" means, in this case, that you could follow what was going on; "bold" means that there was plenty of wholehearted clutching and grop-ing; "disciplined" means that the clutching and groping was never gratuitous or irrelevant. Julie Bovasso came down from New York to play Irma the madam; James Edmund Brady designed costumes that featured a bit of vinyl, a good deal of leather, and plenty of flesh (plus a splendidly virginal black dress, with white at the cuffs and a high collar, for the ingénue-prostitute Carmen); Brooks Jones' staging brought out Genet's careful counterpointing of impersonation and "reality."

In 1967–68, the company is playing in repertory for the first time, but the list of plays is noticeably more conventional than those of previous years: *Hamlet, The Member of the Wedding, The Royal Family* (by George S. Kaufman and Edna Ferber), *The Devil's Disciple, An Enemy of the People* (in Arthur Miller's adaptation), *Waiting for Godot,* and a bill of short plays. The long-range future plan is the usual one: a new home in an urban-renewal project downtown, with a main auditorium seating about eight hundred people or thereabouts, and a 300-seat experimental theatre. As far as the resident theatres are concerned, that is the American Dream.

The Theatre of the Living Arts (Philadelphia)

This theatre began in 1964 when two Philadelphia ladies named Jean Goldman and Celia Silverman decided to try and establish an Off-Broadway-type theatre in Philadelphia. They wanted to put on Brecht's *Galileo* with Elia Kazan or Harold Clurman directing, but both these gentlemen had other commitments. Then they decided to have a young director, but William Ball was busy, and so their choice finally fell on Andre Gregory, a young Harvard graduate who had produced and directed off Broadway. After that, one thing led to another, and when *Galileo* opened on January 6, 1965, in a 407-seat converted movie house in a Negro slum, it was as the first production of a new resident professional theatre that already had 6,700 subscribers; Mr. Gregory was the new theatre's artistic director.

In its brief existence, the Theatre of the Living Arts has attracted an extraordinary amount of attention. A couple of fairly well-known New York playwrights have expressed interest in writing for it. Robert Brustein, the dean of the Yale School of Drama, invited the company to give its production of *Endgame* at Yale. The New York and the national press have taken notice. Some of this attention is attributable to the fact that the theatre is only about an hour and a half from New York; but a good deal of it, I think, comes from the air of excitement that—sometimes at least—has prevailed there. And this, in turn, came mainly from Mr. Gregory, right up until he was fired (or did he quit?) in February of 1967.

Mr. Gregory is a member of the Actor's Studio, and acknowledges its influence on his work. But he appears to be free of the various kinds of corruption (whatever they are—opinions differ) for which the Studio is justly or unjustly famous—perhaps because he has spent time in Europe, and worked with the Berliner Ensemble. "Just doing plays well is nice," he says. "It's a value, but it's not a prime value." He wanted his theatre to be the place where the community came to question itself. One of the purposes of the Living Arts should be, he believed, to "shock and seduce—but more shock—into thinking. Things have been much too rigid in this town. . . . People have got to feel about problems that concern them."

This, of course, is more or less what most resident-theatre leaders say they want, though they usually express it in less militant language, without the emphasis on shock. But it is a tall order. One wonders how often an evening at the theatre changes anybody's mind, or causes him suddenly to begin thinking about something that had never occurred to him before. I would tend to believe that the important effect of the theatre is subliminal and cumulative, that it builds up in a man's mind like a coral island. But I would guess that at least during Mr. Gregory's tenure, it built up faster at the Living Arts than at most resident theatres.

Not that I agree with all of Mr. Gregory's choices. I was not enthusiastic about *The Last Analysis*, Saul Bellow's self-consciously raffish attempt at intellectual farce, which I saw in May of 1966. The play concerns itself with a washed-up Jewish TV comedian named Bummidge, a "serious buffoon" who wants to broadcast the story of his life over closed-circuit television to an audience of psychoanalysts gathered at the Waldorf-Astoria. It was directed with high competence by George Sherman, then the theatre's associate director. Bummidge's broadcast itself, as staged by Mr. Sherman, was a hilarious nonsense fantasia on themes from Freud. Fred Voelpel's set filled the spacious Philadelphia stage with an intriguing collection of clutter. Tom Brannum as a grotesquely weedy ex-ratcatcher and Merwin Goldsmith as a plaintive tailor were particularly good in a generally satisfactory supporting cast. As Bummidge, David Hurst was splendid: light and deft, very funny, unflagging but never forced, elfin but never overcute.

Mr. Bellow has loaded Bummidge with *Weltschmertz* and *Angst*; students of modern literature will have a field day comparing him to Herzog. But Herzog is not so noisily pretentious, and even Herzog is not so intolerably self-obsessed as Bummidge. The latter has a few good lines here and there: "Oh Doctor," he cries, "why can't I live without hope like everyone else?" But for the most part, Bummidge is not a lovable *idiot savant*; he is somewhat of a nuisance. Around him Mr. Bellow has written a repetitive, meandering script, full of lame jokes and peculiarly unidiomatic dialogue: "Curse that interfering Winkleman! I know he wants to exploit me." "Good riddance to that square old stuff." "Nonsense. There's too much riding on Bummy for us all." There is a great deal of talk about the human condition, but very little is said about it. Mr. Bellow's foray into farce reminds me of the essay in which T. S. Eliot longed to be a music-hall clown, so that he could really reach the masses. I thought when I saw the play in New York, and again when I saw it in Philadelphia, that Mr. Bellow was slumming.

Poor Bitos, Jean Anouilh's acute and subtle study of the revolutionary temperament, is a play far more my taste (an avowal which will give me a black eye in certain critical circles). The Living Arts production, directed by Mr. Gregory, showed, for better and for worse, what this theatre could do. Anouilh's Bitos is a Communist public prosecutor in a small French town, graceless, uncultivated, fanatically dedicated, and ruthless; in a flashback he turns into Robespierre, his prototype. He hates the frivolous, decadent aristocrats of the town, yet would love to be like them; when invited to one of their parties, he comes, but the party has been arranged specifically to torment him.

Mr. Gregory made it quite a party. In rehearsal, he provided a phonograph and had his actors improvise to jazz and rock 'n' roll; the phonograph, the music, and a good bit of the improvised material ended up in the performance. The result, influenced perhaps by *La Dolce Vita*, was probably the most obscene, degenerate orgy ever seen in Philadelphia. I particularly remember an actress in a skintight scaly-silver sheath wriggling passionately on the floor and doing God knows what to Bitos' feet. These abandoned revelers had little in common with Anouilh's elegant aristocrats, and the pathos of poor clumsy Bitos, the washerwoman's son who never knows which fork to use, passionately envying the cool, assured, exquisite Beautiful People around him, was lost amid all the hotly spectacular goings-on; but in its place we got a vivid picture of a lone puritan trying to preserve himself in the midst of a debauch.

Even more than John Hancock with A *Midsummer Night's Dream* in San Francisco and Pittsburgh, or Douglas Seale with *The Chinese Wall* in Baltimore, Mr. Gregory went all out for shock. He was brilliantly aided by Eugene Lee's constructivist wooden setting, with its floor sloping crazily in several directions at once, by Mr. Lee's hallucinatory lighting, and by the unhackneyed sensuality of Adam Sage's costumes. A crucial moment in the play was marked with a deafening scream of electronic music and a blinding flash from bright lights focused directly into the eyes of the audience. One of the revolutionary ladies in a flashback scene performed with one breast exposed. (We were demurely informed in a program note that this lady used to appear that way in real life.) It was an audacious production, very contemporary, very immediate, very vivid, and I admired it.

But it was a production in which the scenery, lighting, costumes, music and special effects were more interesting than the acting. George Bartenieff with his febrile raging was often intriguing as Bitos, but rather mannered, with a tendency to tense up and gabble indistinctly in moments of crisis. As his chief tormentor, Anthony Zerbe was competent enough, but in accordance with the director's scheme he coarsened the elegance of the character. The Broadway production, on the other hand, and the London production before it, had no special effects, no *dolce vita*, no shocks, only two superb performances by Donald Pleasance and Charles D. Gray as Bitos and his opponent. It focused, as the Living Arts production did not, on two men fighting with everything they had, which is what drama is really about.

The Theatre of Cruelty can be highly exciting; bare breasts and blinding lights have their place in the theatre, especially when used, as Mr. Gregory used them, for purposes beyond themselves; but nothing will ever replace good acting. *Bitos* in Philadelphia had an air not just of urgency, but almost of desperation, as if Mr. Gregory feared that ordinary theatrical methods no longer work, that an audience must be shocked, galvanized, almost beaten and kicked, before they will pay attention. I do not think that this fear is warranted, and I doubt if Mr. Gregory really thinks so either. But this Artaudian urgency, sometimes verging on hysteria, seems to be a recurrent note in his work.

It cropped up again in *Beclch*, a play by Rochelle Owens, which received its world première at the Living Arts, under Mr. Gregory's direction, on December 20, 1966. (And a Merry Christmas to you, too.) Beclch herself (pronounced "Beklek") is a despotic queen somewhere in a fantastic "Africa of the mind." She is a great big bundle of impulses and desires, all of them nasty. Hardly has the play begun when she has an old woman skinned alive. She persuades an infatuated hanger-on to contract elephantiasis in order that the natives may accept him as their king; the poor fellow walks around for a while with a swollen, rotting leg, but the queen tires of him, and he is forced to strangle himself. Meanwhile Beclch has found a new lover: we know it's the real thing when she pushes him off a platform into the midst of a cockfight. But the new lover sneaks off, and at the end of the play Beclch herself is about to be killed.

Among the samples of dialogue I noted were the following: "There is not one of us without perversion"; "His eyes look like smashed mosquitoes"; "You drop of shit—you pulled hair out of his head"; "No, no—the puke must stay"; "A persimmon is like flesh: it makes a scream when you bite into it"; "Boy, do I love the Negroes, they're proud, proud . . . I could fornicate with a bunch of them"; "Shall a woman's parts be laden with honey yes" (this forms part of a ritual chant); "That's the tune she likes to hear play. The frigging tune of cruelty"; "In each and every pore I want the blood to rain . . . Flies could lay eggs on my body like rotten fruit"; and "I hope I drool like an animal."

Miss Owens reminded me of the Fat Boy in *Pickwick* who said, "I wants to make your flesh creep"—a desire in which she was enthusiastically seconded by Mr. Gregory. In a program note, he quoted a passage from *The Theater and Its Double*, the book in which Artaud developed his vision of a Theatre of Cruelty:*

> . . . In the anguished and catastrophic period we live in, we feel an urgent need FOR A THEATER WHICH EVENTS DO NOT EXCEED . . . It is upon this idea of extreme action pushed beyond all limits that the theater must be rebuilt.

I would take issue with Artaud's implication that this is the *only* kind of theatre we need (so too, presumably, would Mr. Gregory, since the previous Living Arts production had been *Room Service*), but since every kind of human action needs to be reflected in the theatre, "extreme action pushed beyond all limits," which is closer to our hearts than most of us care to admit, should not be excluded. And in fact "extreme action" has been prominent in the theatre since quite a while before Artaud was born. Mr. Gregory acknowledged this, citing *Hamlet, Lear,* and a couple of plays by Seneca; he might have added *The Bacchae, The Jew of Malta, The Revenger's Tragedy,* and, in more recent times, *King Ubu* (an important influence on Artaud). In our own day we have had not only *Marat/Sade,* but also, by the same author, *The Investigation*; the latter is particularly notable for providing "THEATER WHICH EVENTS DO NOT EXCEED" by the simplest of means, dispensing almost entirely with the theatrical razzmatazz that Artaud loved, and relying instead on the cognitive, conceptual, spoken word, which he scorned.

The problem with *Beclch* was that Miss Owens was so bound and determined to make our flesh creep that she constantly overshot the mark. Like the Fat Boy, Miss Owens generated a feeling of adolescent eagerness that was at odds with the somber impression she was trying to convey; hey, she seemed to be saying, if you thought that was disgusting, wait till you see what I've got next! Her fantasies were so fantastic, so luridly preposterous, so up-in-the-air, so divorced from the actual ends and means of human cruelty, that they failed to shock. And shock was *Beclch's* only reason for existence.

---

* *The Theater and Its Double* by Antonin Artaud. Translated from the French by Mary Caroline Richards. Published by Grove Press, Inc., Copyright © 1958 by Grove Press, Inc.

The occasion was partly redeemed, however, by Mr. Gregory's production, which had an authority and amplitude not often encountered in regional theatre. *Beclch* began happening to you from the moment you entered the auditorium. It was dark. On the walls were projected pictures of jungle beasts and birds. A large masklike object hung at the back of the theatre. A network of wires had been strung overhead. Birdcalls and animal roars came over the sound system. (Carolee Schneemann got program credit as "environment consultant.") Ahead, the uncurtained stage was full of dim, pendulous shapes.

The play itself began with a burst of Teiji Ito's percussive music. The lights came up, revealing John Conklin's wild, thick, cluttered, nonrealistic but profoundly jungly setting. Thenceforth there was plenty of savage chanting and ritual dancing, performed not by embarrassed apprentices (as would happen in most resident theatres if they dared to try something like *Beclch*, which they wouldn't), but by the members of a local organization called the Afro-American Dance Ensemble, under the direction of Arthur Hall. These young dancers clearly knew what to do when the jungle drums started beating (*Beclch*'s three live musicians were also members of the Ensemble), and they were thoroughly integrated into the production.

Mr. Gregory offered all kinds of fringe benefits. A great deal of bare flesh was in evidence: during one particularly nowhere-going scene I beguiled the time very happily by watching one young woman's right breast cast a shadow on her ribcage. I was also amused by Mr. Gregory's habit of spilling the action out into the auditorium. This was the only production I ever saw where the actors rolled in the aisles; at one point it looked as if a couple of them were going to miscegenate right at my feet. There was nothing dull about *Beclch* except Sharon Gans's monotonous and strident performance in the title role, and the script.

Later on, Mr. Gregory defended his choice of the play in an article in the *Tulane Drama Review*:*

. . . the theatre is about life and the waters outside the theatre are troubled. We're dropping bombs on children in Vietnam. But Philadelphia isn't ready for a play with the theme of violence. Is

* From "Theatre of the Living Arts," T36 (Summer, 1967), p. 20.

Philadelphia ready for the violence in its own streets? Should we wait for violence to subside, if it will, and do nothing meanwhile? Wait to do the new plays until the writers have become so discouraged from not having their plays done that they are no longer playwrights?

This, of course, leaves the play's inadequacies entirely out of account; and I am far from sure that *Beclch* would have acted as an effective counterirritant to violence even if it had been any good. But I think it expresses what is likely to be a productive viewpoint for a man who runs a theatre, though not by any means a prudent viewpoint.

Beclch closed on January 29, 1967; on February 19, Mr. Gregory was fired as the theatre's artistic director. Why? According to Mr. Gregory:*

The real causes of my dismissal were artistic policy, money, and communication problems, in that order. The Board and I were both working to create a theatre in Philadelphia. The difficulty was that we were trying to create two different kinds of theatre. . . .

. . . This year, after consulting with the Board President, who disliked the play but liked my production ideas, I optioned *Beclch*, our first new full-length American play. And the shit hit the fan.

. . . Contractually the Board had the right to veto any play but could not veto one new American play of my choice each season. However, since there was such a furor, I decided to hold a meeting with the Board to discuss *Beclch*. I spoke for two hours and thought the meeting was a success. I was wrong. I hadn't read the signals correctly.

On the opening night of *Beclch* two leading members of the Board were appalled. Several days later a Board member with a large, local foundation in his pocket resigned. (A year ago, one of the most influential Board members, revolted by Saul Bellow's *The Last Analysis*, walked out of the show and reneged on a $20,000 pledge. This year he resigned from the Board because of *Beclch*.) A Play Reading Committee was reactivated by the Board for next season.

. . . Artistic Directors and Boards of Directors have to get along. An Artistic Director has to be diplomatic. It was no accident that *Beclch* was squeezed in between *Room Service* and *The Time*

* *Ibid.*, pp. 20–21.

of Your Life. At the same time, Artistic Directors must have the right to touch the nerve of their communities, to deal with social and political issues, to go all the way with production styles. Boards of Directors have to be reorganized. They can no longer be Main Liners only; the poor, the intellectuals, the politicians, the artists, the students should also be on the Boards. Repertories should be developed that stretch tastes, that span many interests in the community.

Ideally, Philadelphia should have five permanent theatres, each one with a specific point of view relating to a specific audience supported by a Board which strongly supports that point of view. But this is clearly impossible today. Therefore there must be a lot of give-and-take. *The Time of Your Life* for one part of the audience; *Beclch* for another. Too often our regional theatres are dominated by the taste of the Board and this taste, though it represents money and a certain social milieu, is in no way representative of the *entire* community. Most of the community stays away from the theatre simply because it does not like what is done there.

Now wait a minute. I agree—ardently—that "Artistic Directors must have the right to touch the nerve of their communities," etc. It is true also that the taste of the average board of directors "is in no way representative of the *entire* community." But most of the "*entire* community" wouldn't come to the theatre—any theatre— on a bet, and if they did, available evidence indicates that they would far sooner see something like *The Sound of Music* or *The Beverly Hillbillies* than *Beclch*, and that this would be true even if *Beclch* had been better. What the boards generally *do* represent is that tiny segment of the community that is willing to come to the theatre. I believe that it would be possible to develop a theatre audience that is larger, livelier, and more diverse than the present resident-theatre audience, but that would take many years and a whole lot of money. And money—the money in the community that is available to support a theatre—is another thing that boards of directors tend to represent pretty fairly. These are ugly realities, and they are hamstringing the entire resident-theatre movement, but they have got to be lived with, somehow. To live with them, without losing the kind of urgency that I admire in Mr. Gregory: that is the difficulty everywhere.

There were other difficulties in Philadelphia.

The current authorities at the Living Arts tell a very different story from Mr. Gregory's, suggesting that he flagrantly disobeyed his own precept that "Artistic Directors and Boards of Directors have to get along. An Artistic Director has to be diplomatic." They imply that Mr. Gregory's dismissal was not a matter of artistic policy at all, but rather that it was the result of a power play on Mr. Gregory's part that failed. According to this version of the story, the crisis began when David Lunney, the theatre's managing director, asked for a new contract that would give him the same salary Gregory was getting ($18,000 a year). Gregory supported Lunney; the board turned down the request, making it clear that this was *not* a vote of no confidence in Gregory; Lunney resigned. Gregory demanded the right to select the new managing director, and to replace several members of the board; he told the press that the board had exerted "artistic interference," but provided no particulars. Finally the board fired him on the grounds that he "had breached his contract by acting contrary to the best interests of the theatre" in denouncing the board to the press.

It is clear, at any rate, that Philadelphia had the same problem we have seen, in varying forms, in Washington and Pittsburgh: the plays that the artistic director really wants to do are not those that the theatre's present audience really wants to see. It is a problem that only time, patience, and tact—combined with a certain amount of guts—will solve. More immediately, there was evidently a quarrel as to whether or not the artistic director should be the absolute, total, supreme autocrat at the Living Arts. My own feeling is why not? Mr. Gregory is perhaps something of a wild man, somewhat hard to deal with. But it is clear that any theatre he runs is going to be an exciting theatre, and anyway there have been men who ran important theatres, and ran them successfully, who were far crazier than Mr. Gregory could ever hope to be.

Actually, the whole thing turned out fairly happily, for a while. Gregory and Lunney got a huge federal grant to start a theatre in a ghetto neighborhood in Los Angeles that plays five performances a week, all expenses paid, for high school students, and only three a week for paying adult customers, so they were as nearly free of the ordinary bourgeois resident-theatre audience as they could reasonably expect. Eventually they found that other pressures could be even more onorous, but that is another story (see Chapter Five). Meanwhile in Philadelphia life went on.

As the final production of what was advertised as an "American Retrospective" season, Gregory had scheduled Racine's *Phaedra*, in Robert Lowell's adaptation. He had engaged Diana Sands, the Negro actress, to play Phaedra, and was planning to direct the play as the tragedy of the alien, the outsider. When he left, Stephen Porter was hired to direct *Phaedra*, but the performance gave me the impression that Mr. Porter had no ideas or feelings about the play one way or the other. In the fourth act, Miss Sands suddenly began beating at Theseus' leather breast with her fists, and I sat up: someone was finally *touching* someone. Stand and deliver, oratorio-fashion, is, of course, the traditional French style; but that does not mean it is the right way for Americans to play Racine before other Americans in the twentieth century—only the easiest, most obvious way.

Miss Sands is an actress of real power and grandeur, and she did some breath-taking things, but she seemed to be working in a vacuum. She was magnificently oppressed with *something*, but only at moments did it really seem to be love for Hippolytus in particular that was bothering her. The production appeared to have no impulse behind it: the staging was unimaginative, the sets and costumes unevocative, the supporting cast undistinguished. It was a yawn-provoking evening.

But it would be unfair to judge the future of the Theatre of the Living Arts on the basis of *Phaedra*; this production was a casualty of the upheaval caused by Gregory's departure. All kinds of things continued to go on at the Living Arts. Most theatres shut down altogether during the summer, but during July and August of 1967 the Living Arts sent its production of *Room Service* on a tour of the summer-theatre circuit; meanwhile, the theatre itself was kept open by a film festival.

The budget for 1966–67 was supposed to be $475,000, but ended up being $552,000; in 1967–68 the plan is to cut back to $437,000. But, with the help of some government money, the Living Arts remains active in several directions. Its theatre school, offering courses in acting, mime, theatre games, voice production, dance, stagecraft and stage management, occupies its own building, which it shares with the Afro-American Dance Ensemble (the group which appeared in *Beclch*). Several Living Arts actors have spent short periods in residence at schools in southern Delaware, to read poetry, work with drama clubs, lead workshops for teachers, and do whatever else came to hand. The company's production of *The Caretaker* is doing one-night stands in various places and there are plans for it to tour high schools in eastern Pennsylvania for ten weeks at the end of the season. At the theatre there are dance, chamber music, and rock 'n' roll concerts, and children's plays.

The schedule of major productions for the new season, however, indicated a reaction against Gregory's adventurous spirit. The company went into repertory for the first time (as in Washington and Baltimore), but Art Wolff, the theatre's new "Resident Director" (not artistic director—that had been Gregory's title), programed a season of solid, conventional, safe choices: *The Entertainer* (Osborne), *The Caretaker* (Pinter), *The Importance of Being Earnest, Twelfth Night,* and *The Rehearsal* (Anouilh).

I saw *The Entertainer* at a matinée the day before Christmas, 1967; it was a dispiriting afternoon. Except that the old man in the play was obviously being played by a young actor, the performance as a whole was quite creditable; Mr. Wolff's new company (hardly any of the Gregory-era actors are left) is well above the regional-theatre average. As Archie Rice, the failed music-hall comedian, upon whom shades of the prison-house begin to close as the curtain falls, Harris Yulin was quite good in a soft, buttery, insinuating way. But *The Entertainer* was never really a good play in the first place—too much self-pity and gin, too little progression and pith—and there in Philadelphia, a decade after it was first written, without Sir Laurence Olivier, there really didn't seem any point in putting it on. And one thing about the production particularly disturbed me. When I had seen the play in Boston during its pre-Broadway tryout, one of the music-hall tableaux had featured a gross, flabby, blowzy nude wearing the helmet and holding the spear of Britannia: a stunning image of national decadence. In Andre Gregory's production of *Poor Bitos*, an actress performed with a breast exposed more or less for the hell of it; in Art Wolff's production of *The Entertainer*, Britannia was chastely swathed, even though nudity was specifically demanded in the author's stage directions. Naturally, the point of her appearance was lost.

That evening I saw *The Caretaker*, which fared much better— mostly, I think, because Pinter's script holds up better than Osborne's. *The Caretaker* demonstrates that in any group of three people, there are three possible combinations whereby two of them can gang up on the third: a theme that would seem, considering human nature, to be of permanent importance. Charles Maryan directed a good tight production, and David Margulies was memorably grubby, greasy, seedy, shabby, shifty, scruffy, and sloppy, yet at the same time oddly charming, as the old tramp who becomes caretaker for two mysterious brothers.

The evening concluded with a surprise. As the actors were taking their curtain calls, a group of young people suddenly burst in and began performing a traditional English Saint George playlet, as a Christmas treat. Most of the performers offered more in the way of enthusiasm than finesse (perhaps they were students in the theatre's school), but Mr. Margulies, as a drunken doctor who cures the fallen hero, was irresistible. I had to leave before the little play was over in order to catch my train, but I take it as evidence that some kind of spirit of adventure still endures at the Theatre of the Living Arts.

Further evidence is provided by an interesting change in scheduling. Frequently, a theatre will proudly announce its intention of doing a new play, and then end up producing something like *Twelfth Night*; recently, Mr. Wolff and his colleagues decided to cancel their scheduled production of *Twelfth Night* and substitute a new play, called *Scaffold for Marionettes*, by the theatre's resident playwright, Lester C. Franklin. This is the same *Scaffold for Marionettes*, dealing with the murder of a Negro woman by a white man, that was scheduled to be done at Center Stage in Baltimore (where Mr. Franklin used to be resident playwright), until it was canceled on the ground that it might be libelous. Perhaps the libel laws are different in Philadelphia. At any rate, it seems as if the Living Arts is not, as I had begun to fear, entirely committed to playing it safe.

THE
SOUTH
AND
SOUTHWEST

The Alley Theatre (Houston)

When the resident-theatre movement began to grow, it looked for inspiration not to Cleveland, Pasadena, or Pittsburgh, whose old playhouses plugged away more or less unnoticed, but to a small group of pioneering postwar theatres: the Alley in Houston, the Arena Stage in Washington, and the Actor's Workshop in San Francisco. The oldest of these is the Alley, which was founded by Nina Vance as an amateur group in 1947; in 1954 it signed up with Actors' Equity and became a professional theatre. The first few years were a struggle: "I clawed this theatre out of the ground," says Miss Vance, who is still its producer-director. Lately her task has been easier, since the Alley has become a favorite beneficiary of the Ford Foundation, which has given it $3,500,000 since 1962.

The Alley has been housed since 1949 in a converted fan factory that seats only 230; it usually operates at close to 100 per cent of capacity, and many people are turned away. Yet when I asked about it at my downtown hotel, it took two desk clerks and a bell captain in conclave to figure out where it was. Clearly the Alley needs a new home if it is to play any significant part in the communal life in Houston. And it is getting one. Its new building houses two auditoriums, seating 800 and 300, respectively, and opens in November, 1968. It will be located in downtown Houston where the hotel clerks won't be able to miss it.

Miss Vance says that she started her theatre in unconscious revolt against amateur theatres that devoted themselves to "family plays"; there were other works, she thought, that the American people wanted to see. Nevertheless, for many years she did plays like *Time Out for Ginger*, *The Reluctant Debutante*, and *Holiday for Lovers*. But the Houston audience has evidently grown in more ways than one—or perhaps Miss Vance has. She now believes that "The public is ahead of our ability to keep up with its taste." "I'm less scared to give 'em what I didn't think they'd buy." In the past couple of seasons she has given 'em plays like *The Devil's Disciple*, *Right You Are (If You Think You Are)*, *The World of Sholom Aleichem*, and *The Seagull*, as well as *You Can't Take it with You* and *The Great Sebastians*.

Duel of Angels, Jean Giraudoux's last play, was on the bill when I first got to Houston in April of 1966. It is a curious, subtle, difficult work, dramatizing the conflict between Innocence and Experience, Idealism and Expediency, Chastity and Promiscuity. The Alley had actors who could play Giraudoux—who could display elegance and intelligence, who could deal with the Giralducian irony—but it did not have actors for all the parts in this particular play. There were apparently, for instance, two actresses who could play Experience (or Paola, as Giraudoux calls her). Unfortunately, one of the two had to play Innocence (Lucille), and was too mature, too sophisticated, for the part. The other (Lillian Evans), who *did* play Paola, had a combination of flamboyance and precision that more than compensated for her inability to pronounce the letter "g" when it came at the end of a word. The production in general, cramped on a tiny stage, was neither admirable nor discreditable, but it certainly did not make the most of the play. In her new theatre, presumably, Miss Vance will have a larger, and perhaps even a better, company to cast from.

Even in its present cramped quarters, the Alley is capable of fine work. When I returned to Houston the following season, I found a production of Duerrenmatt's *The Physicists*, directed by Louis Criss, that was well cast (except for a few bit players, who should have been "great ugly brutes" and weren't) and that made excellent use of the Alley's arena stage. A sign in the lobby said, "Notice to guests. Quiet, please! You are in the corridor of Les Cerisiers Sanatorium." And when the sanatorium was suddenly turned into a prison, we heard chains clanking behind the doors we came in by—and hoped, in due course, to get out by. The cramped auditorium was made a positive advantage; it was as if we too were imprisoned.

Duerrenmatt's play deals with the danger that modern science and technology pose to civilization, which makes it a peculiarly appropriate play for Houston, the home of the NASA Manned Spacecraft Center. Very few American theatres have ever tried to function as the consciences of their communities, and the Alley is not one of them. But this production seemed to me a step in that direction. Perhaps the Alley will not be too overawed by its multimillion-dollar new home to think of taking a few more such steps.

The Mummers Theatre (Oklahoma City)

The Mummers was founded in 1949, two years after the Alley; like the Alley, it was begun by local people as an amateur theatre. But its evolution has been slow; it did not go Equity until the fall of 1967. For several years before that it maintained a few ill-paid non-Equity resident actors, but otherwise relied on local talent: two students from Northwest Classen High School had prominent roles in the Mummers' production of Noel Coward's Hay Fever as late as the spring of 1966. One of the girls was intolerable; the other provided a slightly monotonous but competent funny-fat-girl characterization that was almost the best performance of the evening. The leading lady played Coward's glamorous, actressy heroine in a manner reminiscent of Charlotte Greenwood doing Aunt Eller in Oklahoma!; otherwise, the prevailing idea of the proper style for Coward seemed to be based on the English accent that my Uncle Al affects after a few drinks.

Nevertheless, I stopped in Oklahoma City on my rounds the following season, and found a production of Anouilh's Mademoiselle Colombe in which nearly every role was miscast. Anouilh's heroine is supposed to be innocent, but not gawky like the girl who played her; the misanthropic, puritanical, moody, ardent hero was played as if he were a BMOC at the University of Oklahoma; the hero's mother, a raddled, vulgar, screaming termagant, was played by an actress who would probably be very good as an aristocratic but kindly grandmother. Anouilh's super-civilized play about the corruption of innocence, set behind the scenes of a Parisian theatre at the turn of the century, was performed for the most part in broad Oklahoma accents. I managed to enjoy the evening because I love the play and had never seen it, but the production was well below professional standards—or would have been if there were any professional standards in the American theatre.

Perhaps going Equity will bring about an improvement, although only a very hungry actor would want to go to Oklahoma City to work for the Mummers. And perhaps a new building will somehow induce an improvement. The Mummers now functions in an old oil-field equipment warehouse that seats 286 people, but a new theatre is under construction, to open in 1968 or 1969. It will have a main auditorium with 600 seats and a thrust stage, and a smaller auditorium, "a room in which we can alter the actor-audience relationship," seating up to 275 spectators.

The new theatre is being built with the help of Ford Foundation money. Next to the Alley, the Mummers is the Foundation's favorite grantee among the regional theatres; it has been granted $1,785,000 since 1962, most of which will go for the new building and to maintain the company after it moves in. God knows the Mummers can use all the money that the Foundation can shovel in, but does it deserve it? One official of another theatre dismissed the grant as the Foundation's attempt "to plant culture on the prairies." Certainly it would seem that if a theatre of decent quality can be established in Oklahoma City, "in the big fat middle of the Bible Belt," as a local resident observed—Oklahoma City, where the local Baptists picketed *Inherit the Wind* for preaching Evolution—then it can be done anywhere.

The Front Street Theatre (Memphis)

Like the Alley and the Mummers, the Front Street Theatre in Memphis was founded as an amateur group by a local zealot. George Touliatos began it in a hotel ballroom in the summer of

1957, when he was twenty-seven years old. It went Equity in 1959, and moved into its present quarters, a 372-seat converted movie house, in 1961. Mr. Touliatos ran the theatre for the first ten years of its life, and is unquestionably the major figure in its somewhat ambiguous history.

Mr. Touliatos' aim, he told me, was to make his audience "better citizens by alerting them . . . to the most dominant ideas in the world today that can be projected, by showing them problems of the past that are problems in life today, so that they can cope with them and handle them better . . . by entertaining them, by providing a mirror . . . by always showing the dignity of man and the beauty of man in hopes that it will give them strength . . ."

He was aware, however, of a certain disparity between his aspirations and his achievements. "I'm proud of the audience here," he said. "I've been very carefully nurturing them, very slow in developing them." (But if he was so proud of them, why didn't he develop them a little more quickly?) On the other hand, he also said that people in Memphis were "not ready to accept" what he hoped to do. "At this point, there is still the problem of developing audience taste, [and of] economic security." And so he was "somewhat conservative in my selection of plays. I feel a certain guilt about this, I suppose."

In 1964 he had told a local newspaperman, "I think the popular play has a definite place in the schedule. We're not trying to be ultra-arty—I can't stand that." But in 1966 he told me, "We don't do *Life with Father* anymore." Instead he did two musicals a year. He called them "the only true American art form," but maintained that he did them in order to survive: "If we took the musicals out of our subscription package I'm afraid we'd lose half our subscribers." (The subscribers he was so proud of?) Nevertheless he had hopes for the future: once he had to do nine musicals a season, some day, perhaps, he would not have to do any. Mr. Touliatos has evidently been the victim of an advanced case of ambivalence; he is probably not the only resident-theatre director so afflicted, but in him the symptoms were unusually clear.

The day I talked to him, I saw the Front Street production of Anouilh's *Becket*. It was directed by William Woodman, who has also worked at the Cleveland Play House and the Hartford Stage

Company; along with Charles Maryan, Louis Criss, and Stephen Porter, Mr. Woodman is one of a new breed of itinerant directors who turn up at regional theatres all over the map. His *Becket* was quite a creditable job. In spite of all the talk about ensemble acting that goes on in resident-theatre circles, these theatres are often much better off with plays written around one or two characters, because one or two first-rate actors are easier to find than half a dozen or more. Several roles in *Becket* were quite badly played, but the production was held together by the performances of William Shust (jobbed in from New York) as King Henry and Gil Rogers (a member of the resident company) as Becket.

Both parts were unconventionally cast. Becket, the "little Saxon," was six foot three; he had neither quite the lightness for Becket's dandyism at the beginning nor the weight for his archiepiscopal dignity at the end. But he had what was really needed: an air of quiet authority and unpretentious intelligence, and a nice relish for irony. The king was not the usual expansive brute, but a little boy who liked to shock his elders and have his way. Their relationship was clear and credible: a case of passionate adolescent hero-worship, fatally complicated by the fact that the adolescent in question was the king. About every half hour or so there came a reminder that this was not quite what Anouilh had in mind, but on the whole it worked surprisingly well.

In February of 1967 I returned to see the Front Street take on *Macbeth*. The winner was a young actress named Patricia Elliott, who made Lady Macbeth by far the most interesting character in the play. Young as she was, Miss Elliott was *ready*; without being a gorgon, she held sway over Macbeth by sheer strength of character. After the murder of Duncan was discovered, Miss Elliot stood, fetching her breath in convulsive inhalations, waging a terrible, silent fight for self-control, while Macbeth waffled on in the background, until she fainted; it was the high point of the evening.

Miss Elliott aside, the production was undistinguished. Roland Hewgill made a stodgy Macbeth, and the supporting cast was uneven. Grady Larkins, the set designer, produced some spectacular effects: a great roughhewn rock opened to reveal the witches, and when they were done, it closed with a great heaving, sealing them inside. But Curt Reis's staging, with its endless procession of little ingenuities, grew annoying after a while, and the martial hullabaloo at the end was highly unconvincing.

At this time the Front Street was also offering a series of Monday-night productions without décor (Pinter, Williams, Albee, Van Itallie, and Ferlinghetti), and a late-night cabaret show entitled *Money*.

Not long after *Macbeth*, the theatre's deficit caught up with it. A last-ditch, save-us-or-we-close-our-doors appeal for funds managed to raise $35,000, but by the time the dust had cleared Mr. Touliatos had decided to take a two-year leave of absence, leaving the Front Street in the hands of Harvey Landa, its general manager. The last Touliatos season had comprised A *Funny Thing Happened on the Way to the Forum, The Little Foxes, You Never Can Tell, A Streetcar Named Desire, Macbeth, The Miser, Six Characters in Search of an Author,* and a British musical called *Lock up Your Daughters.* Mr. Landa, by contrast, scheduled for the 1967–68 season *Luv, Who's Afraid of Virginia Woolf, The Knack, The Subject Was Roses, The Imaginary Invalid,* and *Twelfth Night.* Four of these plays call for a cast of four or less; the other two are light comedies.

In the fall of 1968, the Front Street will take up residence in a five-hundred-seat auditorium on the campus of Memphis State University; Keith Kennedy, MSU's director of theatre, will become artistic director of the company, and Mr. Landa will continue as general manager. The Front Street has been through a couple of very rough seasons; perhaps at MSU it will find some measure of stability, and maybe even some purpose beyond mere survival.

The Actors Theatre of Louisville

The Actors Theatre occupies an abandoned railway station on the banks of the Ohio River; this provides plenty of atmosphere, but the Louisville group is probably the only resident theatre in the country with a prospective flood problem. The auditorium, with its seats arranged around an open stage in one corner, is serviceable enough, and has recently been expanded to a capacity of 350. Attendance has risen steadily since a native Louisvillian named Richard Block started the theatre in 1964, when he was twenty-six.

The production I saw there of George M. Cohan's *The Tavern* was so ponderously overdirected by Mr. Block, who is still the theatre's producer-director, that it was hard to discern whether the actors had any talent (though I thought I detected a certain panache in Bryan E. Clark, who played the leading role. Mr. Clark doubles as the theatre's business manager.) The performance I saw had been entirely sold out to a local high school, but the house was half empty: an ominous sign.

That was in April, 1966; I've never gone back. The performance I saw may have been atypical, or things may have improved since. (The theatre seemed, when I was there, to be in quite an early stage of development.) Mr. Block has also presented *In White America* and *Slow Dance on the Killing Ground*, which, in the South, would seem to indicate a certain amount of courage.

Theatre Atlanta

Greater Atlanta has a population of well over a million and is growing rapidly, but until November, 1966, when Theatre Atlanta went professional in a splendid new playhouse on West Peachtree Street, the city had no professional noncommercial theatre.

Like the resident companies in Cleveland, Pittsburgh, Houston, Memphis, and elsewhere, Theatre Atlanta began as an amateur organization; it was formed in 1957, when several small amateur groups, "all starving to death," in the words of a local veteran, decided to merge. In 1965, Jay Broad came down from New York to become Theatre Atlanta's managing director. Mr. Broad, a crew-cut young man in his late thirties who looks like a marine, had spent four years running a community theatre in Fort Wayne, Indiana. (In the relevant jargon, "community" means "amateur.") He had also directed at a professional theatre, now defunct, in St. Paul, Minnesota, and had done an Off-Broadway production of *Life Is a Dream* by Calderón. In Atlanta, he supervised the transition to professional status. He recruited a company of twelve Equity actors: six from the Atlanta area who had acted with Theatre Atlanta as amateurs, and six from out-of-state.

Meanwhile, construction was progressing on a big, bright, new $1,250,000 thrust-stage theatre, built by a wealthy local lady in memory of her daughter, who had been killed in the 1962 plane crash that took the lives of so many of Atlanta's prominent citizens. The professional company and the new theatre were inaugurated simultaneously with a production of Peter Shaffer's *Royal Hunt of the Sun.*

In most cities, professional theatres are slightly ashamed of the recourse they often make to local amateur performers. (Many theatres can afford Equity companies; not so many can afford *all*-Equity companies.) At Theatre Atlanta, however, they make no bones about their continuing use of "avocational" actors (as they are delicately called) alongside the professionals. Still, the transition from amateur to professional theatre is necessarily traumatic: a small cozy local institution is suddenly taken over by strangers—who are paid with money raised by those they have in large measure supplanted. The budget shoots up wildly: from $25,000 to $196,000 in Atlanta. The lady who met me at the Atlanta airport, a local matron who does volunteer work for the theatre, was quite touchy about the "paid ones," as she called them. "What's the difference?" she asked. "What *is* the difference?" One index to what's wrong with American acting is that she's got a point.

The quality of the Atlanta company, judging from the performance I saw of Arthur Miller's *After the Fall,* is not significantly below that of most resident companies—which is not saying very much. Miller's autobiographical play walks a thin edge between profundity and meretriciousness; Frederick Congdon, who played the lead in Atlanta, pushed it over immediately into meretriciousness and kept it there. The problem was not that Mr. Congdon is a bad actor, but that he is the wrong kind of good one, always easy, suave, and cool. Miller's hero is tolerable, in his endless concern with his own problems, only because he is really suffering; it was impossible to believe that spruce Mr. Congdon, in his impeccable three-piece suit and repp tie, with his charming little smile, could really be bothered by anything. Certainly nothing in the play had a chance of penetrating his supreme smugness. His performance made me intensely aware of what Jason Robards, the original Quentin, had been able largely to conceal: how Quentin *patronizes* everyone he meets, how maddeningly self-righteous the character is.

Kathryn Loder as Maggie (the Marilyn Monroe part) had a wonderful bodily characterization, swingy-hipped yet vulnerable, but she was limited by the adenoidal, high-pitched voice she affected. It was amazing how much acting Miss Loder was able to do in spite of that voice—she clearly has talent—but I still thought it a wrong choice. The supporting actors contributed some notably unidiomatic performances; watching what appeared to be an all-WASP cast, I was reminded of something Miller himself has had difficulty coming to terms with: the extent to which he is a specifically Jewish playwright. Quentin's mother, for instance, was played by Lila Kennedy, who, I was told, has been for many years the first lady of theatre in Atlanta. Miss Kennedy performed with dignity and poise, but she hadn't a clue about what to do with a line like, "Who knew he would end up so big in the gallstones?" I got the feeling that the company as a whole would look better in some other play.

After the Fall is Quentin's self-analysis, delivered to an imaginary psychiatrist; Mr. Broad staged it explicitly as a psychodrama. He added the psychiatrist to the cast, and wrote him a few lines explaining that a group of people have gathered to help Quentin by acting out elements of his past. The actors spent the evening seated in chairs set around the perimeter of the thrust stage, facing inward; they would get up when required, play a scene, and sit down again. The device did not strike me as intrusive, and it may have made the play clearer to those unfamiliar with nonrealistic dramaturgical devices. But Mr. Broad carried his scheme to the point where it committed him to an unvarying, rudimentary plan of staging, with setting and lighting to match, and this made a dull production duller.

In addition to *After the Fall* and *Royal Hunt of the Sun*, Theatre Atlanta's first season included *Tobacco Road, Waltz of the Toreadors, Caesar and Cleopatra, Boy Meets Girl, Moby Dick* (in Orson Welles' adaptation), and *The Best Man*. (Kathryn Loder who was playing Cleopatra in *Caesar and Cleopatra,* was injured, and Diana Sands, the Negro actress, agreed to substitute for her; that must have been interesting in Atlanta.) The plays are presented in repertory, so that at least two are on view every week. Only four performances are given per week, yet in spite of the novelty of a glamorous new auditorium, in spite of the national publicity attracted by its opening, in spite of the organization's roots in the community, the first season ran at only 55 per cent of capacity. The people just aren't coming. The theatre seats 765; Broad admits that for the present, 400 would have been plenty. But, after all, isn't it shortsighted to build just for the present?

Unfortunately, the power structure and the big money in Atlanta are committed to the Arts Center going up a few blocks away, and have little to spare for the new repertory company. Theatre Atlanta has built for the future, but it is an open question whether it can hold on until the future comes.

Repertory Theatre, New Orleans

Like Theatre Atlanta, Repertory Theatre, New Orleans, began operations in the fall of 1966; like Theatre Atlanta, it is run by a northerner; like Theatre Atlanta, it is having difficulty attracting paying customers. One difference is that the Repertory Theatre is bankrolled by the Federal Government to the extent of about $500,000 a year for its first three years.

The money comes from the National Endowment for the Arts and the U.S. Office of Education; it is part of a pilot project to test whether live professional theatre deserves a place in the high school curriculum. The Repertory Theatre's primary function is to mount a season of four productions, each of which is seen free of charge by virtually all of the 38,000 high school sophomores, juniors, and seniors in the New Orleans area. (There are similar programs, similarly financed, in Providence, R.I., and Los Angeles.) This is not another program to provide "scenes from" this and that to tour high school auditoriums. The Repertory Theatre gives its student audiences full-length, full-scale productions in a 1,500-seat former road-show house; in addition to the student matinées, each production is performed three times a week, at ordinary prices, for the public.

Theatre Atlanta evolved (too quickly for its own good, perhaps) out of an established community group; the Repertory Theatre of New Orleans came into existence by government fiat. Both have been having trouble at the box office. The Repertory Theatre had about 5,000 adult subscribers for its first season, and sold about 5,000 additional tickets for each production over the counter, which means that the adult performances tended to take place before half-empty houses. Stuart Vaughan, producing director of the theatre, complains that "the adult population is extremely slow to respond. . . . I don't think New Orleans would have had a local professional theatre for fifteen or twenty years without government intervention." One New Orleanian I talked to had been to see Mr. Vaughan's production of *Romeo and Juliet*. "It was terrible," he said. "I don't think they changed the scenery three times in the whole production." If this reaction is typical, it would seem that New Orleans has been, as Mr. Vaughan says, "a culturally deprived area."

Mr. Vaughan is a considerable person in the resident professional theater movement. At the age of forty-two, he has been instrumental in founding four resident professional theatres in various parts of the country. He was the first artistic director of the New York Shakespeare Festival, the Phoenix Theatre Repertory Company (New York), and the Seattle Repertory Theatre. In December of 1965, he was suddenly dismissed by the board of directors of the Seattle Rep; shortly thereafter, Roger L. Stevens, Special Assistant to the President on the Arts, picked him to head what became the New Orleans company. Vaughan was chosen as its director before New Orleans was chosen as its location. The company's identity depends first of all on him, and second of all on its primary function of playing for students; the fact that it happens to be located in New Orleans has had very little to do with shaping its nature. In this respect, it is by no means unusual among the resident theatres.

During his days in Central Park with the New York Shakespeare Festival, Vaughan tended toward imaginative, busy productions; he once introduced a miniature circus into *Two Gentlemen of Verona*. Nowadays his work is more scrupulous, more conservative, more austere; some people find it stuffy. Vaughan says:

> I keep being interested more and more in how to make the audience listen to the play on the play's own terms, and less concerned with how to create an exciting success. I think a lot of directors think if you've excited them, you've done it. But I want the audience to see *the play*. If they want to get excited, that's swell too. . . . Naturally one wants to interest, to move, to excite—but with what? For what purpose? How much?

Now, if a director is determined, as Vaughan is, to avoid directorial razzle-dazzle, he had better have a pretty good group of actors, since they're going to be up there with nothing to distract attention from their deficiencies. Vaughan would seem to be in a good position to form such a company; he is an old hand at the trade, with ten years of experience in fishing the New York talent pool, where nearly all the regional theatres look for their actors. No other American director has had so much practice in putting a resident company together from scratch. Furthermore, he has plenty of money at his disposal: he can afford an all-Equity company, and he can afford a top salary of $300 a week. Special guest stars get even more than $300, and so Tessie O'Shea came down to New Orleans to play the Nurse in *Romeo and Juliet,* Parker Fenelley appeared as the Stage Manager in *Our Town,* and June Havoc played Mrs. Malaprop in *The Rivals.*

And yet the New Orleans *Romeo and Juliet,* directed by Vaughan, was not impressive. The first half went well enough, thanks to Miss O'Shea and to Humbert Allen Astredo as Mercutio. Mr. Astredo was a mature Mercutio, looking quite a bit older than his friend Romeo. He made no pretensions to elegance; he was even willing to get laughs by gargling and spitting. But he gargled and spat in a likable manner, and he had the bounce and brio the part needs. Miss O'Shea, a stout English vaudevillian who has appeared on Broadway and done a turn on the *Ed Sullivan Show,* gave her usual performance. But since her usual performance consists mostly of radiating vigorous, vulgar, big-hearted love in all directions, she made a very good Nurse.

After the halfway mark, however, Mercutio is dead, and the Nurse's best opportunities are over; the lovers must carry the play from then on. Vaughan's Romeo and Juliet were attractively youthful, but had not much to offer beyond that. Rex Thompson was, I suppose, a tolerable Romeo of the extreme poetic-exquisite persuasion, in spite of his inability to pronounce the letter "r." But Vaughan says that "identification, or at any rate recognition, is what the art of the theatre is all about." How likely is a New Orleans high school student (or even an adult, from New Orleans or elsewhere) to identify himself with, or even recognize in any positive sense, a Romeo with a distinct tendency toward the namby-pamby? (His "r" problem, aside from intensifying this effect, made it sometimes hard to understand his words.) As for the Juliet (Gretchen Corbett), she was merely slightly insipid.

Vaughan's staging was straightforward and sensible, but the best that can be said for the production as a whole was that it was better than no *Romeo and Juliet* at all. Like the work of Vaughan's that I had seen in Seattle, it was somewhat dry and lacking in impact.

In New Orleans, as in Atlanta and in other cities, the ambitions of theatrical entrepreneurs have—temporarily, one hopes—apparently outstripped both the capacities of the available talent and the desires of the local audience. Until both the actors and the audiences catch up, the resident theatres are in for some awkward years. Repertory Theatre, New Orleans is now protected by U.S. government money; but if that protection were to be removed, the theatre, at this point, would seem unlikely to survive.

THE
PACIFIC
COAST

The Actor's Workshop (San Francisco)

In the summer of 1966 the Actor's Workshop died after four-teen years of stimulation and controversy. It was one of the oldest of the resident professional theatres, but it never lost its adven-turous spirit.

Herbert Blau and Jules Irving, two teachers at San Francisco State College, began the Actor's Workshop in 1952, in a loft behind a judo academy. They were both New Yorkers, both in their mid-twenties; they had met at NYU, where Blau was editor of the *Heights Daily News* and Irving was president of the theatre group. They had in mind a private studio, a workshop, in which to experiment; the results of their experiments were shown, now and then, to a few invited guests. Gradually they turned their attention to the public, went Equity, and rented two theatres in downtown San Francisco. But they retained something of a studio attitude: they had work that they wished to do, and those who shared their tastes could come and see them do it. They wanted a large audience, but were afraid of being corrupted by it; they raised money and peddled subscriptions, but their hearts weren't in it. Many people found them self-righteous; Blau in particular was given to venting his mind in great sweeping manifestoes which won him few friends.

On the other hand, "There are occasions," as Blau says, "when the theatre must do its work against what passes for common consent, to appear to say, 'To hell with society!' "* This service the Workshop learned to perform. It never sought merely to please its audience. Most theatres do at least one lollipop a year—Coward, Kaufman and Hart, Murray Schisgal, if not an outright piece of Broadway merchandise. Almost alone among the resident theatres, the Workshop never did *Under the Yum-Yum Tree* in any way, shape, or form.

It produced Shakespeare, Shaw, Chekhov, Miller, O'Casey, Osborne, and many others, including some new playwrights, but in the years of its maturity it was best known for its productions of Brecht, the Absurdists, and other "difficult" writers. Many of these are now standard fare in the resident theatres, which *Variety* has called "the Beckett and Pinter circuit," but the Workshop was presenting them when no one else would dare. Blau and Irving gave the American premières of, among other plays, Brecht's *Mother Courage*, Pinter's *The Birthday Party*, and *Serjeant Musgrave's Dance* by John Arden. It might be argued that a less adventurous repertory might have done as good or better service for the people of San Francisco, but by introducing these plays the Workshop made itself a force in the American theatre at large.

The results of this combination of courage, high principles, high standards, and bad public relations can readily be imagined. Though the Workshop was widely admired outside San Francisco, though it enlisted the support of the Ford Foundation, though it sent a production of *Waiting for Godot* to New York and to the Brussels World's Fair, its existence was always precarious because it never developed a solid base of financial support from its community. The city government made it an appropriation from time to time—something very few cities have been willing to do for their theatres—but it was never enough to make up for the lack of both a large subscription audience and a few rich patrons.

And so it is understandable that when Blau and Irving were asked to take over the Repertory Theatre of Lincoln Center in January, 1965, they should have accepted; San Francisco had done very little for them. They canceled the rest of their San Francisco season and lit out for New York, leaving Kenneth Kitch, a young

---

* Herbert Blau, *The Impossible Theatre* (New York, 1965), p. 182.

member of the company, as their successor at the Workshop, to keep it alive if he could. But what was there to keep alive? The Workshop had only existed as the lengthened shadow of Blau and Irving. Furthermore, they had taken with them to New York most of the leading Workshop actors (as well as the entire front-office staff, right down to the bookkeeper).

Nevertheless Kitch went ahead. He hired as artistic director a twenty-six-year-old Harvard man named John Hancock (the same Hancock who subsequently stirred up so much controversy in Pittsburgh), and in July of 1965, the Workshop reopened with *The Milk Train Doesn't Stop Here Any More* by Tennessee Williams, directed by Hancock. The author came out to San Francisco to attend rehearsals and do rewrites; the production got a great deal of attention and did excellent business. On the strength of this success, Kitch and Hancock announced their 1965–66 season: Brecht's *Edward II* (an American première), Saul Bellow's *The Last Analysis*, Molière's *Don Juan*, Strindberg's *The Father*, and Shakespeare's *A Midsummer Night's Dream*. In addition, they scheduled a nonsubscription series of weekend productions in their smaller theatre: several new plays, including one by an inmate at San Quentin, and the American première of *The Empire Builders* by Boris Vian.

It was an adventurous program in the Workshop tradition, with several plays that hardly anyone in the audience had ever heard of, and that hardly any other theatre in America would dare to do. When asked about this, Kitch quoted Jules Irving: "I don't want to be doing *Mary, Mary* when the bomb drops." Yet the new directors were more conscious than their predecessors had been of the need for good public relations, and more interested in the techniques of ticket–selling. For their first season they sold 5,100 subscriptions; this is not an impressive number, considering the Bay Area's population and its reputation as a cultural center (in Seattle, with no such reputation and a much smaller population, the local Repertory Theatre had almost 13,000 subscribers), but it was more than Blau and Irving had ever succeeded in selling.

Then in December came another crisis: in spite of good reviews and good business, the Workshop ran out of money. The directors announced that unless $50,000 was raised "within the next few days," the Workshop would close its doors permanently. At the last minute, an anonymous benefactor came through with the final $20,000; the Workshop was saved, and the directors promised no more crises, ever again.

Thus the Workshop was preserved for my visit in the spring, at which time I was confronted by John Hancock's strange version of *A Midsummer Night's Dream*, with sets and costumes by the pop artist Jim Dine—a production that Hancock later restaged, with different casts, at the Pittsburgh Playhouse and off Broadway.

As the play began, a tarpaulin was jerked off a large object prominently placed downstage right, revealing a gaudily lit-up jukebox which emitted Mendelssohn (and Mahler) at intervals throughout the evening. Hippolyta, Theseus' captive mistress, wore only a loincloth, a bra, a great deal of black body make-up, some chains, a sullen expression, and perhaps a wig; she played her first scene in a cage. Demetrius, one of the interchangeable youths, had a light-bulb in his codpiece which flashed on and off whenever he was feeling amorous. And Helena, one of the maidens, was played by a man six feet four inches tall.

All these innovations were lively and theatrical; they got laughs; they "worked." But, surprisingly enough, they were not just gimmicks, not mere effusions of irresponsible cleverness; they were the expression of a consistent artistic intention. The intention was not, of course, Shakespeare's. Jan Kott has pointed out an element of sexual grotesquerie in the play that most directors ignore, but Hancock went whooping and hollering off to the opposite extreme, and scribbled grotesquerie all over what is, after all, an essentially lyrical work. Shakespeare wrote it as an epithalamium, a marriage song. It shows that love is productive of foolishness, confusion, even cruelty and grief, but in the play's scheme these things are transitory. Shakespeare's mockery is affectionate; it does not deny the validity of what is mocked, and the play ends with a powerful blessing on the marriage bed.

In the Workshop production lyricism was exposed as fraudulent, and love was revealed as half itch and half obsession. Mendelssohn was mocked by the jukebox, Demetrius' romantic raptures by the blinking bulb in his crotch. And Hancock's mockery was for keeps. No amount of blessing—particularly not from the Workshop's distinctly *louche* bunch of fairies—is going to straighten out the marriage bed of a six-foot-four-inch male Helena. Shakespeare says,

"Jack shall have Jill, naught shall go ill"; Hancock said that the course of true sex never did run smooth, and what is true sex anyway?

The Workshop production was a denial of the play, a rebuttal, a parody, a blasphemy; it was an anti-*Midsummer Night's Dream*—and a brilliant one. Since it propounded with consistency and clarity (as well as vividness and wit) the notion that man's sexuality makes him ridiculous and grotesque and betrays his pretensions to high-mindedness and beauty, it also fulfilled Matthew Arnold's grand old criterion for a work of art: it was a criticism of life. It was a criticism of Shakespeare as well, but Shakespeare can stand it. The theatre has this advantage, that though one director may decide, for good or bad reasons, to paint a moustache on the *Mona Lisa*, the next director will find the masterpiece as good as new.

Furthermore, no other prudent course was open to Hancock if he was to do this script at all. His company was simply not well schooled enough to present the play adequately in the conventional lyrical manner; on the whole it was very wise of him to use all his tricks to distract our attention from the acting.

Hancock had a difficult row to hoe in San Francisco. The Workshop's old company had been traumatically shattered by the departure of Blau and Irving. The Workshop's facilities were scattered in eighteen different locations, all rented. Financially things were still very shaky; the bailing-out of the December crisis had only postponed the final answer as to whether the Workshop would survive. And so, in the summer of 1966, when Hancock was offered the job of artistic director at the Pittsburgh Playhouse, with three theatres under one roof for his sole use, and a budget of $700,000, he took it (with results for him and for Pittsburgh that have been chronicled in Chapter Three). Once again the Workshop was without an artistic director, and, as usual, it didn't know where its next dollar was coming from. A final appeal to the Chamber of Commerce was rejected, and there was nothing to do but close the doors.

Like nearly all resident theatres (and opera companies, symphony orchestras, art museums, and libraries), the Actor's Workshop ran at a deficit and depended primarily on support from the community—i.e., the local business community—to make up that deficit. There is certainly enough money in San Francisco to support a resident theatre; after the death of the Workshop, William Ball's American Conservatory Theatre was invited to make its home in San Francisco, and its local sponsors have agreed to meet deficits far larger than anything the Workshop envisaged. Why did these same businessmen—or "civic leaders," as they are called when they dabble in culture—allow the Workshop to die?

Part of it, obviously, was the fact that when Hancock left, the Workshop consisted of hardly more than Kenneth Kitch, some memories, and a lot of debts. But I would conjecture that other factors were involved as well. The Workshop was founded without reference to the "civic leaders," and made few compromises with them; they were not encouraged to feel that it was their theatre. The Workshop was one of the most outspokenly anti-Establishment theatres we had, and the more the anti-Establishment forces have to rely upon the Establishment for money, the more they are in danger. He that pays the piper calls the tune.

In San Francisco, moreover, civic leaders were able to occupy themselves with the symphony, the opera, the ballet, the art museums, all nice safe activities which could be depended on not to turn around and bite them. Shortly before its end, the Workshop did a play that might have been about the end of Western civilization. At that time a sign was prominently placed in the theatre, with mockery as its evident intention, saying, " 'Killing, rioting, and looting are contrary to the best traditions of this country'—Lyndon Johnson." The symphony orchestra would never have done that.

But what about other sources of funds? What about the Ford Foundation, which in the days of Blau and Irving had encouraged the Workshop to expand its activities and its budget? Not without reason, the Foundation regarded the post-Blau-and-Irving Workshop as a new organization, and it is Ford Foundation policy to require new organizations to prove themselves before the Foundation will give them any money. While proving itself, the Workshop died. On the other hand, the National Council for the Arts, which disburses U.S. government money, has no such scruples about organizations proving themselves; New Orleans was recently given half a million dollars for a theatre that had not even been organized yet. The Council allotted the Workshop $22,500 in June; it was not enough.

It may be asked why any organ of the Establishment should be expected to support anti-Establishment organizations. The answer is that in this country the Establishment is invulnerable because so many of us have so big a stake in it. There was never any real danger that the Actor's Workshop was going to overthrow the Great Society; the Establishment could have afforded to be generous. The money-powers in this country must be made to feel complacent enough, yet guilty enough, to support dissenting artists, because dissenting artists cannot, in many cases, support themselves, and yet it is a peculiarity of the modern era that the creative art that shows signs of staying power is usually the expression of dissent.

In practical terms, San Francisco has lost nothing. The Workshop has been replaced by the American Conservatory Theatre, a safely eclectic organization that has, nevertheless, performed prodigious feats, and made San Francisco a highly exciting theatre town, as will be seen in Chapter Ten. Nevertheless the fact remains that the Workshop is dead, and the suspicion remains that it was, at least in part, killed because it spoke out too boldly.

The San Francisco Mime Troupe

In 1962, an actor named R. G. Davis, who specialized in mime, left the Actor's Workshop because he thought it was selling out. He thought that the acceptance by the Workshop of a Ford Foundation grant, which enabled it to hire ten New York actors at $200 a week, had been bad for the theatre. Mr. Davis had already founded the San Francisco Mime Troupe in 1959, and he remains its leader to this day. The members of the Mime Troupe support themselves by extra-theatrical jobs, so that they will not have to rely on patronage by government, foundations, or other organs of the bourgeoisie. Thus the Mime Troupe has managed to survive while being far more radical than the Workshop ever wanted to be.

Nowadays the Mime Troupe is not primarily a mime troupe at all, but neither, for the most part, does it mount conventional plays. In addition to works by Jarry, Brecht, and Ghelderode, it has given original plays, happenings, children's puppet shows, and *commedie dell'arte*, plus poetry readings and speeches. It uses *commedia*, vaudeville, and Artaudian shock techniques to comment, as subversively as it can, on American civilization. It is highly admired in some circles, and I have seen it thrust home some barbed shafts; sometimes, on the other hand, its work is vitiated by propagandistic simple-mindedness, and by sheer bad workmanship.

In the fall of 1966 the Mime Troupe made a national tour with a work entitled *A Minstrel Show or Civil Rights in a Cracker Barrel*; I caught it at a one-night stand at Town Hall in New York. "Written by Saul Landau and R. G. Davis from original, traditional, and improvised material," and directed by Mr. Davis, it used the old-fashioned minstrel show to dramatize the state of race relations in this country today. It was performed by a suave, patronizing white Interlocutor and six minstrels in blackface, eyes and lips painted dead-white, wearing silly light-blue shiny satin suits and white gloves. Strutting, shuffling, prancing, grinning grotesquely, they showed us very vividly, at its worst, the mask of degradation that the white man has forced the Negro to wear. And underneath the ingratiating minstrel-manner was a constant threat —just as there is in real life.

The show was full of violence. A white cop killed a black boy, and then two black boys knifed a *black* cop. Three men labeled "Nigger," "Negro," and "White" were gathered together in a men's room; the "Nigger" pulled a knife on both the others. A performer said, "When you live in Watts, man, don' burn down you' own neighborhood. You go fuck up Beverly Hills!" In the intermission, the minstrels went out into the house, mocking and embarrassing the audience, and choosing white girls to come up on the stage and dance with them.

Some people seem to have found the Troupe's shock techniques really shocking. Shortly before I saw them, three members of the company had been arrested during a performance in Denver and charged with "committing a lewd act and using filthy language on the stage." In New York, however, it seemed to me that the Mime Troupe provided the audience with an occasion to congratulate themselves for *not* being shocked. Perhaps it is useful to bring liberals and radicals together for a reaffirmation of their own supposed tough-mindedness, their own willingness to accept their guilt for what has been done to the Negro, and the consequent hatred that the Negro feels for them, but I was reminded of the Feiffer cartoon about the group of white liberals who pay a Negro to come every week and call them names. Maybe that's healthy too. (The Mime Troupe is integrated; Mr. Davis is white.) In any case, I couldn't help thinking that after Genet's *The Blacks*, the Mime Troupe's *Minstrel Show* was slightly second-hand.

The next time I saw the Troupe was on its home ground in San Francisco. Since 1961, it has been setting up its traveling stage in the parks there and playing *commedia dell'arte* free of charge. (There is now a notice in the program, however, that says, "Each performer receives $5 per show. We exist from your donations.") In June of 1967 I saw the Troupe perform in Washington Square Park, a small, green open space between two of San Francisco's hills, in a middle-class neighborhood with Rossi's Drug Store on one corner and a Chinese movie house on another. When I got there, the actors were lounging around in plain view behind a simple platform stage, eating lunch, adjusting their costumes, putting on make-up. A group of kids—white, Negro, Chinese—stood around watching as if this were the show. The performers picked up musical instruments—drum, trumpets, tambourines, cymbals, recorder—and stood on the grass for a while singing folk songs, not too well, as a friendly red dog circulated in the slowly gathering crowd. Finally a couple of hundred relaxed, Saturday-afternoon people were sitting on the grass around the stage, and the show began.

It was called *L'Amant Militaire*. It had been taken from a play by Goldoni, translated by Betty Schwimmer, adapted by Jean Holden, directed by Mr. Davis with Arthur Holden. It was terrible.

The Minstrel Show had the keenness of real wit every now and then; *L'Amant Militaire* was distinguished by witless, quibbling, repetitive nowhere-going dialogue and noisy, clumsy, effortful performing. Shouting and stumbling about are not the same as comic acting, and denunciation is not the same as satire. Pantalone, the Mayor of Spinachola, was a capitalist with a Jewish accent, in cahoots with the Spanish "Generale"; their preoccupation as well as their style was exemplified in a line (I forget whose) that went, "As Lyndon Johnson once said to Bing Crosby, screw the poor." The play's message for our times was summed up in another line: "Nothin's gonna change unless you get up off your ass and do something." And for earthy, vigorous, popular humor, how about: "[She:] No one can feel my despair." "[He, rubbing her belly:] I feel it, my darling."

Sometimes the performance displayed a commendable tendency to adapt itself to the immediacies of the audience. "I've come to water the flower children," said one actor, sprinkling nearby spectators. Another exchange went: "You're pretty big for an Italian." "I grew up in the country, not in North Beach." But mostly the performers just flailed gracelessly on and on and on. After a while I couldn't take it any longer, and left—the first time I have ever voluntarily walked out on anything. What this country needs, I reflected as I climbed Telegraph Hill in the afternoon sunlight, is an independent, courageous, militant, committed theatre, a theatre like the Mime Troupe, only better.

The Seattle Repertory Theatre

When the Seattle World's Fair was over, among the odds and ends it left behind was a handsome 800-seat theatre. Stimulated by the availability of such a splendid facility, a group of local citizens organized the Seattle Repertory Theatre to occupy it. Stuart Vaughan, who had been the artistic director of the New York Shakespeare Festival and the Phoenix Theatre, was brought out to be artistic director of the new organization, and on November 13, 1963, the company Mr. Vaughan recruited opened in *King Lear*. By that time the theatre already had 9,000 subscribers.

From the first the SRT has been a true repertory theatre, presenting as many as four or five different productions during a single week. Mr. Vaughan's choice of plays was unexceptionably solid, with an emphasis on Shakespeare. In 1965–66, for instance, which turned out to be Mr. Vaughan's last season, the theatre put on *Julius Caesar*, *Long Day's Journey*, *The Importance of Being Earnest*, *Heartbreak House*, *Galileo*, *Ah, Wilderness!*, *The Cherry Orchard*, *Twelfth Night*, and *Hamlet*, plus a children's play, a free, outdoor summer production of *She Stoops to Conquer*, a special production of *Under Milk Wood*, a reading by local poets, and a guest appearance by the Merce Cunningham Dance Company.

In December, 1965, the SRT board of trustees suddenly dismissed Stuart Vaughan from the theatre he had brought into being. It used to be that a theatre was founded by a fanatic who suffered for it, fed it with his heart's blood, and became inextricable from it. But as the resident-theatre movement spreads, more and more theatres are being founded by groups of citizens, without theatrical training or talent themselves, who have decided that a theatre is a good thing for their town, and who raise money and import an artistic director from New York to create a company and to run it. But the citizens retain the veto power over the artists—as they do, ultimately, wherever there are deficits to be met—and occasionally, as in Seattle, they use it.

In Pittsburgh, John Hancock was fired for being too avant-garde, and some people maintain that this was one of the reasons for Andre Gregory's departure from Philadelphia. It does not seem to have been the case in Seattle. Vaughan's sympathizers complained that the board was a bunch of interfering amateurs who wanted to "play theatre." Bagley Wright, the president of the Seattle board, maintained that Vaughan had no conception of teamwork, that it was a mistake for Vaughan to act as well as direct, that two other directors with the company got better performances out of the actors than Vaughan could, that the subscribers were complaining, and that though Vaughan had done a lot for the company, a new artistic director was needed if it was to improve.

Some people associated with the company complained that nine major productions in a season were too many, even if four were revivals from the previous season; Allen Fletcher, whom the board appointed to succeed Vaughan, cut back the number of productions to six, with no revivals from past seasons. One actor with the company told me that under Vaughan they had been "drowning in the mud of classicism." Be that as it may, Fletcher's first season consisted of plays by Arthur Miller, Brendan Behan, Noel Coward, Friedrich Duerrenmatt, Tennessee Williams, and Molière; only one play out of the six was written before 1940. (Having thus righted the balance, Fletcher scheduled Shakespeare, Anouilh, Brecht-Weill, Sheridan, Strindberg, and Kaufman and Hart for 1967–68.)

When I first came to Seattle in the spring of 1966, Vaughan had been gone two months, but the company he had chosen was still there, sedulously adhering to the schedule he had laid out. Brecht's *Galileo,* which Vaughan was to have directed, was staged instead by the acting artistic director, Pirie MacDonald, who had been Vaughan's second-in-command. Much of the acting in it was mediocre in various ways, but the production was redeemed by Thomas Hill's good strong Galileo. *Twelfth Night* was a revival of Vaughan's 1964 production, redirected by MacDonald; it had a reasonably good group of comedians (although the Malvolio tended to gabble indistinctly when he got excited), but Viola and Orsino had little lyricism and less ardor. Shaw's *Heartbreak House,* the production Vaughan was directing when he was fired, was three and a half hours of tedium when I saw it. Most of the actors flourished and brandished their elaborately phony characterizations like small boys in a shower-room trying unsuccessfully to snap one another with heavy, soggy bath towels. Two actresses in major roles had maddeningly grating voices; when, after a long conversation, they were joined by a third actress who had a tense delivery and a pronunciation problem, I was strongly tempted to flee.

When I returned to Seattle a year later, toward the end of the first Allen Fletcher season, things were very much the same, and greatly different. The theatre of course was still comfortable, and the stage still large; the productions, as they had been last year, were lavishly mounted and very good-looking. It was still an unusually large company, mustering fifty-seven strong for *The Visit,* with nineteen Equity professionals (as against seventeen the previous year). The actors were mostly the same ones I had seen last time; they were still not really a very distinguished group; many of them were still bothered with severe speech problems. And yet, under Fletcher's direction, with a few newcomers in their midst, they somehow seemed better; somehow, this year, the productions *worked.*

In *Tartuffe,* one of the ingénues was too old (any girl as sappy as Molière's Mariane had better be young, if only to provide an excuse), and another actress squeaked her way through the important part of the maid in a desperately labored attempt at vivacity. But in spite of some imperfect diction, the cast was at home with the rhymed couplets of Richard Wilbur's translation, and Josef Sommer's Tartuffe was a triumph of grotesque virtuosity: a disgusting, slimy, lip-licking, very funny horror. I had several times seen Mr. Sommer act under Allen Fletcher's direction at the Stratford (Connecticut) Shakespeare Festival, but I had no idea he was capable of anything like this.

Mr. Fletcher's staging also showed a new side of his talent. At Stratford, where he had been artistic director for several years, his work had been scrupulously self-effacing, as if he had feared to leave his own hallmark on a production. But *Tartuffe* was quite elaborately staged, almost choreographed; the director's hand was visible at almost every point, and the performance was all the better for it. Mr. Fletcher and Mr. Sommer made it a funny show, and an SRO house enjoyed it greatly. (There is more in *Tartuffe* than a funny show, of course, but in half a dozen productions I have never seen that "more" made manifest on the stage, not even at the Comédie Française. I hear that Roger Planchon's production . . . Meanwhile, I am willing to settle for a funny show.)

Night of the Iguana gives off a sense of Tennessee Williams playing his old familiar tune. It was probably a mistake of Mr. Fletcher to pace it so slowly; the play doesn't deserve it. But, like some of his heroines, Williams' plays are moving even in the depths of their grandiloquence and wallowing self-pity, and this one is no exception. Again, the Seattle production was far from unexceptionable. Williams wrote a play about a man and two women, one a dignified lady and one a blowsy slut. In this production, the script to the contrary notwithstanding, it became a play about a man and two dignified ladies.

But, again, on the whole, it worked. To play the hero, Fletcher imported another actor who had worked for him at Stratford: a tall personage named Frank Converse, who was just about to find fame on television, although no one knew it at the time. He was a bit young to play an unfrocked minister approaching middle age who had been through a great deal, all of it bad, since his unfrocking, but it was a highly interesting performance all the same. Skinny and shaky, he looked like a marionette constantly threatening to fold up; his deep, very slightly adenoidal voice and cultivated diction suited the grandiloquence of his dialogue; his falling-apart fatigue and his desperate fury were both believable.

Robert Darling's set—a light, delicate, slightly fantastic tumbledown tropical hotel made of scrim—lit by Barbara Nollman, was beautiful to look at, perhaps even too much so. And the tropical storm in the first act was splendid: I could almost smell it.

For *The Visit*, Mr. Darling designed another brilliant set, this one harsh and mechanistic in style. Again, the acting was of no inordinate distinction, but Pirie MacDonald, who directed, made good use of his huge stage and his huge company, and the point of Duerrenmatt's dark fable came across strongly.

The SRT appears to be prospering under Mr. Fletcher's stewardship. Attendance in 1966–67 was 77 per cent of capacity, as against 63 per cent the year before. A multifaceted student program, begun under Mr. Vaughan, continues. Actors are sent into the schools to work with the teachers, read poetry, talk about theatre, and make themselves useful in other ways. Unsold tickets are available to students (as they are at several other theatres) for $2 at curtain time; it is a pleasure to see long lines of kids, even on rainy nights, waiting to get in. In addition, in the spring of 1967, there were three weeks of performances for students, at the theatre, of *Tartuffe* and *The Crucible*, paid for by federal funds. The SRT has also continued to give free performances in the city parks; in 1967 it presented *The Merry Wives of Windsor* for six weeks in Seattle and other Puget Sound cities. And once again there were bonus programs for subscribers: a bill of Chekhov farces, and an e. e. cummings show.

In the fall of 1967, the SRT inaugurated a second smaller auditorium, where it plans to do new scripts and other experimental work, in addition to some conventional small-cast plays. There will be one small production for each major one, to utilize the actors not needed on the main stage. For the future, there are plans—or hopes, at least—for a tour of the Pacific Northwest.

All the SRT needs now are better actors; in the meantime, it is very odd how well Mr. Fletcher has managed to do without them.

The Center Theatre Group (Los Angeles)

There has been resident theatre in the Los Angeles area since long before the Center Theatre Group, or its predecessor the UCLA Theatre Group, came into existence. The Pasadena Playhouse, traditionally one of the leading American community theatres, was founded in 1917, and began using professional actors many years ago. Over the years it has lost impetus, however, and in the summer of 1966 it was seized by Internal Revenue agents for tax arrears of $31,000. Since then, under a new "executive producer-director," former TV producer Albert McCleery, it has come a long way toward recovery, but it seems to have decisively lost its position of leadership.

The Theatre Group was founded in 1959 under the sponsorship of the extension program at UCLA, to utilize for serious theatrical ends some of the many talented people attracted to the area by the movie and television industries. It was not tied in to the university's theatre arts department, and the university took no financial responsibility for it. It put on its shows in university buildings, but could use these buildings only when they were not wanted for other purposes, which necessitated a limited and somewhat sporadic production schedule.

John Houseman (Orson Welles' colleague at the Mercury Theatre; the producer of the movie *Julius Caesar*; former artistic director of the American Shakespeare Festival at Stratford, Connecticut) was artistic director of the Theatre Group from 1960 to 1963; in 1964, Gordon Davidson joined the Group as assistant director for its production of *King Lear*, and stayed on to become its managing director. From the beginning, the Group has been adventurous in its choice of plays, and successful in persuading people to come to them. In 1965, it scheduled a bill of one-act plays by W. B. Yeats, predictably one of the world's all-time all-star audience-losers, which played to 74 per cent of capacity; no other production that season fell below 90 per cent.

The Theatre Group's production of Rolf Hochhuth's *The Deputy*, a big hit in Los Angeles in 1965, was one of the few resident-theatre productions ever to be booked for a coast-to-coast tour of road-show theatres in major cities; I caught up with it in Chicago. After the Los Angeles run, several actors had left the cast, but the production had been recast and re-rehearsed by the original director, Gordon Davidson. It was vividly staged, with a very effective use of sound and light, and it was well designed by Peter Wexler. But it was not, on the whole, well acted. Hochhuth's hero, an idealistic young priest who goes around telling various Church officials that the Nazis are killing the Jews, is a little on the simple-minded side at the best of times, but Robert

Brown played him as Jack Armstrong in a cassock. No less than three actors in prominent parts, Mr. Brown included, had difficulty pronouncing the letter "s," and there was some strenuously hackneyed emoting going on. Being based in Los Angeles, the Group is almost the only resident theatre that can exist independently of the New York talent pool, but judging from *The Deputy* this is not much of an advantage.

After its 1966 season (which included *Next Time I'll Sing to You* by James Saunders, the Bernstein-Hellman-Wilbur-Latouche-Parker version of *Candide, The Birthday Party,* and *Poor Bitos*), the Theatre Group left UCLA and moved downtown to the new Music Center, where it became, in effect, a part of the Center Theatre Group. The Music Center is Los Angeles' answer to Lincoln Center, and the Center Theatre Group is its legitimate-theatre organ. The Group had been somewhat of a stepchild at UCLA; now it enjoys the golden embrace of the Los Angeles cultural Establishment. The chairman of the board of directors of the Center Theatre Group is Mrs. Norman Chandler, the famous "Buffy" Chandler, wife of the owner of the Los Angeles *Times,* and the moving force behind the Music Center. The president of the Center Theatre Group is Lew R. Wasserman of MCA. The official adviser to the board is Robert Whitehead, founder of the Repertory Theatre of Lincoln Center. And the director of the Center Theatre Group is Elliot Martin, the producer of *Nobody Loves an Albatross* and *Never Too Late.*

The Group has two theatres under its jurisdiction; it is responsible for a thirty-seven-week subscription series in the 2,100-seat Ahmanson Theatre, and a thirty-six-week subscription series in the 750-seat Mark Taper Forum. The Ahmanson opened in April, 1967, with a touring company of *Man of La Mancha,* but that was by way of a *vorspeise.* Its first subscription season, in which four attractions are to be mounted on a two-million-dollar budget, opened on September 12, 1967, with the American première of *More Stately Mansions* by Eugene O'Neill, directed by José Quintero, and starring Ingrid Bergman, Arthur Hill, and Colleen Dewhurst. This was followed by a new musical comedy based on *The Happy Time,* starring Robert Goulet and David Wayne, and then by the Royal Shakespeare Company (of Stratford-on-Avon and London) with a repertory of *As You Like It* and *The Taming of the Shrew.* The fourth production is to be the world première of

"*Catch My Soul,* A Blues Musical Version of *Othello,* A 'Popera,' words by William Shakespeare, music by Ray Pohlman, conceived and directed by Jack Good." Don't knock it until you've tried it, I guess.

The Ahmanson operation, of course, is not a resident professional theatre at all; its policy is evidently a little of this and a little of that, with an eye on what can be sent to Broadway. (*More Stately Mansions* and *The Happy Time* have already turned up in New York; no word yet on the popera.) In the Mark Taper Forum, on the other hand, of which Gordon Davidson is the artistic director, the policy of the old Theatre Group is being continued—in lavish surroundings, on a million-dollar budget, with a deficit of $250,000 to $300,000 expected for the first season, although there are 29,600 subscribers (a huge number for a resident theatre; only the Repertory Theatre of Lincoln Center has more).

The Forum opened on April 14, 1967, with *The Devils,* a play by the late John Whiting that deals with Life, Love, Sex, Sin, and Suffering, often in capital letters. In London and New York I found it pretentious and diffuse, but also intelligent, unhackneyed, and not without theatricality. In Los Angeles, Frank G. Bonnelli found it "dastardly." This would not matter very much except that Mr. Bonnelli is a member of the Los Angeles County Board of Supervisors, and the county owns the land on which the Music Center is built. As Mr. Bonnelli put it, "We don't want to be complete censors, but . . . " This summer the supervisors approved a new five-year lease for the Ahmanson and the Mark Taper only after Mrs. Chandler assured them that in future an expanded standards committee would review all productions. Gordon Davidson remarked, "I don't approve of censorship of any kind, but I think it is good that the Music Center itself will be responsible for the content of the productions, rather than any outside agency." So far, no incidents of actual censorship have been made public. So far.

The Devils was succeeded at the Forum by the world première engagement of Romulus Linney's *The Sorrows of Frederick,* which I was able to see. It turned out to be a chronicle play about the life of Frederick the Great of Prussia, presented by the Forum by arrangement with Robert Whitehead and Albert Marre; Mr. Marre directed, and Mr. Whitehead was thinking about bringing it to Broadway. It was one of those fluid affairs, constantly flashing backward and forward. It showed us Frederick as a pathetic three-year-old child; as a neurotic young man, self-pitying, desperately avid for flattery, a trifle effeminate; as a liberal monarch in his prime; and as a wry, hard-nosed old campaigner. The real Frederick was a man of considerable style, and this was captured in Mr. Linney's writing and in Fritz Weaver's virtuoso performance. Meanwhile all kinds of lively theatricalities were going on: Frederick's decrees abolishing torture, establishing freedom of the press and of religion, and reforming the judiciary and the army were read out as the king played his flute and conducted a concerto of his own composition. Mr. Marre made extensive use of films and projections (designed by John Hoppe and Ralph Alswang, and coordinated with Mr. Alswang's sets and lighting) for all kinds of special effects; every year, on my Shakespeare-festival rounds, I see worse ways of evoking battles. (Stratford papers, please copy.)

There was some fine stuff in *The Sorrows of Frederick*, including a very funny scene in which the aged Frederick dispenses justice to a soldier condemned to death for having sexual relations with his horse. "A mare, I hope," says Frederick, and then gives judgment: "Pardoned—transferred to the infantry." But sometimes the writing provided at least an occasion for sentimentality, and here Mr. Marre made the worst of things; there was somewhat too much of Frederick at center stage, weeping bitterly because someone has been taken from him. At one crucial point in the play, that someone turns out to be a dog: ". . . my angel," says Frederick, . . . our two heads on one pillow . . . Now you've gone away and left me . . . Good-by, my angel." It is hard to say how Mr. Linney wanted us to take this astonishing scene, but Mr. Marre staged it all out for pathos, with no apparent awareness of the grotesque comedy inherent in it—which is odd, considering that zoophilia had already been employed in the play for explicitly comic purposes.

Moreover, the play never reconciled Frederick the philosopher with Frederick the butcher. How did this unhappy, intelligent, enlightened, well-intentioned man come to keep Europe aflame with war for so many years? "We always become the last thing we ever wanted to become," says someone in the play. But why? how? The play ends with a newsreel of Hitler and a display of Nazi flags. It might have been a powerful final image, but it was not prepared for; the play did not lead up to it. *The Sorrows of Frederick* was an erratically entertaining spectacle with some strong scenes and funny lines, offering some vivid glimpses of a fascinating character about whom someone, someday, ought to write a really good play.

The leading roles in *The Devils*, played in New York by Jason Robards and Anne Bancroft, were played at the Forum by Frank Langella and Joyce Ebert, two young actors who made their names Off-Broadway and in the resident theatre. *The Sorrows of Frederick* employed the services of such non-Hollywood actors as Mr. Weaver, Albert Dekker (as Frederick's loathsomely boorish father), Nancy Marchand (as his dowdy queen), and George Coulouris (as Voltaire). *The Marriage of Mr. Mississippi*, by Friedrich Duerrenmatt, the third Forum production, featured Nan Martin, Jack Albertson, and David Hurst. Clearly Mr. Davidson knows where good actors are to be found, and clearly he has enough money to hire them. None of the first three scripts he chose are favorites of mine, but they are adventurous and serious choices. A Monday-night experimental series is attracting capacity audiences. The Forum itself provides the facilities to do just about anything that can be done on a thrust stage, though its auditorium might well have been much larger. During the first season 87 per cent of the 750 seats were pre-sold by subscription, which would tend to indicate a larger audience than the theatre has room for. Looked at another way, of course, that 87 per cent is a happy statistic, considering all the half-empty regional theatres there are in this country. If Mr. Davidson can keep the censors off his neck, and generally resist the temptations of affluence, he may do very well.

The Inner City Repertory Company (Los Angeles)

Before his first season at the Forum was over, Mr. Davidson already had competition—of a rather different kind from that offered by the Pasadena Playhouse. On September 14, 1967, the Inner City Repertory Company opened its first six-play season at the new Inner City Cultural Center, under the leadership of Andre Gregory and David Lunney. Having done some exciting work at the Theatre of the Living Arts in Philadelphia, having left

Philadelphia after a dispute with their board of directors, Messrs. Gregory and Lunney were given $600,000 by the federal government to set up a resident theatre to play for high school students. Thirty-five thousand youngsters are being brought to the theatre by bus to see four plays a year, free of charge, during school hours, as part of the regular school program. Students see rehearsals as well as performances, and the actors will visit schools to perform scenes and to discuss the plays. There are also three performances a week for the ordinary theatre-going public to which admission is charged, and two productions during the season are to be mounted for adult audiences only.

Analogous federally-funded projects to give high school students a chance to see live professional theatre were begun last year in Providence and New Orleans, but the Inner City venture is the only one of the three that is oriented explicitly toward minority groups. (Mexican-Americans, Orientals, and Negroes are mentioned in the Center's literature—in that order, perhaps because Mexican-Americans and Orientals don't riot. The Jews, presumably, can take care of themselves by this time.) The enterprise is housed in the former Fox Boulevard Theatre, which is located, says a press release, "in a minority community." In addition to a 900-seat auditorium for the professional company, the Center will also contain a professional school of the arts, and a library of material concerning minority-group culture in Los Angeles; other theatrical activities in "the minority community" will also be able to use the premises.

It was courageous of the government to let Mr. Gregory loose on the teenagers of Los Angeles, especially considering Los Angeles; he is one of the very few men in the resident-theatre movement who is seriously interested in making use of the theatre's power to provoke. For openers, he directed a production of *Tartuffe* in which, he said,

> Tartuffe is being played by Louis Gossett as a white-black man who wants to make it in an upper-middle-class white world. We are setting the play in Monterey 1842 in order to create an upper-middle-class environment in American terms.

I am far from sure that this is any way of doing justice to *Tartuffe*, and it has occurred to me in the past that Mr. Gregory might be more interested in what he could do with a play than in what actually was in it. (The same, of course, could be said of Meyerhold.) But I would like to have been around when this production was discussed in ghetto high schools; it might have made a few Negro students feel, for a change, that the school was actually trying to talk to them about something important. It might also have been interesting to hear that production discussed in the pleasant suburban high schools, surrounded by playing fields and parking lots, out in Goldwater country. Perhaps it shook them up a little.

It certainly shook up the Los Angeles Board of Education, which forced Mr. Gregory to remove certain slides of nude art works that formed part of the production and to clothe an actor in long underwear when he took an onstage bath. (A bath? In *Tartuffe?*) In fact, the board found Mr. Gregory rather hard to take altogether. As his second production for the students, he had scheduled Brecht's *Caucasian Chalk Circle;* the board vetoed this on "moral grounds." (The moral of *The Caucasian Chalk Circle* is as follows:

That what there is shall go to those who are good for it,
Thus: the children to the motherly, that they prosper
The carts to good drivers, that they are well driven
And the valley to the waterers, that it bring forth fruit.*

If ideas like this ever got around in Los Angeles, who knows what would happen?) Mr. Gregory was told to substitute either *The Glass Menagerie* or *A Raisin in the Sun.* He chose the former, and cast a Negro actor as the Gentleman Caller. When the board demanded that this actor be disguised as a white man, Mr. Gregory decided that he had had enough of its meddling, and resigned. It is perhaps rash to comment on the rights and wrongs of the matter from a distance of three thousand miles, but it appears that Mr. Gregory was trying (as is his custom) to create a theatre that was urgently relevant to the concerns of its audience, and that this was exactly what the Los Angeles Board of Education did not want. What will happen henceforward with the Inner City Repertory Company, I have no idea.

* Translated by Eric Bentley and Maja Apelman, published in *Parables for the Theatre* (Grove Press, New York, 1948), p. 189.

6

MINNEAPOLIS

*

The Tyrone Guthrie Theatre

It is astonishing, when you come to think of it, that most of the resident theatres were founded by people whom nobody ever heard of. Without the resources of professional prestige, the founders were forced to begin on a very small scale, with small budgets, small, makeshift quarters, small audiences, and small companies of obscure actors; most resident theatres are still small-scale operations. The great exception is the Tyrone Guthrie Theatre in Minneapolis.

The co-founder and for three years the artistic director of the Guthrie was Dr. Sir Tyrone Guthrie himself. Dr. Guthrie had had previous experience in starting new theatres: in 1953, after decades of success at the Old Vic, at Sadler's Wells, at Covent Garden, at Stratford-on-Avon, at the Edinburgh Festival, in the West End, on Broadway, at the Metropolitan Opera, in Tel Aviv, in Helsinki, and elsewhere, he had helped to found the Shakespearean Festival at Stratford, Ontario, and had made it one of the foremost theatres in the English-speaking world. His partners in the Minneapolis venture were Oliver Rea, a Broadway producer, and Peter Zeisler, a stage manager and theatre technician. All three had been successful in the commercial theatre, and all three had had just about enough of it. They determined to found a resident profes-

105

sional theatre somewhere in America, and invited applications from interested cities. (The story of the Guthrie Theatre's founding is told more fully in Dr. Guthrie's own book, A *New Theatre*.)

To bring Dr. Guthrie and his partners to Minneapolis, local citizens raised more than two million dollars to build a 1,437-seat theatre. (This would be the capacity of a large Broadway house; some resident theatres, even today, have less than 250 seats, and few are as large as the Guthrie.) For the first season, in 1963, a company of forty-two actors was recruited; at its head were Hume Cronyn, Jessica Tandy, George Grizzard, Rita Gam, and Zoe Caldwell. Almost 22,000 season tickets were sold before the theatre opened, and the total paid attendance for the first season was 193,344; the operating budget was $715,000. The following year, the attendance passed the quarter-million mark, and in 1965 the theatre had its first million-dollar budget. Nowadays it employs about 155 people at the height of the season, including over thirty Equity actors. As resident theatres go, it is a very large-scale operation.

It is difficult to measure the impact of a theatre on a community, but a phenomenon like the Guthrie is much harder to ignore than most resident companies. There is some reason to believe that the theatre has helped Minneapolis to think of itself as a metropolis. One small indication came, a few years ago, from the fashion column of the New York *Herald Tribune*. It seems that Dayton's Department Store in Minneapolis had opened America's first authentic mod boutique for men. Is Minneapolis ready, wondered the *Herald Tribune*. To which a Dayton's buyer replied that "Minneapolis hasn't been the same since Tyrone Guthrie moved his repertory theatre here."

The Guthrie is not only big, it is also good: one of the very best in the country. The asymmetric thrust stage of its large theatre is an unusually interesting playing area, on which designers, actors, and directors have done memorable work. The company *is* a company: there was a particularly large turnover after the 1966 season, but still no less than sixteen actors returned in 1967; four performers have been with the theatre for every one of its five seasons, without going stale. Directing can be a problem when Dr. Guthrie is not around, but Dr. Guthrie has been around for four out of the first five seasons, and he is one of the foremost figures of the English-speaking stage.

When I first turned up in Minneapolis in 1965, the jewel of the repertory was Dr. Guthrie's production of *The Cherry Orchard.* Chekhov thought, or said he thought, that *The Cherry Orchard* was "a comedy, and in some spots even a farce"; Stanislavsky, on the other hand, said flatly: "This is not a comedy; this is a tragedy." Dr. Guthrie took an intermediate point of view. Madame Ranevskaya and her brother Gaev, who allow their ancestral cherry orchard—and the way of life it represents—to slip through their fingers, were aristocratic spoiled children, too weak and silly for tragic purposes. But though the comic side of their difficulties was acknowledged, and much was made of the out-and-out absurdity of their friends and servants, the seriousness of their plight was not scanted or burlesqued.

Lee Richardson as the upstart Lopahin showed no signs of ever having been a peasant, and thus obscured Lopahin's position in the play; but for the most part the acting was admirable. Ken Ruta played Trofimov, the "perennial student," as a drowsy, plaintive, bewildered spaniel puppy. Nancy Wickwire was a touching Varya: sober, fretful, sharp-tongued, with incipient spinsterhood hanging over her like a cloud. Hume Cronyn was gloriously funny as the *schlemiel* Epihodoff. As Ranevskaya and Gaev, Jessica Tandy and Robert Pastene moved through twin hazes of dreamy disconnection. Miss Tandy had nothing to offer quite so interesting as Mr. Pastene's exquisitely detailed vaguery, until the climax of the play, when Lopahin bursts in with the news that the cherry orchard has been sold. Ranevskaya has nothing to say in this scene; in the Guthrie production she simply sat in an armchair, facing front. As Lopahin shouted and carried on behind her, she listened, tried not to cry, and failed, and did so with such grace and such power as to make the scene, and the evening, hers. (Of course, I was sitting in the center of the auditorium, directly facing her. What was it like, I wonder, for the people who sat at the extreme side, who could see hardly anything of Miss Tandy's face? Perhaps from where they sat they saw an equally moving scene; but I doubt it. The thrust stage is not without its disadvantages.)

The other productions I saw in Minneapolis that season were of less interest. Nobody could say of Hume Cronyn as Richard III, as Tennyson said of Henry Irving, "Where did you get that Plantagenet look?" Little Mr. Cronyn was not very kingly, nor very formidable; he did not catch much of Richard's perverse heroism. The production got by well enough, however, on Mr. Cronyn's good timing and general professionalism, and on Dr. Guthrie's gift for theatrical excitement.

Douglas Campbell's production of *The Way of the World* did manage to prove how beautifully actable this Restoration masterpiece is. Zoe Caldwell was often exquisitely delectable as the flirtatious Millamant, though her energy level was sometimes dangerously low. Robert Milli as her lover Mirabell, though a little lacking in glamour and sparkle, was in period without being foppish, and made it clear that Mirabell is the play's standard of value, the only man in it who deserves respect. But one of Congreve's most marvelous feats in this play is to make fashionable wit into a language of love more erotically alive than any endearments; since the two Minneapolis lovers never seemed particularly in love, the play's central relationship lost much of its urgency and fascination. What was left, however, was still quite enough for a good evening's entertainment: a great deal of brilliant dialogue, well rendered, and several funny fools (notably Ken Ruta as Witwoud and Ed Flanders as Petulant: a poodle companioned with a hedgehog). Few American companies could do even as well as this.

After the 1965 season, Dr. Guthrie, evidently feeling that his Johnny Appleseed work had been done, resigned as artistic director; the 1966 season was the first under Guthrie's long-time associate and chosen successor, the Scottish actor-director Douglas Campbell. Most of the acting was, as it had been, admirable; the stage, again, was cleverly used. But something was wrong. Mr. Campbell is a splendid showman, but he seems to have more feeling for the theatre than for the drama. *The Skin of Our Teeth* and *As You Like It* were produced with plenty of lively theatremagic, but the productions tended to obscure the plays. In both cases the director seemed to have had insufficient faith in his material—a common, and crippling, affliction in the American theatre.

Mr. Campbell, who staged *The Skin of Our Teeth*, went all out for yocks and got them. What he could do with a brass band, a crowd of merry-makers at a convention, or a procession of animals on their way to the ark, was a pleasure to behold, but the play's emotional impact was diffused by all the goings-on. As Mr. and Mrs. Antrobus, Thornton Wilder's eternal Adam and Eve, Lee Richardson and Ruth Nelson spent the first act cavorting heavily, like old-fashioned vaudeville comics. They never entirely recovered the dignity thus forfeited—dignity that these characters need if the play is to make its point. The Fortune Teller, whose voice of doom dominates the second act, was very weakly played by Evie McElroy. The best work of the evening came from Nancy Wickwire as Sabina, the comic maid, voice of the Philistines, and eternal home-wrecker.

Edward Payson Call, at that time associate artistic director of the Guthrie, directed *As You Like It* very cleverly; there were many moments when words and action were most effectively counterpointed. His Rosalind, Ellen Geer, was a bit strident, but Len Cariou was an excellent Orlando: blunt, rustic, high-spirited, good-natured, with an odd capacity for dominating the stage without apparent effort. Ed Flanders as Touchstone, the jester, substituted wry detachment for pranks and gambols, and made even his most trivial quibbles entertaining.

This might have been a very pleasant production if only Mr. Call had known when to stop, but many of his bright ideas turned out to be annoying distractions. He set the play in the American South at the time of the Civil War, an arbitrary device that did nothing to elucidate either the play or the war. It was an innovation with absolutely nothing to recommend it, unless you subscribe to the theory that poor old Shakespeare has written another bomb that needs all the help a director can provide. This was an *As You Like It* for people who can't stand *As You Like It*.

Under Mr. Call's scheme the melancholy Jaques, for instance, whom Shakespeare designed as a bit of a poseur but a keen-witted commentator nonetheless, became a cross between Robert E. Lee and Don Quixote, his keenness lost in clouds of fake pathos. Mr. Call needed fake pathos because he did not know where in the play the real pathos is. There is a subtly poignant moment in the script when a time-serving courtier, experiencing a moment of wistful decency, says to Orlando, who is out of favor: "Sir, fare you well. Hereafter, in a better world than this, I shall desire more love and knowledge of you." Mr. Call got an easy laugh, and obscured the point, by having the courtier played as a screaming fag. The relation of screaming faggotry to the Civil War was one of the production's many unanswered questions.

Strindberg's *The Dance of Death* is a rarely done work by one of the seminal modern dramatists; it was directed, in earnest for a change, by Douglas Campbell, and it was admirably acted by Robert Pastene and Nancy Wickwire. (When you have seen Miss Wickwire in *The Dance of Death* at a matinée, giving a formidable performance in the authentic grand manner, and seen her again that evening in *The Skin of Our Teeth* perking about as Sabina, Thornton Wilder's bird-brained bit of fluff, then you know what versatility is.) But it occurred to me nevertheless that the reason why *The Dance of Death* is so seldom done, is that it is not really very good. The play is about a sick marriage; it appears to be the model for *Who's Afraid of Virginia Woolf?*, but it seemed to me that Mr. Albee has greatly improved upon his predecessor. Strindberg's dialogue (at least in Norman Ginsbury's translation) seemed colorless in comparison to Albee's. Strindberg's main combatants are not so much fully rounded characters as they are mere vessels of hatred; Albee's characters hate too, but they hate in a richly individual fashion. Most important, Strindberg has his characters tell us about "love-hate" which "comes from the hell inside us," and demonstrates it with a lot of melodramatic plotting, whereas Albee shows us this love-hate with such subtlety and power that he has no need to editorialize about it. On the other hand, Sir Laurence Olivier has recently had a great success with *The Dance of Death* at the National Theatre in London; he is said to have played it as a black comedy. Perhaps there is something that I don't know—and that Mr. Campbell didn't know either.

It is said that Mr. Campbell feels a special affinity for the works of George Bernard Shaw; he managed, nevertheless, to make a botch of his production of *The Doctor's Dilemma*. As the dullish Dr. Ridgeon, who has to decide who shall live and who shall die, Lee Richardson did all that could be done, and Robert Pastene was suitably crisp and dry as a surgeon who thinks that the answer to everyone's problem is to operate and remove the "nuciform sac." But with these exceptions, every important part was in some measure miscast.

Ken Ruta played Sir Ralph Bloomfield Bonington, the fatuous society doctor, in an ecstasy of burbling self-esteem; in twenty years he will be ideal for the part, but in 1966 his white hairs and padded belly obviously did not become him. Mr. Ruta was so funny that only a perfectionist would have been unwilling to forgive the fact that he was not the one young actor in a thousand who can play an elderly man with complete conviction; but the other miscastings were more serious. As the oldest doctor of all, John Cromwell was certainly old enough (and what a pleasure it was to see a genuine old man on the stage of a resident theatre), but the character is written to be sharp and gruff, and Mr. Cromwell's hesitant, gentle delivery tended to smother his laughs. As the dishonest, doomed young artist and his fascinating wife, Ed Flanders and Nancy Wickwire—brilliant actors both—were both, among other disabilities, too old. The wife is supposed to be an unworldly, ardent girl from Cornwall, with more passion than brains; Miss Wickwire was unmistakably a shrewd, self-possessed American woman with more brains than passion. Mr. Flanders handled his comedy with irresistible cheeky ebullience, but his death scene was a long failure. In spite of all his rascality and all his jokes, this is supposed to be a twenty-three-year-old genius dying of tuberculosis before our eyes—think of Keats. If this scene is to work at all it must touch our emotions somehow, but Mr. Flanders was totally lacking in the gallantry and youthful glamour that might have made it pathetic.

Multiple miscasting was not the production's only fault. It might be asked, in a theatre crawling with speech teachers, with a company capable of handling to perfection the half-dozen or so different accents required in O'Neill's *S. S. Glencairn,* why one single way of pronouncing the English language might not have been adopted for *The Doctor's Dilemma,* instead of allowing each member of the cast to speak English English or American English as he pleased.

The Guthrie Theatre's stage, moreover, is far from ideal for drawing-room comedy, and Dahl Delu's settings were not much help. Mr. Campbell's staging was often a positive hindrance. For long stretches of crucial scenes, I was nearly driven distracted wondering when some actor was going to get his broad back out of the way so that I could see what was going on. And when this consummation finally came about, it often served to block the view of another group of would-be spectators. Mr. Campbell is usually good at making the most of the thrust stage, but here his acumen deserted him. *The Doctor's Dilemma* was only rescued by the sheer professionalism of the actors, which was evident through all the miscastings, and by the enduring sparkle of Bernard Shaw's dialogue.

The final production of the 1966 season was *S. S. Glencairn* by Eugene O'Neill. This is the over-all title for four early O'Neill plays that deal with the crew of a freighter plying between Great Britain and the West Indies; the faults of the Guthrie production, directed by Mr. Campbell and Mr. Call, were too minor to mention. Paul Ballantyne, Lee Richardson, Ed Flanders, Ken Ruta, John Cromwell, Len Cariou, Sandy McCallum, and almost everyone else in the large cast dealt with O'Neill's sweaty realism as if they had been born to it. Shipboard life with its coarseness and closeness, its bickering and idling, was easily and unselfconsciously evoked.

Dahl Delu's settings and the uncredited lighting provided all the assistance our imaginations needed to turn the stage into the deck or the fo'c'sle of the *Glencairn*. The actors, principals and bit-players alike, singing sea chanteys in deep-throated chorus, performed the set-changes most entertainingly before our eyes. But surely something is more than slightly askew when the set-changes are more fun than the plays themselves. O'Neill's early études in the naturalistic manner are, I guess, worth reviving when they can be revived this well; but they are not genuine classics, nor do they represent a voice from the past that at this moment we particularly need to hear.

I was not the only one dissatisfied with the 1966 season at the Guthrie. Attendance fell off from the 1965 figure of 239,833 for 214 performances to 214,182 for 223 performances. In each of its first two seasons, the Guthrie had made a small operating profit; in 1965 it had lost $82,000; in 1966 it lost a record $170,377. There was no question of cutting back; the theatre planned for 1967 a budget of $1,200,000, a 20 per cent increase over 1966, and decided to expand its activities into neighboring St. Paul. But change was in order.

The Guthrie had been rather conservative in its choice of plays. Up through 1966, there had been a play by Shakespeare every season, and always a well-known one. The other Guthrie authors in those first four seasons were Chekhov (two plays), Shaw (two plays), Miller, Williams, Ben Jonson, Congreve, Brecht, Wilder, Strindberg, and O'Neill. The Guthrie is a large house to fill, and the obvious way to try to fill it is by giving the people plays, or playwrights at least, that they have heard of before. I see nothing reprehensible in this, though the management had been attacked for it; most of these playwrights are well known by name, but how many people in the upper Midwest have ever seen their work? Even if the plays had been familiar to the audience, would they not be worth seeing again?

The danger of this policy is expressed by Peter Zeisler, the company's co-founder and managing director: "We started out as primarily a classical repertory theatre—and it's a hell of a lot easier to do a new play well than it is to find some kind of validity and some kind of statement to make with the big whoppers. What we constantly have to be careful is not doing the whoppers for the sake of doing the whoppers." In planning the 1967 season, Mr. Zeisler said, "We wanted to shake things up a little." They decided on no Shakespeare, and nothing from the Chekhov-Strindberg-Shaw bag. They were already committed to one production: *The House of Atreus*, a new adaptation of *The Oresteia*, directed by Dr. Guthrie, which had been postponed from the fall of 1966. Their other four productions were a new musical version of *The Shoemakers' Holiday* by Thomas Dekker (1599), *Thieves' Carnival* by Jean Anouilh, *Harpers Ferry* by Barrie Stavis (the world première of a new American play about John Brown), and *The Visit* by Friedrich Duerrenmatt.

The Shoemakers' Holiday is about Simon Eyre, "the mad shoemaker of Tower Street," who rises to become Lord Mayor of London by saying things like, "Peace, Firk; peace, my fine Firk! Stand by with your pishery-pashery. Away!" The play praises jollity, constancy, and other simple shoemaking virtues, and celebrates the Romance of Business (a poor boy can become Lord

Mayor and have the King to breakfast) with a vernal forthrightness that makes its clichés seem fresh again. One early fan of *The Shoemakers' Holiday* was Queen Elizabeth herself, who, we are told, "graciously accepted" it "for the mirth and pleasant matter" it contained. Her Majesty to the contrary notwithstanding, it was never a really good play, being somewhat simple-minded and slapdash; but for these very qualities—and also because it is sentimental, full of gusto, not without charm, and in the public domain—it would seem to be highly eligible material for musicalization. The Guthrie version, affectionately directed by Douglas Campbell and John Olon-Scrymgeour, was fairly successful; the set was drab, the singing often weak, and the music not very tuneful, but the play's good nature came through.

Thieves' Carnival is a delicate, feather-light, preposterous farce about pickpockets and heiresses; Stephen Porter's production had all kinds of little things wrong with it, but was delightful anyway.

Harper's Ferry, on the other hand, the first new play presented publicly by the Guthrie in its five-year history, turned out to be a badly crafted piece of simple-minded liberalism. Barrie Stavis, who wrote it, is obviously an earnest, well-disposed gentleman; his good intentions are all over the play like a rash. "I believe in the ultimate goodness of the people of this land," says somebody, and this kind of empty rhetoric is as close as Mr. Stavis comes to an insight into the fascinating and ambiguous career of John Brown. The dialogue is peculiarly unspeakable, like a bad translation: "My boredom grows heavy." "Does it distress you, Father, that I debate this subject?" "You grieve too sorely." Every important plot-point is made again and again and again. The dramaturgy is so clumsy that Brown's handling of the attack on Harper's Ferry seemed almost comic in its ineptitude; it was hard to understand why anyone should have placed his life in the hands of such an oaf. Edward Binns made matters worse by playing this great, grim fanatic as an ordinary nice fellow; a look at the picture of Brown on display in the lobby—cadaverous, ruthless, awe-inspiring, more than a little mad—made clear what was wrong with Mr. Binns's amiable, professional performance.

Except in his work with Mr. Binns, Dr. Guthrie's direction subtly and surely made the most of the material. The story of John Brown, of course, is superbly dramatic in itself, and some of that intrinsic drama could not help coming through. A John Brown play is a fine idea—perhaps some day someone will write a good one. (It was subsequently announced that 27,000 high school students would be treated to special matinée performances of *Harper's Ferry*, to be paid for by a $100,000 federal grant.)

And then there is Dr. Guthrie's production of *The House of Atreus*, which stands by itself. It is the only genuine revival of a Greek tragedy that I have ever seen; all the other attempts, in comparison, have been mere exhumations. *The Oresteia* was freely adapted for the occasion by John Lewin, but the result was still Greek tragedy, Aeschylus' drama and not Mr. Lewin's; Dr. Guthrie succeeded—uniquely, I daresay, among modern directors —in conjuring up a considerable vestige of those dark tremendous forces that the Athenians encountered in the Theatre of Dionysus. And, in doing so, he gave us probably the nearest thing to a Theatre of Cruelty spectacle, as Antonin Artaud imagined it, that we have ever had in this country. Dr. Guthrie has never been close to the avant-garde among whom Artaud is a hero, but his own path has taken him in a strikingly similar direction.

The Theatre of Cruelty is the ideal theatre of Artaud's imagination, an ideal that can never be realized entirely. It is exciting to talk about "an image that will shake the organism to its foundations and leave an ineffaceable scar," "a serious theater, which, overturning all our preconceptions, inspires us with the fiery magnetism of its images and acts upon us like a spiritual therapeutics whose touch can never be forgotten";* it is worthwhile aiming at such a theatre, because a man's reach should exceed his grasp; but could it ever really happen? (And even if the theatre, or anything else, could overturn *all* our preconceptions, would that be such a good idea? Aren't at least some of our preconceptions correct?)

But just what did Artaud have in mind when he talked of a Theatre of Cruelty? Not what might be superficially expected.

With this mania we all have for depreciating everything [he wrote], as soon as I have said "cruelty," everybody will at once take it to

* All quotations of Antonin Artaud in this chapter are from his book *The Theater and Its Double*, translated from the French by Mary Caroline Richards, published by Grove Press, Inc., Copyright © 1958 by Grove Press, Inc.

mean "blood." But . . . it is not the cruelty we can exercise upon each other by hacking at each other's bodies, carving up our personal anatomies, or, like Assyrian emperors, sending parcels of human ears, noses, or neatly detached nostrils through the mail, but the much more terrible and necessary cruelty which things can exercise against us. We are not free. And the sky can still fall on our heads. And the theater has been created to teach us that first of all.

And that, first of all, is what Greek tragedy teaches us.

Artaud sought to bring back to the stage at least "a little breath of that great metaphysical fear which is at the root of all ancient theater."

> The theater must make itself the equal of life—not an individual life, that individual aspect of life in which CHARACTERS triumph, but the sort of liberated life which sweeps away human individuality and in which man is only a reflection. The true purpose of the theater is to create Myths, to express life in its immense, universal aspect . . .
> . . . great social upheavals, conflicts between peoples and races, natural forces, interventions of chance, and the magnetism of fatality will manifest themselves either indirectly, in the movement and gestures of characters enlarged to the statures of gods, heroes, or monsters, in mythical dimensions, or directly . . .
> These gods or heroes, these monsters, these natural and cosmic forces will be interpreted according to images from the most ancient sacred texts and old cosmogonies.

All of this sounds as if Artaud was calling almost explicitly for a revival of Greek tragedy, which, more than any other kind of Western theatre, deals with "life in its immense, universal aspect." But he was not. ". . . we shall try," he said,

> to concentrate, around famous personages, atrocious crimes, superhuman devotions, a drama which, *without resorting to the defunct images of the old Myths* [italics mine], shows that it can extract the forces which struggle within them.

The key assumption here is that the "images of the old Myths" are "defunct." Anyone who has seen English-language productions of Greek tragedy would be likely to agree. In our time and country only Dr. Guthrie has been able to infuse these images with the fullness of life.

Artaud himself was entirely unable to see that Greek tragedy might be the foundation for the kind of theatre he sought to build, because he was in violent revolt against the French theatrical tradition of reverence for the classics, which was—often still is—expressed in static stagings in which the actors merely stood and declaimed the sacred text. A theatre in which this took place, "a theater which subordinates the *mise en scène* and production, i.e., everything in itself that is specifically theatrical, to the text," was, according to Artaud, "a theater of idiots, madmen, inverts, grammarians, grocers, antipoets and positivists . . ." Throwing the baby out with the bathwater, he raised his famous cry, "No more masterpieces!"

> Masterpieces of the past are good for the past: they are not good for us. . . . If the public does not frequent our literary masterpieces, it is because those masterpieces are literary, that is to say fixed; and fixed in forms that no longer respond to the needs of the time.

But a work of dramatic literature is "fixed" only on the printed page; in the theatre it can take many shapes. Artaud demanded "a theater which eliminates the author in favor of what we would call, in our Occidental theatrical jargon, the director; but a director who has become a kind of manager of magic, a master of sacred ceremonies." But what if the director could function in this manner *without* eliminating the author? That is exactly what Dr. Guthrie has done with *The House of Atreus*. The significance and power of his production come from his success in evoking "a little breath of that great metaphysical fear," "life in its immense, universal aspect," "gods . . . heroes . . . monsters . . . natural and cosmic forces"—just those central elements of Greek tragedy that are absent from most productions. The import of *The House of Atreus*—an import felt in the first place by some more primal, basic faculty than the reasoning mind—is that tremendous powers are loose in the world, compared to which an ordinary mortal is a puny creature indeed. In other words—Artaud's words—"We are not free. And the sky can still fall on our heads."

Dr. Guthrie's means, as well as his ends, were on the whole quite Artaudian. He did not, of course, fulfill the entire Artaudian prescription. I did not notice, for instance, a "physical rhythm of movements whose crescendo and decrescendo will accord exactly with the pulsation of movements familiar to everyone," or "the physical action of light which arouses sensations of heat and cold," or "absolutely new sounds, qualities which present-day musical instruments do not possess." A rather more significant dictum was also unfulfilled:

> We abolish the stage and the auditorium and replace them by a single site, without partition and barrier of any kind, which will become the theater of the action. A direct communication will be reestablished between the actor and the spectator, from the fact that the spectator, placed in the middle of the action, is engulfed and physically affected by it.

But though stage and auditorium remain separate areas at the Guthrie, they are at least in the same room, and not separated by the wall-with-a-hole-in-it that we call the proscenium arch; and though the spectator is not in the middle of the action, the Guthrie's asymmetric thrust stage brings the action into the midst of the spectators.

In other respects, however, *The House of Atreus* came far closer to what Artaud wanted. The prophet called for a theatre that "turns words into incantations." He demanded

> cries, groans, apparitions, surprises, theatricalities of all kinds, magic beauty of costumes taken from certain ritual models; resplendent lighting, incantational beauty of voices, the charms of harmony, rare notes of music . . . concrete appearances of new and surprising objects, masks, effigies yards high, sudden changes of light . . .

All these Dr. Guthrie supplied, and few of them failed in their effect.

Human individuality was not, as Artaud demanded, entirely swept away. Mr. Lewin's adaptation elaborates on Aeschylus' occasional hints for intimate details: the grim reminiscences of a soldier back from Troy, the feeble wailing of Orestes' old nurse. Dr. Guthrie deftly brought out the individuality of certain major characters: Agamemnon's slightly cheap arrogance, Clytemnestra's bitchiness, the forlornness of Cassandra. Yet these towering figures were not thereby diminished; the production was Artaudian in spirit because of the successful boldness with which Dr. Guthrie used anti-realistic, hieratic, bizarre devices to establish it on a superhuman plane.

The actors were not dressed in the white crypto-mini-skirts and dainty draperies that traditionally serve for Greek tragedies; Tanya Moiseiwitsch, the designer, swathed them in bulky costumes of coarse, earth-colored fabrics and covered their faces with masks. The choruses seemed human, more or less (except, of course, for the Furies). The major characters were more than life-size; with their rigid, stately gestures, they looked like huge, awe-inspiring dolls. Yet even they were dwarfed by the tawny gates that dominated the set, and by the tremendous figures of the gods, who were right out of human scale altogether. Orestes was a heroic figure, and grim enough when he killed Clytemnestra, but in the shadow of great golden Apollo he looked like a small boy clinging to his father for support.

All the actors, except some in the chorus, were men, which placed the action at a further remove from ordinary life. Douglas Campbell as Clytemnestra brought an incongruous touch of Lady Bracknell to the proceedings, but his ironies were vibrant and sharp, and he rose to climaxes of brazen power. Robin Gammell doubled successfully as Cassandra and Electra. Among the men who played men, the most notable were Lee Richardson as Agamemnon and Apollo, and Len Cariou—one of the finest young classical actors now working in this country—as a powerful Orestes.

The actors who made up the choruses were notable because they were not riffraff whose only distinction is that they come cheap (as they would have had to be off-Broadway, or in most regional theatres); many of them have played important roles in the Guthrie Theatre repertoire. In his staging for the chorus, Dr. Guthrie completely avoided the one-two-three-kick danger, employing instead a fluid series of stylized, asymmetrical groupings. The choral speaking, like that of the principals, rose easily from almost-colloquial speech through chanting to outright song. I doubt if there is another company in this country that would be capable of executing Dr. Guthrie's tremendous intentions.

Mr. Lewin has condensed the trilogy so that it can be played in three and a half hours; it seemed far shorter. *Agamemnon,* the first play, made an impressive prologue. The second play, which Mr. Lewin entitles *The Bringers of Offerings,* rose to heights of power that I never thought a Greek play could attain in the twentieth century. There was a grimly infectious sequence of ritual, wild yet controlled, as Orestes worked himself up to the murder, and a towering moment near the end, when Orestes cried "Spread it out!" and the fatal net that entangled his father was dragged hugely open over the stage. (Miss Moiseiwitsch's special talent for theatrical images centered around one huge, single element on an otherwise bare stage was much in evidence throughout the production.)

The third play, here called *The Furies,* was less successful than either of the others. The Furies themselves, those evocations of primitive ferocity and horror, were an unsolved problem. When Aeschylus first produced the play, we are told by an ancient writer, the Furies "so terrified the crowd that children died and women suffered miscarriages." In Aeschylus' time, of course, the audience's own beliefs worked to increase the emotional impact of these grim goddesses—an advantage that a modern director lacks. As if acknowledging that nowadays the Furies are a liability, Dr. Guthrie kept them out of sight as much as possible: a prudent recourse, not a daring one. Unfortunately we could still hear them, and they were nowhere near as terrible as the script keeps insisting they are; they sounded like the witches in most productions of *Macbeth,* and just as unconvincing.

Another problem was the goddess Athena, who presides at the epoch-making trial that finally breaks the great chain of murder. Enthroned and tremendous, she looked like the radiant principle of justice she is supposed to be, but Douglas Campbell played her as a world-weary ironist, not even seriously interested in the case unfolding before her. In every play there are certain places where any suggestion of mockery, however immediately effective, can only tend to undermine the final effect; this trial is one. Furthermore, the final ceremony of order which ends the trilogy, which should be a sublime climax representing the emergence from darkness into light, was not, in Dr. Guthrie's staging, nearly equal to the rites of chaos that went before it.

Aside from these particular difficulties with *The Furies*, the production's limitations, as well as its virtues, were those demanded by Artaud. There are certain functions of theatre in which the prophet was aggressively *not* interested. Myths, dark forces, "life in its immense, universal aspect" were everything to him. "It is not on the social level that the action of theater unfolds. Still less on the moral and psychological levels." Such a pronouncement would cut off whole dimensions of implication from *The Oresteia*, and that is what happened in Dr. Guthrie's production.

The Oresteia is not of overwhelming interest as a psychological drama, but on the social and moral plane (the two are impossible to separate) it has much to say. In a pamphlet published by the Guthrie Theatre, the poet Robert Bly writes:

> In *The House of Atreus*, Aeschylus, a genius ten times over, describes what it feels like for a family or a nation to be caught in its own past mistakes. And what is the mistake that this ruling family made over and over again? It was the *refusal* to forgive, expressed as the *inability* to forgive. . . . Like the characters in *The House of Atreus*, our whole nation is now being pulled into the bottomless mud because of our past mistakes in Southeast Asia. . . . We cannot forgive North Vietnam nor the Vietcong; they in turn cannot forgive us. We are in the House of Atreus.

With this in mind, several members of the theatre published an advertisement in a Minneapolis paper inviting Vice-President Humphrey, then in town, to come and see the production.

But I doubt if he would have been very much edified, not, at least, about Vietnam. We could never be in *this* House of Atreus; it was a house of giants, not of men. In Dr. Guthrie's production, the trilogy had no existence as a problem play, a hypothetical case, a discussion of issues, though Aeschylus has included, and Mr. Lewin has preserved, all these things in it. At the Guthrie Theatre, *The House of Atreus* was simply a rite, an evocation of something high and formidable, an image of magnificence. Perhaps it could not be anything else and still be this; at any rate, it was enough. In our time we have hardly known it possible that such a thing could be created in the theatre, which is why Artaud was so frustrated. Artaud was too unpredictable and irrational, and too bitterly opposed to a verbally oriented theatre, for it to be safe to say that he would have loved *The House of Atreus*. But it did realize, however imperfectly and partially, some of his dearest dreams.

I was not the only one who admired Dr. Guthrie's titanic production. A local critic called it "A monumental feat . . . The performance is certainly the high peak of the current season and one of the shining achievements of [the theatre's] whole five-year career." A Chicago critic said it was "rich and provocative and immensely stageworthy." *The New York Times* said, "The ensemble style so long sought by the Guthrie Theatre is becoming an actuality, and this massive *House of Atreus* is one of its finest accomplishments," and Walter Kerr in a Sunday piece called it "extraordinarily impressive." And, perhaps for the first time in two thousand years, it turned out that Aeschylus was box-office. As I write, the season is not yet over; attendance is running about 80 per cent of capacity (as against 66.8 per cent last year). And the most popular play in the repertory is *The House of Atreus*.

Meanwhile the company prepares for its first winter season. So far, in deference to the Minnesota climate, it has opened in the spring (latterly with thirty or so student performances before the regular season begins) and played in repertory until late fall. But on December 26, 1967, it began a fifteen-week repertory season at the Crawford Livingston Theatre across the river in St. Paul. (I ought to admit here that, officially, it is the Minnesota Theatre Company that has been appearing at the Tyrone Guthrie Theatre and will now add a season at the Crawford Livingston Theatre. But everybody has always referred to the whole operation as "The Guthrie.") The Crawford Livingston is the former home of a now-defunct professional company called Theatre St. Paul; the Guthrie authorities have enlarged it to a capacity of 655 spectators. Three plays are to be presented: *Enrico IV* by Luigi Pirandello, *She Stoops to Conquer* by Oliver Goldsmith, and *Tango*, a black comedy by the contemporary Polish playwright Slavomir Mrozek. Thus the Guthrie becomes, for the first time, a year-round operation. If the arrangement works, it will presumably be continued in future years.

At the moment, then, things are looking good in the Twin Cities, thanks in particular to the tremendous success of Dr. Guthrie's *The House of Atreus*. But Dr. Guthrie will not always be around to pass a miracle whenever the theatre that bears his

name is in need of bailing out. Mr. Campbell, his successor as
artistic director, resigned at the end of 1967. Peter Zeisler, the
theatre's managing director, has hired Edward Payson Call
(formerly second-in-command to Mr. Campbell) and Mel Shapiro
as resident directors. The Guthrie has an excellent company,
splendid physical facilities, and tremendous resources generally;
given the right leadership, it could be a great theatre. *The House
of Atreus* has given it some indication, at least, of what greatness
looks like. Where its new leadership will take it remains to be
seen.

The Firehouse Theatre

As far as I know, the Firehouse Theatre in Minneapolis is the
only genuine avant-garde theatre between New York and the
West Coast. Its artistic director, Sydney Schubert Walter, came
from the Open Theatre in New York, and many of its authors—
Megan Terry, Jean-Claude van Itallie, Sam Shepard—are prominent on the Off-Off-Broadway scene. The Firehouse "hopes to
evolve a new style of theatre through experimentation with new
staging techniques." It is interested in nonverbal use of the voice
and non-naturalistic use of the body, in ritual, and in "frank and
intimate contact with the audience" so that "the entire auditorium become[s] the stage."

Four young local zealots remodeled an old firehouse and started
the Firehouse Theatre in the summer of 1963; it opened with *The
Connection* (by Jack Gelber) two months after the Guthrie
opened with *Hamlet*. Until the fall of 1965, when Sydney Walter
became artistic director, the Firehouse was an amateur group;
since then it has been a semi-pro operation, with a small group of
actors, who are required to perform various backstage and front-of-
house chores in exchange for the derisory pittance ($75 a week)
which they receive. This "Actor-Worker arrangement," as the
theatre's prospectus whimsically observes, "insures a real commitment to the idea of the theatre on the part of company
members." Productions are cast from a workshop group that
meets at the theatre twice a week; its members include the actor-
workers and a number of local amateurs.

The Firehouse's eight-production, ten-and-a-half-month season
balances avant-garde classics (Beckett, Ionesco, Pinter) and new

works. In 1966–67, the theatre presented *Waiting for Godot, The Sideshow* by Frederick Gaines, *Viet Rock* by Megan Terry (the season's most popular play), Ionesco's *Victims of Duty*, Pinter's *The Birthday Party, Ranchman* by Megan Terry, a Beckett triple bill (*Play, Acts without Words I* and *II*, and *Krapp's Last Tape*), and *The Thing Itself* by Arthur Sainer.

The novelty in the Firehouse production of *Godot* was the use of stroboscopic lighting effects, the vogue for which has spread in various directions from the wonderful world of mixed media. Every few minutes throughout the play, the action (or inaction) was interrupted, the ordinary stage lighting went off, some flashing stroboscopic lights came on, and the actors made inarticulate noises and strange gestures indicative of distress; finally one of them would manage to blurt out his next line, the strobes went off, the ordinary lighting came on, and the play resumed. About halfway through the evening I caught on that these stroboscopic interludes were supposed to show us that the desultory conversations of Didi and Gogo are a desperate defense against inner terrors that break through whenever the conversation breaks down; these terrors can only be subdued by resuming the conversation. It is a perfectly valid point, but as conveyed in this production it never got through to my emotions; the stroboscopic terrors never became terrible to me.

Strobes aside, the Firehouse *Godot* was adequately directed by Sydney Walter, and rather well acted. Marlow Hotchkiss played Didi with a Chaplinesque walk and a certain droopy elegance; Paul Boesing was pleasantly floppy as Gogo. David Saunders played Pozzo as a tweedy Englishman with knee-boots and pince-nez; as Lucky, mournfully lugging his suitcases, Don Young looked rather like Willy Loman. But the production could have used more comedy, more pathos, more imagination; perhaps Mr. Walter was distracted by his strobes from dramatizing the characters' relationships more fully, and from making better use of the opportunities for vaudeville-style clowning that Beckett has so abundantly provided.

I returned to Minneapolis in time for *The Thing Itself*, a "theatrical collage" by Arthur Sainer. *The Thing Itself* had a little bit of pretty nearly everything: films and slides on overlapping screens, strobe lights, electronicky sound effects, singing, dancing, guitar-, tambourine-, and drum-playing, animal noises—you name it. So open was the form of Mr. Sainer's collage that when a couple of spectators got into the spirit of the thing and began talking back to the actors, I assumed (incorrectly, as it turned out) that they were part of the show.

Some subject matter was occasionally discernible. A bearded agitator talked about his desire to "assassinate the city." A young woman who liked to eat fruit was arrested—"Are you Harold Queer?"—and beaten up by two men in trench coats. A couple of people got shot at close range. (Used gunpowder smells awful.) A young woman in a striped mini-dress received, and rejected, several young men in her bedroom.

There were indications that some profound significance is intended to lurk in all of this. The title is a German philosophical term (I think). "In our theatre," says one of the characters, "there is no stage and no story, only human life, pushed into a corner, threatened . . ." A program note by Mr. Walter, who directed, was awash with profundity:

> The Thing Itself. To touch it is to know the wellspring of life, the single, simple source from which flows all experience, all images, all sensations, all emotions. But The Thing Itself can only be approached through the baffling complexity of the images and experiences that flow from it. The approach must be intuitive, not rational.
>
> This play presents the experience of one man attempting to grapple with The Thing Itself. . . .

Well, I was there (not at the world première, granted, but at the preview the night before), and I didn't see much of all that. For me there was no Thing Itself in *The Thing Itself*, only a grab-bag of odds and ends. I may be hung up on rationality (". . . a rational ordering of experience . . . never leads to The Thing Itself," says the program), but all I saw was Mr. Sainer having his fantasy-funsies.

However, thanks in large part to a zingy production, Mr. Sainer's funsies often became my funsies as well. In between a lot of dull parts, I enjoyed the sex, some of the violence, the songs (music by Paul Boesing), and a lot of the sound-and-film magic by Marlow Hotchkiss, particularly the transformation of the stage into a cathedral by means of projections and sound tapes, and a funny film that was shown instead of curtain calls. A couple of the girls in the cast could have been more assertive and energetic; otherwise I had no fault to find with the acting. (Paul Boesing, a bushy-black-bearded personage with a great deal of presence and polish, continued to be the most interesting performer in the company.) And the occasional felicities of the dialogue were Mr. Sainer's own: "Poundcake corrupts, but absolute poundcake corrupts absolutely." My only real objection to *The Thing Itself* is that the fun parts were rather too widely spaced. A mixed-media revue should have more hit numbers.

Items like *The Thing Itself* would be fairly esoteric stuff even in New York; you may well ask whether there is much of an audience for it in the upper Midwest. The answer is no. The Firehouse gives only three performances a week, in a theatre that seats only 147, yet attendance for the 1966–67 season hovered between 50 and 60 per cent of capacity. (The previous season it had been about 33 per cent, so the trend is up.) This means that though the budget is low ($45,715 projected for 1967–68, about the same as it has been for the last two seasons), the deficit is high ($29,095 projected for 1967–68). A recent $10,000 grant from the federal government through the National Endowment for the Arts will help, and fortunately, Marlow Hotchkiss, the theatre's co-founder and managing director, has an independent income; when push comes to shove at the theatre, he borrows on his stocks.

And so the Firehouse forges ahead down the path it has chosen. A new season opened on September 29 with (of all things) *Peer Gynt*, which was followed by *Mortality* by Ken Kelman, *Happy Days* by Samuel Beckett, *Woyzeck* by Georg Büchner, *Jack Jack* by Megan Terry, a triple bill consisting of *Three* by Nancy Hotchkiss, *Chicago* by Sam Shepard, and *The Rime of the Ancient Mariner*, and an outdoor production of *A Man's a Man* by Bertolt Brecht.

I have not greatly enjoyed my visits to the Firehouse; I seem to be somewhat fixated on plot and character, and the Firehouse is not very interested in either. But I've watched them experimenting with improvisation, ritual, and direct address to the audience in workshop sessions, and they are not just messing around. The techniques they are working with are not entirely new, but they are searching, conscientiously and not without talent, for new ways of using them.

7 ELSEWHERE IN THE MIDWEST

*

The Manitoba Theatre Centre (Winnipeg)

Winnipeg, Manitoba, is Canada's seventh largest city, with a population of 265,429 at the last census (487,000 in Greater Winnipeg). Located far out on the prairies, it is cut off from the rest of the world by blizzards in the winter, floods in the spring, and sheer distance at any time. What is not available there, in the way of culture, is available nowhere for hundreds of miles; by the same token, Winnipeg's cultural institutions must function as a lifeline to the outside world, alleviating the city's sense of isolation, enlivening the gloom of those long winter nights. It cannot be easy to run a resident professional theatre out there in the middle of nowhere, but such a theatre is in a position to make a greater difference to the life of its community than could a theatre in a city like, say, Philadelphia.

In the summer of 1958, the Winnipeg Little Theatre, an amateur group that had recently acquired an old movie house as a home, and Theatre 77, a fledgling professional group, decided to merge. They called the new organization the Manitoba Theatre Centre: "Centre" because it "was meant to be more than a theatre"; it was to "become a focus for all theatrical energy and resources in our community." The Centre has been true to this purpose. In addition to major productions in the large theatre, and experimental productions in a small studio theatre, its activities now include an annual performance on local television; three school touring programs (one each for senior high, junior high, and elementary schools) that visited 184 institutions in 1966–67; a high school drama festival; a children's theatre with a history of producing new plays; the Manitoba Theatre School with over four hundred students, aged seven and up, and a special workshop for schoolteachers; a scholarship fund to send talented students from Winnipeg to the National Theatre School of Canada; a lecture series on such topics as Aristophanes and George Steiner's *Death of Tragedy*, with illustrative scenes read by members of the company; another lecture series, for subscribers, on the season's plays; miscellaneous readings and recitals; and an advice service for amateur groups.

Such a program requires a budget of over $500,000; less than half of that comes in from the box office (the 828-seat theatre operates at an average of about 81 per cent of capacity), but heavy government subsidies make up most of the difference.

Next to the Stratford Shakespearean Festival, the MTC is perhaps the leading English-speaking resident professional theatre in Canada (there are others in Halifax, Toronto, Vancouver, and elsewhere). Its connections with Stratford have in the past been quite close. Many Stratford actors have appeared in Winnipeg. John Hirsch, who served as artistic director of the MTC until January, 1966, has directed at Stratford for three seasons. (Mr. Hirsch is a remarkable man. He came to Winnipeg from Hungary in 1948, a seventeen-year-old refugee orphan; ten years later he became one of the founders of the MTC. Beginning with the 1968 season, he will be artistic director with Jean Gascon at Stratford, and he also works frequently at the Repertory Theatre of Lincoln Center in New York.)

In 1966, Winnipeg and Stratford presented two plays in collaboration. The last two plays on the MTC spring schedule were replaced by *Nicholas Romanoff* by William Kinsolving (a new work about the Russian Revolution by a young American playwright) and *The Dance of Death* by Strindberg; *Nicholas Romanoff* was directed by Michael Langham and *Dance of Death* by Jean Gascon. The plan was to move the two productions to Stratford for the summer. (M. Gascon was also at that time the artistic director of the Théâtre du Nouveau Monde in Montreal. In Montreal, Winnipeg, and Stratford he played the leading role in *The Dance of Death* under his own direction. In Montreal the production was in French; in Winnipeg and at Stratford, in English.)

Nicholas Romanoff, which I saw in Winnipeg, was the most lavish and expensive production in the MTC's history. It looked splendid, although a bit cramped, on the MTC's stage, and it was well acted by William Hutt as Czar Nicholas, Frances Hyland as the Empress Alix, and Leo Ciceri as Rasputin. (All three are Stratford regulars, but all three had appeared at the MTC previously.) The play is an uninspired but competent chronicle; its central point is that Czar Nicholas was not an evil man but a very ordinary man caught in a situation that was too much for him, and the dramatist did not altogether avoid the obvious danger involved in writing a play about a very ordinary man. *Nicholas Romanoff* never got to Stratford; another play about the Russian Revolution was produced there instead.

Within two years, the Stratford Festival will become a year-round operation, and its actors will not be so readily available to other theatres in the winter. Lately, however the MTC has established an informal connection with the Shaw Festival at Niagara-on-the-Lake, Ontario. Paxton Whitehead, the Shaw Festival's artistic director, has acted for the MTC, and Mr. Gilbert has directed at the Festival. A production of *Major Barbara*, directed by Mr. Gilbert, opened at Niagara in August, played a stand at Expo '67, and moved westward to open the 1967–68 season at the MTC.

In the past, the MTC's choice of repertory has been somewhat timorous; it has produced *The Solid Gold Cadillac*, *The Fourposter*, *Once More, With Feeling*, and a number of other commercial scripts. But it has also done, in nine seasons, four original Canadian plays and a Canadian revue as regular productions (and several more original plays in its studio theatre); few American theatres have been willing to take even so many chances with new plays. The Winnipeg audience does not seem overly given to pap: the hit of the 1964–65 season was *Who's Afraid of Virginia Woolf*, which did 97 per cent of capacity; *Mother Courage* did a respectable 81 per cent. In 1965–66, the most popular production was *The Threepenny Opera*; the Canadian première of *Andorra*, Max Frisch's play about anti-Semitism, was not far behind. *The Importance of Being Earnest* and *The Tempest* also did well; *The Private Ear* and *The Public Eye*, the season's only concession to *kitsch*, did not.

Edward Gilbert, the young Englishman who took over from Mr. Hirsch as artistic director, proposes "to lead and not follow. . . . I'm being paid, amongst other things, . . . to offer people experiences which they are unlikely to undergo if I weren't here."

Well, I guess so, considering Winnipeg, though his 1966–67 season's schedule would be considered conservative in some theatres. He offered *Charley's Aunt*, *The Rainmaker* (abject *kitsch*, but perhaps more pertinent on the prairies than in most places; the last rainmaker passed through Winnipeg only about fifteen years ago), *Galileo* (with Tony Van Bridge, the Stratford actor who played it so magnificently in Boston; this production toured Canada as part of the Centennial festivities), *A Funny Thing Happened* . . . (the season's most popular show), *Romeo and Juliet*, *Lulu Street* by Ann Henry (a new play), and *Luv*.

Lulu Street, the new play, was a Centennial project, commissioned by the Manitoba Chapter of the Imperial Order of the Daughters of the Empire, the Canadian DAR. Eddie Gilbert told me, "I can't do any old new play. They have to be—big letters—OURS. They must offer the opportunity of a creative activity and process that takes place *here*. Just receiving a script from New York isn't much help to me. I'm doing *Lulu Street* not because I think it's any better than other new plays that have been written, but because it's about Winnipeg. . . . It's an ordinary family domestic drama set in the time of the General Strike of 1919, which took place here."

The play takes its name from a real street in Winnipeg. Its hero is a union leader named Matthew Alexander, and his rather peculiar daughter is an important character; in the program was a picture of the author's father, Alexander Henry, addressing a meeting in Victoria Park during the General Strike. The strike itself seems to have been one of the great traumas in Winnipeg's history, featuring riot, arson, the army, and the Northwest Mounted Police.

But though the theme is local and personal, the treatment is traditional. Perhaps Miss Henry had been reading Sean O'Casey; *Lulu Street* reminded me strongly of *The Plough and the Stars*, another play about a violent upheaval in the midst of a city and the wrenching effect of that upheaval on the personal relationships of the participants. A main theme in both plays is the old theme of love and honor, private responsibilities versus public ones: should a man stay home with those he loves, or go and join his brothers in the streets? Jack Clitheroe, his wife Nora, and the Easter Rising, O'Casey's fatal triangle, are reincarnated in Matthew Alexander, his daughter Elly, and the General Strike.

O'Casey's play, however, is far wiser, far subtler, far less obvious. The climax of *Lulu Street* takes place at a big party in the second act; just when the revelry is at its height, a messenger bursts in with News: "Stop, stop! Matthew, they've arrested all the strike leaders. There is rioting at City Hall . . ." And Matthew of course replies, "Tell 'em to hold the line; I'll be along." In the last act, the dialogue drops into the hoary clichés that have become traditional in this sort of play, or movie, or TV show: "If men didn't dream, and believe some day that dream would come true, well, we couldn't go on then, could we?" "It's life that counts, and the key is love. And that word—it's a mystery and a revelation."

Lulu Street has substantial merits—believable characters, idiomatic dialogue, and plenty of interesting concrete detail—but it is probably too much of a formula piece to be generally viable in its present form (though it might serve as the basis for a good film). Still, I was fascinated to discover that the Royal Albert Arms Hotel, where I was staying, had been used during the strike to put up scabs. And I am almost sure that if I were a Winnipegger, I would have enjoyed the play greatly—not because my standards would necessarily be lower, but because the play would be closer to me, and mean more to me. A play *can*, in the proper circumstances, make up in immediacy for what it lacks in absolute value. Many theatres which are termed "regional" overlook this fact and in so doing limit their value. Interestingly enough, although new plays are traditionally poison at the resident-theatre box office, *Lulu Street* did 86 per cent of capacity, which was well above the season's average.

One important reason for its success, however, was the beautiful performance it received under Edward Gilbert's direction: scrupulously detailed and realistic, yet vigorous and lively as well. One of the hardest things in the world to stage successfully is a celebration, but at the boisterous party in the second act of *Lulu Street*, the merriment never for a moment seemed fake. To play the hero, Mr. Gilbert imported from London a swarthy Celtic type named Robert Cartland, who looked like Richard Burton gone to seed; his daughter was played by a delicate New York actress named Anna Shaler; Sandy Webster, Heath Lamberts, and other Canadian actors played various character roles. All were impeccable individually, and they played together as if they had been doing it for years. The MTC is the only theatre I know that does its casting in three countries, yet in this production, from this heterogeneous group, Mr. Gilbert achieved a far higher degree of ensemble than is usually to be found in resident theatres.

A great deal is talked in resident-theatre circles (and not much is done) about forming permanent companies. The virtues of such a company are an article of faith in these circles: actors who work together over a long period of time, it is believed, can evolve a common vocabulary and an increased sensitivity to one another that make possible a standard of work attainable in no other way. For Mr. Gilbert, on the other hand, a company only makes sense if it espouses a distinct philosophy or theory of acting or staging. "I think to run a company without a philosophic intention is unnecessary," he says. "I think there's a mystique about this word 'ensemble,' and I don't get it. I get it when I see the Moscow Art Theatre, but I certainly don't get it in Boston or Milwaukee." The degree of unity in a production, he believes, depends on the director.

And so the MTC is "basically a jobbing theatre as opposed to a company theatre." Actors are engaged not for a season, but for a play or two or three. The disadvantage is the amount of money spent on air fares. The advantage is that "We cast better. That, I think, is the real key to any standard we achieve compared to other regional theatres. . . . It's easier to get people to come for five weeks than for six months."

He would seem to have a point. The very best work in the resident theatres on this continent is done by genuine resident companies where most of the actors are there for the season and some have been there for several seasons: Stratford (Ontario) and

Minneapolis provide examples. But jobbing has been the salvation of the Repertory Theatre of Lincoln Center, and many smaller theatres have discovered that a full-fledged permanent resident company in the present stage of their evolution is simply an unworkable idea. Some smaller theatres may well be sacrificing the quality of their productions to a dogmatic principle by refusing to job. Mr. Gilbert, being located in Canada, can cast freely in Toronto, New York, and London, as American theatres unfortunately cannot. But the excellence of his production of *Lulu Street* shows how quickly and closely a heterogeneous cast can be integrated.

The Milwaukee Repertory Theatre

Except for the Alley Theatre in Houston, the Milwaukee Repertory Theatre has a longer history than any resident professional company between Cleveland and the Pacific Coast. Founded in 1954 by a group of Milwaukee citizens, it was originally called the Fred Miller Theatre, after a local civic leader. Until 1961 it presented commercial Broadway plays with visiting stars. Then, says the theatre's publicity handout, "it was decided to convert the Fred Miller into a professional resident theatre, a new and exciting kind of theatre gaining great popularity in several larger cities in the United States." In other words, it had become apparent in Milwaukee that resident professional theatre, presenting the classics and serious modern plays, was the wave of the future; summer-stock-in-winter was no longer good enough. As the MRT's producer put it in a subscription brochure, "Professional resident theatre is the 'new look' in entertainment."

Nowadays the MRT's audience prefers the standard resident-theatre plays. "People who come to this kind of theatre," says the MRT's artistic director, "want Culture with a capital C, Message with a capital M. . . . The 20,000 people who see *The Odd Couple* when it plays downtown will never come to this theatre." *Uncle Vanya, Six Characters in Search of an Author, Tartuffe, Mother Courage,* have all been popular; likewise anything by Shakespeare. *Oh Dad, Poor Dad,* Noel Coward's *Design for Living,* and the musical *Once upon a Mattress* all did poorly, but so did the American première of Michel de Ghelderode's *Pantagleize.*

In 1966–67, the MRT played to 80.5 per cent of capacity in its 346-seat arena theatre (a converted movie house in a residential district); in 1968, it will move into a new 515-seat theatre in the inevitable Center for the Performing Arts.

The MRT's productions of *Uncle Vanya* and *Mother Courage* have been greatly admired by visiting critics, but on my first visit to Milwaukee, in the spring of 1966, I saw a production of *The Glass Menagerie* in which all four parts had been miscast. Ralph Williams, who played Tom, the narrator, would have been better suited as a television teen-ager. Mary Doyle (the producer-director's wife) had a husky voice, a funny face, and a gamine quality; she might be very good as Gittel in *Two for the Seesaw*, but she was quite evidently not at her best as delicate, shy Laura Wingfield. Stefan Gierasch gave no indication of those qualities that had made the Gentleman Caller a hero in high school; in his double-breasted, wide-lapeled suit he reminded me of the gangster in *Pal Joey*. Sada Thompson was bigger and more solid than Amanda ought to be; she made her a little less of a lady than usual, a little more of a shrew. Nevertheless, in her Enna Jetticks, her housecoat, and her touching thirties coiffure, she gave a poignant performance—the only one of the evening. Those are the exigencies of resident-company casting, with a vengeance. If you need an actor for Play A and Play C, the temptation to convince yourself that there is a part for him in Play B is almost overwhelming, especially considering that your theatre, as is almost always the case, operates on a tight budget and a large deficit. The problem is by no means confined to Milwaukee.

The Glass Menagerie was directed by John A. McQuiggan, at that time the producer of the MRT. Before rehearsals began, however, it had been announced that he would not renew his contract. (After a short sojourn as co-director of the Trinity Square Repertory Company in Providence, R.I., he is now with the APA.) His successor, with the title of artistic director, is Tunc Yalman, a Turkish director, actor, critic, and playwright (born in Istanbul in 1925) who studied at the Yale Drama School.

Mr. Yalman knows, from personal experience, more about resident professional theatre than most of us. In his teens in Istanbul, he saw "just about every great play ever written." The Istanbul Municipal Theatre, founded in 1915, is a huge company playing in no less than six auditoriums; prices are kept low by huge subsidies. Discussing the *raison d'être* for his theatre in Milwaukee, Mr. Yalman says:

> Mankind has a common human heritage in drama—twenty-five centuries of it. Any play which has lasted beyond its time deals with eternal values and has something to say to mankind. . . . That human heritage . . . has got to be kept alive in a theatre.

In his first season (1966–67), Mr. Yalman offered *Electra* by Sophocles, *The Physicists* by Duerrenmatt, *Design for Living* by Noel Coward, *The Merchant of Venice*, *The Miser* by Molière, *Puntila and His Hired Man* by Bertolt Brecht, and Ibsen's *Hedda Gabler*. To perform in them, he recruited an Equity company of twelve actors, which is about the number that most resident theatres maintain, and kept these actors together for an entire season, which is less usual, "so the company could work together, grow together, so the audience can watch the actors in several parts." During the whole season he employed only one jobber: Boris Tumarin as Shylock. (Local amateurs were used in large-cast plays, as is usual with the smaller resident theatres.) The work I saw at the MRT under Mr. Yalman's stewardship was mostly sound enough, but unexciting.

The Miser was assigned to a guest director, the peripatetic Louis Criss, who led the company to elaborate and comment upon nearly every line of the dialogue. It was a busy, broad, good-natured, frankly artificial production, with a great deal of kissing, goosing, spanking, sobbing, nose-blowing, doubling up with laughter (among the actors), and lying on the floor. This is a sensible enough approach to a farce like *The Miser*; Mr. Criss's ingenuities sometimes justified themselves by the amusement they provoked, and sometimes were a nuisance. There were no particularly good performances, but everybody except one bit-player was satisfactory. I found it a mildly pleasant diversion, but if the play has any particular significance (which I tend to doubt), it did not emerge. The kids in the audience loved it; except for the sex (one scene was played *en dishabille*, which would have astonished Molière), it was really a children's-theatre show.

Nobody, of course, could say that about *Hedda Gabler*, which was directed by Mr. Yalman. The company was rather young for the play, but except for the poor girl who struggled so unsuccessfully to impersonate old Aunt Juliana, this did not matter too much. Gregory Abels, who played foolish George Tesman, was forever showing us just how foolish he was, which is something different from *being* foolish on the stage; I was always aware of the actor characterizing away as hard as he could. Otherwise, the actors coped pretty well, and Erika Slezak, who played Hedda, turned out to be a young actress with the authentic grand manner. Her initial gracious self-possession gave way to nervousness, which gave way in turn to a smiling, blandly mischievous irony, but she always remained a woman of stature. Not only what she said but what she did was full of meaning: nervously pacing the room, or meditatively selecting a mint. Before the evening was over, Miss Slezak ran out of surprises, but the part seems to be written so as to land the actress in this difficulty. And our stage is not rich in young actresses who, like Miss Slezak, can say "It would be better to die!" as if they meant it.

The play (who among us, under the age of forty, has had a chance to see it?) is an elaborate character study of a neurotic woman, unfolded through old-fashioned, Scribean plot-manipulation, involving long stretches of exposition, hidden secrets, melodramatic climaxes. Nowadays, for all its truth, it seems a bit stately and high-flown. For many years we have had no chance to test the theatrical efficacy and significance of the canon of approved dramatic masterpieces; *Hedda Gabler* has not worn altogether well. Ibsen's place in theatrical history is unshakeable; his place in the contemporary theatre is in doubt. (I venture to think that *Brand* might mean far more to us than any of his drawing-room plays.) It may yet turn out that Ibsen's greatest contribution was not the plays he wrote, but the plays his influence enabled others to write. But we will need many more productions of *Hedda Gabler*, and others among Ibsen's plays, in order to be sure.

This problem of whether a script is theatrically viable is a particularly keen one to new playwrights who have had few or no productions. "We're trying," says Tunc Yalman, "to fulfill our obligation to the past, the present, and the future." With the future in mind, he instituted a "Theatre for Tomorrow" series, under which rubric he presented a double bill of plays by Rosalyn

Drexler in the fall of 1966, and a new play by Douglas Taylor in the spring of 1967. A grant of $25,000 from the Rockefeller Foundation paid all expenses. Each presentation gave two performances a week for about two months, at times when the theatre would otherwise have been dark; each was performed by members of the regular MRT company. On the whole, the MRT is a continuous-run stock company, not, strictly speaking, a repertory operation. But when a Theatre for Tomorrow play is on, there are two shows in the bill every week, and repertory becomes a fact.

I happened to be in Milwaukee for Mr. Taylor's play, which was entitled *The Sudden and Accidental Re-education of Horse Johnson*. Horse Johnson turned out to be a warehouseman who walked out and went home one day to think about solving the world's problems. The comedy in the play—and there is quite a fair amount—comes largely from the incongruity between Horse's warehouseman's mannerisms and his messianic aspirations, as he alternately picks his teeth and talks about poetry. But the author seems to have no idea of what an overbearing, self-infatuated ass his hero is. Horse Johnson is not worth listening to in himself, and neither are the people who surround him, since they are stupid enough to take him seriously. And his chastisement in the last act brings him only the most elementary and hackneyed insight; he is capable of no other kind. He discovers that it is impossible for one man to solve the world's problems by himself; Mr. Taylor trumpets this forth as his message, but some of us knew it all along. The whole play is predicated on the assumption that however misguided Horse Johnson is, he is a man of stature; but this assumption is never justified.

The production was carefully naturalistic, with water coming out of faucets and celery getting chopped. But one actress was slightly uncomfortable with proletarian diction, and another was far too young to play a "gettin' old" character with any conviction. Michael Fairman was not really hulking enough to play Horse Johnson—not the kind of man anyone would nickname "Horse" —but he made the character's plight more interesting than perhaps it deserved to be, and made both his warehouseman aspect and his messiah aspect believable as parts of the same person.

The Rockefeller Foundation has renewed its grant, and there

will be more Theatre of Tomorrow productions this year. Perhaps Mr. Yalman will find some scripts that are more than "promising"; even if he does not, the Theatre of Tomorrow program will at least continue to offer a few American playwrights a valuable chance to learn from their mistakes.

The Detroit Repertory Theatre

Bruce Millan started the Detroit Repertory Theatre in the spring of 1967. He was thirty-seven years old and a native of Detroit, and he had been producing children's theatre in the Detroit area for eleven years. His new project is not a lavish affair: the theatre is located in a not-very-attractive Negro district, the seats are folding chairs nailed to wooden bleachers, and the producer himself sells refreshments during the intermission. The acting company was Equity, but it was not good; the performances I saw of Duerrenmatt's *The Marriage of Mr. Mississippi* and Molière's *Tartuffe* were mediocre-to-poor. Audience response was almost nil. In the Detroit Repertory's short season of forty-two performances, total attendance amounted to just 1,168, which means a 160-seat theatre operating at about 20 per cent of capacity. Detroiters who want to go to a resident theatre patronize the John Fernald Company at Oakland University in suburban Rochester (which will be discussed in Chapter Eleven). Mr. Millan has announced that he will reopen in January, 1968, but the survival of his Repertory Theatre is very much in doubt.

Yet all this has very little to do with the real value of Mr. Millan's work. The Repertory Theatre's real function is to provide a sort of front for the aspects of this work that he is most interested in. He is cynical about the resident theatres in general, since they reach, in most cases, such a tiny percentage of the community. He is determined to go after the other 98 per cent. This he has been doing since 1956 with his "backyard" tours, which bring children's shows into all sorts of community places in Michigan, Indiana, Ohio, and western Pennsylvania, since the productions do not require fully equipped theatres. More recently, Mr. Millan has been reaching about 50,000 children in the Detroit area with another touring program that has visited sixty junior and senior high schools, financed by $150,000 from the federal government transmitted via the Detroit public school system.

I went along with the company on a visit to Durfee Junior High School, not far from the theatre. It was for all practical purposes an all-Negro school; I saw only one white student, out of several hundred. (I wonder how he felt?) The student body could hardly have been more segregated in Mississippi itself; clearly these children saw, in their own lives, very little evidence that integration was possible. Into schools like this—and other kinds of schools as well—Mr. Millan brings a completely integrated company: two white men, a black man, a white woman, a black woman. "We've got to put Negroes on that stage," Mr. Millan says, "men especially. . . . Just to have a Negro man walk on that stage creates a tremor right through the audience. We're not talking about theatre. We're talking about starving people looking for something to identify with. Good artists be damned, we've got to have somebody black on that stage."

The longer of the two items on the program was *The Case of the Crushed Petunias*, an uncharacteristically whimsical little fable by Tennessee Williams. The heroine, a prim New England spinster named Miss Simple, was played by a white actress. The traveling salesman for "Life, Inc.," who persuades her to break out in search of experience and love, was played by a black actor.

The Case of the Crushed Petunias was selected by the school system as being suitable for students; I was more interested in its companion piece, which was written and directed by Bruce Millan. He calls it a "Living Text." There was no set; the actors played in street clothes, switching from role to role every few moments. The Living Text began with the words, "The Civil War is over." "Ain't no slave no more," the actors chanted. "Gonna see my missus every night," said one, and the audience got the point. They laughed and cheered and applauded and stopped the show. When it resumed, one actor, suddenly switching from black to white, yelled, "Nigger, you're going to miss your slavery!" The rest of the show dramatized how the white man regained ascendancy over the black. Throughout, the casting was completely nonracial; the actors, black and white alike, were constantly switching from playing blacks to playing whites, and back again. At one point, a white southern judge played by a Negro actress sentenced a Negro prisoner played by a white actor. When the judge called the defendant "boy," there was liberating laughter. The kids were shown, for once in their lives, that in spite of the terrible history of race relations in this country, racial barriers need not always be absolute.

Mr. Millan's Living Text lasts only seventeen minutes, but it wastes no time and pulls no punches. It is lucid without being simple-minded. It does not patronize or platitudinize. It is not noticeably rigged or slanted. It is vigorous, fast-moving, absorbing, and it shows clearly what the white man has done to the black man in this country. Finally someone is leveling with at least a few American students about this matter, without any ameliorative Booker T. Washington crap. Finally black students are hearing and seeing something in their schools that bears an immediate relationship to what they hear and see outside.

According to Mr. Millan, one principal complained that after a visit by the company, the school had to suspend the regular curriculum for one whole day to answer the kids' questions about the play. This by itself should serve to indicate that Mr. Millan's school tours are doing an important job. In 1968, federal funds are harder to come by, and nobody knows how, or whether, these tours can be financed. But in any case, Mr. Millan has shown, far better than some companies with far greater pretensions, what the theatre can do, what it is for.

The Playhouse in the Park (Cincinnati)

The Playhouse in the Park began in 1960, when a little pavilion in Eden Park was saved from impending demolition and turned into a neat thrust-stage theatre: an indoor auditorium surrounded by porches and lawns that serve as lobbies. Located on top of a steep hill overlooking the city, the Playhouse is very difficult to reach except by car; this tends, of course, to cut it off from poorer Cincinnatians. But nearly all resident theatres, no matter how easy of access, are middle- or upper-class institutions (except for their student programs). And since the Playhouse tends to run at something like 90 per cent of capacity, which means that many people are turned away from many performances, it is clearly reaching just about all the people it can presently cope with. In order to cope with some more, it is currently building a new 650-seat theatre (the present one seats 227). The new theatre will not, for a change, be part of a new Performing Arts Center downtown;

it will be located in Eden Park, adjacent to the old theatre, which will be kept in use for small-scale productions.

Until the new theatre opens, however, the Playhouse must perforce be a small-scale production itself. Its budget for 1967 was only $155,130, amazingly low for a seven-play season; only about nine Equity actors are usually on hand at one time; the maximum salary for actors is $150 a week, also a very low figure. But there are few signs of skimping at the Playhouse. The productions I have seen have looked good, and some excellent actors have appeared in them (along with some who were noticeably less than excellent). The Playhouse in the Park is by no means up there with the Guthrie and the very few other first-rate American theatres, but Brooks Jones, its producer, makes his limited resources go re- markably far.

Since Eden Park is probably the pleasantest place in Cincinnati on a summer evening, the Playhouse season very logically extends from April through September. But Mr. Jones does not consider it his function merely to provide light summer entertainment, and his audience appears to feel the same way. When in 1966 he presented *Charley's Aunt,* as a sort of breather between the American première of *Sodom and Gomorrah* by Giraudoux and the American première of *Eh?* by the British writer Henry Livings, the Playhouse was attacked in a local paper for letting down its standards and allowing frivolity and escapism to creep in.

But there are standards in farce as in anything else, and *Charley's Aunt,* with its combination of sure-fire hilarity and Victorian charm, is one of the best. And the Playhouse gave it a happy production. True, the juveniles, though pleasant enough, were somewhat lacking in crispness, and one of them had a slight speech defect. True, one of the ingénues seemed to be doing an introverted Method-thing that had a certain hesitant charm, but nothing to do with this brisk and extroverted play. True, several members of the cast were unable to manage an English accent, though this should be part of the equipment of any well-trained actor. But David Hooks's staging—choreography, really—was beautifully deft, and so was Ed Zang's performance as the Oxford undergraduate who is forced to disguise himself as Charley's aunt. Both Mr. Hooks's staging and Mr. Zang's acting were not only hilarious, but hilarious without heaviness, without overstatement, without sweat. (Mr. Zang is a remarkable actor; I will have something to say in the next chapter about his Hamlet at the Charles Playhouse in Boston.)

In 1967, Mr. Jones presented *The Fantasticks, The Importance of Being Earnest, The Birthday Party,* the American première of *The Cavern* by Jean Anouilh, a double bill of *The Lesson* by Ionesco and *Escurial* by Michel de Ghelderode, *Uncle Vanya,* and a musical version of Schnitzler's *Anatol,* adapted by Tom Jones, using music by Jacques Offenbach. (This last one had been done by the APA and the Milwaukee Repertory Theatre, but has never been seen in New York.) Since I admire Jean Anouilh as the consummate professional among playwrights, I scheduled a visit to Cincinnati to see *The Cavern.*

It turned out not to be one of his best works; it displays the defects of his qualities as well as the qualities themselves. He has always been a facile writer, superbly conversant with the stage and what can be done on it. But there is something somehow insolent, overconfident, about the open manipulation of theatrical devices in *The Cavern.* The play begins with a character called the Author, who explains that this is a play he never succeeded in writing, and who keeps coming back after nearly every scene to complain that this won't do at all. After a while, the joke wears thin.

Still, in an old-fashioned way, *The Cavern* is a viable piece of theatre—old-fashioned because Anouilh has always been an extravagantly romantic writer. That is the secret of his success: the most extravagant romanticism tempered by the most skillful workmanship. He delights in writing exquisite sugarplum idylls (which play much better than they summarize) about poor, beautiful, virginal girls who win the love of rich and handsome young men. But there is another side to Anouilh's romanticism; *The Cavern* is an expression of his taste for lush and violent melodrama, featuring as it does murder, rape, bastardy, abortion, and white slavery. It seems, in this play the Author has never quite written, that the cook in a great house has had, years ago, a child by the duke, her master. She has raised the child to be a priest, and is furious when he falls in love with a kitchenmaid who is already pregnant. The whole situation culminates in homicidal fury and a fatal stabbing.

This may sound in summary like impossible nonsense (and some of it is a bit overripe), but Anouilh has cleverly employed his

Pirandellian scaffolding to prevent us from feeling that we are meant to take the play more seriously than we are willing to take it, without preventing us from being moved by it now and then. The plotting is lively, and so, in spite of much hackneyed gush and tosh about the gulf between upstairs and below stairs, is a good deal of the dialogue. *The Cavern* has an old-fashioned charm, yet it also has moments of revelation about the hardness of life and the cruel, cynical strength that suffering can breed (which in turn breeds more suffering). For all his romanticism, Anouilh has by no means closed his eyes to the real world.

Though the Cincinnati production, directed by Michael Kahn, was uneven, there were sound performances by Emery Battis as the Author, Charles Cioffi as a police detective, and Donald Ewer as a greasy valet. Irene Dailey, imported as a guest artist to play the cook, stomped about in an overobvious attempt to be peasanty, but her performance had a certain rawboned strength all the same. Most of the others ranged from adequate through mediocre to poor.

And as so often happens in the American theatre somebody in charge seems to have had a tin ear. The upper-class characters spoke in upper-class English accents, the valet and the coachman spoke cockney. So far so good. But the detective employed what sounded like a neo-Peter Sellers French accent, and most of the rest stuck to standard American, except for Miss Dailey, who played the cook in Irish-American. Whatever happened to the ideal of a homogeneous ensemble? (The translation, liberally sprinkled with British idioms, only emphasized the inconsistencies. Couldn't someone at least have Americanized the dialogue here and there?)

A flawed play, then, sometimes bordering on the trivial, and inconsistently performed. But the whole occasion was redeemed by a young actress named Lynn Milgrim, who played the pregnant kitchenmaid. Her part was not an easy one: nothing but barefoot meekness until about ten thirty, and then an explosion. For most of the evening Miss Milgrim was a touchingly abject and miserable slavey; but when the explosion came, it was stunning. The girl had swallowed insults and injuries for a lifetime; now her hatreds burst out of her, vomited up with hysterical force, a tremendous indictment that accused us all of complicity in her suffering.

The scene is capably written, in a melodramatic way; but it was

Miss Milgrim who made it eloquent. I left the Playhouse with a sense that something had really *happened* to me—a feeling rare enough in our own theatre, where even "serious" plays are more likely to tickle than penetrate. And perhaps it was not only my connection-seeking turn of mind that made the kitchenmaid's outcry seem to say something about the riots that had, coincidentally, shaken Cincinnati during the run of the play.

The Studio Arena Theatre (Buffalo)

The Studio Arena is another new-old theatre. Founded in 1927 as the Studio Theatre School, it functioned as a school and an amateur theatre for nearly forty years. Then in the fall of 1965, under the leadership of its "Executive Producer," Neal Du Brock, it moved into new quarters downtown, a former night club converted into an excellent 509-seat thrust-stage theatre, and became a professional Equity company. The school continues in the old premises, which also contains a 278-seat theatre that will be used for experimental work.

The Studio Arena's first professional production was *A Moon for the Misbegotten* by Eugene O'Neill, directed by José Quintero, with James Daly and Colleen Dewhurst; its second season opened with George Grizzard as Cyrano de Bergerac. For the most part, however, the theatre tries to get by with its resident company. "Generally," says Neal Du Brock, "we're looking for an actor who has enough training so that he knows how to move and speak, that he has some ear . . ." But he also asks of prospective actors, "What is their interest in this type of theatre?" If an actor asks, "Can I come for just a couple of plays?" then, says Mr. Du Brock, "We don't really want them at all." But well-trained actors willing to commit themselves to a full season on the Niagara frontier are hard to come by; judging by the single production I saw at the Studio Arena in the spring of 1967, a double bill of *The Lesson* by Ionesco and *Antigone* by Anouilh, Mr. Du Brock has not yet been able to find enough of them.

The Lesson came off well enough. Max Gulack, a chubby, jolly Professor, did not build the arc of his homicidal frenzy as firmly as he might have; his culminating violence was not convulsive enough, and so the climax of the play was not very climactic. The play thus became a vehicle for Renee Leicht (wife of Allan Leicht, the director), who really looked like a schoolgirl as she entered, dumpy and cute, grinning, almost aquiver with nervous good will. Mrs. Leicht has revue in her background, and her Pupil was broadly played and funny.

Antigone, Anouilh's modern version of Sophocles' tragedy, fared less well. It had a brilliant setting, designed by Douglas Higgins, of glittering, slippery-looking varnished wood, crazily raked, with geometric, right-angled, clear plastic furniture, which made a cold, hard, unsympathetic world, with no place in it where Antigone could hide even if she would. The costumes, on the other hand (not by Mr. Higgins), detracted from the effect of the production more actively and intensely than any others I have ever seen anywhere. Poor Antigone had to be tragic in a shiny white mini-skirt, and Haemon, that upright youth, was outfitted in tight bright white-on-white bell-bottoms and cream-colored boots, which made him look like a refugee from the Andy Warhol ménage.

Linda Selman, who played Antigone, has an attractive, husky voice and an air of something special about her that might someday take her far. She can say, "Save your tears . . . you may still need them," with the right kind of vibrations. But her performance never quite came to a climax; surely at some point in her ordeal, Antigone should cry out. And everything she said was undermined by the fact that she lisped; like not a few resident-theatre performers, she is in desperate need of the attentions of a speech therapist. As Creon, that scrupulous and conscientious tyrant, Gerald Richards, with the gray in his hair obviously artificial, looked too young. He was a bit self-conscious in his imposingness, and did not really seem urbane and intelligent enough to be saying the lines that Anouilh has written for Creon. Elaine Kerr played Antigone's sister Ismene as a Newyorky bitch, for no good reason that was apparent to me, and Russell Drisch as Haemon was somewhat of a lump.

The only justification for the *Antigone* is the familiar last resort: that is is better than no production of *Antigone* at all. (The sparse audience at the matinée I attended was comprised mostly of high school students; whether they were interested, polite, or intimi-dated I cannot be absolutely sure, but they were quiet and gave every indication that they were listening to this highly cerebral piece.) As always when I have been able to see only one production at a theatre, I may have lit by chance on one that was highly atypical (though this possibility is diminished in theatres, like the Studio Arena, which rely on a permanent company). And, of course, it is always possible for a theatre to get better (though it is not inevitable).

The Studio Arena runs a "Summer Straw Hat Series" that in 1967 presented *Barefoot in the Park*, *Beyond the Fringe*, and *Luv*, a good selection among recent light entertainments. On the whole, however, says Mr. Du Brock, "I don't think Buffalo audiences are asking me for comedies." In programing the regular season, he tries to include "A little something for everyone in order to attract those people we still don't have as subscribers. . . . Plays that we like, we feel are worthwhile. . . . Our biggest consideration is what we can do best."

His 1967–68 season will include the world première of a pair of one-act plays by Edward Albee, entitled *Box* and *Quotations from Chairman Mao Tse-tung*, directed by Alan Schneider: quite a coup for Buffalo. The other plays on the schedule are *The Threepenny Opera*, *The Imaginary Invalid* (Molière), *H. M. S. Pinafore*, Pirandello's *Henry IV*, *A Delicate Balance* by Mr. Albee, Pinter's *The Homecoming* (if the rights are released in time), and *Charley's Aunt*. This is by no means a trivial program. Perhaps Mr. Du Brock will manage to find the resources to pull it off.

NEW
ENGLAND

The Charles Playhouse (Boston)

The Charles Playhouse, which celebrated its tenth anniversary in 1967, is the oldest of the five resident theatres in New England; for most of its career it was the only one. Its artistic director, Michael Murray (who resigned in January, 1968), grew up in Washington and knew the work of the Arena Stage, but when he and Frank Sugrue (a lawyer who is now the theatre's full-time managing director) began their operation, they were, says Mr. Murray, "Off-Broadway oriented." At that time there were a few resident theatres isolated here and there across the country, but little sense of a "movement"; it was Off-Broadway that was going to revitalize the American theatre. How long ago that seems!

In the spring of 1963, however, the Ford Foundation sent Murray and Sugrue off to Washington, Houston, San Francisco, and Minneapolis to take a look at the Arena Stage, the Alley Theatre, the Actor's Workshop, and the Guthrie Theatre, and around that time the Playhouse began to bill itself as a resident professional theatre. Recently it has given up casting each production from scratch; it now has a resident company of about twelve Equity and seven non-Equity actors; the latter are used for the high school touring program and the afternoon children's shows, as well as for small parts in the major productions. Even in the old days, of course, the Playhouse used to employ certain performers over and over again; it was founded with a nucleus of actors from Boston University. But now there is much more emphasis on the idea of a company; and the high school and children's programs, both fairly new, indicate that the Playhouse will in future look upon itself, as do most resident theatres, as a wide-ranging community institution.

The first home of the Playhouse was a loft over a fish market near the foot of Beacon Hill; after the first season, however, this was abandoned in favor of a downtown building (in an alley behind the Shubert where the big musicals play) that was formerly a night club, and before that a church. It has a good-sized thrust stage and 525 seats; within a few years, says Frank Sugrue, it will be too small.

The Charles presents the solid, standard resident-theatre repertory of plays, with a touch of unconventionality in the programing now and then. In 1966–67 it offered *Love for Love, The Balcony, Hamlet, Mother Courage, Oh! What a Lovely War,* and *Inadmissible Evidence,* plus a nonsubscription summer production of *Macbird!* The 1967–68 season is devoted to American plays: *America Hurrah, Awake and Sing!,* a bill of one-acts (*Dutchman* by LeRoi Jones, *The Madness of Lady Bright* by Lanford Wilson, and *The Nine O'Clock Mail* by Howard Sackler), *The Old Glory, Room Service,* and one to be announced. The planners have obviously been influenced by the "American Retrospective" season in Philadelphia; still this looks as if it will be one of those rare seasons where the plays illuminate one another. A pity they can't play in repertory.

Early in 1966 I turned up in Boston, after several years' absence, to have a look at the Playhouse's production of *Galileo.* (This was after the play had been done in San Francisco, Washington, D.C., Cleveland, and Philadelphia, but before it hit Seattle or New York's Lincoln Center.) There were good supporting performances by Edward Zang and Edward Finnegan, Charles Playhouse stalwarts whom I remember from my student days around Boston in the late 1950's. Mr. Finnegan, a portly old gentleman with a red face, is a highly authoritative and lovable actor, and something of a legend in Boston. But some of the other performances were hopelessly bad, and Mr. Murray's staging made very little of the opportunities for theatrical flamboyance that Brecht provided in this as in so many of his plays.

As an ensemble effort, the Boston *Galileo* was mediocre, but it was redeemed—almost transfigured—by the star performance (in the best sense) of Tony van Bridge in the title role. Someone in the play says of Galileo, "He has more enjoyment in him than any man I ever saw. He indulges in eating, drinking, and thinking to excess." Not many actors could live up to this description, but Mr. van Bridge gave us a joyously sensual man and a keenly intelligent one, for whom food and wine and science all provided the same kind of deep, visceral delight. Mr. van Bridge is a member of the Shakespearean Festival company at Stratford, Ontario; if the American resident theatres could tempt more Stratford actors south of the border during the winter, the standard of acting at our theatres would be higher than it is.

When I returned to Boston in the spring, the Playhouse was doing *The Tiger* and *The Typists*, Murray Schisgal's pair of short two-character plays. They are slight works and not very entertaining unless the actors come through with zany but accurate caricatures of middle-class urban types, the kind of people you see on the subways. In Boston, only Lynn Milgrim's typist was extravagant and specific enough. Looking wonderfully awful in a wig and false eyelashes, Miss Milgrim went from girlish crudeness to frumpy middle age as a funny-pathetic quintessence of the second-rate working girl. The rest of the acting (including Miss Milgrim's performance in *The Tiger*) was pleasant and professional, but too bland and general, without the necessary relish for idiom and milieu.

Interestingly enough, *Galileo* and *Poor Bitos*, two "talky" historical plays, were the box-office hits of the season at the Charles; Mr. Schisgal's easy-to-take, close-to-home pair of trifles did less well.

The Charles Playhouse *Hamlet*, which opened in December, 1966, was a strange sort of Christmas present, a stark black-and-white production that showed us the Danish court as a cold, poor, desolate place. The set by William D. Roberts was a couple of simple black platforms with a thing like a bat's wing overhead; his costumes were more or less modern, vaguely central European or Russian: greatcoats, boots, persian-lamb-collared jackets, fur hats, black turtle necks. Edward Zang's Hamlet was a strange, unheroic prince: waspish, a little effeminate, obviously intelligent, vibrating with keenness and nervousness, with a slim, delicate-looking body, receding hairline, bony fingers curling and working, and a strange clumping walk in his boots. After the Ghost scene, Mr. Zang was *really* distracted, as Hamlets seldom are; he said, "Now, Mother, what's the matter?" with an offhand insolence that wasn't really offhand; and surely no Hamlet can ever have been better at baiting Rosencrantz and Guildenstern. But "the glass of fashion and the mold of form," Mr. Zang wasn't.

It was, as I say, a strange *Hamlet*, with an imaginative, intriguing, yet not perverse or gimmicky production-concept. Mr. Zang is an actor worth watching, whatever he does; he can play certain sides of Hamlet extremely well. But Michael Murray's direction was better in conception than execution. Not everything quite fitted together; the big, populous, crucial court scenes were not clearly staged; and, as seems to be usual when the Playhouse attempts a large-cast show, some of the acting was quite, quite bad. A vulgar Claudius is a good idea; a Borscht-Circuit Claudius is not.

Hamlet, for all the influence of Peter Brook's *King Lear*, had a real creative impulse behind it; *Oh! What a Lovely War*, which came along in the spring, was a somewhat spiritless attempt to recapture the rapture of Joan Littlewood's original production. When the material was strong enough to carry the performers, it worked; fortunately, that was most of the time. The ironic contrast implicit in the title, between the frivolousnesss of the form (vaudeville) and the grimness of the content (World War I), made enough effect to justify the evening. *Oh! What a Lovely War* in Boston was both entertaining and timely: its confident announcements that victory was about to be won—actual quotations from General Sir Douglas Haig—were weirdly reminiscent of the pronouncements of some later generals.

Lovely War was directed by Eric House, another veteran of the Stratford, Ontario, Shakespearean Festival, who remained in Boston to play the leading role in *Inadmissible Evidence*, the season's last production. John Osborne's play is a hymn of hate, a *Look Back in Anger* gone sour, devoid of the peculiar exultation (in youth, in sex, in rhetoric, in the power to feel) that informs the earlier work. It depicts the crack-up of an angry middle-aged lawyer who drinks, takes pills, fornicates, and vituperates endlessly, and does all these things with the same compulsive joylessness. It is built like Haydn's Farewell Symphony: one by one, everyone around Bill Maitland quietly leaves the stage, until Maitland is alone. The problem with the play is that after a while it is easy to see what's coming, and we find out nothing about Maitland that we didn't know before.

I enjoyed the play more in Boston than I had in New York, mostly, I think, because the theatre in Boston was more intimate. Mr. House was plaintive and waspish rather than furious, as Nicol Williamson had been in New York: more an unhappy terrier than a mad bull. But his performance, though smaller in scale, was no less valid, and it carried the play. The other characters are the merest straight men for Maitland (which is another of the script's problems). They were all well played in Boston, under Mr. Murray's direction; the actors who played Maitlands' office staff carefully brought out the shallowness, the lack of receptivity, in their characters, and a girl named Swoosie Kurtz provided a particularly vivid caricature of a mini-skirted, bottom-twitching, new-generation sexpot.

Inadmissible Evidence was the only one of these five productions about which I did not have serious reservations; the Charles Playhouse would appear to have a very uneven company, not very well directed. But even without being able to set a consistent standard of good quality, even with bad acting and dull staging, it somehow manages to do quite a bit of interesting work. It would seem that if they have the right chemistry, the resident theatres can perform a service even before they get good. Thank God.

The Theatre Company of Boston

Since July, 1963, when David Wheeler started the Theatre Company of Boston, the Charles has had a rival. The newer company is the smaller (226 seats—increased to 400 in 1967—as against 525; seven Equity actors instead of twelve; a budget of about $145,000 as opposed to $400,000), and, by deliberate design, the farther-out. The Charles has done the conventional avant-garde playwrights—Brecht, Ionesco, Genet, Beckett, Pinter—but the Theatre Company calls itself "the only professional resident-theatre company in the United States that is firmly committed to the new and the experimental." It has done its Pinter (I saw a decent production of *The Birthday Party* there), and its Beckett, just like everybody else, but it has also done a good deal to live up to its claim.

In 1964 it gave the American première of *Live Like Pigs*, John Arden's play about a group of gypsy-like tinkers and their catastrophic impact on a housing development—about, in other words, the wild instinctual life in conflict with the necessary restraints of civilized living. The production did so well in Boston that it was moved to an Off-Broadway theatre in New York, where it was again a success; it was also the first presentation of any John Arden play in New York. It was a respectable but not a good production; the characters tended to come out smaller, tamer, more ordinary and less vivid than Arden had written them.

In the spring of 1966, with the aid of $10,000 from the Rockefeller Foundation, the Theatre Company presented a "Festival of New Plays": eight plays (mostly one-acts) by nine American authors (one play was a collaboration), grouped into four bills, presented for two weeks each. The playwrights included one from Off-Broadway (Adrienne Kennedy), two from Off-Off-Broadway (Sam Shepard of the Café La Mama and Rosalyn Drexler of Judson Memorial Church), two novelists (Miss Drexler and John Hawkes), one poet (Lawrence Ferlinghetti), and four whose names were previously unknown to me: Geoffrey Bush, George Dennison, and Andy and Dave Lewis.

And here we come up against a problem for which I can offer no solution. Clearly the American theatre needs new playwrights; clearly the resident theatres could perform a tremendous service by helping to develop them. Yet people do not want to see new plays: the Theatre Company does close to 50 per cent of capacity (which is its break-even point) when it presents Pinter or Brecht, but only 25–30 per cent when it does new plays. Sunday matinées are traditionally ill-attended, but at one during the Festival there were only twenty-one people in the audience. And after seeing *The Wax Museum* by Mr. Hawkes and *The Investigation* by Mrs. Drexler, I could only congratulate those who stayed away.

The Wax Museum was one of those plays in which two characters swap identities; it ended as it began, only with a different girl fondling the wax statue of a Mountie which she called George. The play was feebly whimsical and feebly nasty; it seemed to need, though not to deserve, a livelier, more imaginative staging than Mr. Wheeler gave it.

In *The Investigation,* a detective has sex-and-violence fantasies which horrify a young prisoner who is accused of rape and murder. The detective talks to a girl's bloodstained dress, takes it in his arms, dances with it, finally kisses it; later he induces the prisoner to vomit; still later he makes the young man re-enact the crime. If only there had been some point to it all, it might perhaps have horrified the spectators, or even amused them. (Mrs. Drexler displayed a pleasantly corny turn of phrase in her musical comedy *Home Movies,* which was transferred from the Judson Church to a regular Off-Broadway house; *The Investigation* has some of the same quality.) But the play simply wambled self-indulgently here and there as its author's vagrant fancy took it; nothing seemed to be done for any reason, and very little was good enough to be its own excuse for being. Are plays like these really worth presenting to the public? And if there are better ones, where are they?

In 1966–67, the Theatre Company presented *Marat/Sade* by Peter Weiss, the American première of *Armstrong's Last Goodnight* by John Arden, *Tiny Alice,* *The Caucasian Chalk Circle,* a double bill of new American plays by Geoffrey Bush and Daniel C. Gerould, a double bill of *Krapp's Last Tape* by Samuel Beckett, *The Undertaker* by John Hawkes, and *Desire Under the Elms* by Eugene O'Neill.

I saw only the last. The script strikes me as one marked for mortality; in a few years it will be unrevivable. The company did it, as they do everything, on a small open stage with the audience clustered tightly around on three sides; under these circumstances, it was an achievement to keep the play from being ridiculous. David Wheeler's direction was elaborately naturalistic, with plenty of nodding, grunting, sighing, scratching, and stretching, real bread and milk at the supper table, real water to wash the dishes in, and a real chamber pot under the bed. Which is the kind of staging the play demands. Several scenes worked quite well, and the climax was almost terrible.

As Eben Cabot, O'Neill's land-hungry, sex-hungry, mother-fixated hero, Larry Bryggman performed in the manner customary for such roles: guttural shouts followed by heavy breathing. But he did it pretty well, and how else is the part to be played? As his father, that septuagenarian tyrant, Ralph Waite was too young and hopelessly o'erparted; the role needs the kind of actor who could play Lear, and these are in short supply.

As Abbie Putnam, the New England sex-bomb, Bronia Stefan was miscast. She was too civilized to be the wild woman who kills her own child to prove her love for its father, and for all her rawboned beauty and glorious chestnut hair, she did not project Abbie's serene confidence in the power of her body to attract menfolk. Her Abbie was intelligent and ironic, but vulnerable and shy, with a fineness of spirit that did not really belong in the play. But it was a lovely performance.

After *Desire Under the Elms*, the company went off to Kingston, Rhode Island, for its second annual summer season in residence at the University of Rhode Island. In November, 1967, it opened its regular Boston season in its new permanent head-quarters, a former movie house in Back Bay. The first production was a double American première: a double bill of *The Dwarfs* by Harold Pinter and *The Local Stigmatic* by Heathcote Williams. This was followed by still another American première: *Left-Handed Liberty*, John Arden's play about Magna Carta, the third Arden play to be introduced to America by the Theatre Company of Boston. *Left-Handed Liberty* was presented in collaboration with Boston University, at the B.U. theatre (which is more than twice as large as the company's own new house), with several advanced B.U. theatre students in the cast; this is intended to be the beginning of a continuing alliance between the theatre and the university.

The Trinity Square Repertory Company
(Providence, Rhode Island)

When I first went to Providence in April, 1966, the Trinity Square Repertory Company, then in its third season, looked like the ninety-seven-pound weakling of the resident theatre move-ment. Except for its Shakespeare matinées, financed with $15,000 from the Rockefeller Foundation, which played to 40,000 high school students, Trinity Square was a small-scale operation, with a budget of only $125,000 and only 1,865 subscribers; its auditorium was upstairs in the parish house of a church.

On that first visit I saw a rather in-and-out production of *Playboy of the Western World*. A talented, beautiful girl named Katherine Helmond was spirited and lyrical as Pegeen Mike, who can't find anyone in her little Irish village worth marrying; William Neary, a stocky, curly-haired youth with a nice smile, might someday play the Playboy very well, but he was whiney and overcute on this occasion; the supporting cast had its moments, but was on the whole not authoritative. There was a general air of cutting corners, of pinching pennies, of making do.

By the following fall, however, Trinity Square had become prosperous and expansive. Its annual budget had zoomed to $700,000, It refurbished its old 293-seat Trinity Square Playhouse, and also leased the 938-seat downtown auditorium of the Rhode Island School of Design. At the height of the 1965–66 season, there were about ten Equity actors in the company, and the total number of people on the payroll (nobody seems to have the exact figure) was something like twenty-four; at one point in the following season there were eighty people on the payroll, including thirty-one Equity actors dispersed among two productions, one playing for students in the afternoon, the other for adults in the evening. The season was expanded from twenty-eight to thirty-seven weeks, and the total season attendance jumped from 30,810 to 197,182.

There was just one reason for this dramatic change: a grant of $535,000 from the United States government to produce plays for high school students. As it had done the previous season, Trinity Square mounted a seven-play subscription season primarily for adults. Under the terms of the grant, however, four of those seven plays—*Saint Joan, Ah, Wilderness!, A Midsummer Night's Dream,* and *The Three Sisters*—were given forty extra student matinée performances apiece. At these matinées, each play was seen, free of charge, as a part of the curriculum, by *all* of the nearly 40,000 sophomores, juniors, and seniors in *all* the public, private, and parochial secondary schools in the state of Rhode Island. (One exception must be noted: the students of Woonsocket High School were kept away from *Ah, Wilderness!* because the Woonsocket superintendent of schools thought that "parts of it are pretty raunchy.") The government paid all costs for these productions, which meant that the theatre's own money was left over for the three adults-only productions and for other expenses. As a result, the whole atmosphere of the organization changed. Money is no guarantee of quality in the theatre, but it does tend to help.

There was one further reason for the change in the company: John A. McQuiggan, formerly producer at the Milwaukee Repertory Theatre, became co-director in Providence with Adrian Hall, who had been in sole charge there since 1964. (Mr. Hall, a Texan, had worked for Margo Jones, and directed several Off-Broadway successes; Mr. McQuiggan had begun his career at the age of sixteen with the Antioch, Ohio, Shakespeare Festival, and had been a founding member of the APA.) Mr. Hall had built up a small nucleus of good actors in Milwaukee, and brought a number of them with him when he came east; and two nuclei are better than one. Nearly all of the resident companies have a few good actors; hardly any of them have enough. (Mr. McQuiggan subsequently resigned, and some of his actors followed him.)

The season opened in October, 1967, with an uninspired but effective production of *Saint Joan,* directed by Mr. Hall, with Mr. McQuiggan's wife Mary Doyle in the title role. Shaw's Joan is half peasant, half saint; Miss Doyle played the peasant very well, the saint not so well. Stefan Gierasch made Bishop Cauchon an aged, tottery, highly imposing prelate: a formidably detailed character performance of the kind that only English actors are supposed to be able to do. I saw the show at nine thirty in the morning in the presence of nine hundred lively teen-agers who laughed and applauded and listened and enjoyed themselves; so did I.

While *Saint Joan* continued to play for the students at the larger auditorium, a production of *A Streetcar Named Desire,* for regular audiences only, opened at the smaller theatre. At the performance I saw, the orchestra floor was mostly filled by solid doctor-lawyer types and their wives, but the balcony was full of college kids. They were a knowledgeable audience, talking about how Brando yelled "Stelluuuuh!" in the movie, and about how Stella is supposed to be, you know, a passive type of personality in contrast to Blanche.

Blanche was beautifully played by Katherine Helmond, but Miss Helmond was twenty years too young for the part, and it mattered. So much of the play is devoted to talk about Blanche's age, she herself is so obsessively concerned with it, that it becomes very important to see her desperately holding together the ruined remains of her beauty, whereas Miss Helmond was obviously an attractive young girl with nothing to worry about. Donald Gantry as Stanley was a boy sent to do a man's job; he turned our most famous image of gross, coarse virility into a clean-cut Joe College type. It showed that you can't become a male animal just by hitching up your pants every now and then. These are the exigencies of resident-company casting: good actors forced to play parts that they are not ready for. Still, the production held its audience for three and a half hours, and at the end the applause was enthusiastic.

The most ambitious of the season's productions was the world première of a musical version of Truman Capote's *The Grass Harp*, a gentle southern fable about some childlike people who take refuge in a tree from the pressures of contemporary life. The book and lyrics were by Kenward Elmslie, the music by Claibe Richardson; Adrian Hall directed. There were vague plans or hopes to do the show in New York at some future date, and Barbara Baxley, Elaine Stritch, Carol Brice, and Carol Bruce had been lured to Providence to appear in it.

Since its Providence engagement, however, the show has never been heard of again, and this is a pity. When I saw it, it was misproportioned, discontinuous, sometimes confusing, sometimes overcute and sticky, and generally in desperate need of work, but charming and touching all the same. It had some poignantly beautiful songs, with unhackneyed lyrics and titles like "Cool Cool Elbow" and "A Genteel Sufficiency of Abundance." Providence was lucky.

I saw the Trinity Square production of *Ah, Wilderness!* at nine fifteen in the morning with an audience of students from the Moses Brown School, a fashionable private school for boys, and East Providence High School, a coeducational public high school in a lower-middle-class suburb. The production was handsomely mounted and pretty well acted, and I enjoyed it, especially Stefan

Gierasch's gorgeously funny performance as bibulous Uncle Sid. But I enjoyed the audience too, and found their reactions more significant than anything in the play itself.

It is a strange thing to sit in an auditorium with nine-hundred-odd teen-agers, waiting for a play to begin: the place is alive with undischarged energy. And as soon as something—anything—happens on the stage, this energy is focused explosively on it. The kids make an unruly audience, but their noisy responses are for the most part signs of involvement, not of indifference. As one of the actors in the company points out, "They're honest. They tell you right off. They like it—whoopee! They hate it—ecch! The kids are not judging anything like the scenery, the costumes, the acting. They're really watching the play. They're involved with the characters as people."

Ah, Wilderness! deals with the joys and sorrows of a sixteen-year-old boy named Richard, who is struggling—as the adolescents of Rhode Island are struggling—to define himself in relation to his parents and to the opposite sex. Being part of the school curriculum, the play was an offering of Adult Authority, yet it depicts the acting out, by an adolescent, of some of those sexual and rebellious impulses that Adult Authority is generally at pains to ignore, deny, and suppress. (That is perhaps why the superintendent of schools in Woonsocket felt it incumbent upon him to protect his students from this "raunchy" entertainment.) Adult Authority, in its official messages to the young, is constantly implying that sex is either discreditable or nonexistent.

Teen-agers know that this is not true. But because of the inhibitions that surround us all, it is seldom easy for individual adults to admit the truth of the matter to individual adolescents. *Ah, Wilderness!*, for all its cozy sentimentality, functioned as such an admission; the kids received it as such, and were delighted. It confirmed their feelings about the rightness of their own impulses and the element of hypocrisy in the restraints imposed on those impulses.

Thus when Richard's father, in a moment of high spirits, slaps Richard's mother on the behind, the audience whistles and cheers, delighted to see the old folks so frisky. (Probably they have always suspected that the dignity of maturity, the impression adults tend to give of being the Army of Unalterable Law, was mostly pose.)

But when the father says to Richard, "You watch that damfool talk," there is a murmur of disapproval at this exercise of authority. And when Richard says, "I'll show them!" and strides out defiantly for a night of sin, there is a delighted tempest of whistling and applause.

In the next act, as a prostitute undoes Richard's tie, someone in the audience shouts "Ah, no!" in tones of bewildered delight; when she kisses him, a voice cries, "You turn me on!" clearly they are following the action. When the prostitute suggests that Richard's innocent girl friend Muriel is probably "out with a guy under some bush this minute, giving him all he wants," they send up a roar of appreciation at the chance to confront, under the auspices of Authority, the kind of image that Authority has taught them is not to be put into words.

Later on, thinking about his experience with the prostitute, Richard says, "But I didn't go upstairs with her," and continues, "Muriel and I will go upstairs . . ." and there is a tremendous burst of applause and whistling. When Richard and Muriel finally kiss, the house goes wild, as if to say "SEX LIVES! LONG LIVE SEX!"—which is the essential message of all these outbursts. Thus the performance becomes the occasion for a lively and good-humored demonstration of adolescent rebelliousness.

Now it may be argued (it probably would be argued in Woonsocket) that all this is perfectly appalling, that a spirit of rebellion is never to be encouraged in the young, that it is likely to lead to insolence, misbehavior, and God knows what. (The Woonsocket superintendent has already noted, in a statement made to the local paper, that one boy in neighboring Pawtucket, sent to the principal's office for using obscene language, argued, "I heard worse than that in *Ah, Wilderness!*") But even in the midst of their rebellious enthusiasm, the students acknowledge that restraints are necessary. Robert J. Colonna, who played the Bartender in *Ah, Wilderness!*, reports that there is one place where the audience was always quiet. When the prostitute tries to get Richard to come upstairs with her, Richard replies, "I don't want to"—and they never laugh. They respect his refusal.

I would conjecture that most members of the student audience accepted and appreciated *Ah, Wilderness!* as an expression of adult interest in their concerns. In our society it is often very difficult for adults and adolescents to converse frankly on subjects of real importance; I believe that the performance of *Ah, Wilderness!* I saw in Providence was such a conversation. I wish more adults could have had an opportunity of listening.

Thanks to the federal grant, Trinity Square is enabled to supply the schools not only with the performances themselves, but with scripts, recordings, pictures, pamphlets, films, and various other materials to help tie the plays securely into the curriculum. More important, actors and staff members of the theatre are constantly visiting schools all over the state to talk with the students about the plays and about the theatre in general. I went along on a visit to Rhode Island Vocational and Technical High School, and what I heard and saw there confirmed my impressions as to the success of Project Discovery, as the Providence student program is called.

Most of the students at Rhode Island Vocational had never seen a play before, but a group of them had been inspired by *Saint Joan*, the first Project Discovery production, to form a drama club and produce a play of their own. Some of the students were even stimulated to buy tickets for the Trinity Square non-student production of *A Streetcar Named Desire*. Nearly all of them, however, preferred *Ah, Wilderness!* to *Saint Joan*. Like a number of students from other schools whom I had talked to, most of them had been particularly bored by the tent scene in *Saint Joan*, in which a nobleman and a bishop analyze Joan as a Protestant and a Nationalist; they objected to all the talk. (I wonder what they made of *The Three Sisters*? But that raises a very complicated question.)

They liked *Ah, Wilderness!* because it dealt "with the same problems we have now." "This here showed a family, showed what really happened." "In *Ah, Wilderness!* the father—you could compare it to *your* father." "Right now we're at a stage where everything revolves around sex, and *Ah, Wilderness!* revolved around this too."

But they were aware of the extent to which things have changed since the time (1906) in which the play is set. They were aware of the increase in sexual freedom: referring to the love scene on the beach between Richard and his girl friend, one said, "I don't think nowadays they would have just sat and talked." They were also aware of the change in parent-child relationships: "These days parents don't worry about drinking." "Nowadays parents can't do that to the kids. They just jump in the car and take off. Or nowadays the kids have a weapon: they go upstairs and play the record-player." But perhaps the change had not been entirely for the better: "Usually now the father and the sons don't confide in each other."

Clearly, for these students, the performance had not been just an occasion for blowing off steam. They had understood the play and thought about it, and by its means they were stimulated to think and talk freely and cogently about problems very close to them. Woonsocket to the contrary notwithstanding, they appeared quite uncorrupted by it. And yet, on the other hand, they clearly did not regard Project Discovery as simply an adult imposition. One of the boys even offered help to the visitors: "If you've got any problems, the kids would be glad to build it for you."

Project Discovery, and the analogous projects in New Orleans and Los Angeles, have been planned as three-year programs (though their future is uncertain, since Congress has to appropriate their funds annually). By the end of that period, if all goes well, tens of thousands of students, from all social and economic classes, will have seen ten or twelve full-scale professional productions. If any sizable proportion of those students are impelled to come back for more on their own, it would prove that the theatre has something to offer to a far larger percentage of the population than it has been able to reach for many years.

The Hartford Stage Company

Before he decided to found his theatre in Hartford, Connecticut, Jacques Cartier considered five or six cities as possible sites. "I came to Hartford," he says, "because Hartford looked like the best place to get a theatre started"—and besides, it was not too far from Smith College, where he was teaching at the time. The younger breed of resident-theatre directors have no particular commitment to the cities in which they happen to find themselves; either they have been fished out of the New York talent pool by some board of directors in the hinterlands, or else, like Mr. Cartier, they have calmly chosen a city they considered suitable, and gone to work. (But the old theatres, which were started and which are still run by local zealots, are no more "regional" in their orientation than the new ones.)

Mr. Cartier raised $100,000 from private contributions, found a building downtown that he could get for a nominal rental, converted it into a pleasant theatre with a thrust stage, and opened for business in April, 1964. He quickly found an audience; attendance has been, on the average, well over 80 per cent of capacity, and some seasons it has run over 90 per cent. The problem is that the Hartford Stage Company has almost the smallest auditorium of any resident theatre, seating only 225 people. Even though Mr. Cartier's budget for the 1966–67 season was just under $300,000— modest by resident-theatre standards—he was left with some $84,000 to raise from private sources. But relief may be in sight: there is talk of a new civic arts center in Hartford, which might, if it gets built, include a new theatre for the HSC, seating about 675 or maybe 750. Meanwhile the board of directors struggles with its deficit. As for Mr. Cartier, he is resigning in June of 1968 because he feels that "the time has come for me to move on and give my attention to other projects."

Mr. Cartier says that he was once only interested in plays that could help to make a better world. Then he was caught up in magic: to make an exciting theatrical occasion. Now, he feels, he is trying to wed the two. In other words he is an eclectic, like most resident-theatre men; most of them are even less committed to a particular kind of play or style of playing than to a particular locality. (This is probably just as well: most of these theatres are the only ones for miles around, and if they do not provide their communities with a balanced diet, there is nobody to supplement it.) Mr. Cartier's statement of purpose for the HSC is a very sound but quite general one, to which, I think, most of his colleagues in other cities would subscribe: "I would like to expose people here in Hartford to points of view about life, about people, that they don't find themselves exposed to ordinarily."

This purpose, however, was only indifferently served by the torpid production of *The Importance of Being Earnest* (staged by a guest director, Mel Shapiro) that I saw there in March, 1966. The two young heroes, as played by Henry Thomas and Paul Weidner, were exquisitely polished Wildean men-about-town.

The resident theatre in general needs more stylishness, but on this occasion these actors needed less of it; so exquisitely polished were they that they managed to convey a profound lack of interest in anything that was going on—an attitude that is always quick to spread from the stage to the audience. Period style, even for a play where languor and detachment are so appropriate, does not necessarily involve such a dampening lack of energy. The young women, in their way, were worse than the men; Gwendolyn was merely pallid, but Cecily resembled a Hollywood starlet.

I got back to Hartford later in the spring, and this time I saw, somewhat to my surprise, a production of *Twelfth Night* that had just the consistent professionalism that resident-theatre productions, of period plays especially, tend to lack. In such productions there are frequently several performers in important roles who cause the play to die a little every time they open their mouths; here only a servant or two, seen little and heard less, ever let down the side. Everyone else spoke the verse and the quibbling Elizabethan prose clearly, smoothly, pleasantly, and naturally, as if it were their customary means of expression. Paul Weidner, who directed, went all out for prettiness and got it; since *Twelfth Night* is, among other things, Shakespeare's prettiest play, this is a sensible way to approach it, especially as Mr. Weidner managed also to avoid having too much prettiness.

Earnest and *Twelfth Night* were both designed by an extraordinary young man named John Conklin. The orthodox way to design for a thrust stage is to use just a few carefully chosen, meaningful props or scenic units, and leave the rest to the costuming and the audience's imagination. Mr. Conklin can create on a thrust stage the kind of elaborately pictorial effects usually associated with the proscenium stage (and often thought outmoded even there), yet his settings are carefully planned with the necessities of the thrust stage in mind, and seem perfectly at home on it. His single set for *Twelfth Night* was a nineteenth-century dream of Mediterranean romance. As a backdrop, covering the stage's one wall, he gave us a lushly painted seascape, framed by flat cut-out foliage wings at the sides and foliage borders overhead. In front of this, on the thrust itself, was a lovely Italian garden of stone steps and platforms, benches, balustrades, and urns, all decked with vines and flowers. Under Peter Hunt's lighting (effulgent sunshine and shadow-dappled night) it was as artificial and idyllic as the play itself—perhaps even a little more so.

The following season the company offered a labored, ponderous, smirking version of a Victorian melodrama called *Under the Gaslight*. It was highly popular, playing to 96 per cent of capacity; I was disgusted by it, although—or perhaps because—I find this kind of play hilarious when not hammered home by main force.

After this, I was not eager to see the Hartford production of *The Servant of Two Masters* by Carlo Goldoni, even though the play had been the hit of the Venetian theatre season of 1743. Unless it has suffered severely in all three of the translations I have encountered, it is a piece of goodhearted, simple-minded fooling, heavily dependent upon the comic resources of its executants. It is firmly rooted, moreover, in the *commedia dell'arte* tradition, about which American actors know even less than they know about most kinds of theatre. Sighing lovers, bumbling servants, farfetched coincidences—all the paraphernalia of classical comedy—are not so much in demand nowadays as they were in Goldoni's time, especially when, as in this case, they are adorned with no poetry and very little wit.

But I went to Hartford all the same (it was on my way to Boston, and I had a free night), and I saw their *Servant of Two Masters*, and it turned out to be, in its modest and cheerful fashion, something of a revelation. The Hartford performers were not (God knows) highly experienced, specially skilled actor-acrobats, like the troupe for which *The Servant* was written, but Paul Weidner, the director and translator for the Hartford production, found a kind of life in Goldoni's old farce that American actors can project.

He realized that the *commedia* was fundamentally a popular art form. Its natural habitat was the streets, where traveling companies, most of them grubby and second-rate, would set up a stage and do their stuff before a noisy, rowdy, macaroni-and-garlic crowd. Mr. Weidner used Goldoni's play as a means of evoking the vigorous, exuberant life of the Italian streets, which, it was implied, has not changed very much over the last two hundred years.

As you came into the theatre, the thrust stage was bare except for a large rubber-tired cart, piled high with junk and surmounted by a crate of live chickens. At about eight fifteen, a couple of *ragazzi*, looking like the laborers and loafers you see in working-class neighborhoods in Italy today, appeared and started to unload the cart; one of them chewed bubble gum, making popping noises as he worked. As they arranged the stage for the performance, other men and women drifted in; they were the actors. Some of them called "*Buon giorno*" to the house. One girl was wearing a mini-skirt; another, whose breasts were practically jumping out of a scoop-necked blouse, offered her small dog to be petted by members of the audience. Tinny music started coming out of a loud-speaker: "Santa Lucia," mandolin selections, and Verdi.

The actors drifted off again to put on their costumes. To beguile the time, one of the scene-shifters did some second-rate acrobatics, yelling "Bravo!" for himself whenever he brought off some simple feat. Actors drifted on again; there were arguments; a fight broke out and was quelled; and by not too long after eight-thirty an attractively scruffy aggregation of traveling players (or so we were willing to believe for the nonce) was ready to present *The Servant of Two Masters*.

It was all a gimmick, of course, and by no means an original one; I have seen this strolling-player idea applied to *The Taming of the Shrew* (where it is written into the script), *The Comedy of Errors*, and *The Rivals*. But on this occasion it provided more fun before the play proper began than some productions manage in an entire evening. Furthermore, it provided a context within which both actors and audience could relax and be comfortable with each other and with Goldoni's play, which through all the goings-on was never, so far as I could tell, distorted or demeaned.

The performance itself was in keeping with what had gone before: earthy and energetic, with little time wasted on subtlety, and no precious powdered-wiggery. A porter, underpaid and kicked, made the "*Va fongul!*" sign, fist to inside of elbow, as he walked off. A servant saw a half-eaten apple, and grabbed it. Traveling players understand about hunger.

Goldoni's script demands to be elaborated with a great deal of business, and this Mr. Weidner supplied, drawing upon the traditional *lazzi* (sight-gags) of the *commedia*, and upon the immemorial repertory of pratfalls, kicks, and miscellaneous mayhem that unites Aristophanes with Tom and Jerry. All of this was neatly and zestfully executed, and most of it was extremely funny.

Truffaldino, the eponymous servant who causes so much confusion for both his masters, was played by Macon McCalman, a veteran of many seasons at the Front Street Theatre in Memphis. Much of the more elaborate business fell to him: it was he who became so hungry that he killed an invisible fly, cooked it over a match, and ate it (this is very traditional); it was he who got his face pushed into a bowl of pudding, from which it emerged covered with goo (this, of course, is even more traditional). Mr. McCalman was as funny as he needed to be, and had an agreeable, easygoing, country-boy quality. (Truffaldino is, after all, both traditionally and as Goldoni wrote him, a hick from Bergamo.) The production's one really brilliant performance, however, was given by Henry Thomas as Pantalone, the father of one of the lovers: a conventional old-man characterization, raised to a hilarious pitch by sheer comic virtuosity.

But the production succeeded as an ensemble effort. All the actors appeared to be functioning on the same easy, informal, happy wave-length. The initial convention was never forgotten. Caley Summers' costumes were just the kind of gaudy but dubious eighteenth-century outfits that a hand-to-mouth company in Italy might improvise: one of the lovers, for instance, wore a scarlet eighteenth-century coat over a brown T-shirt and green corduroy pants. The set-changes featured the same seedy *ragazzi* who began the evening; they worked to memorably tinny recordings of Verdi's "Questa o Quella," Rossini's "Largo al Factotum," and other song hits you love. Even Mr. Weidner's translation was flavored with a combination of operatic and ice-cream Italian: "*Piano, piano, momento, signor,*" *Me misericordia!*" "*Buono dio!*" "*Si,*" "*Bella,*" "*Scusi,*" "*Prego,*" "*Molto honorato,*" "*Maldetto!*" "*Assassino!*" The atmosphere was maintained right through the happy ending, when all the confusions were cleared up and all the lovers reunited, to the waltzing finale and curtain call (to the tune of the "Brindisi" from *Traviata*).

By presenting to us the idealized image of a sunny, expansive style of life, at the opposite pole from our tight bourgeois ways, the production served, I think, a purpose beyond simple merrymaking. It is about time that somebody besides the hippies reminded us of what we miss by being good, busy, success-oriented Americans. The standard of work at Hartford appears to be wildly erratic, but this production, at least, fulfilled Mr. Cartier's statement of purpose: "to expose people here in Hartford to points of view about life, about people, that they don't find themselves exposed to ordinarily."

The Long Wharf Theatre (New Haven)

The brief history of the Long Wharf Theatre shows how much a couple of assiduous and clever young men can accomplish in a short time in these days of "cultural explosion"—and also indicates some of the pitfalls that attend such accomplishment.

Harlan Kleiman, the first executive director of Long Wharf, is a Brooklyn boy with a master's degree in industrial administration from Yale; by special permission, he earned a number of credits toward his degree by taking courses at the Yale Drama School. Jon Jory, the theatre's first artistic director, is the son of the actor Victor Jory. The younger Jory began acting in summer stock as a child; after college he spent two years in the Army directing plays for Special Services, and two years studying playwriting at Yale.

The two founders decided to locate their theatre in New Haven by a process of elimination; they thought it had possibilities as a theatre town, and, after all, it was where they were. "Then," says Kleiman, "the spieling started." It was the fall of 1964; Jory was twenty-six, and still a graduate student at Yale; Kleiman was twenty-four, and unemployed. They had successfully run a season of summer stock in a small town near New Haven, but neither had any professional reputation, and neither had local connections. And they proposed to raise $125,000 in the New Haven area to give the city something called a resident professional theatre.

"At no time during the first four months of this saga," says Kleiman, "did I ever ask anybody for money." Who would trust a couple of kids that nobody had ever heard of? They talked to 250 or 300 people in those early months, telling them about their plans and asking them two questions: "Can we use your name?" and "Will you give us names of other people who might be interested?" One of Kleiman's maxims is "Always use people to get other people." "Almost all the money that was raised," he says, "was raised by putting this one in contact with that one, pulling strings, learning where the pockets of gelt are." They tried to find people whose energies exceeded their commitments, and commit them to work for the theatre; they tried to get in touch with the widest possible variety of social, political, economic, and ethnic groups.

Around January they set up a system of pledge cards, to be collectible only when pledges for $30,000 were in hand. On February 1, 1965, they incorporated; at that point they had only spent a total of $200 on the project. Before the end of February, they were able to call in the pledges.

Meanwhile, after scouring New Haven for a site, they reluctantly decided to locate in the new Long Wharf Terminal Market. It was cut off from the rest of New Haven by the railroad tracks on one side and the Connecticut Turnpike on the other, but there was no alternative, and the partners made up their minds to set up shop in a long, low, unadorned modern building, other sections of which were tenanted by the Ideal Printing Company, the Kahn Meat Company, and the Lamberti Sausage Company. It turned out to be an ideal site for the automotive age: plenty of parking, and easy access from the turnpike without fighting city traffic.

Meanwhile the wearisome job of raising money went on. The partners made some seven hundred appearances at parties and club meetings; until the theatre opened, they had never less than two speaking appearances a day between them, and sometimes as many as six. According to Jory, people began to think, "These are interesting and dedicated boys, and they shout and scream so much that they should have a chance to do this." They made the most of Jory's father's friends; Robert Preston, Eli Wallach, Henry Fonda, Lloyd Nolan, and half a dozen others were prevailed upon to lend the new enterprise their names as members of a "Theatrical Advisory Board." A fund-raising brochure was mailed to 10,000 people. Interested ladies were formed into a fund-raising organization called "Hands," which stands for "Helpers and Supporters." (Nowadays the Hands ladies sell subscriptions, sew costumes, find props, decorate the lobby, run a newsletter, and provide yet more speaking engagements for the directors.)

In late April, work began on turning a slice of the Terminal Market into a theatre with a good-sized thrust stage and 441 seats (picked up cheap from an old New Jersey burlesque house—another Kleiman coup). The first subscription drive began in early May. Four productions were announced for an eight-week summer season: *The Crucible, The Hostage, Little Mary Sunshine,* and Peter Shaffer's double bill, *The Private Ear* and *The Public Eye.*

The first performance was on July 6, 1965. In ten months, Kleiman and Jory had raised $122,000 (out of the $137,000 they found that they needed for capital expenses) and founded a theatre. That's how it's done nowadays.

The summer season played to more than 99 per cent of capacity, and almost broke even. It ended on August 29; on October 22 began the eight-play winter season, which presented works by Sean O'Casey, Ben Jonson, Gilbert and Sullivan, Euripides, Noel Coward, Chekhov, Sheridan, and O'Neill. The winter season attracted 84,760 people, more than 85 per cent of capacity.

During its first year, Long Wharf began more auxiliary activities than many theatres have after a decade. The Long Wharf Children's Theatre gave five productions for matinée performances at the theatre. The high school touring company visited thirty-six schools with a program called *Comedy through the Ages.* Over 17,000 students from 110 schools in seventy-five towns came in groups to see regular performances; a study guide to the plays was offered free to all the high schools in the state. (I might as well confess to a personal interest here, having written a large part of that study guide myself; in fact the founders of Long Wharf are old acquaintances of mine.)

With a $50,000 grant from Community Progress, Inc. (an organization financed by the Ford Foundation and the federal poverty program), the theatre and the New Haven Board of Education established a program for eight hundred culturally deprived high school students, and for over two thousand elementary school students from the poverty-impacted inner-city schools. The high school students came to the theatre for regular performances; the younger children were brought in for special matinées of the children's shows. The elementary school program "was designed to use the theatre as an instrument to raise the motivation of poorer children for learning in general, and for facility with language in particular." Special teachers worked with the children to prepare them in advance, and had them write essays and do art-work based on what they had seen. Each child was sent to see four out of the five Long Wharf children's shows, and many were inspired to go to the fifth one on their own. Six ten-year-olds walked two miles to the theatre to see *Gabriel Ghost*, and then walked two miles home; fifty children saved money for four months so that they could afford to see *Thumbelina*.

Some of these activities are perhaps unique to Long Wharf; most are copied from other theatres. But Long Wharf has probably started more of them more quickly than anybody else. (It even has a program, financed by a small grant from the New Haven Foundation, to bring old people to its Sunday matinées.) Why? "It gives us a great many more mechanisms to get to the public," Kleiman says. If a child goes to the Long Wharf Children's Theatre, the child's mother will know about Long Wharf, and is likely to think it a good thing. Children, of course, are the audience of the future, and the resident theatre, with its aspirations to permanence, can and must look ahead. Anyway, the Children's Theatre showed a profit. Furthermore, as Kleiman points out, no foundation is going to give a theatre in its first year a grant just "for art." On the other hand, as somebody (not Kleiman) has said, "There's money in poverty nowadays." Finally, Kleiman seems to believe in the intrinsic validity and usefulness of these programs, and to have enjoyed setting them up.

After just a year, then, Long Wharf was a going concern, going in several directions. Kleiman, at the age of twenty-five, was the boy wonder of the regional-theatre movement (though with his three-piece suits, his pipe, and his expansive manner—part con man, part tycoon, and part Jewish comedian—he does not look much like a boy wonder). He was widely recognized as an expert on how to set up a theatre, and was asked to teach theatre administration at NYU.

Long Wharf's first season, then, was a spectacular success—except for the productions themselves. It seems as if Jory, who did most of the directing, and David Hager, who designed most of the sets, had not learned how to use their big stage; several productions wandered around uncomfortably on it. And while Jory showed himself to be an inventive director, he tended to overuse his own creative powers, and not to trust the playwright.

The best of the six Long Wharf shows that I saw during that

first year was the summer production of *The Hostage*. "The action takes place," said the program frankly, "in the Long Wharf Theatre which is got up as an Irish brothel." Before the play began, the actors roamed the theatre, ad-libbing in their own persons. ("I'm the oldest juvenile in the business," one of them assured me.) During the intermissions, rock 'n' roll came over the loud-speakers, and the actors danced with the spectators. The performance, under Jory's direction, was full of improvisations and bits; the presence of the audience was frankly recognized. Every night some member of the public sitting in the front row was handed a freshly opened beer by one of the actors. The tenderness in the play, the ripening relationship between the captured British soldier and the Irish servant girl, suffered lamentably, but there were plenty of compensations; this is a play made to be improvised on. But O'Caseys' *Plough and the Stars*, Coward's *Hay Fever*, and Sheridan's *The Rivals* were all partially disfigured by overelaborate staging and by broad, styleless, sometimes actively annoying performances.

In almost every production that I saw, however, there was at least a performance or two worth remembering. In *The Plough and the Stars* and in *The Trojan Women* I was greatly impressed by Eda Reiss Merin, a middle-aged lady with a dumpy body and a crow's voice and tremendous warmth and tremendous passion. As Hecuba in *The Trojan Women*, she did not look like a queen or sound like a queen; she didn't have to; she *was* a queen. In *The Rivals*, the two pairs of young lovers were more or less washouts, but the production was redeemed by the boobs and rubes who surrounded them. William Swetland was easy and deft and very funny as the hot-headed Sir Anthony Absolute; Walter Rhodes (who had been well-nigh intolerable in *Hay Fever*) was wildly hilarious as the rustic suitor Bob Acres.

In its second summer, Long Warf asked for trouble. Instead of taking the summer off to lick wounds and prepare for the next campaign, they mounted a "Summer Première Festival": four productions of new plays in eight weeks. All the plays but one were new works from playwrights associated with the theatre; the exception was *The Happy Haven* by John Arden, which received its American première. "We are risking our shirts on this God damn summer season," said Jory, "and I'm inordinately proud of it." "Another production of *Little Mary Sunshine*," said Kleiman, "is not going to make the world a better place to live in."

The summer season opened with a double bill of plays by David Kranes. We might have been spared the first of these, *The Loon Hunt,* an exercise in portentous whimsey which dealt with yet another prosperous suburbanite whose life is a sham because he never finished writing his novel. The whimsey comes in because the hero insists on playing elaborate cute games (no hanky-panky, however) with a fatiguingly ardent and pure-hearted sixteen-year-old baby-sitter. The second play, *I'm Nobody,* dealt with a girl brought up in isolation and passivity, who, on her own for the first time, picks up a young man. It had a number of boggy soft spots, but it also had some good pathetic comedy and some viable straight pathos. Done badly it might have been maddening, but at Long Wharf I was gradually but firmly drawn in by Margaret Cowles' grave and beautiful performance. Naïve ingenues tend to drive me up the wall, but Miss Cowles captured a very rare quality: absolute candor, absolute innocence. The two plays were given excellent productions, with atmospheric and serviceable settings by David Hager, and direction by Jory that strengthened the plays without distracting attention from them. Still, an uneven evening. Mr. Kranes is worth encouraging, but these particular plays demand rather more indulgence than an ordinary audience can be expected to supply. This is a frequent resident-theatre dilemma; the best answer seems to be a special series of experimental productions, on dark nights or in a special small auditorium, where the audience understands that it is there to take its chances.

John Arden's play was another matter; Arden is one of England's leading dramatists. But the word had not reached southern Connecticut; for all the interest his play aroused, he might have been another beginner. *The Happy Haven* was rejected by the local critics, by the public—by just about everybody except me.

Arden's plays have a way of being disappointing in production: obscurities, diffuseness, and miscellaneous difficulties tend to emerge that were not so apparent in the reading. But with *The Happy Haven,* it was the other way around. The script has the dignity, the distinction, the beauty of language and fineness of mind, that are characteristic of Arden's work; but it seems, all the same, to be an odd, rather dry, somewhat baffling dramatic-comic whatzit. In Douglas Seale's New Haven production, however, it became considerably clearer, sometimes insidiously powerful, often amusing, and almost always highly intriguing.

Arden's plays tend to maintain a delicate balance between two groups or forces or ideas. *The Happy Haven* is set in an old people's hospital; it poises the hospital's superintendent against the patients. The superintendent, Dr. Copperthwaite, is young, crisp, and very scientific; he regards the patients in his care merely as objects on which to experiment; during the course of the play he discovers an elixir of youth that he proposes to try out on them. There are five patients: Mrs. Phineus, Mrs. Letouzel, Mr. Golightly, Mr. Hardrader, and Mr. Crape. (Listen to the uncanny sound of those names; you can sometimes tell a good deal about a writer's sense of style from the names he gives his characters.) These old people are variously self-deluding, stupid, selfish, lazy, and/or malevolent, but they demand recognition of their humanity; in the end they take a grotesque revenge on the doctor.

The play embraces farce, fantasy, satire, serious dramatic conflict, ritual, direct address to the audience, mordant prose, eloquent rhymed verse, and songs in the ballad tradition. How to find a style of presentation that will bring all these disparate elements together? Here Mr. Seale triumphed. "The play is intended," says Arden, "to be given a formalized presentation," and Mr. Seale is fertile in formal devices. The doctor's introductory monologue was illustrated with slides; performers left the thrust stage and came up among the audience; one actor accompanied a song with a bit of the old soft-shoe. Sometimes Mr. Seale's invention flagged; more might have been done in the way of direct recognition of the audience, more might have been made of the doctor's experimental apparatus with its test tubes, retorts, Bunsen burners, and colored liquids. But from the moment the play began—there was a scream, and a patient lying on a mobile table was practically flung across the stage—it was clear that this was a medico-fantastic extravaganza, farcical but also grotesque.

Arden specifies that the old people are to wear masks, and these were experimented with in New Haven; at the performance I saw, however, masks had been abandoned in favor of heavy, masklike facial make-up, with a thick line drawn around it to emphasize its artificiality. Thus the point was made that photographic portraits were not being attempted, that naturalism was out of the question, without denying the actors their facial mobility.

In the last analysis, however, what made the play work (for me anyway) was the boldness and clarity of the cartoons drawn by each member of the cast. David Byrd played Mr. Crape with a limp, a nasty grin, a gutteral voice, and a strange accent; Marcie Hubert played Mrs. Phineus as a great blob of indolence, gluttony, and mischief, like a fat spoiled child. Both were brilliant in contrasting ways: Miss Hubert was grotesquely funny, while Mr. Byrd's incisive, menacing malevolence gave the play its backbone. Kate Wilkinson, Robert Gaus, and Walter Rhodes were the other three patients. We knew that none of these five actors were really old, but they never tried to fool us into thinking that they were, and so their work seemed natural and unforced. It was amazing that with less than two weeks of rehearsal, Mr. Seale and his actors should have achieved such unity, such mastery of an unfamiliar style.

The "Summer Première Festival" played to 56 per cent of capacity—somewhat of a comedown from the previous summer's 99 per cent—and lost $40,000. Jory had not been kidding about risking their shirts.

For its second winter season, Long Wharf scheduled an almost ideally typical resident-theatre list of plays: *Oh, What a Lovely War* (a musical, but not an ordinary Broadway musical), *The Three Sisters* (very big: also done that same season in Providence, Hartford, Pittsburgh, and Oakland, Michigan, for a grand total of fifteen sisters), *The Man Who Came to Dinner* (the APA's successful production of *You Can't Take It with You* had started a Kaufman-and-Hart boom), *Misalliance* (Shaw is always a good bet), *Mother Courage* (Brecht is In nowadays), *The Tavern* (George M. Cohan's parody-melodrama: another boom started by an APA revival), and *The Night of the Iguana* (Williams is Williams, and sex is sex). It was a carefully balanced season: comic, serious, comic, comic, serious, comic, serious. It included no play written before 1900. And all seven plays were at least reasonably good of their kind.

Misalliance, in particular, comes close to being the ideal resident-theatre play, as the resident theatres and their audiences are now

constituted. It is full of shrewd observation and intelligent discourse, yet it is easily assimilable and full of fun, and it does not
make too great demands on a company. Everybody says—or used
to say—that Shaw's plays read so much better than they act, but
Misalliance is one of the most actable plays ever written. It has no
plot, and no subject in particular, but plenty of sure-fire goings-on,
including an airplane crash, an attempted murder, and a love-chase
that is spied upon by an eavesdropper concealed in a portable
Turkish bath. Its fifty-year-old wisecracks and farcical bits and
running gags still work as well as anything Neil Simon ever
wrote—and Shaw is smarter than Neil Simon. Even so light a
work as this is still a criticism of life, and the criticism is not
merely the center of a sugar-coated pill but a vital part of what
makes the play delightful.

Shaw's theatrical skill is proof (more or less) against all but a
thoroughly bad production; in the good but far from flawless
revival at Long Wharf, the play positively blossomed. It was by no
means well cast. One actor was too dignified and imposing for his
part, another not dignified and imposing enough; one actress was
far too young, and so elegant that when she said she was an ex-
shopgirl there was no question of believing her. This sort of thing
had seriously damaged the Long Wharf production of *The Three
Sisters*, but in this respect Shaw is made of sturdier stuff.

It is a nuisance, however, that Long Wharf, like many other
resident theatres, cannot put together a company that can manage
consistent and unforced English accents. (This should be a basic
part of every actor's training, though nobody has ever yet learned
it from Lee Strasberg.) Oddly enough, the Chekhov play, which
needs a very relaxed, shirt-sleeved sort of acting, suffered instead
from some highly elocutionary King's English performances. It
would appear that Long Wharf, again like many other theatres, is
forced to make do, in many cases, not with the actors it needs, but
with the actors it can get.

Arvin Brown, who directed *The Three Sisters*, was defeated on
that occasion by a play that exposed the weaknesses of the Long
Wharf company; *Misalliance*, again under Mr. Brown's direction,
made the company look good. (Not that it was altogether the
same company; there has been a good deal of turnover from play
to play at Long Wharf, as—again—at many other theatres.) The

Misalliance performance had an easy zest; the pace was brisk but not forced; the staging was fluid and sometimes inventive, but never tried to compete with the text.

It was a happy evening, the kind that makes friends for the theatre that provides it. To make friends in such a fashion is not the highest function that a theatre can have; still, I think, it is an achievement worth being proud of. If it's not, the whole resident-theatre movement is largely a fake.

By the time of *Misalliance*, the Long Wharf needed all the friends it could get: it was in the midst of a financial crisis and a "Save the Theatre Campaign" to raise $90,000 and avert bankruptcy. New Haven is one of the smallest communities in the country to have a resident theatre, and Long Wharf has to compete for its audience with the old Shubert downtown, which books Broadway shows, and the resurgent Yale School of Drama (see Chapter Eleven). In its second season, the bloom of novelty was off it; subscriptions had fallen off from about 8,000 to about 5,000, and attendance was running at about 65 per cent of capacity instead of 85 per cent. The deficit was mounting. In January, 1967, the board of directors panicked and asked the Yale Drama School to take the theatre off their hands. Yale appeared willing, but when the matter was leaked to the local paper, public outcry was sufficient to induce the board to change its mind and decide to make a fight for it.

The drive succeeded, and the theatre was saved—for the moment at least. During the season, Jory resigned to be a free-lance director; a few months later, Kleiman resigned to produce in New York. Each was succeeded by his second-in-command: Jory by Arvin Brown, Kleiman by Douglas Buck. For the 1967–68 season, Long Wharf will operate on a tight budget, concentrate on small-cast shows, and try to survive.

I went up to New Haven in December of 1967 to see Mr. Brown's production of Anouilh's *The Rehearsal*. There was some competent work in it, but competent in the wrong style. The cast was defeated by the Henry James syndrome: in our day as in his, Americans have no gift for beautiful decadence, for exquisite corruption, and just precisely this decadence and corruption (contrasted, as usual in Anouilh's plays, with radiant virginal innocence) is the subject of *The Rehearsal*. The best performance in the production was given by Leo Ciceri, a Canadian who has worked extensively in England, and even Mr. Ciceri has done better work during his years at Stratford, Ontario. The Countess and the Count's mistress, those two cold, glittering, glorious creatures of artifice, became mere café-society bitches in sunglasses. And the actors were not helped by a set that transformed the drawing-room of the Louis XV château of Ferbroques into an ersatz-California-Spanish garden.

People do not seem to be flocking to Long Wharf; the competition from the new professional company at Yale is deeply felt. It may be unfair, but there is no doubt that Yale has more prestige, more money, more freedom to take risks. Unless it turns out that there is room in New Haven (population 152,000) for two resident professional companies, Long Wharf's chances are not good.

NEW YORK: THE COMÉDIE FRANÇAISE THAT WASN'T

The Old Regime at Lincoln Center

In the fall of 1963, when the company of the Repertory Theatre of Lincoln Center assembled for the first time, Elia Kazan told them:

> We have come together to make a theatre. . . . Since we are Americans, this will be an American theatre. It will be centered in New York City, but it will not be aimed at one section or group in our country. We hope it will be a world theatre, expressing the way we Americans see the world. . . . Finally, we hope, it will speak for all men by expressing what is deepest and most enduring in the lives of all men.*

To implement these dreams, mighty resources of talent, energy, and prestige were gathered together. Elia Kazan had directed *A Streetcar Named Desire, Death of a Salesman,* and many other Broadway plays; Kenneth Tynan had said, overstating the case remarkably little, "There is only one trend in the Broadway theatre, and its name is Kazan." Robert Whitehead had been for many years among the most substantial and respectable of Broadway producers, with *Member of the Wedding, Separate Tables,*

* *Theatre: The Annual of the Repertory Theatre of Lincoln Center,* Barry Hyams, ed. (New York, 1964), Vol. I, p. 77.

Bus Stop, A Man for All Seasons, and many other plays to his credit. Kazan and Whitehead were the directors of the new institution. As their "executive consultant," the two leaders hired Harold Clurman, director of *Member of the Wedding, Bus Stop, Tiger at the Gates,* and *Waltz of the Toreadors,* respected critic, and co-founder of the Group Theatre. To design sets, and to act as co-designer for both their temporary and permanent theatre buildings, the duumvirs hired Jo Mielziner, the foremost among Broadway designers. Their acting company was headed by four Broadway stars: Jason Robards, Jr., David Wayne, Hal Holbrook, and Ralph Meeker. Arthur Miller was the Repertory Theatre's resident playwright, as Odets and Shaw and Molière and Shakespeare before him had been resident playwrights of other theatres. Kazan affirmed that Miller was "as much a part of our group as Bob Whitehead or myself or any actor."*

These are some of the most famous names in the American theatre, yet the life of their collective enterprise was unsatisfactory and brief. Shortly after the beginning of the Repertory Theatre's second season, Whitehead was dismissed by the theatre's board of directors, and Kazan resigned in his support. Their successors, Herbert Blau and Jules Irving (the founders of the San Francisco Actor's Workshop), made no bones about their determination not to build on the foundations bequeathed them, but to start all over again almost from scratch. Thus in spite of all the talent, all the money, all the high hopes, good wishes, and great dreams, the result of the Kazan-Whitehead enterprise, after only six productions in two seasons, was failure, failure in every sense. Whose failure was it?

As always, there is no one answer. It was not only the failure of Whitehead and Kazan. The philanthropists are implicated, and so are the critics. Ultimately, however, the first Lincoln Center debacle (there was another one later, as we shall see) represented the final failure of the serious wing of the postwar Broadway theatre, of which Whitehead and Kazan and their colleagues had been for many years among the leaders. The Repertory Theatre experiment was an unsuccessful attempt on the part of the Broadway Establishment to find a viable alternative to the Broadway system. The failure indicates that this middle-aged theatrical gen-

* *The New York Times,* August 9, 1964.

eration reached its peak with the Broadway productions of *Street-car* and *Salesman,* and has been on the decline ever since. At Lincoln Center this generation had its opportunity to surpass this peak, and muffed it. The fault was largely history's, in that our theatrical life has been so meagre and so chaotic—but it was history that this very generation had been instrumental in making.

More than anything else, the Lincoln Center Repertory failure was a failure to break free from the old Broadway attitudes, a failure of vision, of nerve, of dedication. "The trouble with the whole thing," said a Broadway producer to Kenneth Tynan five years before the Repertory Theatre opened, "is that there's nobody in it who really gives a burning damn."* The melancholy history of what might be called the first Repertory Theatre of Lincoln Center proves this anonymous commentator to have been more right than wrong.

Traditionally, an art theatre begins with a theatre artist profoundly dissatisfied with the lack of opportunity for meaningful work offered by the commercial theatre, and willing to sacrifice years of his life to create new opportunities for himself and others. Sometimes there are two such fanatics; sometimes a group. Thus Antoine founded the Théâtre Libre in Paris, and Copeau the Théâtre du Vieux Colombier; thus Stanislavsky and Nemirovich-Danchenko founded the Moscow Art Theatre. In our own country, there have been Judith Malina and Julian Beck at the Living Theatre in New York, Joseph Papp at the New York Shakespeare Festival in Central Park, and Herbert Blau and Jules Irving at the Actor's Workshop of San Francisco. There are other ways: the Canadian Stratford Festival—now the leading North American Shakespearean company—began in the imagination of a small-town booster, and the British National Theatre was founded by the government (in response, however, to long-continued pressure by the theatrical community). But the Repertory Theatre of Lincoln Center must be one of the very few theatres ever to have begun as a slum-clearance project.

It seems that in 1955 the Mayor's Slum Clearance Committee, headed by Robert Moses, had twenty-five rundown acres north of Columbus Circle that it wanted redeveloped; knowing that both the Metropolitan Opera and the New York Philharmonic-Sym-

---

* Kenneth Tynan, *Curtains* (New York, 1961), p. 375.

phony Orchestra were looking for new homes, Moses offered them part of the site. They accepted, and John D. Rockefeller, III, agreed to head a committee that would consider how the scope of the project might be expanded. Eventually the committee became the governing body of the Lincoln Center for the Performing Arts, Inc., of which Rockefeller became the first president. Thus Lincoln Center was from the very beginning a creation of the municipal, financial, and artistic Establishments.

Under Rockefeller's leadership, it was decided that the Center should include a repertory theatre, but nothing much was done about it until a department-store heiress, the late Mrs. Vivian Beaumont Allen, gave three million dollars to start the repertory ball rolling. "I have long been interested in the American theatre," said Mrs. Allen. "It has been my cherished hope that our country might one day have a national theatre comparable in distinction and achievement to the Comédie Française." In an interview with a *New York Times* reporter, she outlined her ideals and beliefs concerning the theatre in general:

> A good play is such a refreshing thing. And I don't mean the unpleasant plays of Tennessee Williams. And why would anybody put on such a dreadful thing as Molière's *Médecin Malgré Lui? The Diary of Anne Frank* is my idea of a beautiful play. And *The Music Man* was cheerful and enjoyable, although nothing else.

Somehow, in spite of her three million dollars, it is hard to believe that Mrs. Allen gave a burning damn.

It was only after the three million was in the till that Whitehead and Kazan were invited by Rockefeller and his colleagues to found the theatre. The initiative came from the businessmen; it was they who called in the artists, dangling their millions as an inducement. This primacy of the businessmen was to cause trouble later. It is perhaps utopian to demand that philanthropic businessmen should have no say in how their money is being spent, but that merely points up the difficulties involved in depending on philanthropic businessmen—as the Repertory Theatre, like nearly all resident professional companies, was from the first committed to doing.

In the summer of 1960, plans for the Vivian Beaumont Theatre, the Repertory's permanent home, were announced. The new theatre was to have nothing but the best. Its stage would be far larger and better-equipped than any on Broadway. The whole thing ended up costing something like 9.25 million dollars. (The Tyrone Guthrie Theatre in Minneapolis, by comparison, which has room for a considerably larger audience, cost only 2.25 million dollars.)

There was only one thing wrong with the new theatre—but this one thing was the first hint of a portentous oversight. John D. Rockefeller, III, had insisted from the beginning that "Lincoln Center is for the many."* It would seem to follow from this that the Repertory Theatre should have the largest possible seating capacity, to make room for as many of the many as possible and to help keep the prices low enough so that the many could afford to come. Thus the Théâtre National Populaire in Paris has 3,000 seats, and even the Comédie Française has 1,438; the Festival Theatre in the little town of Stratford, Ontario, seats 2,258. The capacity of the Vivian Beaumont Allen Theatre varies between 1,070 and 1,100, depending on whether the thrust stage is in use. So much for the many.

The price scale, when announced, reinforced the testimony given by the capacity of the theatre: it was very little lower than that prevailing on Broadway for straight plays. Whitehead and Kazan talked long and bravely and well about their ideas for their new theatre, but said curiously little about the audience. Whom did they expect to come to their theatre? How were these people to be attracted? The two directors seem never to have thought through this question.

At a number of performances I attended, the few cheap seats were filled while large gaps remained among the many expensive ones, but during the first season nothing was done to fill these gaping rows of unused seats with those who might have wanted to come, but could not afford $5 or $6 or $6.50 a ticket. Finally, in the Repertory's second season, seats were halfheartedly made available to students at a special rate—but only to the universally denounced production of The Changeling which nobody wanted to see anyway. This is all that the first Repertory Theatre did toward implementing a thick stream of public statements about

* The New York Times, December 14, 1956.

Lincoln Center's special concern for students. Even the Shuberts have a better record than that. Whitehead and Kazan did nothing to allay a widespread suspicion that Lincoln Center was to be the exclusive preserve of the upper middle class and the rich.

But we are getting ahead of our story. In the fall of 1962, Whitehead and Kazan went to work full-time on their new project, forsaking all other commitments—except that Kazan had a movie to finish, which occupied him intermittently for many months. It was discovered that the Beaumont Theatre would not be ready in time, and a temporary theatre was built in Greenwich Village, a "steel tent" with a highly serviceable open stage. Here, on January 23, 1964, the Repertory Theatre of Lincoln Center opened with the world première performance of *After the Fall*, Arthur Miller's first play in nine years. The next morning Howard Taubman asked in *The New York Times*:

> Which to celebrate first? The return of Arthur Miller to the theatre with a new play after too long an absence? Or the arrival of the new Repertory Theatre of Lincoln Center with its high promise for a consecration to drama of aspiration and significance?

and answered:

> Celebrate the conjunction of events, for together they may mark a turning point in the American drama. . . . The new company proclaims a fresh affirmation.

It was a great occasion—the last in the history of the Kazan-Whitehead regime.

By the end of the first season, the honeymoon was over. Everybody knew that the Repertory Theatre was in trouble. The *Village Voice*, a Greenwich Village weekly that concerns itself extensively with the theatre, gave it an award "for outstanding disservice to the American theatre." Even the faithful Howard Taubman said, "The first season, despite its accomplishments, has left doubts, and the future is full of questions."*

Elia Kazan was on the defensive; he complained bitterly in the *Times* about the "venom" from "intellectuals and especially within

* *The New York Times*, March 22, 1964.

our profession . . . The attacks started long ago—in fact before we actually did a production."* He had a case. As the Establishment theatre par excellence, the Lincoln Center Repertory was sure of the good will of Establishment spokesmen such as the *Times* and Mrs. Lyndon B. Johnson. ("I thought it was agonizing," said Lady Bird of *After the Fall*, "terrifically written and terrifically acted.") † But it came in for a great deal of ill-will, even hatred, as well. Part of this was sheer jealousy. No American theatre had ever had so much given to it: so much recognition, so much real estate, so much money, so much power to do as it wished; and many people, especially in the theatrical profession, just couldn't stand it. Another part of the ill-will came from deep and widespread suspicions, cherished especially by the intellectuals, against anything identified with the Establishment—suspicions that events often prove to be not unfounded. And the very expectation that the new theatre aroused was in constant danger of turning into disappointment: of him to whom much is given, much—sometimes impossibly much—is demanded.

Though the intellectuals and the theatre professionals led the attack, the audiences were right behind them. The first season had been quickly oversubscribed; for the second, subscription orders fell off by nearly 50 per cent.

The problem was not the acting, nor the directing, nor the splendid new stage; it was the choice of plays. Kazan and Whitehead had fallen victim to the widespread delusion that, as Kazan expressed it, "There is a whole repertory of American plays, written over the last forty years, that have become contemporary classics."‡ Most of our theatrical and literary potentates and powers came to maturity during the twenties and thirties, and are unaware of how harshly time has dealt with the plays they discovered in their youth and young manhood. The harm this kind of misprision has done to the American drama is incalculable. When pinchbeck is so widely taken for gold, the standards for new work inevitably become corrupted. The faults of the between-the-wars playwrights—pretentiousness, simple-mindedness, and bad rhet-

---

* *The New York Times*, August 9, 1964.
† *Ibid.*, January 21, 1964.
‡ *The New York Times Magazine*, "Lincoln Center Section," September 23, 1962.

oric—are widespread also among contemporary playwrights. *After the Fall* might have been a far better play were it not for the example of O'Neill.

Nevertheless, I would defend the choice of *After the Fall* as the Repertory's opening play—and not only because a great many people turned out to want to see it. The play has become, like *J.B.* before it, one of those shibboleths that separate the high-brows (Elizabeth Hardwick, Robert Brustein), who loathe it, from the middle-brows (Howard Taubman, Lady Bird Johnson), who admire it. But perhaps there is something to be said for an intermediate view. The play is a three-hour potted psychoanalysis of the author, with all his memories acted out in fragments—most of them too brief to make any clear statement—and commented upon by the author-narrator-hero-patient—murkily, and at too-great length. Like so much fictionalized autobiography, it is full of self-indulgence; what Mr. Miller takes to be his perceptions are often only his obsessions. And yet, underneath the rhetorical fat, the bones are those of a genuine drama. Three hours of attention to it are not wasted; Mr. Miller has something to tell us about the difficulties of living with our own capacities for destruction, and every once in a while—just often enough—illumination comes through the fog.

It has been argued that irrespective of the merits of *After the Fall*, the Repertory Theatre should have left it alone, because it could just as well have been done on Broadway, where it need not have drawn on the funds of a subsidized operation, but could actually have made money for all concerned. To which it has been counter-argued that the play needed the long rehearsal period that only a repertory theatre can afford (Kazan, in several interviews, has harped on the fact that he had only nineteen days in which to rehearse so difficult a play as *J.B.*); that the play benefited by being done on an open stage thrusting into the audience, which no Broadway theatre can provide; and that, conclusively, Miller would never have finished the play if the Repertory Theatre had not existed. And yet, considering that Miller's great fault is his strenuous desire to be a genius, his play might, paradoxically, have been improved by an exposure to the mean practicality of Broadway.

As for the other two presentations that first season, hardly anybody wanted to see them, and they were quickly dropped from the repertory, leaving *After the Fall* to run all summer by itself. O'Neill's *Marco Millions* was beautiful to look at; José Quintero, the director, and David Hays, the designer, found a mode of simplified, suggestive spectacularity that suited the new stage very well. But *Marco* has always been regarded as one of O'Neill's lesser plays; nobody has an investment in its status as a classic, and so there was no reason to overlook the cliché-laden ponderosity of this galumphing thirty-seven-year-old parable.

But for Whom Charlie, the last of the first season's productions, is not one of the drawing-room comedies that S. N. Behrman wrote during the thirties, but a new essay by Mr. Behrman in the same old style. The subject matter is postwar—it deals with a foundation that subsidizes writers—but the self-conscious urbanity and the simple-minded bourgeois liberalism are heavily redolent of the plays that Behrman wrote for Ina Claire. It has been widely maintained that the play needed a realistic drawing-room set, which the Repertory's temporary theatre, with its open stage, could not accommodate, and that it was not well cast from the Repertory company. But the real problem was the play: not only was it one long banality, it was a banality thirty years outmoded.

How, we may ask, did the Repertory Theatre, that vibrant new departure, get itself stuck in S. N. Behrman's rut? The answer is disquieting. The play had been on Whitehead's Broadway agenda, and Kazan had been engaged to direct it. When the two transferred their energies to the Repertory Theatre, they simply brought the play along.* This does not seem to display much of a determination to do in their lavishly subsidized new theatre what could not be done in the commercial theatre. It proved easier to take Whitehead and Kazan out of Broadway, than to take Broadway out of Whitehead and Kazan.

Aside from the much-debated success of *After the Fall*, did the Repertory Theatre have *anything* to show for its first season? It had a temporary theatre which augured well for the permanent one that was still a-building. The open stage of this theatre had been used sometimes well, sometimes badly; its qualities and

* S. N. Behrman, "The Common Sense of Insanity," in *Theatre: The Annual of the Repertory Theatre of Lincoln Center* (New York, 1964), Vol. I, pp. vii–ix.

limitations were now known. Some interesting actors—Jason Robards, Jr., and David Wayne, most notably—had been seen in two contrasting roles apiece during a single season, and had displayed hitherto-unfamiliar aspects of their talents. In *But for Whom Charlie*, Mr. Wayne played a seventy-year-old writer with his usual charm, and an impeccable technique; he could not have been more convincing had he actually been seventy. Mr. Robards was a tower of strength in the tremendous leading role in *After the Fall*; only after seeing another actor play the part did I realize how his craggy honesty kept the play—and the part—from seeming as meretricious as it often is. Then in *But for Whom Charlie*, he played a meek Jewish *schlemiel* as if he had made his career playing nothing else. One of the great weaknesses of the American theatre is that even our best actors are so seldom seen—how often on Broadway does Robards or Wayne or anybody else get to do two roles a season? If only their roles at the Repertory Theatre had been in all cases worthy of them!

And if only some of the other actors had proved more worthy of their roles. For the second season of the Repertory—which the original directors did not survive—revealed a new and profound deficiency. It turned out that the acting company, selected and trained with such care and publicity, was inadequate to its high purposes.

The program for the second season was, on paper, quite an interesting one: Whitehead and Kazan had clearly determined to stop dodging the challenge presented by the plays of other countries and other times. This is a challenge that American theatre people have long found dauntingly formidable; the Group Theatre —with Harold Clurman and Lee Strasberg as its directors and Kazan in its acting company—never faced it. Yet it is a challenge that a repertory theatre worth its salt must finally conquer.

The Repertory Theatre of Lincoln Center did not conquer this challenge; instead, the challenge overthrew it.

The season began with *The Changeling*, a post-Elizabethan bloodbath (1624) by Thomas Middleton and William Rowley. The play is widely admired by students of Jacobean drama; hardly anybody else has ever read it. And nobody has seen it; as far as anybody could figure out, the Repertory Theatre production was the first professional showing the play has ever received in this country. (The recent, successful, London production was the first there in three hundred and some odd years.) And yet it is a magnificent play, with much to say to us. It may be the first Existentialist drama: "Y'are the deed's creature," says a murderer to the woman who has suborned him, enunciating the Sartrian creed that we define ourselves by what we do.

It is a play that deserves to be seen, and which never would be seen unless there was a repertory theatre with the courage to do it. An ideal choice for this repertory theatre then—assuming that the audience, and the company itself, were ready for it. In the event, the company certainly was not, and the choice turned out to be wildly foolhardy.

Marco Millions and *But for Whom Charlie* had been mistakes; *The Changeling* was a fiasco. Critics called it "deeply embarrassing," "shot through with glaring deficiencies," "a sorry start."* Word quickly spread through New York that the production was not merely bad but *terrible*, and attendance was so poor that a number of performances were canceled.

Actually it was not quite so bad as all that. It was no worse than some of the shows that Joseph Papp puts on at his much-lauded New York Shakespeare Festival in Central Park. David Hays's intricate setting was admirable; there was a spectacular murder; a young actor named Barry Primus played a leading part as if better direction might have enabled him to play it well. Kazan, who directed, was reasonably faithful to the script, and did not play games with it as American directors so often do when let loose on a classic.

Yet it is undeniable that *The Changeling* was badly done. Kazan's famous gift for abnormal psychology had deserted him. There was plenty of kissing and clipping and jumping into an onstage bed, and plenty of mayhem and mutilation (something too much of all this for some of our delicate critics), but the emotions and desires, the tangle of loves and hates, the discoveries and internal transitions, that give meaning to the bed-bouncing and bloodletting—all this was less clear. It is no wonder that some critics, in their ignorance, took the play for mere Grand Guignol.

But the worst of it was the sheer unprofessionalism of the

---

* Walter Kerr, *Herald Tribune*; Howard Taubman, *The New York Times*; John McClain, *Journal-American*. All October 30, 1964.

acting. According to Kazan, this was to be the show that would give "the kids" a chance; many of the kids were not remotely ready for it. For all their months of research on the period, for all their elaborate program of classes in acting and voice and diction, several of the leading actors seemed like clean-cut American college kids who had bitten off far, far more than they could chew. The weakness of the company was cruelly exposed.

It was not so exposed again, though the subsequent Kazan-Whitehead productions were by no means distinguished. With the next production the company was on safe, familiar ground: a new play by Arthur Miller, entitled *Incident at Vichy*. Whereas *After the Fall* had been long and diffuse, *Incident at Vichy* was short and tightly focused, but both plays indicated that nothing good had happened to Mr. Miller's talent in the long years of silence that preceded them.

With *Incident at Vichy*, he employed the assistance of a powerful collaborator: history. The mere invoking of the Nazi horror is enough to arouse emotion in many people; the rabbi of our synagogue, years after the war, had only to scream "Dachau!" from the pulpit on Yom Kippur to start the pledges rolling in for the U.J.A. But Mr. Miller, unlike the rabbi, did not merely rely on history to do his work for him. He contrived a simple situation which served, like a burning glass, to focus and concentrate the horror. In a detention room at Vichy in 1942, a group of men, mostly Jews, sit and wait. They have been rounded up by the Germans and their French collaborators, and now they wonder what will become of them. One by one, they are taken inside for interrogation, from which most do not emerge. It was like a sinister and desperate slow-motion game of Ten Little Indians; it could be felt in the pit of the stomach even by one who is left unmoved by the ordinary Nazi-horror-mongers; it was in the highest degree dramatic.

Unfortunately, Mr. Miller was not primarily interested in this kind of drama. He did not precisely scorn and spurn his situation, but he seemed to be mainly using it as a pretext, almost a come-on. It seemed as though Miller did not really want to write plays any more; he wanted to talk to us directly. The impulse behind *Incident at Vichy* appeared to have been primarily ideological.

Now I do not mean to do a Walter Kerr, and imply that the

worst thing the theatre has ever done was to go whoring off after the delusive delights of ideology. It is just that Mr. Miller is less than a first-rate ideologue. And so the audience had to listen at length to a Communist spouting Communist clichés; to a gentle Austrian prince who asseverates repetitively that human decency still exists; and to a psychoanalyst who insists that all men are guilty. (As everybody knows, Mr. Miller is feeling pretty guilty himself these days; and while all forms of misery love company, none is quite so compulsively sociable as guilt.)

Mr. Miller's ideas did not insult the intelligence, but neither were they very stimulating. However, when the playwright deigned to punctuate his discourse by tightening his dramaturgical screws, he did it so successfully that the tension held through long stretches of idea-mongering, almost until he was ready to tighten them again. In overvaluing his capacities as a thinker, Miller neglects his great gift, which is precisely for dramaturgy in its best sense: for creating meaning through *action*. The Nazi "professor" in *Incident at Vichy*, who comes out of the interrogation room to the frightened line of victims and says "Next!" is not only more dramatic than all the sententious lucubrations in the script; his appearances also *say* more about the implications of Nazism. Actions, in the theatre, do not always speak louder than words; but in Mr. Miller's plays they do.

Harold Clurman directed *Incident at Vichy* with absolute, total fidelity, as if determined that the audience should accept it on the author's own terms or not at all. The play was given without intermission (it lasted an hour and three-quarters). Mr. Clurman ignored the temptation to constant movement imposed by the open stage of the Repertory Theatre's temporary home; his staging could have been transferred virtually intact to a proscenium house. It took courage to allow half a dozen or so performers to remain static for so long in a row on a bench, and Mr. Clurman's courage was in good part rewarded. Insofar as the play was capable of doing what Mr. Miller wanted it to do, the direction was successful.

In climactic passages, however, the director's fidelity served only to aggravate the author's pretentiousness. Mr. Miller's prose only occasionally caught the sound of human speech, tending instead toward abstractness, sententiousness, and self-consciousness, with a particular weakness for the pseudo-apothegm. "We 've learned the price of idealism." "But can one wish for a world without ideals?" —so runs a typical exchange. Now this is not terrible—compared, for instance, to much of O'Neill—but Joseph Wiseman as the psychoanalyst and David Wayne as the prince brought out its worst qualities by belting it in the most earnestly self-indulgent oratorical style, with plenty of the histrionic equivalents for *italics* and exclamation marks! and CAPITALS.

This left David J. Stewart in an awkward position, since he was *supposed* to be playing a ham actor. But Mr. Stewart projected his character's false attitudinizing and genuine fright with great clarity and tremendous conviction. And it is only fair to note that Mr. Wiseman did convey an impression of strength, and that Mr. Wayne's peculiar, effortless charm—which was highly relevant to the character as written—seemed to be not merely a theatrical commodity but a genuine attribute of the soul.

Incident at Vichy, then, was an ambiguous half-success; *Tartuffe*, which followed it into the repertory, was dubious in a different way. Michael O'Sullivan's grotesque little Tartuffe, with stringy hair, buck teeth, chinless chin, and knock-knees, was comic even when he was not doing very much of anything. Unfortunately, he didn't do not much of anything very often. He wooed his patron's wife with busy clumsiness, in the vaudevillian spirit of Jack Gilford goosing chorus girls as the mute King Sextimus in *Once upon a Mattress*—except that Mr. O'Sullivan was anything but mute. He sobbed, he shouted, he screeched inexhaustibly throughout the play, occasionally becoming inarticulate from sheer excess of effort. Low comedy, of course, is far from antithetical to the theatre of Molière, which is deeply grounded in the *commedia dell'arte*—the Orpheum Circuit of the seventeenth century. And O'Sullivan's first wooing scene was very funny indeed. After that, however, the law of diminishing returns set in. Worse still, the point of the play got lost in his vociferations.

There was one beautiful moment in the production which showed what the rest of it lacked. Tartuffe is slapped in the face. And although he had just been trying to seduce the wife of his benefactor, Mr. O'Sullivan assumed an expression of sickly, unctuous piety, and—carefully, elaborately, making sure that nobody, onstage or in the audience could miss the significance—turned the other cheek. This bit of pantomime is not in the script Molière has left us, but it grew naturally, not only out of the action, but also out of the theme of the play. It dramatized the essence of hypocrisy, by showing in action that to use heavenly things for earthly purposes is blasphemy. The laughter evoked was an expression of feeling not only about the character and the situation, but about the great issue with which Molière was concerned.

But for the most part, this *Tartuffe* hardly seemed to be about hypocrisy at all. Perhaps an American audience would merely have been bored by the famous *tirade* in which Tartuffe explains that adultery is perfectly all right if an expert like himself is on hand to square things with Heaven. Perhaps. But William Ball, who directed, was taking no chances. The *tirades* were spoken, or screamed, but we did not attend to them; they were obscured by a continuous series of farcical elaborations.

As if aware that the core of the play was missing, Mr. Ball took great pains with its periphery. He seemed to have gone for inspiration to Vermeer, and in collaboration with his designers (David Hays for the set, John Gleason for the lighting, Jane Greenwood for the costumes), created warm, beautiful seventeenth–century genre pictures of his own, which were enhanced by Lee Hoiby's flute-and-harpsichord music. By skillful and lavish (sometimes overlavish) use of pantomime, employing three supernumerary servants, two pleasant children, and a babe in arms, Mr. Ball evoked the life of the Orgon ménage as it can seldom have been evoked before. If only Tartuffe had not, for all the noise he made, been such an obvious weakling, if only we could have believed, as the plot demands, that he represented a genuine menace to the household whose head he had so egregiously duped, we might really have come to care about the numerous, prosperous, lively, affectionate, and attractive family that Mr. Ball created.

Tartuffe is a comedy of bourgeois life, and in this production it was played as such, without an excess of mincing and flitting. Yet the cast almost never lapsed into ordinary modernity. They spoke Molière's couplets, in Richard Wilbur's rhymed translation, with a reasonable approximation of having been born to them; and they generally displayed the ability to make themselves seem at home in another century than our own, and in another theatrical convention than that of modern realism—an ability sorely lacking among

American actors in general, and, heretofore, among the Lincoln Center troupe in particular.

The reason for this was that the *Tartuffe* company was essentially a different one from that which was appearing on alternate nights in *After the Fall* (held over for a second season), *The Changeling,* and *Incident at Vichy*. Mr. Ball had had no previous connection with the Lincoln Center Repertory, and he brought in no less than seven actors new to the company. Six of these were never seen with the company in any other play; the seventh, Mr. O'Sullivan, returned only when the Repertory Theatre was under new management. Considering what the main company had shown of itself in *The Changeling*, bringing in new actors for *Tartuffe* was the better part of valor. But it made hash of the repertory ideal of an ensemble, a group of versatile actors developing a common style by working together in play after play. By allowing Ball to bring in his own actors, Whitehead and Kazan implicitly admitted that their own company was incapable of performing *Tartuffe*.

Why? Why, with so much time, so much talent, so much money at their disposal, did Whitehead and Kazan so egregiously fail to develop a classical ensemble? The easy answer is the one about America's having no tradition for the performance of the classics, so that our actors are unfamiliar with them and untrained for them. This explanation will serve for most resident theatres. But the Repertory Theatre of Lincoln Center was founded in order to do something about precisely this situation, and was given plenty of money to do so. And the fact remains that in spite of everything we *do* have good classical actors in this country, if you know where to look for them. William Ball found a number of them for his pickup *Tartuffe* who put the regular company to shame.

The true answer, perhaps, is that Elia Kazan came late to the classics, and, in spite of his intelligent defense of his choice of *The Changeling,** never developed a genuine commitment to them. Kazan had been directing for nearly thirty years. For fifteen or twenty of those years he had been at the top of his profession, in a position to do almost any play he wished. And yet before *The*

* *Show*, January, 1965.

Changeling he had *never* directed a noncontemporary play. After all those years, he came to *The Changeling* as a novice. This is what the Broadway theatre does to those who work in it—unless, perhaps, it was men like Kazan who made the Broadway theatre in their own image. Probably it was a little of both.

Kazan was quoted as saying, only a few years ago, "that he would never produce Shakespeare because, 'I am more interested in the life that is around me.' "* —a statement that would indicate that he had neither the ability nor the desire to head a repertory theatre that would include the classics in its purview. What induced him to change his mind? "He wanted to go down in history," suggests an ex-member of the company. Perhaps.

At any rate, it was as a novice at classical drama and a newcomer to repertory theatre that he chose his company. It certainly seemed as if they were chosen with little regard for the special abilities that noncontemporary drama demands. The Repertory Theatre provided an eight-month training program for the younger actors before rehearsals began, and voice and diction classes running concurrently with rehearsals and performances. We need many more such programs if more than a small minority of our actors are to be fully equipped with professional skills. But a few months of voice and diction study cannot be relied upon to make silk purses out of sows' ears.

A charter member of the Repertory Theatre charges that its actors were not really selected to be part of a company, not chosen for the flexibility and versatility that repertory demands, but, in large part, simply cast for roles in *After the Fall*. Certainly the company never looked so good again as it did in that play. Here again Kazan may have been bound by decades of habituation to the Broadway system whereby every production is a self-contained entity, and nothing is done with an eye to permanence.

In the early days of the Repertory Theatre, Kazan had spoken of it as a "family." At about the time *The Changeling* opened, however, he was evidently finding the permanence of family life somewhat irksome. Though still willing to direct for the company,

---

* Robert Brustein, "Repertory Fever," *Harper's*, December, 1960; reprinted in Brustein, *Seasons of Discontent* (New York, Simon and Schuster, Inc., 1967), p. 206. This quotation and all other quotations from the book are reprinted by permission of the publisher.

he withdrew from active management, leaving Whitehead single-handedly in charge. It was just about a year since the company had begun rehearsals for its first play—not a long tenure. Evidently, when Kazan spoke of the company as a "way of life," he did not mean a way of life for himself. The conditioning of twenty-five foot-loose years on Broadway was too strong for that.

Whitehead remained; but he did not remain long. In December of 1964 it was revealed that the theatre's board of directors was busily trying, behind his back, to replace him with Herman Krawitz of the Metropolitan Opera—whose boss, Rudolph Bing, broke the story. Whitehead declared that he had been wrongfully discharged; Kazan, Arthur Miller, and Harold Clurman ended their connection with the Repertory Theatre as a gesture of solidarity. The old regime had ended. Krawitz prudently decided to stay with the Met, and the Repertory Theatre was headless for several months until, after an exhaustive search, Blau and Irving were chosen.

The whole affair made it clear that the ultimate authority at the Repertory Theatre was its board of directors, a group consisting mostly of businessmen, and led by the president of the theatre, Robert L. Hoguet, Jr., executive vice-president of the First National City Bank of New York. Hoguet is in no sense a man of the theatre; he seems not even to be particularly interested in it. He believes in culture, however, and in the obligation of the business community to the community at large. He assumed the presidency of the Repertory Theatre out of a desire to serve, as another businessman might interest himself in the affairs of a university or a hospital. After many generations of dubious respectability, the theatre is coming up in the world when men like Mr. Hoguet and John D. Rockefeller, III, take an interest in it, but this advancement is not unattended with danger. Universities have suffered before now from the restrictive influence of their boards of trustees and regents.

When asked what he and his fellow businessmen had to contribute to such a theatre as that of Lincoln Center, Hoguet named fund-raising—for he realizes that a noncommercial theatre cannot be expected to show a profit—help in the thousand nonartistic problems that come up in the course of such a sizable operation, and bringing their "objectivity" to bear on the selection of the theatre's management personnel. It was presumably in the exercise of the last function that Whitehead got the gate.

However, according to Harold Clurman:*

> The brute fact is that none of the criticisms—justified or not— leveled at Whitehead and Kazan were the causes for the overthrow of their regime. The board of directors were eager to retain Kazan and Miller on the theatre's roster. Whitehead was the target. And this was due not to any administrative negligence or to such calamities as *The Changeling* about which Whitehead was as unhappy as anyone else, but to the fact that he had literally forced the board's hand in building the ANTA-Washington Square Theatre [the Repertory company's first, temporary home], an action to which the most powerful member of the board was unalterably opposed.

This would seem to indicate that businessmen, for all their "objectivity," can be every bit as vindictive as any artist.

Objectivity, in this case, tends to look like just another name for ignorance. It is evident, at least, that Mr. Hoguet and his colleagues had no clear idea of what kind of men they thought were needed to run the Repertory Theatre. The first directors were a Broadway producer and a Broadway director. To succeed them, the board tried to engage an administrator with no artistic pretensions at all, who had not worked in the legitimate theatre for eleven years, and who had passed those years in the employ of one of the most profoundly conservative artistic bodies in existence, the Metropolitan Opera. Only after he had turned it down was the job offered to Herbert Blau and Jules Irving, two anti-Broadway radicals whose work had been accomplished three thousand miles west of both Broadway and the Met. If the board members gave a burning damn, they were apparently in a state of considerable confusion as to what they gave a burning damn about.

Pragmatically speaking, putting aside the question of their motives, were they "right" in replacing Kazan and Whitehead with Blau and Irving? We shall never know. Kazan insisted all along that it would take at least three years to develop a company; he and Whitehead were cut off after less than two. During those two years they made serious mistakes, recognized them, and

* *The Nation*, May 16, 1966, p. 584.

showed some capacity to learn from them. They had splendid plans for the first season at the Vivian Beaumont Theatre, which was built for them.

It is hard not to be wistful about Kazan's production of the *Oresteia*, in an adaptation by Robert Lowell, and Franco Zeffirelli's production of De Musset's *Lorenzaccio* (a sprawling drama of almost Shakespearean richness, almost unknown in this country) —which we had been promised,* and which now we will never see. Whitehead and Kazan and their Broadway colleagues possess vast reserves of talent; it is unhappy for them, and for everyone in America who goes to the theatre—or who has stopped going to the theatre because of the inadequacy of what he finds there—that the great experiment in harnessing these talents for a higher purpose has, for whatever reason, failed.

The New Regime at Lincoln Center

When Whitehead and Kazan departed the Lincoln Center Repertory in December of 1964, less than a year after the company's gala opening, they had three plays running in repertory and *Tartuffe* in rehearsal. *Tartuffe* opened on schedule in January; *The Changeling* was dropped, and the three remaining productions finished out the season. Meanwhile, on March 1, 1965, Herbert Blau and Jules Irving moved in from San Francisco as the new directors, and began planning for the future.

The replacement of Kazan and Whitehead by Blau and Irving was not simply a change in management but an entirely new beginning. The new leaders were of a different generation from the old (Blau was thirty-eight, Irving thirty-nine); they brought to their work a very different kind of experience and had built their careers on the repudiation of much that the old leaders stood for. Kazan and Whitehead had been pillars of Broadway; Blau and Irving were pioneers of the regional theatre, which had been born largely out of disgust at the inadequacies of Broadway, which Blau has called a "graveyard." In a letter to their San Francisco subscribers, Blau and Irving promised, ". . . ideologically we shall remain as we have always been, three thousand miles from Broad-

* *The New York Times,* August 9, 1964.

way. . . . We have been given a mandate to do at Lincoln Center what we have done here, and more so . . ."

Irving denies that he and Blau ever intended simply to transplant the Actor's Workshop to New York. He points out that of thirteen major roles in *Danton's Death*, the first Blau-Irving production at Lincoln Center, eleven were played by actors who had not been members of the Workshop. He and Blau were feeling frustrated in San Francisco, he says, because of the limited funds available to them there, and the difficulty of getting and keeping gifted actors. What Lincoln Center represented to them was the opportunity to take "a significant step forward. Any artist worth his salt wants to function on the highest artistic level possible."

Still, certain facts remain. Blau and Irving brought with them a dozen actors from the Workshop (including Mrs. Blau and Mrs. Irving), and quickly got rid of the entire Kazan-Whitehead acting company. They switched the Repertory Theatre from a repertory to a stock system of operation, like that which had been in effect at the Workshop (though the Workshop too, on occasion, had played in repertory). The Workshop had been a young company without big names, performing plays of which a large percentage were unknown to the public, although admired by avant-garde academicians; the same was true of the new Lincoln Center company as Blau and Irving reorganized it. (Since the Workshop had successfully produced Brecht, Beckett, Pinter, and Genet when these worthies were still considered wildly esoteric, Blau and Irving had some reason for confidence in their own taste.) As Blau said when their new appointment was announced, "Our production concept will be the same as that we followed at the Workshop."*

On the other hand, the new directors displayed from the beginning a determination to mix their San Francisco actors with New York actors, and to make full use of the elaborate technological facilities of their new theatre.

The new policy didn't work. In each of the new management's first two seasons, three productions out of four were failures; Blau and Irving were reported to be on the verge of being fired; Blau resigned; Irving got rid of the old Workshop actors, or reduced

---

* *The New York Times*, January 31, 1965.

them to small roles, and got big names from outside the company to play leads, and put on popular plays. And again we are reduced to asking, why? What happened *this* time?

First of all, some of the scripts were very badly chosen. Some, perhaps, were scripts whose deficiencies became especially apparent in a New York context, while their merits were obscured; one or two simply stank on ice. Paradoxically, Blau and Irving were just as guilty of ignoring the play's relevance to its audience as the ordinary resident-theatre hack who puts on *The Importance of Being Earnest* because it has a small cast, and it's a comedy, and people have heard of it, and what the hell, it'll sell.

Some of the plays they did, however, deserved to be done. *Danton's Death* by Georg Büchner, *The Country Wife* by William Wycherly, and *The Alchemist* by Ben Jonson are by no means void of meanings and fascinations for us today, and could, I think, be accepted by a New York audience. But since these plays are unfamiliar both to the critics and to the public, they are objects of suspicion to both groups, and this suspicion can only be overcome by really first-rate productions. The Blau-Irving productions, though extensively denounced, were no worse than what a lot of resident theatres have been getting away with for years. The directing tended to lack imagination, theatrical flair, and strong production concepts, but it was neither gimmicky nor unduly clumsy. The acting was not distinguished, but the performers could at least move and talk; they seemed to be at least minimally well-trained professionals, as had not been the case with the actors in *The Changeling*. The standard of work was merely mediocre; but under the circumstances mediocrity was not good enough.

On October 21, 1965, a production of Büchner's *Danton's Death*, directed by Herbert Blau, marked the opening of both the first Blau-Irving season and the Vivian Beaumont Theatre, built (to the specifications of Kazan and Whitehead) expressly to be the home of the Repertory Theatre of Lincoln Center. The theatre had been designed by Eero Saarinen and Jo Mielziner, who had sought flexibility above all. It can be used for proscenium-style productions, but in front of the proscenium is an apron curving out twelve feet into the audience, and in front of *that* a removable thrust stage projecting fifteen feet further into the audience, who would thus, when the thrust stage is used, surround the playing area on three sides. The auditorium proved to be comfortable, if somewhat candy-boxy and over-plush; both the proscenium and the thrust-stage arrangements work pretty well. And the theatre has been equipped with all the magical playthings that modern theatrical technology has evolved.

Danton's Death was written in 1835, when its author was twenty-one. It is a sprawling, multi-scened chronicle of the French Revolution, built like a Shakespearean history play but permeated with Büchner's peculiar, brooding, Romantic sensibility; it had not been seen in New York since Orson Welles did it in the thirties. The Lincoln Center production was full of shouting and running about and theatrical things and stuff, as if Blau wished to demonstrate that, bookish and austere as he was, he could be as theatrical as the next man when he wanted to be; scenery swung in and out and roundabout on turntables and wagons, as if Blau and Jo Mielziner, the designer, were eager to show what their new theatre could do. Paul Mann (one of the few holdovers from the Kazan-Whitehead company) and Roscoe Lee Browne were a splendidly fanatical couple of revolutionaries, but Alan Bergmann and Robert Symonds in the leading roles of Danton and Robespierre, though competent enough, were scarcely the mighty opposites that the script envisions. As one who is interested in the play, I found myself moderately, casually interested by the production; but Büchner has few fans in New York, and the whole enterprise was extensively condemned.

A small incident connected with Danton's Death gives an indication of Blau's and Irving's insecurity and willingness to please their new public. (They had been famous for their unwillingness to cater to their San Francisco public.) In a mimeographed program distributed at previews, Blau wrote, "Terror, according to Robespierre, Castro, Verwoerd, Mao Tse-tung and President Johnson, is the moral whip of virtue. This is not to equalize all aberrations of power, but to recognize—as Buechner did at twenty-one—that nobody has a premium on tyranny. By fault or default, from whatever good motives, we are all executioners." The Times ran an article quoting several playgoers who had been incensed at seeing President Johnson's name in such company*—too incensed, presumably, to notice the care with

* The New York Times, October 14, 1965.

which the implied comparison was qualified. The offending article, temperate as it was, was quickly withdrawn; the program for the performances carried only a historical note that could offend no one.

Danton's Death was followed by a not-bad but colorless production of Wycherly's *The Country Wife*, directed by an old Workshop stalwart named Robert Symonds. It was another critical failure. (With 39,300 subscriptions sold before the season began, the company was insulated from the usual indication of failure with the public.)

The American première of *The Condemned of Altona* by Jean-Paul Sartre made it three in a row. Sartre's play deals with a German family haunted by guilt for its share in World War II, and by implication with France's guilt for the Algerian War and perhaps also our guilt for the war in Vietnam. This is the kind of theme we need repertory theatres to deal with, and Sartre has in the past written some highly interesting plays. But here his characters operate from motives so abstract and finespun that their actions are impossible to follow, which reduces the play to a series of grand but meaningless gestures, like a film of De Gaulle with the sound turned off. I understand from a philosophy student I know that it all makes excellent sense if you've read Sartre's *Being and Nothingness*, but *Being and Nothingness* is over six hundred pages long, and the game hardly seems worth the candle. The fact that Sartre wrote the play lends a certain significance to the reasons for its badness, but does not make it any better. Herbert Blau's production seemed to me quite good, but a play like this has enough boredom built into it to defeat any production. The most frivolous of comedies could hardly have communicated less to its audience than this piece of abortive high seriousness.

The succession of disasters was finally broken by the last production of the season: the first production in New York of Brecht's *The Caucasian Chalk Circle*, directed by Jules Irving. The play is a diffuse and sprawling parable that deals with many things, but its most immediate subject is mother-love. The only thing that can hold it together through its ins and outs and wanderings is a transcendent performance by the actress who plays Grusha Vashnadze, the kitchen maid who earns her right to keep the governor's child by caring for him and making sacrifices for him after his parents have abandoned him. Elizabeth Huddle, who played the role at Lincoln Center, was pleasant, competent, and well cast, but a radiant incarnation of mother-love she wasn't. The actress who plays Grusha must carry the play, and Miss Huddle was not quite up to this.

But she was good all the same, and so was most of the cast, and Mr. Irving showed that he knew how to stage a spectacle. James Hart Stearns's beautiful sets, costumes, and masks—the sets simple and primitive in style, the costumes elaborate, stiff, and gaudy— were beautifully lit by Richard Nelson. The play had a pleasant folk-tale air about it; everybody by that time wanted a chance to be nice to poor battered Blau and Irving; the critics liked the production; its run was extended. Still, a big black question-mark hung over the lavish new theatre.

It got bigger and blacker after the 1966–67 season opened with Jules Irving's leaden production of *The Alchemist* by Ben Jonson. This time the play was eminently stageworthy, and some pretty good actors had been assembled for it. But Irving seemed to have no idea in particular of what to do with them. A good farce director is a sparkling fountain of imagination; Irving showed himself a dry hole. There was nothing terribly *wrong* with his work; it was just insufficient. The alchemist himself, for instance, made an entrance in a white wig and a gown, clashing a set of finger-bells. So far, so good; but what then? Why, nothing in particular. The actor floated about the stage and clashed his bells, but nothing much came of it, no telling variations were made on it, no farcical climax was built from it.

Most of the actors seemed to be doing whatever they habitually fell back on when they couldn't think of anything else to do. Michael O'Sullivan as the cozening alchemist displayed his buck teeth frequently (and very formidable they were); changing his disguise the better to cheat each new victim, he provided several skillful but not-very-funny sub-characterizations. (Every time I see Mr. O'Sullivan, I get the impression that he would be marvelous in some *other* role.) In the tiny part of Lovewit, the London gentleman who comes in at the very end of the play to find that his house has been scandalously misused in his absence, Philip

(Right) Zelda Fichandler, founder and producing director of the Arena Stage, Washington, D.C. *(Photo by George de Vincent)*

(Far right) Sir Tyrone Guthrie, first artistic director of the Stratford (Ontario) Shakespearean Festival, co-founder and first artistic director of the Tyrone Guthrie Theatre, Minneapolis.

(Right) Jules Irving, co-founder and co-director of the Actor's Workshop of San Francisco, now director of the Repertory Theatre of Lincoln Center.

(Far right) Paul Baker, managing director of the Dallas Theatre Center.

(Right) Robert Brustein, dean of the Yale School of Drama.

(Far right) Ellis Rabb, founder and artistic director of the APA Repertory Company, in the title role of *Pantagleize* by Michel de Ghelderode, as produced by the APA. *(Photo by Eileen Darby–Graphic House)*

(*Left*) William Ball, founder and general director of the American Conservatory Theatre.

(*Right*) Joseph Papp, founder and producing director of the New York Shakespeare Festival. (*Photo by George E. Joseph*)

(*Left*) Michael Langham, artistic director of the Stratford (Ontario) Shakespearean Festival, 1957–67. (*Photo by Peter Smith*)

(*Right*) Jean Gascon, executive artistic director of the Stratford Shakespearean Festival, now also known as the Stratford National Theatre of Canada.

John Hirsch, co-founder and former artistic director of the Manitoba Theatre Centre, now associate artistic director of the Stratford Shakespearean Festival.

(*Right*) Scene from *The Great White Hope* by Howard Sackler at the Arena Stage, Washington, D.C., December, 1967. James Earl Jones, second from left, Lou Gilbert, third from left. Directed by Edwin Sherin; costumes by Marjorie Slaiman.

(*Below*) Scene from *Serjeant Musgrave's Dance* by John Arden at the Arena Stage, Washington, D.C., March, 1966. Directed by Edwin Sherin; scenery by Robin Wagner; costumes by Nancy Potts.

Sharon Gans in the title role of *Beclch* by Rochelle Owens at the Theatre of the Living Arts, Philadelphia, December, 1966. Directed by Andre Gregory; scenery by John Conklin; costumes by Eugene Lee.

Stage and auditorium of the Tyrone Guthrie Theatre, Minneapolis, during a performance of *The Three Sisters* by Anton Chekhov, 1963.

Douglas Campell as Clytemnestra and Robin Gammell as Cassandra in *The House of Atreus*, adapted by John Lewin from the *Oresteia* by Aeschylus, at the Tyrone Guthrie Theatre, July, 1967. Directed by Sir Tyrone Guthrie; designed by Tanya Moiseiwitsch.

(*Below left*) Lee Richardson as Apollo and Len Cariou as Orestes in *The House of Atreus*.

(*Below right*) Douglas Campbell as Clytemnestra in *The House of Atreus*.

(*Above*) Scene from *The Cavern* by Jean Anouilh at the Playhouse in the Park, Cincinnati, 1967. Directed by Michael Kahn; scenery by Douglas W. Schmidt; costumes by Caley Summers.

Irene Dailey as the Cook and Lynn Milgrim as the Kitchenmaid in *The Cavern*.

(Above) Scene from *Twelfth Night* by William Shakespeare at the Hartford Stage Company, Hartford, Conn., April, 1966. Directed by Paul Weidner; scenery and costumes by John Conklin.

Scene from *The Servant of Two Masters* by Carlo Goldoni at the Hartford Stage Company, March, 1967. Jacqueline Coslow as Clarice and Henry Thomas as Pantalone. Directed by Paul Weidner; scenery by John Conklin; costumes by Caley Summers.

Scene from *After the Fall* by Arthur Miller at the Repertory Theatre of Lincoln Center, New York, January, 1964. Jason Robards, Jr., seated far left, as Quentin. Directed by Elia Kazan; setting by Jo Mielziner. *(Photo by Inge Morath–Magnum)*

Scene from *The Caucasian Chalk Circle* by Bertolt Brecht at the Repertory Theatre of Lincoln Center, New York, March, 1966. Robert Symonds as Azdak, seated at right. Directed by Jules Irving; scenery, costumes, and masks by James Hart Stearns.

Morris Carnovsky as King Lear in the American Shakespeare Festival's 1965 revival at Stratford, Conn. Directed by Allen Fletcher; scenery and costumes by Will Steven Armstrong.

(Below) Scene from *Journey to Jefferson*, adapted by Robert L. Flynn from *As I Lay Dying* by William Faulkner, at the Dallas Theatre Center. Directed by Paul Baker; scenery by Virgil Beavers; costumes by Mary Sue Fridge.

The APA Repertory Company in *You Can't Take It with You* by George S. Kaufman and Moss Hart, New York, 1965. Rosemary Harris as Alice and Clayton Corzatte as Tony, seated foreground. Directed by Ellis Rabb; scenery by James Tilton; costumes by Nancy Potts.

Scene from *Pantagleize* by Michel de Ghelderode in the APA production, New York, December, 1967. From left to right: Nicholas Martin as a Poet, Ellis Rabb as Pantagleize, Sydney Walker as Innocenti, Patricia Conolly as Rachel Silbershatz, Keene Curtis as an Anarchist, and Nat Simmons as Bamboola. Directed by John Houseman and Ellis Rabb; scenery by James Tilton; costumes by Nancy Potts. (*Photo by Eileen Darby–Graphic House*)

(*Above left*) Rosemary Harris as Lady Teazle in *The School for Scandal* by Richard Brinsley Sheridan in the APA Repertory Company production, New York, November, 1966. Directed by Ellis Rabb; costumes by Nancy Potts.

(*Above right*) Helen Hayes as Mrs. Candour, Ellis Rabb as Joseph Surface, and Rosemary Harris as Lady Teazle in *The School for Scandal.*

Tony van Bridge in the title role of *Galileo* by Bertolt Brecht, with Brian Norman as the young Andrea Sarti, at the Charles Playhouse, Boston, January, 1966. Directed by Michael Murray; scenery and costumes by William D. Roberts. (*Photo by Joseph C. Towler, Jr.*)

Scene from *Six Characters in Search of an Author* by Luigi Pirandello in the American Conservatory Production, San Francisco, 1967. From left to right: Jennifer Nebesky as the Girl, Frank Kelleher as the Boy, Barbara Colby as the Step-Daughter, Paul Shenar as the Son, Josephine Nichols as the Mother, and Richard A. Dysart as the Father. Directed by William Ball and Byron Ringland.

Rene Auberjonois flies through the air as Lord Fancourt Babberly in the American Conservatory Theatre production of *Charley's Aunt* by Brandon Thomas, San Francisco, 1967. Directed by Edward Hastings; scenery by Stuart Wurtzel; costumes by William French.

(*Above*) Rene Auberjonois in the title role of *Tartuffe* by Molière, with DeAnn Mears as Elmire, in the American Conservatory Theatre production, San Francisco, 1967. Directed by William Ball; scenery by Stuart Wurtzel; costumes by Jane Greenwood.

Paul Shenar as Brother Julian in the American Conservatory Theatre production of *Tiny Alice* by Edward Albee, San Francisco, 1967. Directed by William Ball; scenery by Stuart Wurtzel.

(*Above*) The Delacorte Theatre of the New York Shakespeare Festival in Central Park. The crowd, half-hidden by the trees, is lined up almost all the way around the lake.

Scene from Shakespeare's *Measure for Measure*, produced by the New York Shakespeare Festival at the Delacorte Theatre, July, 1966. Directed by Michael Kahn; scenery by Ming Cho Lee; costumes by Theoni V. Aldredge.

The Mobile Theatre of the New York Shakespeare Festival. Onstage is A Midsummer Night's Dream, directed by Jack Sydow, 1964. (*Photo by George E. Joseph*)

(*Right*) The new Florence Sutro Anspacher Theatre, opened October, 1967: the first of three auditoriums to be completed at the new Public Theatre of the New York Shakespeare Festival.

Stage and auditorium of the Festival Theatre, Stratford Shakespearean Festival, Stratford, Ontario. (*Photo by Peter Smith*)

Scene from *Mahagonny* by Bertolt Brecht and Kurt Weill at the Stratford Shakespearean Festival, Stratford, Ontario, July, 1965. At left, Muriel Greenspon as Mrs. Begbick. Directed by Jean Gascon; designed by Brian Jackson. (*Photo by Peter Smith*)

Bosco displayed more authority and panache than anyone else in the cast.

One down.

Shortly after *The Alchemist* closed, a significant event didn't happen at Lincoln Center. At the Vivian Beaumont there was, and is, a highly serviceable second auditorium downstairs, with 299 seats and a thrust stage, intended for experimental performances and called The Forum. Although they had operated two auditoriums simultaneously in San Francisco, Blau and Irving ignored The Forum during their first season in New York, evidently feeling that they had enough on their hands as it was. Finally they announced that The Forum would open on December 3, 1966:

> The opening production, *In 3 Zones* by Wilford Leach, is the first in a series of new plays by American writers planned for the season. A new play will be done in The Forum because it is searching for something original in form or because it has a lot on its mind or because it exercises a writer of considerable promise who may have a good deal more to say another time. The Forum is a place for a hearing, a place to exercise the imaginations of writers, painters, sculptors and musicians. It is a center for an active dialogue with new voices.

In 3 Zones was duly put into rehearsal under Herbert Blau's direction, and it actually played a few previews. Then mechanical difficulties set in, and the production never opened. The Forum remained unused for the rest of the season. The reasons for this were financial, Irving says; but even in the theatre, when there's really a will there tends to be a way.

Meanwhile, Blau and Irving unveiled their next major production: Federico Garcia Lorca's tragedy of *Yerma*—another failure. Lorca wrote some plays that show distinct signs that they might be viable in English, but *Yerma* is not among them. I am willing to believe that were I a Spaniard, born to an understanding of the society in which Lorca's tragedy is rooted, and to an appreciation of Lorca's richly metaphorical style undistorted by translation, I might admire it greatly. Lacking these advantages, I can still get occasional intimations of its quality from reading or seeing the play in English; but on the whole I find it alien to the point of ludicrousness, and an execrable choice for a repertory theatre that exists to play in English in New York.

Yerma herself is a Spanish peasant woman who spends an hour and forty minutes saying "Ai! Ai! I cannot have a child!" or words to that effect, after which she strangles her husband. In the Age of the Pill, at a time and place where more and more people are occupied with the question of how *not* to have children, Yerma's problem seems extremely remote. It is impossible for us (for me, anyhow, and I doubt if I'm alone) to understand a woman being driven out of her mind by the fact that she has no child. Her monomania rapidly becomes a nuisance.

The production was quite creditable, as lost causes go. Gloria Foster could still have used some work on her diction, but she was strong and never embarrassing in the title role. Her husband was played by a lean, dark, graceful young man named Frank Langella, who must be one of the very few American actors capable of playing convincingly a character who talks about his "honor" in the Mediterranean sense. Both actors were new to the company; neither, to date, has appeared with it since. The director was also new: John Hirsch, co-founder of the Manitoba Theatre Center, and an important figure in the affairs of the Stratford (Ontario) Shakespearean Festival. This was the first time that Blau and Irving had brought in an outside director, and Mr. Hirsch accomplished a production that should have satisfied anyone who wanted to see *Yerma* in English. But who *would* want to see *Yerma* in English, except students of Spanish literature and amateurs of the impossible?

Two down.

During the run of *Yerma*, Herbert Blau resigned from the Repertory Theatre because, he said, "the climate is no longer right for me to do what I came to do in the form I had in mind." Jules Irving, Blau's partner for fifteen years, was left to carry on alone. The parting was amicable. It must have been clear to both of them that the attempt to run the Repertory Theatre of Lincoln Center with a company of young unknowns, doing the tough plays admired by the academic avant-garde, had been a failure. Blau had always been the rigid idealist; he resigned. Irving, the supple, practical one, remained.

Less than two weeks after Blau resigned, Irving booked a Broadway show into the Vivian Beaumont Theatre for the following fall. *The New York Times* carried the news that an all-star revival of *The Little Foxes* by Lillian Hellman, directed by Mike Nichols, and already announced for Broadway by the producer Saint Subber, would open instead at the Beaumont. It would be the first play on the 1967–68 subscription series, but Mr. Subber would supervise the production, and the Repertory Theatre's acting company would have nothing to do with it. Now I myself do not believe that anything labeled "Broadway" is necessarily poison. *The Little Foxes* is not a profound play, but it is a powerful one; I would far rather see a good production of it than a bad production of *The Alchemist,* or any production of *The Condemned of Altona* or *Yerma.* But Blau and Irving had promised, "ideologically we shall remain as we have always been, three thousand miles from Broadway"; now Irving had broken that promise.

Of course, *The Little Foxes* will sell a lot of subscriptions. And if Broadway is not the bogeyman, and the play is a sound one, perhaps taking it in at the Beaumont is a sensible compromise, a refusal to be prevented by dogmatic rigidity from doing what is best for the theatre and its audience? If it were merely a matter of using the theatre when it would otherwise lie idle (as was the case with Peter Ustinov's play *The Unknown Soldier and His Wife,* booked in for the summer of 1967), I would agree. But *The Little Foxes,* as Irving says, "takes me off the hook of doing a fourth production." It is another disturbing indication that Irving is not really very eager to produce plays himself. Moreover, it egregiously violates the principle that a subsidized theatre, a theatre that receives a tax-break and competes with charities for the philanthropic dollar on the grounds that it is performing a public service, should not do what commercial organizations could and would do just as well, when it could be performing services that nobody else can provide.

The Little Foxes can best be defended on the premise (which we all hope, and believe, is no longer true) that the less the Repertory Theatre has to do for itself, the better off we all are. This view was given considerable support, however, by its next venture after *Yerma:* the world première of *The East Wind* by one Leo Lehman, which happened on February 9, 1967. At last the Repertory Theatre was doing its duty by a new play; were it not for the theatre's previous record, expectation might have run high. I am able to report that *The East Wind* was about a couple of European refugees who didn't like each other very much; but, although I saw the thing, I am baffled as to what else I can say about it. How were we supposed to take this peculiar chronicle? Why were we supposed to take it? I am absolutely mystified by what the Repertory Theatre authorities, or the author, or anybody connected with the enterprise, could have had in mind.

Three down.

The East Wind was followed, none too soon, by the first unqualified artistic success that the Repertory Theatre has had since it was founded: *Galileo* by Bertolt Brecht, directed by John Hirsch, with Anthony Quayle in the title role. (*Galileo* was originally to have been directed by Herbert Blau, and the title role was to have been played by Rod Steiger; even before Blau left, the principle of outside star casting had been accepted. But Steiger called in sick, and we know what happened to Blau.)

The production was beautifully designed. Robin Wagner's set was a big square platform with a large scaffoldy tower at each side, more scaffolding overhead, a screen at the back, and a sign that said "GALILEO." When the action moved to Florence, a pictorial map, with Brunelleschi's dome prominent in the center, came down from the flies, along with a sign saying "CIVITAS FIORENZA"; the elegant grandeur of papal Rome was clearly established with a few hangings, a few candelabra, and a few richly costumed extras. Martin Aronstein's lighting made the most of Mr. Wagner's work.

Mr. Quayle's Galileo was slightly lacking in charisma, but had the keenness of mind and the gusto that the part calls for. He was very moving as the old, broken Galileo, clutching at his shawl, and probing with pathetic irony for some indication that his recantation had not stopped the progress of science altogether. (Brecht would probably not have wanted this scene to be so moving, since he wished, above all, that we should reject Galileo for having recanted; but it would have been misplaced piety to allow Brecht's ideological commitments to get in the way of his talent.)

Mr. Hirsch created some beautiful theatrical moments. When Galileo destroyed his daughter's chance of marriage by defying her aristocratic fiancé in the interests of scientific freedom, the poor girl was left standing pathetically in her wedding dress before a huge, red image of the sun. And when the Pope finally gave his consent for Galileo to be interrogated by the Inquisition, he had a long, pointedly papal exit in his glorious robes.

The production disproved a Brechtian dogma by being no less lucid and stimulating for being emotionally involving as well. It was *because* we were moved by the effect of Galileo's recantation on his disciples that we were prepared to understand its significance. At the end of the play, the applause was real and enthusiastic, and Mr. Quayle was deservedly bravoed. If the Repertory Theatre can maintain this standard, it will be one of the finest in the country (which, considering the resources at its disposal, is exactly what it ought to be).

This last production of the theatre's 1966–67 season adumbrated a viable policy for the future: good and significant plays for which the audience is ready (they have heard of Brecht by now and are prepared to accept him), performed by a resident company augmented, when necessary, by well-known—but well-cast and highly talented—actors from outside. This is not noble and foolhardy, as the old Workshop policy may have been. It leaves to others the tasks of discovery and confrontation that the Workshop seems to have performed. But it is a useful and sensible way to run the Repertory Theatre of Lincoln Center.

Irving himself is eager to defend his policy, and he makes a strong case for it, with the aid of words like "practical," sensible," and "pragmatic." "My objective here," he insists, "is exactly the same as it was in San Francisco, but I think the fundamental difference is the way we go about achieving this objective"—the objective being the development of a permanent company. "Ideologically, I don't think I've changed one iota from what I was in San Francisco, but I've recognized that I'm in Rome, and when in Rome you've got to do it as the Romans do it."

In San Francisco, there was "a commitment for slow growth without the demand for instant success." It was possible, therefore, to start with a body of actors and stick to them. Whitehead and Kazan, he feels, did essentially the same thing by signing actors for up to two and a half years, and building the repertory around them. At the beginning of their reign at Lincoln Center, he and Blau also worked on this principle, signing actors for an entire season on an as-cast basis.

But at Lincoln Center, amid the travertine and the tile and all the other manifestations of the Edifice Complex, "instant success" is demanded. "There is an expectation in these surroundings . . . the problem here, very simply stated, is to create a theatre in the glare of the spotlight . . . I think it's going to be a question of time before the identity of the company emerges fully . . . During that time of development I must maintain the highest standards possible." Therefore, during the period of growth, theatre artists will be accepted into the company for a season, or for three shows, or for two, or one. "The previous policies were exclusive. The present one is catholic. The theatre is open to the best outside talents available." The hope is that those actors and directors who work well with the company will be induced to return, and eventually to become part of the company. (Anthony Quayle, for instance, will return to direct *Tiger at the Gates*.) Thus a nucleus of artists will evolve that will grow larger and stronger with time. Irving does not demand total devotion. "I think it's healthy for an actor to identify with his company, but to be free to do something else if the schedule permits it. But in no sense does this negate the long-term objective of forming a company."

Irving does not feel that his policy in regard to play-choice has changed significantly. "My philosophy of the theatre is pragmatic. I produce plays which excite me, which I would like to work on." He wants the Repertory Theatre to be "committed to putting on the most meaningful and exciting plays, and that's not any different from what we did in San Francisco." He does concede one thing: "The only change might be the embracing of a *Danton* at an early stage in the history of a theatre might have been too early a choice." Which indicates, rather faintly, what is obviously a reality for the immediate future at least: a go-slow policy on "difficult" plays.

The 1967–68 season began with Mr. Nichols' star-studded guest production of *The Little Foxes*, which turned out to be both very popular and very good. It was followed by the Repertory Theatre's own production of Bernard Shaw's *Saint Joan*, with Diana Sands in the title role. The fact that Miss Sands is Negro functioned, if anything, to her advantage in this part: Joan is an outsider, a village girl among lords and kings, and Miss Sands' color served as a sort of metaphor for this. (Its effect was somewhat diminished by the presence of other Negro actors in the cast.) Her Joan had, in addition, plenty of genuine emotion, plenty of individuality, and plenty of authority. But though Miss Sands is very talented, I came away with the impression that Saint Joan was not her part. Her Joan was somehow not vulnerable enough; I was never caught up short by the realization that here was a little girl confronted by tremendous and terrible realities. And, perhaps because she was never a very spiritual Joan, never really rapt in the love of God, her climaxes never burst into incandescence.

What was most remarkable about this production was the quality of the supporting cast. The old crew from the Actor's Workshop were mostly relegated to bit parts and understudy assignments; the major roles were taken by a sort of resident-theatre all-star team. John Hirsch, who directed, brought William Hutt and Tony van Bridge with him from Stratford, Ontario; Mr. Hutt as the Earl of Warwick beautifully combined urbanity and toughness, while Mr. van Bridge was a splendidly formidable Bishop Cauchon. As Dunois, the Bastard of Orleans, Philip Bosco of the American Shakespeare Festival proved, as he has done so often, that masculinity and lyricism are not mutually exclusive. ("Lyricism" means that words tend to sound like poetry when Mr. Bosco says them; "masculinity" means, in this case, that it was nevertheless easy to believe that Mr. Bosco's Bastard commanded an army.) Edward Zang, of the Charles Playhouse in Boston, must have been the most nervous, fidgety, peevish, skinny Dauphin ever seen; his performance was right at the edge of caricature, and did not evoke much sympathy for the poor put-upon kinglet, but it was a delicate, vivid, and highly entertaining piece of character-work. And Stephen Joyce, formerly of the New York Shakespeare Festival, the American Shakespeare Festival, the San Diego Shakespeare Festival, the Seattle Repertory Theatre, the Arena Stage, and the Los Angeles Theatre Group, brought tears to my eyes with his reading of Brother Martin's description of the burning. Already, it would seem, the resident professional theatre has developed some remarkable talents; it was pleasant to see so many of them assembled in one place.

After *Saint Joan* in the Repertory Theatre's schedule come *Tiger at the Gates*, directed by Anthony Quayle, and *Cyrano de Bergerac*, with Richard Basehart in the title role. According to Mr. Irving, "These three selections have a common theatricality and sweep ideally suited to the size and scope of the Beaumont main stage. They are plays designed for audiences, and the comment they make upon our times is compelling without being didactic. Each of the plays is about an unrelenting individualist who maintains his or her integrity in the face of the corruption surrounding him." Furthermore, all three plays are nice safe choices; unlike the plays of previous seasons, they have all been consumer-tested in New York within the last ten or fifteen years. But I have been maintaining throughout this book that the fact that a play is popular does not *necessarily* mean that it is not worth doing. *Saint Joan* and *Tiger at the Gates* have as much to say to us as any play that the Lincoln Center Repertory has ever done. As for *Cyrano*, well, as Max Beerbohm says, "even if *Cyrano* be not a classic, it is at least a wonderfully ingenious counterfeit of one."

I have as yet found no opportunity to mention the programs that the theatre mounts annually to tour high schools in the New York area or the arrangements for selling tickets to students at $1.50 apiece; these were instituted under the Blau-Irving administration, and will be continued.

Furthermore, Mr. Irving has finally bestirred himself to activate The Forum, having been given $25,000 for the purpose by the Rockefeller Foundation. In addition to a series of Monday night performances without décor, presented before an invited audience, there are to be four full public productions there every season, "with an emphasis on new American writers," says the handout. The first of these productions, which opened in November, 1967, was a bill of two mediocre short plays by a television writer named Mayo Simon. The first one, *Walking to Waldheim*, accurately subtitled "a comedy almost to the end," might have been written by a second-rate Jewish Thornton Wilder. It depicts a carload of relatives on their way to a funeral; one by one they get out and walk, by which we are meant to understand that they are dead.

Walking to Waldheim has some good, idiomatic Jewish writing, and there isn't anything much wrong with it, but there isn't anything very interesting about it either, and good acting by Aline MacMahon and others was not enough to sustain it all the way. The second play, *Happiness,* was a dialogue between a feeble old man (Jacob Ben-Ami) and a lively old bag in a red wig (Lili Darvas). What they were doing together I never understood; the tone of their activities was more or less comic, with pathetic overtones.

Clearly the Repertory Theatre does not intend to stint on The Forum; it placed some first-rate performers at the service of Mr. Simon's little efforts. But why did Mr. Irving choose to open his experimental theatre with such a couple of pallid, conventional scripts? Once again it looks as if he is determined to play it safe. But playing it safe can sometimes, in the long run, be dangerous. The Repertory Theatre has proudly announced that ten per cent of all seats in The Forum will be available free of charge to students "and young people from low socio-economic areas." The poor, in other words. But plays like Mr. Simon's are likely to drive young people back to the movies for life.

Upstairs, however, in the main auditorium of the Beaumont, where it is possible to play it safe and still produce first-rate scripts, things are going better. I was restrained in my admiration for the Repertory Theatre's *Saint Joan,* but it was certainly superior to most of what preceded it on that lavishly-equipped stage: good enough, even, so that it might be worth passing up a movie to go and see it. I find it hard to admire Mr. Irving's courage, but it is possible to respect his shrewdness. And shrewd, prudent men, however uninspiring their example may be to contemplate, have their uses. Jules Irving seems to have a gift for survival. He seems to have concluded, from bitter experience, that his job at Lincoln Center is to run an Establishment company. But the National Theatre of Great Britain is an Establishment company, and they're doing all right. Not to mention the Comédie Française.

THE
NONRESIDENT
PROFESSIONAL
THEATRES

One of the recurrent themes of this book is that a theatre derives its nature far more from the man who runs it than from the city in which it happens to find itself. The most extreme cases of this tendency are three theatres which have passed all or most of their careers as touring organizations without any fixed residence at all. Two of these theatres have more or less settled down, confining their touring to the summer months; the third was intended from the beginning as a touring group, and has every intention of remaining one.

The APA Repertory Company

"APA" stands for "Association of Producing Artists." The full name must have meant something to somebody once, but nowadays the company is universally known by its initials. It was founded in 1960 by Ellis Rabb, at that time a twenty-nine-year-old character actor who had also done some directing. Mr. Rabb is still its artistic director; what the APA is, he has made it.

The new organization's first engagement was in Hamilton, Bermuda, where it opened on May 12, 1960, with a repertory of three plays: an adaptation of Schnitzler's *Anatol*, with music taken from Offenbach, directed by Mr. Rabb; *Man and Superman*, directed by Allen Fletcher, and *The Seagull*, directed by Mr.

Rabb. Things were sparse in the early days. Rosemary Harris, who was Mr. Rabb's wife and the company's leading lady until 1967, used to pitch in and sew costumes. Jack McQuiggan, who has lately rejoined the company after working at the Milwaukee Repertory Theatre and the Trinity Square Playhouse in Providence, remembers when the APA office was half of his apartment; he and the organization split the rent. After Bermuda came a short tour on the summer-stock circuit, and a stand at Princeton University. There, during the fall of 1960, the company mounted eight plays in seven weeks—plus five plays by Shakespeare, all new productions, in eight weeks beginning in February, 1961. After another summer-stock tour, the company spent the fall of 1961 at the Fred Miller Theatre in Milwaukee (now the Milwaukee Repertory Theatre).

On March 21, 1962, after nearly two years of slogging, Mr. Rabb brought the APA into New York for a six-week stand at the Folksbiene Playhouse, the most inaccessible of all Off-Broadway theatres. From this engagement I remember rather dimly a modern-dress production of *The Seagull*, which seemed to me ill-advised. The one moment which has remained vividly in my mind is the appearance in the last act, in a black raincoat, of Miss Harris as Nina. In the third act of *The Seagull*, Nina is still a girl; in the fourth act, two years later, she has had a disastrous love affair and borne a child who died, and she has become a woman. All this Miss Harris conveyed; by some art too deep for analysis she made you see and feel that she had been profoundly changed by suffering, that she had become a different person. In later years, when Miss Harris has sometimes seemed to be merely engaged in peddling her (admittedly irresistible) charm, the memory of this performance has reminded me that she is a real actress, and a rare one.

The company spent most of the 1962–63 season at the Ann Arbor campus of the University of Michigan, with time out to tour the Michigan countryside. It returned to Ann Arbor in the fall of 1963, and in March, 1964, it opened at the Off-Broadway Phoenix Theatre in New York. Its repertory consisted of *Right You Are* by Pirandello, *The Tavern* by George M. Cohan, a double bill of *Scapin* and *Impromptu at Versailles* by Molière, and *The Lower Depths* by Maxim Gorky. *Right You Are, The Tavern,* and *Scapin* had all been mounted by the APA at Princeton in the fall of 1960; the APA is one of the few American companies that are serious about amassing a permanent library of productions which can be revived again and again over the years. Except for *The Tavern*, I saw all the APA's productions that season; my impression was of a sound, workmanlike company from which something, some element of sparkle, was missing.

When Mr. Rabb and his colleagues returned to New York in December, 1964, after another fall season at Ann Arbor, I realized that the missing ingredient had been Rosemary Harris, who had accepted an invitation from Sir Laurence Olivier to spend the 1963–64 season at the British National Theatre. At the Phoenix in 1964–65, she dominated all three plays in the repertory. She was exquisite as Ann Whitefield in *Man and Superman* (a character she had been playing, at intervals, since the old Bermuda days), intriguing as the title character in Giraudoux's baffling Biblical drama *Judith*, and delightful as Natasha in an adaptation of *War and Peace*.

Ellis Rabb's direction of *War and Peace*, and the adaptation itself (made by Alfred Neumann, Erwin Piscator, and Guntram Prufer) were distinguished for an effective manipulation of theatrical devices; the Battle of Borodino, for instance, was described by a narrator who moved dolls to illustrate his points, while the actors playing Napoleon and General Kutusov stood above and made pronouncements. The fine cast included Donald Moffat as Andrei and Ronald Bishop as Pierre; Sydney Walker as fierce old Prince Bolkonski was particularly vivid and lovable.

Man and Superman, however, had problems, the greatest of which was Mr. Rabb's performance as John Tanner. Mr. Rabb is unbelievably tall and unbelievably thin; he looks like Plastic Man. His special talent as an actor is for grotesquerie, both comic and serious; he has given brilliant—unsurpassable—performances in parts such as Smee, the meek pirate who spends his time at the sewing machine in *Peter Pan*, and Tiresias, the blind seer in *Oedipus the King*. But John Tanner is not like that; "a certain high-chested carriage of the shoulders," says Shaw, "a lofty pose of the head, and the Olympian majesty with which a mane, or rather a huge wisp, of hazel-colored hair is thrown back from an imposing brow, suggest Jupiter rather than Apollo." Mr. Rabb's demeanor in this role was distinctly swishy, which gave Tanner's anti-feminine outbursts a nasty tinge that Shaw did not intend and that worked against the play. One problem with having an actor in charge of a company is that actors are not always the best judges of their own talents.

It is only fair to add, however, that the ideal of the company is important to the APA; it is most emphatically not a mere pretext for one or two actors to spread themselves. Important roles in *Man and Superman* were double-cast; at many performances Donald Moffat played Tanner, Nancy Marchand played Ann, and Miss Harris took the small part of Violet. As the company grew, so did this practice of multiple casting, until nowadays two, three, or even four actors are ready to go on in every role. It might even be said that in this zeal for artistic democracy, the talents of the company's leading players are under-utilized. Robert Brustein reports, for instance, that at the performance he saw, Miss Harris played Violet "with such elegance and *esprit* that Nancy Marchand, playing Ann, seemed leaden by comparison—and the production was thrown out of balance."*

Nevertheless, this second season at the Phoenix was a roaring success with the critics and the public alike. The engagement was extended through the summer, and the APA played to near-capacity houses at the 299-seat Phoenix for nearly three hundred performances. The next step was obvious. The Phoenix management, which had been running a noncommercial theatre in New York since 1964 (with several changes of mind as to what kind of theatre it ought to be), prepared to give up its premises (in more ways than one) to devote itself exclusively to sponsoring the APA on Broadway and elsewhere. The official billing now reads, "APA–Phoenix . . . presents the APA Repertory Company."

Meanwhile the company went off to Ann Arbor as usual for its fall season at the University of Michigan; there Ibsen's *The Wild Duck*, *Herakles* by Archibald MacLeish (a world première), and *You Can't Take It with You* by Kaufman and Hart were added to the repertory. Unfortunately there was not enough money available to bring a full repertory season to Broadway as planned; but to keep the company's hand in, as it were, *You Can't Take It with You* was brought in for a continuous run. In November, 1965, it

* Robert Brustein, *Seasons of Discontent* (New York, 1967), p. 266.

opened at the 995-seat Lyceum Theatre on Forty-fifth Street. The production received what press agents refer to as "unanimous raves" from the critics, and had an eminently successful thirty-one-week run. After five years of hand-to-mouth wandering, the APA had successfully challenged the commercial theatre on its home grounds, and triumphantly withstood the comparison.

You Can't Take It with You had not exactly been neglected in the twenty-nine years since its first production. Generations of high school drama clubs had galumphed their way through it, causing many citizens to regard it with some degree of dubiety. The APA's deft and affectionate revival made it seem less like a warhorse and more like a minor classic. The Sycamore ménage, that durable collection of eccentrics, turned out to resemble a band of drugless proto-hippies of all ages, each gently engaged in doing his thing. In fact they embody the hippie ethic rather better than the hippies themselves, since instead of opting out of bourgeois conformity into a new conformity with rigidities of its own in which everybody's "thing" turns out to look suspiciously like everybody else's, they have used their freedom from the rat-race to develop their own individualities. Thus Grandfather goes to commencements, throws darts, and raises snakes; father and his friend Mr. De Pinna (who came eight years ago to deliver the ice, and stayed) make fireworks; daughter Essie dances and makes candy; son-in-law Ed prints, makes masks, and plays the xylophone; mother Penny writes plays because eight years ago a typewriter was delivered by mistake.

The effect was strangely ingratiating; the Sycamores, as played by the APA, were so lovable that they just escaped being too lovable. Donald Moffat played Grandpa as Robert Frost; Dee Victor was Penny the playwright; Gordon Gould was at the xylophone, Jennifer Harmon was in the toe-shoes, Sydney Walker and Joseph Bird were in the cellar making fireworks. The juvenile and the ingénue, two rather weakly written parts, were vivified by Clayton Corzatte and the ineffable Rosemary Harris. But no performance overshadowed the others; it was an ensemble success.

Mr. Rabb directed the play as a period piece. From all accounts the thirties were pretty awful to live through, but now that they're over they have acquired, when viewed in a certain light, a very winning sort of dowdy charm. Mr. Rabb and the company, with the help of James Tilton's set and Nancy Potts's costumes, made the most of this charm without detriment to the play's abundant hilarity. A few stretches of sentimentality and sententiousness are built into the script, and there was—there must of necessity be—a certain air of escapist light-mindedness about the whole thing. Still, reviving this play at this time performed the always useful function of reminding a "success"-fixated society that there is an alternative to the compulsive imperative of the Protestant Ethic, that there is something to be said for going off and doing your thing even if you are over thirty. And since the APA company has been doing just that quite arduously for several years, they had in a sense earned their right to say so.

The success of *You Can't Take It with You* made the idea of the APA playing repertory on Broadway seem more viable than ever. And so, after visits to Los Angeles, Ann Arbor, and Toronto, the company opened a thirty-week season at the Lyceum in November, 1966, this time to present not a single production but a rotating repertory of six plays. The company of thirty-three included many familiar APA faces and one notable new recruit: Helen Hayes. The foremost surviving representative of the pre-Method generation, of the genteel tradition in the American theatre, had been moved to place her decades of experience, her splendid professionalism, her talent, and her limitations at the disposal of a young company striving to create a new tradition. For the APA it was an augmentation—and a definition.

The company, to its credit, did not re-structure itself around Miss Hayes; it might be said indeed that her abilities were not given the scope they deserved. In *The School for Scandal*, which opened the season, she took the small part of Mrs. Candour; attention was focused on Rosemary Harris as Lady Teazle and Ellis Rabb as Joseph Surface. Miss Harris was, of course, irresistible. As somebody once said about somebody else, "There's language in her eye, her lip, her cheek—nay, her foot speaks." Especially her dainty foot, flashing beneath her skirt as she kicked it forward in delicately hoydenish glee. (One of the finest touches in the performance was the way she showed us the bouncy country girl under the enthusiastically fashionable town lady.) It was easy to see what old Sir Peter, her husband, saw in her; but Miss Harris, in the delight she took in teasing him and playing cute for his benefit, showed us also (which is far harder) what she saw in him. When Lady Teazle's indiscretions were exposed in the famous screen scene, her remorse was not just a gesture, but a beautiful moment of pathos. In rapidly spoken passages, Miss Harris has a way of fetching breath in great desperate gasps that sometimes makes it painful to listen to her; a couple of times, in *The School for Scandal*, she seemed on the verge of strangulation. If she could cure this technical defect, she would be unsurpassed in this kind of part. As for Mr. Rabb, he played the hypocritical Joseph with sneaky-snakey nastiness.

American actors are famous for their inability to play what used to be called "old comedy"; a lot of people hoped that in the APA we finally had a company that could do an eighteenth-century play like *The School for Scandal* with the same perfection of style that, say, Abe Burrows and his troops were able to bring to *Cactus Flower*—with the same complete command, in other words, that the APA itself exercises over *You Can't Take It with You*. In the event, these hopes were not quite fulfilled, even though the company had been doing the play for four years.

This sort of material demands prettiness and grace from all concerned, yet James Tilton's sets were cheap-looking and drab. None of the acting was really bad, but several small parts were given substantially less than their full value. The play begins slowly, with a great deal of exposition and gossiping about gossip, and Mr. Rabb, who directed, found no way to make all this particularly interesting. Shortly before the intermission, however, things fell into place, and the second half of the evening was a pleasure. The production as a whole was less polished than John Gielgud's Broadway revival, but it lacked the peculiar brittle coldness of the Gielgud version. Gielgud made the play an exquisitely executed verbal ballet; in Mr. Rabb's hands it became—thanks largely to Miss Harris—more of a play about people.

In addition to *The School for Scandal*, the repertory included three other revivals of previous APA productions, and two productions new to New York. *Right You Are*, Pirandello's shell game with reality as the pea, was given a highly polished performance. Helen Hayes was the unhappy Signora Frola, making an entrance like Queen Victoria, all dignity and bereavement; Sydney Walker was her distraught son-in-law, and Clayton Corzatte was Lamberto

Laudisi, Pirandello's *raisonneur*. Well done as it was, the play struck me as cold and dry, more important for its influence on theatre history than for its intrinsic merits. *War and Peace*, another revival, looked as good as ever in the larger theatre. Clayton Corzatte, Donald Moffat, and Rosemary Harris were once again the Narrator, Andrei, and Natasha. But it occurred to me that this pleasant, sentimental pageant, full of hand-kissing and heel-clicking, flags and uniforms, did not have over-much to do with Tolstoy. About the third revival, *You Can't Take It with You*, nothing further needs to be said.

The first new production, *We, Comrades Three*, was not a play at all, but a staging of Walt Whitman's poetry, adapted by the late Richard Baldridge and directed by Ellis Rabb and Hal George. It was not simply a poetry-reading; the five costumed performers had been given plenty of action. There was no dramatic structure, however, and no characters to speak of. At the production I saw (this production, like the others, was extensively double-cast), Marco St. John, Sydney Walker, and Will Geer played Whitman at various stages of his career, and Helen Hayes and Patricia Conolly played various women. Miss Hayes was her familiar self even when, wearing a crown and a red-white-and-blue, starry-and-stripey cape, she was forced to stalk about the stage brandishing a sword and pretending to be "Columbia." Few actresses, forced to impersonate the Gem of the Ocean, could escape being ridiculous, but Miss Hayes, petite and feminine as always, was never for a moment in danger of losing her dignity. The other performers were also entirely professional.

The problem was the material. Whitman's habit of making his points several times over did not conduce to a lively evening. Ideas and perceptions unremarkable in themselves were expanded into long catalogues of indiscriminately chosen detail. It was an evening of remorselessly public rhetoric. I left the theatre with the feeling that old Walt must have been somewhat of an old gasbag, and I was evidently not alone in this; *We, Comrades Three* was the only production of the season that was not a critical success. The public didn't buy it either, and it was soon dropped from the repertory.

The other production new to New York (it had been done in Ann Arbor) was *The Wild Duck*, directed by Stephen Porter. The play is Ibsen's own satire on Ibsenism: into the Ekdal household, which is living a fairly satisfactory life patched up out of all kinds of illusions, comes an awkward, fanatic interloper who tries to force them to "build a completely new mode of life—a way of living together in truth, free of all deception," and causes nothing but trouble.

It occurred to me while watching *The Wild Duck* that the APA has the best collection of twiddly actors in America. Where else could you find so many elaborately detailed, nicely executed character performances, so entertainingly full of twitches, fidgets, grunts, and nods? (Sydney Walker, in particular, made a memorably decayed, shuffling, floppy hulk out of poor drunken Old Ekdal.) Unfortunately, twiddling is not quite all that *The Wild Duck* requires. It is highly commendable, for example, that Clayton Corzatte, who usually plays juvenile leads for the company (though he is getting a bit old for them nowadays), can transform himself into such an interestingly odd little man when he plays Gregers Werle. But he was not really ugly and uncharming enough for Gregers, and his performance lacked the necessary cutting-edge of neurosis. It was never clear that meddling in the affairs of the Ekdals was the most exciting thing that had ever happened to Gregers, that he belonged to the dangerous breed of those who derive their keenest satisfactions from manipulating others. Mr. Corzatte's performance was one of several excellent, highly polished pieces of acting that did not really answer the demands of the play.

It has not been the APA way to *grapple* with things; its style is more of a graceful glide. Mr. Rabb and Stephen Porter have directed most of its recent productions; Mr. Porter's work has been uniformly uninspired, and even Mr. Rabb, except in the case of *You Can't Take It with You*, has seemed unable to get beyond flashy showmanship. As an acting company, the APA is an oddity in the American theatre because it is stronger on technique than guts. These actors seem to have a bias toward high comedy; they excel at playing refined ladies and gentlemen or picturesque eccentrics. The company has had Helen Hayes, Rosemary Harris, several other good actresses, and several superbly proficient but lightweight actors. So it seems, at any rate; I suspect that there is more in some of these performers than the APA plays and directors have been able to liberate. Or perhaps the APA authorities have very cleverly worked to conceal the limitations of their actors. Or perhaps both hypotheses are partly true.

After a stand at Expo 67 in Montreal as the official representative of the United States, the APA began its second annual Broadway repertory season in November, 1967, with *Pantagleize*, "A Farce to Make You Sad," by the modern Belgian playwright Michel de Ghelderode, who has had a small vogue among the theatrical-academic avant-garde. *Pantagleize* turns out to be a helter-skelter fantasia about a sweetly imbecilic fellow who accidentally gets caught up in a revolution. The APA production, with Mr. Rabb in the leading role, was finely acted and the staging by John Houseman and Mr. Rabb was full of theatre magic: a brilliant parade, for instance, consisting mostly of a few flags passing and repassing behind a wall. The sets and costumes, by James Tilton and Nancy Potts respectively, were all in stark blacks, grays, and whites, luridly lit by Mr. Tilton. As a show *Pantagleize* was effective, but underneath the razzmatazz the play seemed compounded of mediocre comedy and wan pathos, with nothing in particular to say.

To accompany *Pantagleize* in the repertory, the company mounted *The Show-Off* by George Kelly, an American comedy of the twenties, in what looked like an attempt to repeat its successes with *The Tavern* and *You Can't Take It with You*. *The Show-Off* was well-acted: Helen Hayes dominated the stage as a tetchy, gabby matriarch, working-class but formidably respectable, and Clayton Corzatte as the show-off himself was skillful and personable enough to keep this unpleasant character amusing. The production was enthusiastically reviewed, and has been very popular, for reasons I do not altogether understand. Mr. Kelly had a good ear for the banalities of ordinary conversation, and managed to derive a few chuckles from them, but in this he is greatly surpassed by Chekhov, Ionesco, and Pinter. His play struck me as a very mild little domestic comedy, with an admixture of rather arbitrary domestic drama: giving the family breadwinner a stroke seems to me a somewhat too easy way of inducing pathos. This sort of cozy, milk-and-water theatre may appeal to the middle-aged, but tends, I think, to drive young people to the movies. It made me think longingly of the violent delights of *Bonnie and Clyde.*

The third new production of the APA season was Ionesco's *Exit the King,* in which the gradual decay and ultimate death of King Berenger the First made a rather obvious metaphor for the decline and fall of each individual life, and if you like, of Western civilization or mankind in general. Had it lasted only twenty minutes or even a half an hour, it might have been greatly touching, but M. Ionesco has padded it out to a running time of an hour and a half. In the APA production, Richard Easton played the King with plenty of technique and not much emotional intensity; and if the King's death mattered so little to him, how should it matter very much to us? Rouben Ter-Arutunian's setting (a lofty, shimmering chamber with plastic walls) was the most entertaining element of a tedious evening.

Both *Exit the King* and *Pantagleize,* however, are new to New York, and represent a kind of material with which the company had not previously concerned itself. Its fourth and last new production of the season is *The Cherry Orchard,* directed by Eva Le Gallienne, who also plays Queen Marguerite in *Exit the King.* Uta Hagen plays Madame Ranevsky. These two, plus Miss Hayes, comprise a formidable assemblage of Great Ladies of the Stage; Rosemary Harris, however, having divorced Mr. Rabb, has left the company, and nobody can say when or whether she will return.

Up to now, in spite of the prestige it has lately acquired, the APA has not really been a fully-equipped general-purpose repertory company. There is something slightly superficial, slightly precious about it, a lack of urgency, of thrust, for all its enormous proficiency. Enormous proficiency is, of course, a hard item to find in the theatres this book is about; but the APA seems best suited to a city where other companies are available to handle the heavier reaches of dramatic literature.

The American Conservatory Theatre

On September 6, 1967, after more than two years of wandering and wondering, the American Conservatory Theatre announced that it would make its home in San Francisco. The ACT, then, is no longer a nonresident theatre, but I include it in this chapter because of those two years, during which it played in cities and towns from coast to coast (often not knowing where, if anywhere, it was going to play next), and because its character was firmly established long before San Francisco adopted it. Although it was set up with the Pittsburgh Playhouse in mind, it was always *at* the Playhouse rather than *of* the Playhouse. As William Ball, the ACT's managing director, has said, "The initial impetus for the group was for a structure that had continuity separate and independent from location, so the artists could perpetuate their own work whether or not a city or a board of directors happened to subscribe to it."

Unlike most American theatres, the ACT has a personality, and that personality is Mr. Ball's. Before everything, the ACT has always been Bill Ball's company; no other theatre in the country expresses its leader so intensely.

William Ball was a successful Off-Broadway director, on the threshold of fame and fortune, when he turned down *Fiddler on the Roof* and *Royal Hunt of the Sun* in order to start a theatre of his own. To help him achieve this goal, the Rockefeller Foundation came through with a grant of $115,000; additional money was raised from other sources, and on July 15, 1965, the Ball company made its debut at the Pittsburgh Playhouse. Reviews were enthusiastic; whether or not the Pittsburgh public turned out in droves is unclear, since several sets of figures seem to be in circulation. But in any case, Mr. Ball and the Playhouse management got along spectacularly badly, and when the first six months were over, the ACT left the Playhouse forever and went on the road. (The Pittsburgh part of the story is told, from another point of view, in Chapter Three.) The company's nomadic existence, said Mr. Ball, would continue until some community was willing to give it a permanent home on acceptable terms. It played engagements in Michigan, Connecticut, California, and Illinois before it was finally able to settle in San Francisco.

According to Mr. Ball, his aim in founding the ACT was to establish "an artistically creative, fertile ground, free from the pressures of intense financial operations. . . . I would like," he says, "somehow dignity and joy to be possible for the actor in his work." Having met Mr. Ball, however, I doubt if a disinterested desire to improve the lot of the actor was his only motive. He must have been aware that even a successful Broadway director is only an employee of the producer, and that once a Broadway production opens, the director's job is substantially over. For a man who likes to spread himself, a man who likes the taste of power, a permanent company of his own can offer far more scope for his inclinations—and his talents—than even the gaudiest career in other kinds of theatre. And Mr. Ball is not a shrinking violet.

The autocrat of the ACT is a strange and picturesque creature: slim, pale, exquisitely dressed (a small, elegant black sombrero perched on top of his bald head), disorganized, hypnotic, and charming. The charm, however—what I saw of it, at least—appears to be merely a performance. When I was finally, suddenly granted an interview with him, the hard-won product of half a dozen long-distance phone calls, he immediately threw an arm around my shoulder (though we had only met once before, and then just for an instant), and quoted whimsically from *Twelfth Night:* "Hast ever seen the picture of 'We three?'" (his other arm being around someone else's shoulder). Yet there is something vague in his manner; sometimes his soft voice will just trail off . . . He seems to assume that he is the center of the world, the observed of all observers. "Can I talk to you again later?" I said to him, as our very brief interview was halted at curtain time. "That depends," he replied, "on how self-assertive you are. I'll be around."

But if Mr. Ball were not slightly mad, the ACT would probably not be the exciting company it is; indeed there might be no ACT. Mr. Ball's policies are utterly, wildly impractical, yet somehow they get carried out, and they have made his company one of the finest in the country.

These policies are peculiar in two significant respects. First, the company's name—American Conservatory Theatre—was not selected merely for the sake of the acronym it makes. Several theatres maintain training programs for their actors, but the ACT really is a conservatory. Five people are listed on the roster as teachers; several other members of the theatre teach classes; guest-teachers are brought in from outside. It is claimed that every actor in the company is in training all the time. They study:

Voice Production	Stage Movement
Nonverbal Communication	Mime
Suspense	Objects and Senses
Rhetoric	Basic Acting
Scansion	Improvisation and Games
Phonetics	Jazz, Tap, Flamenco
"Yat" [that's what it says]	Histrionics
Sight Reading (Music and Dialogue)	

and also a mysterious phenomenon called the Alexander Technique, the purpose of which is "to direct the flow of energy into a state of dynamic relaxation." (A full-time Alexander trainer is on the payroll.) Naturally, all this is expensive. The ACT figures on an annual deficit of about $600,000 ($600,000! Hardly any theatres in the country even have *budgets* that big!); $500,000 or so of that sum is needed to support the training program. But Mr. Ball thinks it is worth it, and who is to gainsay him? (Mr. Ball doesn't get gainsaid very often.)

The other expensive peculiarity of the ACT is the sheer number of productions it puts on. In its six-month Pittsburgh stand, playing repertory in the two theatres of the Pittsburgh Playhouse, it mounted twelve productions in six months. In a twenty-two-week San Francisco stand early in 1967, it presented sixteen productions, again in two-theatre rotating repertory. During that San Francisco season forty-seven actors played a total of 187 characters, an average of four per actor; two members of the company played eight roles apiece (all this, presumably, in addition to their participation in the training program). I was talking to an ACT actor one day when a lady came up and told him, "I thought you were wonderful last night." "Last night?" said the actor. "What was I in last night?"

The copiousness, the drunken-sailor prodigality of the programming, is obviously not an unmixed blessing. I remember sitting at certain ACT performances, watching Actor X struggling with a role he was not quite right for, and thinking how good Actor Y might have been in the part; but Actor Y was over at the other theatre, playing another part. And such an intensive schedule can hardly help but impose a strain on everybody concerned. But in spite of variations in quality, much of the acting is exceedingly good. And the fantastic, unnecessary richness of the schedule helps to create the air of excitement, emanating in the first place from Mr. Ball, that envelops the company.

Ball is the American Reinhardt. He is eclectic, committed to no particular kind of drama or style of acting or social role for the theatre. He will try anything; he often seems determined to try everything. His only commitment is to the Theatre Theatrical, with the emphasis on the director; he loves to create "ostentations" and "wonders," to use two of his favorite words. There are, of course, other American directors whose primary commitment is to showmanship, but with Mr. Ball there seems to be a peculiar unbroken continuity of flamboyance extending from the way he lives his life to the way he runs his company to the way he directs his productions. And yet even this commitment is not absolute. He seems to be less insensitive to the integrity of the plays he directs than most American directors of the Genius School. And he cleverly hires less spectacular directors, notably the scrupulously unobtrusive Allen Fletcher, to direct for the ACT; the quietude of Mr. Fletcher's work makes a very nice balance with the whizz-bang flashiness of Mr. Ball's.

I first encountered the ACT at the Westport Country Playhouse in Westport, Connecticut, in the spring of 1966, about four months after its hegira from Pittsburgh and ten months after its debut. Confined for the moment to one auditorium, it was offering only six productions.

Allen Fletcher's *Death of a Salesman* could have done with a little more directorial flair at a couple of big moments, and it seemed to suffer here and there from the exigencies of repertory casting. But on the whole the production did ample justice to Arthur Miller's best play, thanks largely to the beautiful acting of Richard A. Dysart as the doomed salesman. Mr. Dysart's repertory of nervous gestures when he was uncomfortable, and his salesman's con man's tricks when he was operating; his shuffling, weary walk and his little vaudeville swagger; his lips, forming an O as he gazed off into the past, or pushed together into a pout as the pressures of the present became difficult to bear; his wheezy laugh; his quick, clear, completely motivated transitions: a multitude of little things, finely controlled yet perfectly spontaneous, were fused into a most moving image of desperation desperately fought.

The ACT frequently rehearses more than one actor in a role, and in the case of Mr. Fletcher's *Uncle Vanya* there was a pair of alternate performers for each of the major roles. Therefore I cannot categorically say that the ACT's *Vanya* was a dreary bore; I can only say that it was a dreary bore on the night I saw it, with the second team in. The pace was slow, even for Chekhov; Mr. Fletcher seemed to have been working for lethargy, apathy, humidity, and stultification—not exactly theatrical qualities. The acting was not bad, exactly, but only the very best is good enough for Chekhov. The Astrov (Ramon Bieri) was coarse, and the Sonya (Jacqueline Coslow) was pretty and cold instead of plain and warm. Vanya (Jay Doyle) was interesting at first: seedy, rumpled, dazed, with wild eyes. He looked as if he might explode, as Vanya must do when he tries to shoot the Professor; but when the time came, his vocal attack was not sharp enough, nor his emotion high enough, and the explosion was something of a dud. *Vanya* was the only ACT production done at Westport that had its première there (the others had all been done previously in Pittsburgh or elsewhere); maybe it improved later on; maybe the first team was better. In any case, *Uncle Vanya* was the only ACT production done at Westport that was not in the repertory during the first San Francisco season.

The four young men who performed in the ACT's *Beyond the Fringe* were proficient and personable, though sometimes shaky about the British accents required. Rene Auberjonois, who directed the show (and also appeared in it), did not strive unduly to be original, but on the other hand the actors did not strive unduly to imitate the first performers of this intelligent and amusing small revue.

The other three ACT Westport productions were William Ball productions. *Under Milk Wood* by Dylan Thomas (which I did not see) and Pirandello's *Six Characters in Search of an Author*—two shows which Mr. Ball had directed successfully off Broadway—were directed for the ACT by Byron Ringland after Mr. Ball's "Original Conceptions"; Edward Albee's *Tiny Alice* was directed by the Master in person.

Six Characters is Pirandello's fantastical think-piece about a group of "Characters" from an unfinished play who descend on an acting company in the middle of a rehearsal to demand that the actors help them to put their predicament onstage. It has always struck me as a rather gimmicky and spun-out piece. And whenever people come onstage and say, in effect, as they do in *Six Characters*, "I'm suffering, look how I'm suffering," I tend to begin suffering myself. But at Westport my sufferings were alleviated by a great deal of very jazzy theatre-magic.

In Paul Avila Meyer's brilliant adaptation, Pirandello's second-rate Italian theatre company, rehearsing another Pirandello play that is almost unknown in America, becomes the ACT itself, rehearsing *Charley's Aunt*. There were some funny jokes about American rehearsal methods, and the artificial frivolity of *Charley's Aunt* (with Austin Pendleton dragging about in a long rehearsal skirt as the fake aunt) contrasted effectively with the somber agony of the Characters.

The production was full of ostentations and wonders. I remember especially a moment at the end of the play, after the Characters seem to have disappeared forever. The Actors have gone home disgusted; the Director (that is, the actor who plays the Director) is left alone on a darkened stage. Then suddenly the Characters materialize out of nowhere, looking exactly as they did on their first appearance: grouped tightly together as if posed for a Victorian family photograph, in a strange green light. They do not speak; then suddenly, silently, they disappear forever. And we sense that they are like the Flying Dutchman, and will never be at rest.

Richard A. Dysart and Janis Young were good as the two leading Characters; so was Robin Gammell as the Director; so, more or less, was the rest of the cast. The play and the production offered rich opportunities for a lighting designer, and Jules Fisher seized them admirably. But it was a director's show.

So was *Tiny Alice*, a play that needs all the help a director can give it. Mr. Albee spins his plot around affable, compliant Brother Julian, who is given by his Cardinal into the hands of the mysterious Miss Alice and her two fishy colleagues, a Butler (named Butler) and a Lawyer (unnamed). The playwright presumably meant that this mishmash of sex, religion, and betrayal should have some profound metaphysical significance—otherwise he has wasted a very great deal of fancy rhetoric—but all I got out of it, on Broadway or at Westport, was that lay brothers ought to be very careful while making house calls.

The play made somewhat more sense at Westport than it had on Broadway, since Brother Julian (Paul Shenar) was young and handsome, instead of being John Gielgud. This accounted, to some extent, for both his naïveté and the attraction he held for Miss Alice. But there is too much in *Tiny Alice* that dare not tell its name, and even Mr. Ball could not make very much sense of it. What he could do, and did, was to reward the audience for sitting through all the rhetoric by providing bursts of splendid zap-zap theatricality at frequent intervals.

A fat Cardinal sprawling in his sleep—a great blob of red on a huge throne—made an arresting image to begin the play with. Later on, the Lawyer flung down the Butler belly upward across the huge model of Miss Alice's palace that took up a large part of the set; the Butler's head was dangling over the edge of the model toward the audience; his arms were spread wide; the Lawyer was leaning fiercely over him, about to commit who knew what? Among the possibilities implicit in the moment were strangulation, crucifixion, and rape. None actually happened (not onstage any-way), and I now forget entirely, if I ever really understood, what the Lawyer and the Butler had fallen out about; but moments like this at least kept one awake. At the end, when Brother Julian, having finally been shot, takes an unconscionable time a-dying because the playwright has given him what must be pages of stuff to spout, Mr. Ball saved the occasion by arranging a veritable orgy of light and sound to accompany Julian's throes.

Paul Shenar as Julian, DeAnn Mears as Miss Alice, Ray Rein-hardt as the Lawyer, Al Alu as a wildly swishy Butler, and Harry Frazier as the Cardinal comprised the entire cast; all were highly commendable, but all were brilliantly outshone by Mr. Ball. This seems to happen fairly often when Mr. Ball directs. I am not quite sure that I should be happy about it if I were one of Mr. Ball's actors (though he seems able to do his stuff without preventing them from looking good too), but as a member of the audience I have no complaints.

After Westport, the company spent two weeks at the Good-speed Opera House in East Haddam, Connecticut, with *Beyond the Fringe;* then came a repertory engagement at the Stanford Summer Festival on the campus of Stanford University in Palo Alto, California, then another repertory stand at the Ravinia Festival near Chicago. The response at both Stanford and Ravinia was so enthusiastic that groups in San Francisco (just up the Peninsula from Palo Alto) and Chicago became interested in establishing the ACT permanently in their cities. In both cities, however, there was a certain reluctance about assuming responsibility for the company's staggering deficit. So a compromise was arrived at. The company would become a resident theatre with two residences; it would play annual seasons of about twenty weeks in both San Francisco *and* Chicago. (As things worked out, it never got to Chicago.)

The ACT opened its first San Francisco season on January 21, 1967. There was no attempt to start slowly and build support gradually; the ACT came to San Francisco under conditions that made it, by almost any measure I can think of, larger than any other remotely comparable theatre in this country. With sixteen productions in twenty-two weeks, it was certainly the most prolific; during the last week of the season, it presented eighteen performances of fourteen productions in two theatres in San Francisco, plus eight performances of a fifteenth production in Los Angeles. (The Los Angeles stand was part of an extensive "Out Rep" program whereby the smaller productions in the regular repertory give performances in miscellaneous odd places scattered around the California countryside; there was even a performance outdoors at a winery.) The smaller of the two theatres the company used in San Francisco (seating 640) had been the larger auditorium of the old Actor's Workshop; the ACT's larger theatre was the 1,448-seat Geary, normally a road-show house. The two theatres combined gave the ACT a total seating capacity of 2,088: more than any other American resident theatre except the New York Shakespeare Festival. There were some fifty actors in the company, and about 175 people on the payroll. The budget for the twenty-two-week season was a whopping $1,250,000; I can't prove it, but it's my guess that the ACT spends more money per minute than any other company in America.

This colossal gamble paid off. *Variety* headlined, "Ball's ACT in Smash Frisco Bow, With Rave Reviews and Boff Biz." There were 12,000 subscribers before the season began (though the Actor's Workshop, which preceded the ACT in San Francisco, had fewer than 5,200 subscribers in its best year). The season opened with Molière's *Tartuffe;* the San Francisco *Examiner* called it "magnificent," while the *Chronicle,* less conservative, proclaimed it "a screaming, bellowing, unbelievable triumph." Immediately another thousand subscribers signed up. Attendance for the season ran to 1,448 people every night in both theatres combined, which has got to be some sort of record. Total attendance for twenty-two weeks (note: an ordinary resident-theatre season runs about thirty-six weeks) came to 222,685: a figure exceeded, as far as I can discover, only by the New York Shakespeare Festival, the Stratford, Connecticut, Shakespeare Festival and the Guthrie among American theatres.

How to explain such an immediate, massive popular response? Guilt over the death of the Actor's Workshop may have had something to do with it (and probably had a good deal more to do with the willingness of the San Francisco business community to meet the large ACT deficit). But where the Workshop had tended to keep the San Francisco audience at arm's length, the ACT embraced it enthusiastically. "San Francisco has measured up to everything we hoped for," said Mr. Ball, "except one thing. People haven't come backstage—no one comes to say hello to the actors. I'm going to take down the sign at the stage entrance that says 'No admittance' and say 'Welcome backstage.' We must have contact with the people for whom we perform."

He was similarly accommodating as to the repertory of plays. Many people had found the Workshop's repertory too formidable for their tastes, but Mr. Ball is such an eclectic that he can produce, with no loss of integrity, plays that Blau and Irving could not have done without feeling that they had sold out. "To succeed," said Ball, "a theatre must have an audience! ["Give an audience a chance, and it will certainly be wrong."—Herbert Blau*] We try to pick plays with enough variety to reach a wide range of audiences. We cannot be worthy of the subsidies that we have received, and others that we hope for, unless every theatre seat is filled within three years." A sixteen-play repertory provides plenty of opportunity for pleasing a variety of tastes. For his first

* *The Impossible Theatre,* p. 166.

San Francisco season, Ball programed eight productions of more or less serious drama, four productions of more or less serious comedy, and four lightweight entertainments. There was a little bit of a great many things, from seventeenth-century French comedy (*Tartuffe*) to the theatre of the absurd (*Endgame* and *Krapp's Last Tape*). (Curiously, only one play on the list was written before 1900.)

A significant factor in the company's success was, of course, the quality of the productions. Not all of them (God knows) were good; some were blatantly miscast; but it was clear most of the time that the ACT was a repertory company of very special distinction.

Generally speaking, it seemed to me that the oldest productions were the best: the ones that dated back to the company's Pittsburgh period, or beyond that to Mr. Ball's pre-ACT days in New York. The season opened with a production of *Tartuffe*, directed by Mr. Ball, which had evolved out of the *Tartuffe* he staged for the Repertory Theatre of Lincoln Center in 1964, and had improved in the process. By the time this *Tartuffe* reached San Francisco, it was ready to serve as proof that the wild prodigality of William Ball's ingenuity is one of the wonders of our theatre. Orgon, the paterfamilias, entered to a splendid burst of music from trumpet and harpsichord, and greeted his family (augmented by Ball with two small children); suddenly the familial warmth of the moment was dashed as the moment turned pious, and Orgon turned to bless himself. Later the family gathered around the harpsichord to sing a little song; Tartuffe entered, the lights dimmed, the song stopped; we saw how the interloper acted like a blight on the lives of those around him.

Many of the bits were more explicitly comic, but this was not a hilariously funny *Tartuffe*: just irresistibly vivacious and incredibly clever. It was a pleasure to watch teen-aged kids, sitting in the boxes on cut-rate student tickets, enjoying themselves. But I couldn't help thinking that any play that *needed* all this elaboration could not have much substance in itself. I wonder if *Tartuffe* really is that insubstantial.

The acting was not overwhelmingly good. Judith Mihalyi was tiny and charming as Dorine, the maid, but she tended to push her pertness too far. Ramon Bieri as Orgon, with his silly giggle and his bursts of falsetto, was too foolish to be believed. As his wife Elmire, DeAnn Mears played too broadly in the scene in which she pretended to woo Tartuffe; nobody could possibly have been taken in by such a coarsely obvious parody of passion. The actors were not impeded by the rhymed couplets of Richard Wilbur's translation, but they had not quite learned what to do with the couplets, how to make them a positive asset.

Michael O'Sullivan, who played the title role in Ball's production of the play for the Lincoln Center Repertory Company in 1964, is a member of the ACT, but did not appear in its San Francisco *Tartuffe*; instead, the title role was taken by an astonishing twenty-seven-year-old phenomenon named Rene Auberjonois. Mr. Auberjonois has never acted in New York; since graduating from Carnegie Tech he has worked only for the Arena Stage in Washington and the ACT; in six years he has played fifty roles including King Lear. He is an actor who is not afraid to be larger than life, and he has the talent to justify his boldness. His last utterance as Tartuffe was not in words at all; it was a vicious, guttural exhalation that has no name, and it made a tremendous effect. The things he can do with his body, moreover, are absolutely amazing. And yet there was a hard vein of venomous malice running beneath all his zany antics.

But this Tartuffe, like all the others I have ever seen, was still an awkward, grotesque, ridiculous ass, a patent phony whose pretensions toward piety could never have taken in anybody. I have yet to see a *plausible* Tartuffe, a smart, smooth con man who could conceivably gain the influence over a solid, bourgeois householder that Tartuffe is shown as having. In other words, I have still never seen the play done as high comedy rather than farce. If, as Frenchmen and Francophiles have always maintained, *Tartuffe* is a play of substance and profundity, this would be the way to show it. But if the ACT *Tartuffe* was a victory of theatre magic over dramatic cogency, the quality of the theatre magic justified the venture.

Two other productions given in San Francisco dated back to pre-ACT days: *Under Milk Wood* and *Six Characters in Search of an Author*. *Tiny Alice, Death of a Salesman, Beyond the Fringe,* and *Endgame* survived from the Pittsburgh era. *Endgame* featured spectacular performances by Ken Ruta and Rene Auberjonois; the

Open Theatre in New York and the Firehouse in Minneapolis are experimenting with vocal effects that are past the frontiers of speech, but I have never heard actors giggle, gasp, grunt, bellow, and moan with more audacity and authority than these two. Only beautifully trained actors could make such horrible noises for any length of time without ruining their throats. Mr. Ruta as Hamm (the master) was confined to his chair throughout the play, but Mr. Auberjonois as Clov (the servant) took advantage of his mobility to create a highly imaginative physical characterization; an odd combination of floppiness and stiffness gave him the look of a Raggedy Andy doll in very bad shape. The set by Stuart Wurtzel was interesting too: a very small, high-walled, three-sided room, isolated in the middle of the stage, and obviously made of flats, with canvas peeling off and bracing plainly in evidence. I am not an admirer of *Endgame;* it seems to me that Beckett, having stripped away so many inessentials in writing *Waiting for Godot,* began thereafter to strip away essentials as well; I am reminded of a remark by Henry James or somebody about some writer who was distinguished not only for economy of means, but also for economy of effect. But the production had some highly distinguished work in it.

Two productions dated from the company's engagement at Stanford in the summer of 1966. One was a delightful *Charley's Aunt,* directed by Edward Hastings. Mr. Hastings missed an excellent opportunity for nostalgic charm by paying little attention to the evocation of time and place. Furthermore, the two juveniles and the two ingénues were all lacking in the requisite polish; the older actors were uninteresting; the music was not quite right. In fact, nothing was quite right except Rene Auberjonois, leaping about like a gazellephant in drag as Charley's Aunt. Mr. Auberjonois is a virtuoso of well-nigh-incredible attainments; his gallivantings were hysterically funny, and swept all before them. The drama director of Stagg High School in Stockton, California, took his students to see this production, and reported, "As soon as they saw the ACT show, they realized what I meant by 'throwing yourselves around.'"

Seven new productions were added to the repertory during the San Francisco season itself. *The Torch-Bearers,* an American comedy by George E. Kelly, was quickly dropped from the repertory as a failure; I did not see it, but I doubt if it could have been as bad as Jerome Kilty's highly popular production of *Man and Superman*. Mr. Kilty took every opportunity he could find to sacrifice the integrity of the play for the sake of a few cheap laughs; it looked as if his primary consideration had been to produce what some reviewers like to call a "romp," and to minimize every indication that Shaw had meant his play to be about something. The production was miscast with excellent actors; seldom has a play been done so badly so well. Rene Auberjonois was amusing enough as John Tanner, but he played him as an Oscar Wilde character instead of a Shavian hero, sticking darts with dainty deftness instead of firing off broadsides with exuberant zest. In the famous Hell Scene, as Tanner's alter ego Don Juan, Mr. Auberjonois was downright effeminate, and the scene turned into a swishing match between him and Ken Ruta as the Devil. (In the other half of his double role, as the Jewish brigand Mendoza, Mr. Ruta displayed a quite unnecessarily greasy set of Jewish mannerisms; Shaw was not trying to write another Fagin.) DeAnn Mears, proficient as she is, was wrong for Ann Whitefield; the actress is too old and too solid-looking to get away with the girlish tricks that Ann practices. (Her performance made me realize all over again how exquisite Rosemary Harris had been in this part, and how lucky the APA was to have her.) I am bound to add that the audience just adored every minute of this production, even the archly funnee set-changes, with costumed stage-hand-extras making exaggerated running motions. But it seemed to me that Mr. Kilty and his cohorts had exquisitely castrated the play.

Nothing else that the ACT did was infuriating the way *Man and Superman* was, but I found several other productions disquieting in varying degrees. Mr. Kilty also staged the company's revival of *Dear Liar*, his own adaptation of the correspondence between GBS and Mrs. Patrick Campbell. Sada Thompson, formidable yet witty, with her majestic bearing and tragedy-queen voice, was excellent as Mrs. Pat, but Michael O'Sullivan played GBS as an angry, spoiled, childish, effeminate elf.

In *Long Day's Journey into Night*, Eugene O'Neill's tremendous voyage into his own past, David Grimm and Patrick Tovatt were good as Edmund and Jamie Tyrone (the playwright-to-be and his brother). Angela Paton was also good as their mother, but unfortunately she is a rather chunky lady, without the girlish frailty that can make this character so moving. And Ramon Bieri was totally miscast as the father. James Tyrone is O'Neill's portrait of his own father, who was in his day one of the leading actors on the American stage; the part calls for grandiloquence and a splendid bearing. Mr. Bieri, however, is an unassuming-looking, slouchy gent with a coarsely comic, good-natured face. If there was no actor in the company better suited for the part, surely it would have been better to leave the play undone.

The Seagull, under Edward Payson Call's direction, was a distinctly in-and-out piece of work. Ellen Geer was excellent as Nina: eager, ardent, awkward, girlish, and very attractive. Angela Paton's Arkadina was not a gorgon but a well-preserved woman reluctantly entering middle age; at the same time she was a bitch in the grand manner, trailing a wrap, waving a cigarette holder, even peering through a lorgnette. What was missing was Arkadina's desperation. Out of her desperate need for attention and her desperate fear of growing old, Chekhov's character subjugates her lover and blights the life of her son; when this desperation is diminished to mere concern, the urgency of the play is diminished as well.

The production was further weakened by Austin Pendleton's interesting performance as Arkadina's son Konstantin. Mr. Pendleton is probably America's leading sniveling-brat actor, and on his own terms he played Konstantin quite well. But the whole point about the character is that while his mother, for her own neurotic reasons, must think of him and treat him as an adolescent baby, he is really a talented and troubled young man of twenty-five. In Mr. Pendleton's performance this point was, to say the least, obscured. And so, for these reasons and others, it seemed to me that the poignancy of *The Seagull,* the terribleness of what its people are doing to one another, did not come through, and, as so often happens when Chekhov's plays are less than beautifully done, the Chekhovian tedium communicated itself to the audience.

The other new productions all struck me as successful, in a modest sort of way. In *Arsenic and Old Lace,* directed by Allen Fletcher, I was impressed by how beautifully the lines were played and pointed; it was a splendid exhibition of comic technique, and very funny too. Carol Teitel played sweet, murderous old Aunt

Abbie far better than such a young actress has any right to. The ACT revival of good old lovable *Our Town* was not overwhelmingly distinguished, but it was an affectionate, proficient, and generally charming production; Edward Hastings, who directed, never allowed the play's sweetness to get sickening. Richard Dysart, the company's father-figure, played the Stage Manager; Ellen Geer was Emily. The season's final offering was a well-performed double bill of *Krapp's Last Tape* and *The Zoo Story*. Ray Reinhardt as old Krapp in the Beckett play went in for plenty of quaking, hobbling, open-mouthed detail, well handled if that's what you like to watch. As Jerry, the psychopathic social dropout in the Albee play, Scott Hylands came on with a lot of sexually provocative stuff (hands in back pockets, hands on hips, arms crossed over chest) and a tone of lurking mockery; he played his death scene in the high old style, with plenty of gasps and moans and rhetoric, and made it work.

It was an up-and-down season. Mr. Ball had not directed anything since Pittsburgh, and none of the company's other directors have anything like his gifts. Several actors were badly miscast. The scenery was often perfunctory, and the wigs tended to look like wigs. But in a repertory of sixteen productions, at least five were extraordinary, and several more were good: by no means a discreditable tally. There was quite a bit of very striking acting going on, and even without actually directing anything, Mr. Ball had no trouble in making his presence felt. The general air of exhilaration and success was unmistakable.

During the last week of the season, Mr. Ball called in the press to make an important announcement: the ACT had canceled its plans to spend half of every year in Chicago. It was explained that Actors' Equity had refused to buy the idea of the ACT's dual residency; Equity had insisted that the Chicago stand be regarded as a touring engagement, which meant that about $200,000 per twenty-week season would have to be added to the budget for salaries and per diem allowances. ACT's friends in Chicago were unwilling to commit themselves to raising the extra money. That was the public explanation; there were rumors that the ACT had arranged the situation purposely, in order to stay in San Francisco. Anyhow, the company went off to play summer engagements in Stanford and Ravinia (meanwhile maintaining a 200-hour summer training program in San Francisco, based on the regular ACT curriculum, for forty Bay Area aspirants). And in September it announced happily that it would make its permanent year-round home in San Francisco, playing a forty-week season every year, with a production budget for 1967–68 of $1,500,000, plus $800,000 more for the training program. "Until now," said Mr. Ball, "we have concentrated on survival. At last we can direct our energy toward artistic excellence."

The new season began on October 29, 1967 with a production of *Twelfth Night*, directed by William Ball himself: the first play he had directed in nearly two years. In addition to productions held over from last season, the repertory includes *In White America* (previously mounted by the ACT in Pittsburgh), *Two for the Seesaw* by William Gibson, *Thieves' Carnival* by Jean Anouilh, *A Delicate Balance* by Edward Albee, and *Acting Up*, a one-man show in which Mr. Ball discusses his theories of acting. No less than three world premières are also scheduled: *The Incomparable Max*, adapted by Jerome Lawrence and Robert E. Lee from several works of Max Beerbohm, *Don't Shoot Mable It's Your Husband* by Jerome Kilty, and *Long Live Life*, adapted by Mr. Kilty from the correspondence of Anton Chekhov.

One very peculiar long-term project has also been announced: *The Prince of Denmark*, a cycle of four productions of and about Shakespeare's *Hamlet*, directed by Mr. Ball to be mounted over a two-year period. The first production will be called *Elsinore* instead of *Hamlet*, because says Mr. Ball,

> when one announces *Hamlet*, the audience immediately anticipates a stage filled with Renaissance costumes, torches, drapes, goblets, royal parades, duels, and a swirl of physical activity. Since this will not be a traditional production, we've decided to call the work we're doing on Shakespeare's text by a different name. . . . By placing major concentration on the text, we will have the opportunity to apply Conservatory techniques of verse, scansion, rhetoric, voice production and motionless speech.
>
> My work as a director has been called visual and choreographic. This production represents a directorial experiment in sound. In limiting movement, spectacle, color, lighting and stage composition, we may better explore the resources of the actors' verbal expressivity and achieve dramatic impact in an assault on the emotions through the ear of the audience.

The second production will be a more traditional *Hamlet*. The third will be *Rosencrantz and Guildenstern Are Dead*, a contemporary British play by Tom Stoppard that takes an oblique view of the tragedy. The fourth production, entitled *The Bare Bodkyn*, will use Shakespeare's text, but will be, according to Mr. Ball, "extremely fragmented and imbued with all the absurdities, eccentricities and manic uncertainties of modern life." All this is obviously sheer madness. Only Mr. Ball could think of it; only the ACT, with its prodigious number of productions, could find room in its schedule for four *Hamlets*. Even if all four don't actually get done (two years allows time for many a slip), the plan itself is testimony to the uniqueness of the American Conservatory Theatre. As Mr. Ball modestly observes:

> Our company is on the brink of creating a new form in the theatre that has to do with rhythmics, humor, voice that rises almost to the heights of singing, and movement that creates a union with the ballet and dynamics that can terrify the audience as they have never been terrified before. That is the only way we can get people into the theatre . . . There is now no reason to leave your house unless what happens is so devastating that it cannot happen in your living room.

Could it perhaps be just possible that Mr. Ball might turn out in the long run to be almost as big a genius as he thinks he is?

The National Repertory Theatre

In 1959, a couple of young producers named Michael Dewell and Frances Ann Dougherty sent Tyrone Guthrie's revival of Schiller's *Mary Stuart*, with Signe Hasso and Eva Le Gallienne in the leading roles, on a national tour. They were pleased to discover that there was an audience out there in the hinterlands for classic drama; the production did well generally, and broke box-office records in Washington and Boston. This success set them thinking. "A bunch of us got together," said Mr. Dewell, "and had a sort of group therapy session about why we were in the theatre." All the participants had been successful in the commercial theatre, but they felt unfulfilled. "We decided that what was wrong was that there were plenty of jobs for all of us [but] we wanted to work with each other, in the only theatre that can offer the craftsman his proper tools, and that's the fully professional, fully union Broadway or Broadway-level touring." Nobody had created a Broadway-level classical theatre that they could work in together, so they founded it themselves, and called it the National Repertory Theatre. It has always been a real repertory theatre, presenting two or more productions in alternation. Unlike the APA and the ACT, it was designed specifically as a touring company.

The NRT began its operations in the season of 1961–62 by sending out Eva Le Gallienne and Faye Emerson in a repertory consisting of *Mary Stuart* (again) and Maxwell Anderson's *Elizabeth the Queen*. It was a successful tour, but an exhausting one, visiting sixty cities in thirty weeks. During the season of 1962–63, the NRT did not tour, but made plans for the future. "The great trap," they decided, according to Mr. Dewell, "was to say we're going to go everywhere, because your productions and your work suffer terribly if you do that." They realized that the United States has a number of "regional capitals," where people come for meetings, shopping, and cultural events: Saint Louis, Chicago, San Francisco, Los Angeles, Philadelphia, Cincinnati, and so on. Henceforth the NRT would be "not a bus-and-truck company but a major Class A company that goes and sits for a while in various regional capitals."

This policy has several advantages, according to Mr. Dewell.

You're able to play in the market place, you're able to play in that best touring house in each city, in the place where historically theatre always has been . . . Your audience is sitting in seats that are still warm from the behinds of people who came to see *Hello, Dolly!* and *Barefoot in the Park* . . . You have to entertain first; you're at a safe distance from all the professors and academicians. . . . You also have the opportunity to avail yourself of the mechanisms that already exist: good theatres, good crews, good stagehands, shops with people who can properly dress a wig, mailing lists . . . And your actors can have the freedom from being beaten around by busses and planes and things . . . Our company travels only by jet airplane; they have no non-union personnel at all, thank God.

In 1963–64, the NRT presented Eva Le Gallienne, Farley Granger, Denholm Elliott, and Anne Meacham in *The Seagull, The Crucible,* and Anouilh's *Ring Round the Moon.* I remember poor Mr. Granger as John Proctor in *The Crucible* and Konstantin in *The Seagull;* he had been a Hollywood leading man for so long that now he couldn't *not* be a Hollywood leading man. Though he seemed to be trying as hard as he could, he was unable to break through his own glossy surface. Miss Le Gallienne played Madame Arkadina, Konstantin's mother, in *The Seagull,* with not-very-satisfactory results. Arkadina is a middle-aged actress who inflicts all kinds of damage on those around her, especially her son, in order to maintain her pretense of still being young and beautiful. Miss Le Gallienne was too old to make the pretense convincing, and she was unwilling to exploit the discrepancy for purposes of grotesque comedy, though there is no other way for an actress of her age to make sense of the part. But it was the first national tour for Chekhov since the 1930's, according to Mr. Dewell, and *The Crucible* and *Ring Round the Moon* had never been toured in this country at all.

In 1964–65, Farley Granger and Signe Hasso went out in *Liliom, She Stoops to Conquer,* and *Hedda Gabler;* in 1965–66 it was Eva Le Gallienne, Silvia Sidney, and Leora Dana in *The Madwoman of Chaillot, The Rivals,* and *The Trojan Women;* in 1966–67 the company abjured stars and sent out *Tonight at 8:30* by Noel Coward, *A Touch of the Poet* by Eugene O'Neill, and *The Imaginary Invalid* by Molière. The 1967–68 season will include a fourteen-week stand at Ford's Theatre in Washington, where Lincoln was shot; *John Brown's Body, The Comedy of Errors,* and *She Stoops to Conquer* are to be presented. In future years, the plan is to have two companies in operation simultaneously: one in residence at Ford's, and one on the road.

The NRT is already a big-league organization, with a million-dollar budget. Attendance has grown every year, from 145,000 in 1963–64 to 208,000 in 1966–67. Student groups are admitted at half price; the NRT works with more than 4,000 schools in various parts of the country, providing them with study guides and post-performance discussions. In addition, it spends three weeks every year on the campus of the University of North Carolina at Greensboro, followed by three weeks at Ohio State University in Columbus. It does not merely perform at these universities; company members offer about sixty hours of teaching time at each, plus all sorts of informal seminars, meetings, picnics, and teas.

In the spring of 1967, the NRT presented its repertory **on**

Broadway for the first time in three years, thanks to a $30,000 grant from the U.S. government through the National Endowment for the Arts. It was a mistake. The New York critics were nearly unanimous in their denunciations, and the engagement was curtailed for lack of attendance. This was my own first chance in three years to see the company in action; it seemed to me that it had improved, but not enough. Strong artistic leadership was still lacking. The three productions indicated that the NRT is proficient, lightweight, and genteel: entertaining at times, but exciting, never.

All the productions looked nice, and the actors—no big names among them—seemed to know their business (though it may have been just as well that few of them were faced with any major challenges). Some of them appeared to be genuinely versatile; and if they did not make an impression as a particularly robust group, it must have been at least partly because robustness was so seldom demanded of them by their material. The choice of plays was somewhat peculiar: two second-rate works by major writers, and a set of beautifully crafted miniatures by a minor talent. The one thing all these plays had in common was that they were highly unlikely to offend or perplex anybody.

The Imaginary Invalid is one of those rather mechanical farces that Molière liked to write about old men with obsessions. The title character, a Monsieur Argan, has built his life around his imaginary diseases. He has become a monster of hypochondria, even wishing to marry his daughter to a doctor so as to have one at his side at all times. (When somebody suggests ironically that perhaps he should marry his other daughter to an apothecary, Argan thinks it a fine idea.) There are two ways to play such a character. The actor can go for deep psychological penetration and try to show the terrors and hatreds that might make a man take refuge from reality in purges and pills, or he can use the part as the pretext for a display of comic virtuosity. G. Wood, who played the part for the NRT, took neither course; he simply turned in a competent, uninspired piece of grouchy-old-man acting. As a result, the first forty minutes or so of *The Imaginary Invalid* were slowish going. Things perked up, however, with the entrance of a pair of far-out farcical doctors, played by Denholm Elliott and Geddeth Smith, and from then on the play was quite a nice, pleasant, silly little entertainment, in a wishy-washy sort of way.

A *Touch of the Poet* is the only completed play in what O'Neill projected as a gigantic eleven-play historical saga. It indicates that even at the end of his life, the period during which he wrote his masterpiece (*Long Day's Journey into Night*, of course), he still had not entirely lost his affinity for inflated guff. His hero is a drunken Irishman named Melody, reduced to keeping a second-rate tavern in Massachusetts, who can never forget that he has served as an officer in the Duke of Wellington's army. Melody does his best to ignore the shabby realities that surround him, displays all the airs of a gentleman, and goes on preening before the mirror and reciting Lord Byron's poetry long after we have all gotten the point. Self-delusion and vanity are, of course, the traditional subjects of comedy; O'Neill's attempt to make a tragic hero out of this pompous ass is foredoomed, and the repetitious clumsiness of the dramaturgy does not help matters.

Denholm Elliott as Melody made no attempt to mitigate the character's nastiness, which made the play, paradoxically, less hard to take; the actor, unlike the author, was not trying to put anything over on us. Mr. Elliott encompassed Melody in full spate, and Melody in extremis: Melody as a peacock with claws, and Melody, memorably, as a living corpse. Priscilla Morrill was good as his meek wife, and so was Jeanne Hepple as his spunky daughter (though Miss Hepple was sometimes shrill, and sometimes indistinct); Sloane Shelton was intriguingly cool and poised as an eccentric Yankee lady. The play does undeniably have its moments (as Melody humiliates his daughter Sara, and she responds in kind; as Sara pursues her shy Yankee lover with an interesting mixture of calculation and ardor; as the eccentric old lady narrates the history of her husband's eccentric family), and the company, by and large, made the most of them. People with a weakness for second-rate O'Neill (there used to be plenty of them, though nowadays they must be dying off pretty quickly) must have found this revival highly edifying.

The only NRT production I could praise with any enthusiasm was *Tonight at 8:30*, a bill of Noel Coward one-acters. The first of the three plays, *Ways and Means*, is about an attractive, fashionable, good-for-nothing English couple, who find themselves flat broke on the Riviera. It is a fine example of Mr. Coward in his bitchy vein—and there is no writer in the world who finds bitchiness so exquisitely congenial. John Church and Joan Bassie, in the leading roles, flung their darts quite stylishly, and showed us Toby and Stella as a couple of overgrown, histrionic, witty children. (Considering Mr. Coward's notorious "sophistication," it is remarkable how many of his characters are really big babies.)

Still Life is the play on which the movie *Brief Encounter* was based. A middle-aged doctor and a middle-aged housewife, both as English and as middle-class as anyone could possibly be, meet by chance in a railroad station when he removes a bit of grit from her eye. Though each is quite thoroughly married to someone else, they fall desperately in love, and spend a great deal of time sitting in the refreshment room of the station trying to control their feelings. Denholm Elliott and Priscilla Morrill were fine as the stiff-upper-lipped lovers, but these roles will always belong to Trevor Howard and Celia Johnson, who played them in the movie. The play itself has somewhat faded in certain places; the understated heroics of Alec and Laura ("I can't let you go like this!" "You must!") seem just a bit dated nowadays, and go on just a bit too long. But the comedy scenes for the lower orders, which alternate with the main action, are as fresh as ever.

The third playlet, *Fumed Oak,* is about a little worm of a man, lumbered with a horrible wife, a horrible daughter, and a horrible mother-in-law, who finally turns, tells them all what he thinks of them, and walks out of their lives. The play has a slightly distasteful undertone of cruelty (it is obviously powered by a vicious anti-feminism), but it is a funny little piece all the same, and full of sharp domestic observations. Geoff Garland as the worm played it brilliantly: he began as a sleepy, diffident, mild-mannered little fellow—and stayed that way. The moment of his triumph was rendered all the funnier because he preserved the pathetic air of a man who has had advantage taken of him all his life.

Tonight at 8:30 made a delightful evening's entertainment, but on the whole I found the NRT almost offensively inoffensive. It appears to have a degree of competence, but no imagination and no guts. Its work seems aimed straight at the old ladies who hang out in Schrafft's. This is what Brecht called the "culinary theatre"; do we really need heavily subsidized repertory companies to provide it for us?

THE
UNIVERSITY
THEATRES

I doubt if there exists, nowadays, anywhere in this country, a university or even a college so benighted as to offer no dramatic activity whatsoever. Professional theatre is another matter; but even here various schools have been variously active. Many of them book touring attractions; there is now an established touring circuit for Off-Broadway productions, comprised almost entirely of campus auditoriums. Some schools engage touring repertory companies; the APA, the ACT, and the NRT all play campus engagements every year. Other schools contract alliances with local resident theatres, sending their students to intern at the theatres, and hiring theatre personnel as part-time faculty members. Still others sponsor summer-stock companies of varying pretensions. And a few colleges and universities—just a few—have actually set up full-fledged resident professional theatres of their own; these theatres are the subject of this chapter.

Campus professional theatres make good sense: an academic community should provide an intelligent audience, and academic institutions are at least accustomed to deficit operations. And colleges and universities have in fact taken the primary responsibility for providing serious professional theatre to communities as large as Detroit and St. Louis. Some of the university companies are semiautonomous bodies that exist only to put on plays for the academic community and the larger community that surrounds it; in other cases, the members of the company double as members of the faculty, and students participate alongside the professionals in the productions. For the purpose of this book, of course, I am primarily interested in these campus companies as producing organizations, not as training programs; my focus will be on what they can do for their audiences, not what they can do for their participants.

The McCarter Theatre Professional Repertory Company (Princeton University)

The McCarter Theatre on the Princeton campus, built in 1929, is a substantial, Gothicky building with a proscenium stage and 1,077 seats. It offers hospitality to student productions (notably the transvestite musical comedies of the famous Triangle Club), to a wide variety of visiting artists (Emlyn Williams, Ravi Shankar, Teresa Berganza, José Greco), to a film series, and to Princeton's own resident professional theatre, which performs in repertory on weekend evenings for the public and at matinées for high school groups. The McCarter Professional Repertory Company is entirely a professional operation, with an Equity company of around twenty, plus a few non-Equity journeymen; Princeton undergraduates who want to be in plays have producing organizations of their own.

According to the Faculty Committee for the McCarter Theatre, "The administrative councils of Princeton University . . . are persuaded that the seeing of a play can be an important enhancement to its study, and the McCarter Theatre of Princeton, therefore, is supported by the institution as an educational facility." According to Professor Alan S. Downer of Princeton's Department of English, the aim is that McCarter should "become a 'living library of theatre.'" The Repertory Company is supervised by a committee of the Princeton faculty which, says Professor Downer, "has laid down the guide lines for play selection: during any four-year college generation, a student will have the opportunity to see something of everything the theatre has to offer, from every period and country, in every form." In the Repertory Company's first six years (it was founded in 1960), it presented sixteen plays by

Shakespeare, five by Bernard Shaw, three each by Molière, O'Neill, and Wilder, two each by Brecht, Ibsen, Pirandello, Chekhov, Wilde and Christopher Fry.* In 1966–67, this list was augmented with *Agamemnon, A View from the Bridge, Hamlet, Once in a Lifetime, Waiting for Godot, The Braggart Warrior* (Plautus), *The Tempest, The Emperor Jones,* and *The Servant of Two Masters* (Carlo Goldoni). The company has never produced an original play, though it plans to do so in the future.

The three productions I saw at McCarter in the spring of 1967 were on the drab side, unimaginative in conception and erratic in execution. According to Arthur Lithgow, executive director of the theatre, the Repertory Company provides a "training situation" for professional actors "on the way up." Some of the ones I saw had a long way to go. *The Emperor Jones,* directed by Michael Schultz, came off best: the forest in which Jones regresses to primitive terror was well enough rendered (scenery and lighting by Clyde Blakeley), and so were the hallucinations that visit him out of his personal and racial past (choreography by Lauren Jones and Charles Moore). Even the Witch Doctor, though not terrifying, was never ridiculous, as he easily might have been. Clayton Corbin, who played Jones, has a splendid physique and a capacity for big emotion. But he started his performance in such a state of tension that he was left with nowhere to go in later scenes, and his voice sometimes gave the impression that it was not really as big and deep as he was trying to make it.

Although *The Servant of Two Masters* is two hundred years old, it contains no more profound insights into the human condition than *Barefoot in the Park.* Its only justification is its entertainment value, and the McCarter production was not very entertaining. This is not really the play's fault; Goldoni wrote it for a deft and practiced *commedia dell'arte* troupe, but the actors who played it at Princeton were enthusiastic, ingenuous, and clumsy, more like college kids than professionals. Frederic O'Brady, who directed, supplied or permitted a number of interpolations, a sensible policy for such an easygoing piece. Some of these interpolations ("May I have your attention, please. The owner of gondola number 8450 has parked it on the wrong side of the

* Alan S. Downer, "Repertory Theatre Educates Actor and Audience," *University*, Winter 1966–67.

canal") were funny; the best of them were funnier than anything Goldoni supplied, which is surely an unhealthy sign.

The Tempest, directed by Anthony Stimac, had a nice moment when Miranda, who had never seen a man except for her father, hesitantly touched Ferdinand to see if he was real, and a splendid roaring exit for Caliban right through the auditorium. (The kids loved that.) George Hearn, who played Caliban, is clearly a thorough professional with plenty of thrust, but there was little of the primitive about his monster. The Prospero, Peter Bailey-Britton, was dignified and imposing, and has a good voice, but diction problems made his words hard to understand. The Ariel, Susan Babel, did a lot of balletic posing and seemed generally self-conscious, even a bit pompous. And the Miranda was a pretty, pleasant, properly virginal-looking young girl without a hope of playing the part remotely adequately at this stage of her development. The acting in general was either unpolished and gauche, or labored and overexquisite. The clownery was not very funny (admittedly, Shakespeare has not here provided much to work with in this respect); the austere, geometric set did not encourage lyricism. It was not, on the whole, a very magical production.

The McCarter Repertory Company seems to be run as if just *doing* these plays is enough. The trouble with the "living library" analogy in this case is that, judging from the productions I saw, the emphasis is more on the "library" than on the "living."

The Syracuse Repertory Theatre (Syracuse University)

At Syracuse, as at Princeton, the university had a theatre-building on its hands—in this case a 1,000-seat former movie house not far from the campus. With some financial aid from a local foundation, university authorities decided to establish a professional repertory company, on a two-year trial basis, to share the theatre with various touring and local attractions; as at Princeton, extensive plans were worked out for high school matinées. To administer the building and act as managing director of the new company, the university hired Rex Henriot, who had nursed Theatre Saint Paul in Minnesota from an amateur to a professional company, only to see it fold out from under him. G. F.

Reidenbaugh, head of the university's drama department, became artistic director of the Syracuse Repertory Company.

For an eight-week pilot season beginning in January, 1967, Mr. Henriot and Professor Reidenbaugh hired fifteen Equity actors (including their wives) and scheduled *Love's Labour's Lost* (Shakespeare), *Tiger at the Gates* (Giraudoux), *The Devil's Disciple* (Shaw), and *Slow Dance on the Killing Ground* (William Hanley) to play in alternating repertory.

The Devil's Disciple, directed by Professor Reidenbaugh, was quite bad. Michael McGuire in the title role had plenty of brio and a good sardonic cutting edge, but his abrasive voice worked against him. The leading lady was phony and arch, the character woman overworked, another leading actor emphasized everything a little too much, as if he were addressing deaf people. The actors playing Englishmen (the play is about the Revolutionary War, and the distinction between Englishmen and Americans is not irrelevant) did not bother with English accents, and General Burgoyne, that devastating intellect, was played as an affected ass. It is highly questionable whether a production like this one is better than none at all.

The next day, however, I saw a run-through of what was obviously going to be an admirable production of *Slow Dance on the Killing Ground*, directed by Mr. Henriot. This is the Broadway *succès d'estime* that brings together a guilt-ridden refugee storekeeper, a psychotic young Negro, and a pregnant teen-ager in the refugee's shabby candy-store in Brooklyn. Zouanne Henriot did all the right things in the right way as poor pregnant Rosie; there was a little too much technique in evidence, a slight sense that she was *doing* rather than *being*, but this may well have been ironed out by the time the play opened. The other two performers were impeccable. Gary Gage had just the right sort of profound, slightly flabby solidity for the storekeeper. The Negro boy is a virtuoso part, with two personalities; sometimes he is a sort of professional Negro, hip, sardonic, and dangerous, wielding an Uncle Tom affectation like a weapon, and sometimes he is a gentle, cultured, rather delicate young man with a taste for fancy rhetoric. Roger Robinson, who played the role, was thoroughly equal to both sides of this "self-made schizophrenic," and played each as if the other did not exist, which is just what the character does.

William Hanley, the author of *Slow Dance*, has talent, and his oddly assorted principals grate together in an interesting fashion. But the play degenerates into a self-pity festival, full of pompous talk about Great Issues in a manner reminiscent of Arthur Miller's worst. A three-character play is not, moreover, a very searching test of any company's strength-in-depth. But after *The Devil's Disciple*, it was a relief to know that the SRT had as many as three good actors.

The John Fernald Company of the Meadow Brook Theatre (Oakland University, Rochester, Michigan)

First there was Meadow Brook, the "beautiful rolling estate" (says the souvenir program) of Mr. and Mrs. Alfred G. Wilson, far, far in the affluent suburbs of Detroit. In 1957, the Wilsons donated Meadow Brook, plus two million dollars, to establish Oakland University, an affiliate of Michigan State. New universities, of course, are proliferating all over the country; D. B. Varner, the chancellor of Oakland, is ambitious to make his institution distinguished by creating there "one of the nation's truly great centers of the performing arts." In 1964 the Meadow Brook Festival was founded as the Detroit Symphony's answer to Tanglewood; in 1965 it was joined by the Meadow Brook School of Music. The next steps were a resident professional theatre and an academy for training actors. To set up and supervise both of these, Mr. Varner imported John Fernald.

Mr. Fernald is not a local zealot, not a recent M. F. A. from Yale or Carnegie Tech, not the former director of the Fort Wayne Community Theatre; he is a considerable personage, a mature gentleman (sixty-two years old in 1967) with an international reputation as a director and a teacher of acting. American-born, he made his career in England, directing in the provinces, in the West End, and at the Old Vic. For ten years he was the principal of the Royal Academy of Dramatic Art. He at least is not one of those directors who have never worked anywhere but in their own theatres.

Mr. Fernald recruited twenty-three actors (twelve of them

former students of his) and opened for business on January 4, 1967, with *The Caucasian Chalk Circle;* Brecht was followed by Shakespeare, Shaw, Anouilh, and Chekhov, plus a special children's play for Easter. In October, 1967, the Academy of Dramatic Art opened its doors. It has no academic requirements for admission, and it grants no degrees. The academy is a trade school for prospective actors, and no nonsense about it. A careful line, however, will be drawn between it and the professional company; a brochure for the academy says:

> Students will . . . enjoy the stimulus of being closely linked with the professional theatre, where they will be able to *watch* [italics mine] players trained by the same methods . . . on the stage in a company which, if they successfully complete their course at the Academy, they may be invited to join.

The Oakland undergraduates, of course, will have even less chance to participate in the productions; Mr. Fernald insists on a *"purely professional"* company (italics his). The theatre, he says, is "inside the ambience of the University, as a part of it and yet also as an independent entity."

Oakland University and the Fernald Company are located, so it seemed to me, somewhat inconveniently; there is *nothing* within walking distance of it. I was informed that the campus is within one hour's driving time of six million people, and it appears, not only at Oakland, that as far as the resident professional theatre is concerned, people who do not drive do not exist. In our society, after all, everybody drives except New Yorkers and the absolute poor. Mr. Fernald complains, "It's almost exclusively a very affluent public that we get. I would like to see a more democratic public . . ." and it would not be fair to ask how the democratic public is supposed to get there. The democratic public does drive. It just doesn't drive to the resident professional theatres. But plans are afoot at Meadow Brook to broaden the audience through school programs and other means. And since 7,000 subscriptions were sold for the first season, they seem to be getting along pretty well with just the affluents.

Until its own theatre is ready in the fall of 1968, the company is using a serviceable 608-seat auditorium, with a wide proscenium stage, in the north wing of Matilda R. Wilson Hall. I got out there for the first time in April, 1967, to see the company give an amazingly bad performance of *The Waltz of the Toreadors* by Jean Anouilh, under the direction of Mr. Fernald's associate, Robin Ray. (In most resident theatres such a production would not have been amazing; but I had expected better from Mr. Fernald's company, which ought by rights to have the training that the others lack.) Part of the problem was that the leading actor had fallen sick shortly before the opening. They could have flown in another actor from New York to play General St. Pé, "But," says Mr. Fernald, "that's not the concept . . . It's *within* the company." So another actor was chosen from *within* the company, who was simply unable to play an urbane, middle-aged French general. There are times when the ensemble ideal is far better honored in the breach than in the observance.

But the trouble did not end there. The role of Dr. Bonfant, the general's confidant, was taken by a young man whose efforts at characterization (phlegmy voice with occasional excursions into falsetto, plenty of eyebrow work, an air of oleaginous self-satisfaction) became actively obnoxious; another actor in a (mercifully) smaller part overacted with equal assiduity. Even the set was drab. There was a good performance, however, by Barbara Caruso as the general's mistress, and a brilliant one by Angela Wood as his wife. Miss Wood is one of the very few actresses in America who can play a really formidable virago, a double-barreled, copper-bottomed twenty-one-gun dreadnought, without strain, as if it were her nature to do so. And yet she somehow managed, as Madame St. Pé, to reveal an occasional touch of the woman within the gorgon. I doubt if any comic part ever written for an actress is too heavy for Miss Wood, and I should not be surprised if she could play Lady Macbeth as well.

I came back a month later to see *The Three Sisters*, expecting little, since Chekhov is treacherously difficult, and Miss Wood was not in the cast. Once again I was surprised—this time in the opposite way. Mr. Fernald, who directed, had achieved some remarkable ensemble work. It was clear, for instance, just how Kulygin, the pedant, bored people, and how Solyony, the incipient murderer, made them uncomfortable. Eric Berry was particularly lovable (but not too lovable) as old Doctor Chebutykin, and nearly everyone in the cast acquitted himself well. I have a very pragmatic test for productions of *The Three Sisters*: if the last act makes me cry, I know it's good. I had already seen two mediocre productions of the play in the previous few months, which might have been expected to dull my receptivity, but Mr. Fernald's production passed the test. Clearly he and his company are, at least sometimes, capable of fine work on very demanding material.

The Repertory Theatre of Loretto-Hilton Center
(Webster College, St. Louis, Missouri)

Webster College is a small girls' school in the suburbs of St. Louis, with a Catholic tradition; its president is Miss Jacqueline Grennan (formerly Sister Jacquelin Grennan of the Order of the Sisters of Loretto, but that's another story). Some years ago, Miss Grennan set out to determine just how Webster College could be of the greatest service to its community. Becoming aware that no college or university in the area was particularly interested in the performing arts, and that St. Louis lacked a resident professional theatre, she decided that Webster should emphasize the performing arts in general, and establish a resident professional theatre in particular. Sister Jacqueline obtained $1,500,000 from Conrad Hilton, who had been educated by the Sisters of Loretto, and she used it to build the Loretto-Hilton Center on the Webster campus. The Center has classrooms, offices, studios, rehearsal halls; at its center is a most extraordinary auditorium, essentially a thrust-stage house, but convertible for proscenium staging or theatre-in-the-round. Its capacity can be expanded from 500 to 700 to 1,000 to 1,200 seats by raising a series of mechanically-operated soundproof walls. (When the walls are down, the walled-off sections can be used as classrooms.) Except on special occasions, the theatre is used in its thrust-stage, 700-seat form; in this state it is highly serviceable, and in any state it is handsome and well equipped. This theatre has been occupied, ever since its opening in the summer of 1966, by the professional Repertory Theatre of Loretto-Hilton Center.

"The Loretto-Hilton Center's aim," says Miss Grennan, "is to get our students and our faculty involved in the real world of professional theatre as opposed to the mock-heroic world of the educational theatre." The professional company is much more closely integrated into the curriculum than at Princeton, Syracuse, or Oakland: the professionals teach, and the undergraduates receive academic credit for acting in the productions and working backstage. There are no graduate students. Michael Flanagan, the artistic director of the company, is also the chairman of the college's theatre arts department. One of his public-relations problems, Mr. Flanagan says, is "communicating the idea that these are not student productions, though there are students in them."

Mr. Flanagan is a native of St. Louis, born in 1935, who has taught high school, studied at the famous drama department of Catholic University in Washington D. C., and acted on Broadway. When asked about the purpose of his theatre, he replied, "Quality productions of good plays—or good productions of quality plays, one way or the other. And that covers a great spectrum of plays. I don't think good plays are exclusively classics, or exclusively avant-garde." This, of course, is the standard answer; I have heard it from coast to coast, and I am beginning to think it is really no answer at all.

The company's season is divided into a series of two-month subseasons; during each of these, three plays are mounted in rotating repertory. When I was in St. Louis in the summer of 1967, *The Hostage* by Brendan Behan and *Rashomon*, adapted from the Japanese movie by Fay and Michael Kanin, were playing alternately, and *A Streetcar Named Desire* was in rehearsal. In November and December, a repertory of *The Caucasian Chalk Circle* (Brecht), *The Lion in Winter* (James Goldman), and *The Miser* (Molière) is to be presented; in February and March of 1968 the plays will be *The Merchant of Venice*, *Six Characters in Search of an Author*, and Shaw's *Misalliance*. An eclectic selection: Molière, Shakespeare and the twentieth century.

Mr. Flanagan's production of *The Hostage*, that peerless burst of life-affirming vaudeville, had funny performances by Marian Mercer as Miss Gilchrist, the "sociable worker," and J. Robert Dietz as her gentleman friend Mr. Mulleady; a student actor named Thomas Kampman was quite good as the Cockney hostage himself. (Webster accepts male students in the theatre arts department.) But several performers were miscast (the most prominent among the whores looked as if she would have been more at home playing one of those hard-nosed queen mothers in Shake-speare's history plays), and the general gaiety was often forced. I always enjoy *The Hostage*—how could anyone not enjoy it?—and this was its first production in St. Louis; but it was by no means a distinguished piece of work.

Rashomon was a distinguished piece of work all right; it just wasn't very much fun. It was directed by Louis Criss (a peripatetic artist whose work I had previously seen in Houston and Mil-waukee) in Kabuki style, as the script demands. Four black-clad, hooded, silent figures assisted the principals; a fifth took charge of sound effects. There were long, slow entrances to music, much bowing, much hieratic, formal speech; many passages were half-danced in slow, calm, formal Japanese style. The last half hour or so was a hilarious parody of all that had gone before: when the heroine spat at the bandit, for instance, the sound girl blew a flute and tinkled a bell, after which the bandit wiped his eye. But for the most part, what happened onstage functioned less as a play than as an illustration of Japanese theatre practice; the action got lost amidst all the exotic techniques. It was an interesting experi-ment, skillfully staged by Mr. Criss, but easier to admire than to like.

The Stanford Repertory Theatre (Stanford University, Palo Alto, California)

The founding of the Stanford Repertory Theatre was an-nounced in a handbill, designed for posting on academic bulletin boards, that said:

> Stanford University announces a unique opportunity for drama students in directing, acting, design, costume, and technical produc-tion. The new program includes a professional repertory theatre company and leads to the Master of Fine Arts degree. . . . An artistic director, ten senior actors, and professional designers—all of outstanding professional merit—not only will form the heart of the producing company, but also will serve as teachers throughout the study program. Eight apprentice actors will complete the basic casting, while advanced students also will be invited to work with the professional company.

The company is financed by a $300,000 Rockefeller Foundation grant, allotted at a rate of $100,000 a year, plus (initially) $120,000 a year from the university. Robert E. Loper, head of the Stanford department of speech and drama, became producing director of the new venture, which began operations in the fall of 1965.

Design students as well as acting students are given a chance to exercise their talents in the professional company's productions, and the professionals direct and even act in student productions. But the company is not intended to be merely a training program; it is meant to offer something to spectators as well as participants. It seemed to me, on my one visit, that Stanford was in the middle of palm-planted nowhere, but I am assured that it is surrounded by heavily populated suburbs (San Francisco is just a few miles up the peninsula). When I saw Professor Loper in the spring of 1966, he told me that his audience was 10 per cent student, 5 per cent faculty, and the rest from the civilian population. He had plans to reach low-income groups that traditionally had been suspicious of the university. In a program note, he expressed the hope "that the work of the Stanford Repertory Theatre may be not just an occasional diversion, but a definition, a criticism, and a celebration of our unsafe human condition."

Because it has to share university facilities (a huge 1,700-seat theatre and smaller auditoriums seating 197 and 130) that have other functions as well, the Repertory Theatre has had a somewhat sporadic production schedule. As a result, I have only been able to see one of its productions: a discouraging, and perhaps uncharacteristic, revival of *All's Well That Ends Well*, presented toward the end of the first season. Paul E. Richards was vigorously amusing as the braggart Parolles, and Glenn Cannon coped valiantly with the most discouraging of all Shakespeare's clowns. But the young people in the two leading parts simply spoke their lines clearly, moved around in a more or less appropriate manner, and left it at that. Several student actors (and one or two of the others) seemed to have only a vague idea of what they were doing. Associate Professor William Sharp of Stanford, who was credited with the direction in the program, appeared to have had no views about what really goes on in this odd, difficult "problem comedy," about what it is supposed to do to the audience, about what it's *for.* Certain plays are lucid and accessible enough to survive such treatment, but *All's Well* is not one of them.

The other productions that first season were *That Scoundrel Scapin* (Molière), *The Skin of Our Teeth* (Wilder), a double bill of *The Chairs* (Ionesco) and *The Questions* (John Hawkes), *Prometheus Bound* (Aeschylus), and *The Good Woman of Setzuan* (Brecht). *Prometheus Bound*, directed by Erik Vos, was greatly admired by the critics, and turned out, said Professor Loper, to be "the hit of the season." In its second season, the Stanford Rep offered *Antony and Cleopatra*, a double bill of *A Slight Ache* (Pinter) and *Out at Sea* (Slavomir Mrozek, a contemporary Polish dramatist), *The Beggar's Opera* (John Gay), *The Cherry Orchard*, *Once in a Lifetime*, and *Inadmissible Evidence* (John Osborne). But something happened. The deficit zoomed above the $100,000 mark. Professor Loper stepped out, and Gerald Hiken became acting artistic director.

For the 1967–68 season there will be a drastic cutback. Only three actors have been engaged for the season, though they will be augmented by jobbers. Instead of six productions, there will be five: *The Cavern* (Anouilh), *Candaules, Commissioner* (a new play by Daniel C. Gerould, a San Francisco writer), *Cock-A-Doodle Dandy* (Sean O'Casey), *The Inspector General* (Nikolai Gogol), and a revival of *Out at Sea* on a double bill with *There Is a Meeting Place* by Paul E. Richards. Only one of these will be put on in the enormous Memorial Auditorium, as against four in 1966–67. The university is still committed to having a professional repertory theatre on campus, but its form and dimensions are evidently not yet finally determined.

The Dallas Theatre Center

The Dallas Theatre Center is the lengthened shadow of Paul Baker, one of the best-known figures in American educational theatre. Mr. Baker is a minister's son from Hereford in the Texas Panhandle, who taught drama for twenty-nine years at Baylor University in Waco, Texas. Such actors as Charles Laughton and Burgess Meredith came to Waco to act under his direction, and his production of *Hamlet,* in which the title role was played by three actors including Mr. Meredith, became famous. When a group of Dallas citizens decided to found the Dallas Theatre Center, Mr. Baker was induced to become the head of it; he worked with the architect, Frank Lloyd Wright, on the design of the building (pleasantly located in a park some distance from downtown Dallas), and installed there both a professional company, consisting mostly of people he had trained, and Baylor's graduate program in drama.

In 1963, Mr. Baker resigned from Baylor because the university wanted to censor his production of *Long Day's Journey into Night* (too many swear-words). He was immediately hired by Trinity University in San Antonio, and he brought his entire department along with him; the Dallas Theatre Center dropped its affiliation with Baylor, and became the home of Trinity's graduate program in drama—which is really, of course, Mr. Baker's program, no matter who sponsors it. Mr. Baker spends half the week in Dallas and half in San Antonio, where Trinity has recently built him a splendid new theatre; he commutes by jet.

Nowhere in this country, perhaps, are a professional theatre and a professional training program more closely integrated than at the Dallas Theatre Center. Of the twenty-seven actors, directors, designers, technicians, and administrators who form the permanent company, fourteen hold academic positions on the twenty-member faculty, and most of the remaining faculty members also work in various capacities with the company, as do the students (both the M.A. candidates and those enrolled in a full-time non-degree program). Mr. Baker is a great believer in versatility; the company includes an actor-director-teacher-librarian, an actress-director-designer-administrator-teacher, a designer-director-actor-teacher, and several other multiple-threat talents. And though the Center does not operate under an Equity contract, it has a genuinely permanent professional company, with a core of members who have worked together for years. Productions can be—and are—revived for season after season with the same performers in the major roles.

The Center has a main auditorium with 450 seats, and the "Down Center Stage" in the basement with 74 seats; both are kept almost constantly in action. In 1966–67, the professional company put on eleven plays upstairs, and seven downstairs; four of these were revivals from previous seasons. (*Julius Caesar* has been revived every year since 1962.) Three of the upstairs productions and one of the downstairs productions, plus two more productions from previous seasons, were sent on tour to various places in Texas and Louisiana. In addition, the "Teen-Children's Theatre" and the evening drama classes for adults had productions of their own at the Center. Attendance for the regular productions runs around 61 per cent of capacity (not a high figure), which amounts to about 80,000 people a year, but with tours, children's plays, and dark-night readings of new plays figured in, total attendance comes to nearly 100,000. The Center runs on a budget of $320,000 a year, a modest figure; Mr. Baker and his colleagues make it go a long way mostly, of course, because of the Center's refusal to sign up with Equity).

When I arrived in Dallas in June, 1967, *Barefoot in the Park* was playing in the main auditorium, looking rather uncomfortable on Frank Lloyd Wright's huge and evidently somewhat unwieldy stage. It was a bad production. The staging was copied from Mike Nichols' Broadway prompt book: a tribute to Mr. Nichols that is not undeserved, but an indication that the Dallas director either did not trust his own talent or did not have his heart in his work. Many lines were mistimed; many others were rammed home with ruthless overemphasis. The ingénue was very pretty and voluptuous, but somewhat inhuman; she looked like a hair-dyed, teeth-capped Hollywood artifact, and she had a stage-personality to match. The juvenile was adequate, but showed no particular signs of talent. The actress playing the girl's mother was generally satisfactory, though a bit too young. The remaining principal character was played by a gentleman whose picture in the lobby showed him smiling with Texan amiability and holding a cow skull in his lap, which may suggest something of what was wrong with his performance as a Hungarian *bon vivant*—aside from the fact that he looked a good twenty years too young to play a fading roué.

The State Department or somebody likes to send foreign dignitaries to Dallas to see the work of the Center; in the seat next to me at *Barefoot in the Park* was a charming, courtly old Hungarian theatre historian. Fortunately for the credit of the American stage, he fell asleep shortly after the performance began. As for me, I had a very pleasant time remembering how funny Neil Simon's lines were when other actors spoke them.

In the tiny basement theatre, running concurrently with *Barefoot in the Park*, was an original play entitled *R. U. Hungry (Specialty: Short Orders)*, directed by Mr. Baker himself. It was written by Randy Ford, a student at the Center, who also designed the lighting for it and helped to build the set. (Under Mr. Baker's tutelage, it seems, everybody learns to do everything; according to the program, Mr. Ford had also been active in acting and "industrial ticket sales.") The play was a Texas genre piece, set in a shabby luncheonette. It had overtones of Chekhov, Texas-style (the waitress keeps hoping she'll meet Clark Gable at the supermarket, but he never shows up), and interludes of noisy, busy, unsuccessful farce. Mr. Ford has a real talent for idiomatic, rural, greasy-spoon dialogue, but his play got nowhere in particular and took an unconscionable time getting there.

The title role of R. U. Hungry himself, the proprietor of the luncheonette, was taken by a balding, puckish middle-aged man named Mike Dendy, a member of the permanent company and also the theatre's librarian. R. U.'s wife and waitress, a gabby, blowzy, easygoing bleached-blonde, was played by Judith Davis, who is both a student and a faculty member at the Center, and also its co-executive coordinator. (I don't understand how that works either, but her name appears in the program in all three capacities.) Both Mr. Dendy and Miss Davis were excellent; a student named Johnny McBee had a good bit as a teen-ager, but some of the other students in the cast were a bit out of their depths playing middle-aged people. The Center is an anomalous institution, trying to perform two separate functions simultaneously; *R. U. Hungry*, in spite of some fine acting by some mature actors, made better sense as a drama-school exercise than as a professional production, but the Center does not make any such distinctions among its offerings.

I tend to think, however—I am almost sure—that I came to Dallas at a bad time. Had I arrived a month earlier, I could have seen a production of *The Caucasian Chalk Circle*, staged by the German director Harry Buckwitz of the Staedtische Buehnen in Frankfurt. In the summer, when most theatres are closed, the Center concentrates on Broadway comedies; during the rest of the year its program is ambitiously eclectic. "We are interested," says Mr. Baker, "in anything that's vital and alive and exciting in the world theatre, present and past." In 1966–67 the schedule included two plays by Shakespeare and one by Shaw, plus a French farce directed by a man from the Théâtre de France. The 1967–68 season opened with *Twelfth Night*, and is to include *A Streetcar Named Desire*, *The Homecoming* (if rights are available), and the world première of Paddy Chayefsky's new play *The Latent Heterosexual* (directed by Burgess Meredith, with Zero Mostel in the leading role)—in addition to *The Odd Couple* and *Charley's Aunt*.

Unlike most regional theatres, moreover, the Center always has a few writers around, actually on the premises; it does not have to rely for new scripts on what comes in the mail from New York. Since its founding, the Center has presented no fewer than twenty-nine original plays. Some of them were probably no better than *R. U. Hungry*; I should be surprised if all of them were as good. But one of them was the internationally famous *Journey to Jefferson*, adapted by Robert L. Flynn (who works for Mr. Baker in the drama department of Trinity University in San Antonio) from William Faulkner's novel *As I Lay Dying*. This is the production that won the Special Jury Prize at the Théâtre des Nations festival in Paris in 1964. It was revived in Dallas in January, 1967; I wish I could have seen it. But it is pretty clear in any case that the Center's capacities are by no means circumscribed by *Barefoot in the Park* or even *R. U. Hungry*.

The Yale Repertory Theatre (*Yale University, New Haven*)

In the early nineteen-sixties, when I was a student at the Yale Drama School, this prestigious institution had become a temple of stagnant mediocrity. Its leadership had long since stopped asking itself what purpose the school should serve, and how it might best serve that purpose; things were done merely because they had always been done that way. Then in 1966 Robert Brustein, the dramatic critic of the *New Republic*, became dean of the Drama School, and changed all that. Opinions vary about Mr. Brustein— he is perhaps the most controversial figure in the entire American theatre—but it is clear that something—a whole lot, in fact—is finally happening at the Drama School.

Mr. Brustein has complained with some justice of the tendency to review *him*, rather than the work done at the Drama School. But the work done at the school is, in a sense, his work (there was little enough done there before he came). Mr. Brustein obviously aspires to become an important force in our theatre, and he has already succeeded; in any case, he is a symbol of forces larger than he is. He came to New Haven fresh from a furious seven-year war, waged mostly in the pages of the *New Republic,* against the *status quo* in what he considers our "debased theatre." Perhaps he is something of a fanatic, but the theatre has always owed a great deal to its fanatics. It is not necessary to agree with him all the time to acknowledge the service he has rendered as a leader of our theatrical insurgents.

It must be a depressing business for a man who is devoted to the theatre, as Mr. Brustein unquestionably is, to see its American manifestations through Mr. Brustein's eyes. It is understandable that lately he should have grown weary of denunciations. Having proved abundantly and repeatedly that the art of the theatre has been betrayed and prostituted by Broadway and the Broadway mentality, he has lately turned to scanning the non-Broadway horizons with great eagerness for signs of possible redemption. It is obvious that he regards his new position as dean of the Drama School as an opportunity to participate in the great redemptive work, and to help bring about the "third theatre" he has written about, which will combine reality and joy. "We'll settle for nothing less than changing the whole face of the theatre," the *Times* quotes him as saying.

All this represents, I believe, no ignoble disposition on Mr. Brustein's part. It would have been easy for him to go on as he had done, holding his nose at the top of his voice. He was good at it (as indeed he still is); in fact he was becoming famous for it. And God knows, there was—and is—a need for it. Mr. Brustein had his function as denunciator neatly and successfully marked out; it took courage, therefore, for him to go out on a limb with some positive assertions as well, and to be willing to use his new resources to turn assertion into action.

One of his basic innovations at Yale has been his program of professional productions. (Traditionally, the Drama School's major productions had been performed by student actors.) "With its 1966–67 season," said Dean Brustein,

> the Yale School of Drama initiates a new program, offering—in addition to the customary student workshop presentations—visits by the more enterprising theatre troupes around the country, and major productions of new and established plays by professional theatre artists. Eventually these major productions will be performed by our own resident repertory company, largely staffed by designers and playwrights trained at the school, but until the new course of study is fully under way, the interim program will try to satisfy the hunger for theatre at Yale.
>
> The purpose of this program is twofold: to provide our students with bold examples that might expand their own resources, and to introduce local theatregoers to adventurous plays and production techniques in an atmosphere free of commercial pressures. Our aim is to join two links that have long been separated—the American theatre and the literate audience—at the same time exposing the university community to the more radical, experimental forms now being tested by isolated groups and individuals. A few of these works may well stimulate controversy, and we welcome that—for it is not by bland acceptance but rather by combat and contention that the modern theatre has always inched forward.

Mr. Brustein began his tenure in October, 1966, by importing the company of Philadelphia's Theatre of the Living Arts to present Samuel Beckett's *Endgame,* in a production, directed by Andre Gregory, that made extensive use of improvisation. The following week brought the Open Theatre from New York with *Viet Rock* by Megan Terry, which had originated in the Open Theatre's work. The Open Theatre people spent four weeks at Yale; they rehearsed for two weeks and performed for two, but they found time to work on improvisational exercises, their specialty, with the students.

After *Viet Rock* had departed for New York, where it played a controversial engagement off Broadway, the Drama School mounted the first of its own professional productions: *Dynamite Tonite,* an antiwar comic opera with book by Arnold Weinstein and music by William Bolcom, which Mr. Brustein had praised when the Actor's Studio presented it briefly off Broadway. After its run in New Haven, the Yale production opened off Broadway to give the work a second chance there, but it did not prosper.

The next Drama School offering was its own production of Ben Jonson's *Volpone*. The roles of Volpone and his parasite Mosca were played by David Hurst and Ron Leibman, who had appeared at Yale in *Endgame* and had subsequently been hired by the Drama School to teach acting and serve as resident actors. They are both talented performers, but they were rather odd choices as exemplars for students, and as leading actors in a production of *Volpone*, since Mr. Hurst proved unwilling or unable to shake his Jewish accent, and Mr. Leibman lisped. Through sheer technical inadequacy they made hash of Jonson's heavily gorgeous verse, and thus forfeited the play's element of grandeur—the implication of something heroic in the very baseness it depicts. This is not just a matter of form; when the verse is botched, the play's meaning is diminished.

Still, the production was by no means without interest. "The world which Jonson satirized and attacked," wrote the director, Clifford Williams of the Royal Shakespeare Theatre, "is very much our own world; a riot of imagination and creation on the one hand—materialism gone mad and spiritual poverty on the other hand. Images of this confusion are all around us—the pop scene, *haute couture*, *dolce vita*, the jet groups, the trend setters. This is an ambience which we recognize, and it seems the natural one for a modern production of *Volpone*, if we are to appreciate the relevancy of the play to our own society." And so he put the play into modern dress, more or less.

Volpone at Yale did not look or sound as if "a riot of imagination and creation" was part of the world it dealt with. But the play is, before everything else, a scream of rage against "materialism gone mad and spiritual poverty," and that, from time to time, was reflected forcefully in the production, which brought forth some vivid images of greed, malice, and hypocrisy. Mr. Leibman, looking like a cross between Paul Newman and Milton Berle, glistening with slimy innuendo, was degeneracy incarnate. In the scene where Volpone and Mosca worship their gold, Mr. Leibman *licked* a large gold ball affectionately before putting it back into its shrine.

Jonson has provided Volpone with three retainers: "Nano, a Dwarf," "Castrone, an Eunuch," and "Androgyno, an Hermaphrodite"; Mr. Williams made the most of them. Nano resembled a spider; Androgyno was a leatherette-clad Warholian nonesuch who belted rock 'n' roll into a hand mike (lyrics by Jonson, except for an occasional "ram sham bap shoo wa da"); Castrone was a memorably disgusting drag queen. They threaded in and out of the action as recurrent reminders that this society was not only evil but sick.

Perversion, disgustingness, *dolce vita*, and rock 'n' roll are of course very fashionable nowadays, and it might be asked where cogent contemporaneity ends and mere modishness begins. It would be a hard question to answer, since even what is merely fashionable is an expression of the age. Mr. Williams' production concept looked to me like a legitimate attempt to grapple with the play, not to evade it by gimmickry. But somehow he failed to carry it far enough, and the performance gradually ran out of steam. Rumor has it that Mr. Williams came to New Haven prepared to direct the play in a more or less seventeenth-century context, met the actors, and only then decided to update it. The production certainly looked as if that had been the case; the settings were "period," and so were some of the costumes. And certainly the updating helped Mr. Hurst and Mr. Leibman, by providing plenty of scope for their talents (Hurst's for clowning, Leibman's for Actor's Studio-style sardonic menace), and by distracting attention from their deficiencies. I hesitate to think what these actors would have done to a more conventional *Volpone*. If the production was not, on the whole, a success, it was at least not afraid of the play's enormity. It did manage, now and again, to express Jonson's colossal rage against human depravity. And it made an encouraging contrast to the sterility of the recent production of Jonson's *Alchemist* at Lincoln Center.

Volpone was followed, in May of 1967, by the world première of Robert Lowell's adaptation of Aeschylus' *Prometheus Bound*, in the Drama School's own production. Mr. Lowell's adaptation is a very free one—"Half my lines are not in the original," he says in a program note—and the play belongs really to the American poet-playwright, not to his Athenian forerunner.

For quite some time, Mr. Lowell has been interested in reworking, for his own modern purposes, material bequeathed to him (and, of course, to all of us) by writers of past ages. Concurrently, he has been feeling the peculiar fascination that the theatre has traditionally exercised over poets. Some years ago, these two tendencies found simultaneous expression in a trilogy of one-act plays, based on stories by Hawthorne and Melville, and entitled, with all kinds of ironies, *The Old Glory.* Two-thirds of Mr. Lowell's trilogy was produced in 1964 at the American Place Theatre in New York, and one play, a dramatization of Melville's novella *Benito Cereno,* found wide favor.

Its particular champion was Mr. Brustein, who wrote in the *New Republic*:

> The social-psychological theatre of the thirties, which culminated in the Actors Studio and Lincoln Center [then under the management of Robert Whitehead and Elia Kazan], has now proved itself utterly incompetent to deal with a serious work of the imagination, or anything other than Broadway and Hollywood commodities. And the American theatre will never find itself again until all these outmoded methods and limited visions have been swept away.
>
> Just such a renewal seems to be occurring now at the American Place Theatre where Robert Lowell's *The Old Glory* is currently enjoying an inspired production by Jonathan Miller.*

And thus Mr. Lowell's *Prometheus Bound,* directed by this same Jonathan Miller, the culmination of Mr. Brustein's first year of deanship at Yale.

Prometheus Bound did not strike me as a very long step toward the Third Theatre, which is to combine reality and joy. The play is marked from end to end by Lowell's fineness of mind; it has a peculiar purity about it; it has dignity without pretentiousness; it has moments of great eloquence. And what a pleasure it was to meet in the theatre (of all places) a modern American writer who can absolutely be depended upon never to lapse into cliché. The play was given an admirable and lavish production (financed in part by a U.S. government grant). Yet it did not, as we say, "work."

Prometheus, of course, is the archetypal rebel, maintaining a

* Reprinted in Robert Brustein, *Seasons of Discontent* (New York, 1967), pp. 255–256.

posture of splendid defiance, asserting the primacy of the individual against the system. As such, he has frequently been reincarnated by modern dramatists—by that dwindling band of modern dramatists, at least, who keep hold of their Romantic heritage and refuse to concede that significant action is impossible. In our century, Bernard Shaw, T. S. Eliot, Arthur Miller, and Robert Bolt have all created Promethean heroes. Usually Promethean drama resolves itself into a rousing paean to the heroism of the martyr for conscience's sake. Mr. Lowell's Prometheus has his moments of splendid defiance (hard-bitten in their irony, never pompous or smug), but on the whole Mr. Lowell seems interested in something else. What? I find it hard to say (although some clue may be afforded by the fact that around the Drama School they referred to the play as *Waiting for Prometheus*).

The new *Prometheus Bound*, like the original, lacks dramatic thrust, progression, suspense—in a word, plot. At the beginning of the play, Prometheus gets fastened to a rock; he receives several visitors; long speeches are delivered back and forth; at the end a new punishment begins. I do not maintain that every play should keep us diverted with plenty of plot; but plot is the strongest kind of through-line a play can have, and the dramatist who dispenses with it had better provide us with plenty else to hold onto. The static dramaturgy inherited from Aeschylus makes it particularly unfortunate that at a first hearing of *Prometheus Bound*, it was often difficult to make sense of what Mr. Lowell's characters were saying.

There were moments when the writing was economical and precise. An old man (an old god, literally speaking, but all Lowell's characters function as men), who has sold out to the tyrant Zeus, says: "I have grown old and carefree by learning how to give in." Prometheus himself says of Zeus: "Suppose he is powerless to pardon, and only almighty in his ability to inflict pain"—which may or may not be a reference to the escalation of the war in Vietnam. (In the early part of the play several references to Zeus made him sound like President Johnson. "No contemporary statesman is parodied," Mr. Lowell insists. "Yet I think my own concerns and worries and those of the times seep in." And the President is well known to be one of Mr. Lowell's concerns and worries.)

But there was something peculiarly evanescent about large parts of the play. I found myself at many points wanting to stop the action (or rather, the talk) and say, "Can we have that again?" Enlightenment—some idea of how the speech currently being spoken related to the rest of the play—usually seemed just around the corner, but there, for the most part, it stayed. Finally, the play got boring.

I am tempted therefore to dismiss Mr. Lowell's *Prometheus* as closet drama—but I wonder if any play completely without theatrical value could have given rise to so beautiful a production as *Prometheus Bound* received under Jonathan Miller's direction at Yale.

In Mr. Miller's program note he says: "There is a ghastly piety about most productions of the Greek drama . . . an empty classicism which reflects scholarly respect more than any direct engagement of the imaginative sensibility." We all know what he means: a lot of actors in white nighties posturing before a temple front. Mr. Miller has reformed this altogether, "setting the play in a shattered seventeenth-century castle-keep," with stained and dusty costumes that would not be out of place in a production of *Mother Courage*. Setting and costumes were designed by Michael Annals, who teaches scene design at the Drama School, and the lighting was by Phil Dixson, a student; their work looked magnificent. The set seemed to extend up to infinity, and down almost as far; its detailing was copious, yet its outlines strong; as the lighting changed, it constantly took on new fascinations. And, majestic as it was, it seemed in accord with Mr. Lowell's evident intention of making Prometheus a human hero, not a demigod.

Prometheus himself was played brilliantly by Kenneth Haigh, who created the role of Jimmy Porter in *Look Back in Anger*. Since then, he has never quite won the recognition his talents deserve. With his gift for irony, and his air of virile intelligence, why have we never seen him play Hamlet? His Prometheus was a stocky, tousle-haired, unpretentious fellow, with a kind of bitter zest to him, no less a hero for being at the same time a *Mensch*. Irene Worth was splendid as Io, persecuted by Hera for having been loved by Zeus. The Drama School's two resident professional actors were both, this time, highly effective in smaller parts: David Hurst as Ocean (a sleazy time server in the Zeus administration) and Ron Leibman as Hermes (a braying thug). Indeed all the acting was admirable; nowhere in this country, I dare say, could the play have been done better.

Some of Mr. Miller's ideas were questionable, but throughout the production there was the sense of an audacious yet responsible mind, and a skilled hand, at work. But Mr. Miller, for all his talents, was unable to make Mr. Lowell's *Prometheus* viable for the theatre (I doubt if anybody could), and so the event as a whole must be called a failure. But it was a stimulating failure, a vigorous, serious, intelligent failure—just the sort of failure that a drama school ought to have now and then.

The following fall, Mr. Brustein's Yale Repertory Theatre officially became a reality. Its first season opened in October, 1967, with *'Tis Pity She's a Whore*, John Ford's seventeenth-century tragedy, directed by Kenneth Haigh. This was followed by the world première of *We Bombed in New Haven*, Joseph Heller's first play, which I went up to New Haven to see. Since Mr. Heller is the author of *Catch-22*, which I regard as a glorious comic master-piece, I found it hard at first to think that his play was ir-remediably flawed. "It needs work," I said very wisely throughout the intermission. But a play needs work when it is sound at the core and weak around the periphery; *We Bombed in New Haven* has some first-rate periphery, but its core is a mess.

Only toward the end of the play did we discover what Mr. Heller was really trying to do, but then it turned out that *We Bombed in New Haven* is essentially a grindingly conventional military problem-play. Poor weak-but-decent Captain Starkey is torn between his soldierly duty and his humane impulses: how long will he be able to continue obeying orders that oblige him to send men to their deaths on futile bombing missions? The question is raised, and raised again, and raised some more, in a whole series of crises and showdowns, none of them very effective. Much of the writing in these scenes is amazingly bald and clumsy-earnest; the play turns into a simplistic antiwar tract, on an intellectual level not far above the late Oscar Hammerstein's preachments about brotherhood.

Fortunately, the plot and the theme do not surface until the play is three-quarters done. As if in an unconscious attempt to avoid confronting the hackneyed simplicities of his premise, Mr.

Heller procrastinates for about an hour and a half before getting down to business. Some of this time is taken up with ham-handed Pirandellicism: "I'm not really a soldier. I'm an actor playing the part of a soldier." "None of this of course is really happening. It's a play. It's a show." (The play's title is a pun, embracing the theatrical as well as the military sense of the word "bombed.") For most of its length, however, We Bombed in New Haven seems to be an aimless but very funny military comedy. In between going off to bomb Constantinople or Minnesota, the soldiers spend their time just hanging around, talking and grousing, eating the lousy doughnuts and drinking the lousy coffee provided by "the second prettiest girl on the base," and playing various games. The dialogue is full of Mr. Heller's characteristically goofy cogency: "Today we're going to bomb Constantinople right off the map!" "Why don't we just bomb the map?" and "You know what I love best about you?" "My coffee?" "No, your body." And "Why don't you let the men smoke?" "Because they want to." Perhaps, if he abandons We Bombed in New Haven, Mr. Heller could salvage long stretches of it for use in some more viable context.

In the meantime, the Drama School's professional company, under Larry Arrick's direction, gave the play the benefit of some remarkable ensemble acting: unaffectedly masculine and smooth yet electric in its rapport, like a basketball game. Stacy Keach, the original Macbird, did all that could be done with poor Captain Starkey, who is caught in Mr. Heller's moral cleft stick. Ron Leibman played his chief antagonist very effectively as a Jewish wise guy. Anthony Holland and John McCurry made a couple of picturesque soldiers: Mr. Holland's persona, as Mr. Brustein once pointed out in a review, "is that of a shrill, red-headed Jewish sissy";* Mr. McCurry, an enormous Negro, gained a place in the hearts of many connoiseurs some years ago for the authoritative, the magisterial, the definitive way in which, as Sam in The Connection, he would rumble, in that huge, deep, resonant voice of his, "Sheeeeiiit." The quality of the acting was consistent all through; the Drama School students who played the supernumerary characters identified in the program as "Five Idiots" were

* Seasons of Discontent, p. 77.

always funny-dumb whenever I looked at them, but I never caught one of them mugging unduly.

Later in its season, Yale Repertory Theatre has scheduled Pirandello's *Enrico IV* (a one-hundredth-birthday present to its author), *The Three Sisters*, and Shakespeare's *Coriolanus*, with Stacy Keach in the title role. Alvin Epstein, Paul Mann, and Barry Morse are also listed as members of the company. At least seven of the professional actors will double into the classroom, and students will continue to play small roles in the professional productions.

In a recent article in *The Times*,* Mr. Brustein advocated:

> an alliance between the resident theatre movement and the great universities. This . . . could provide a solid base of operations, and a relative freedom from the pressure to produce immediate results or to meet the entertainment demands of a community. Under the umbrella of the university, men in science and the humanities have traditionally conducted research, with the time to pursue their work and the facilities to pursue it efficiently. Why should this not be possible in the theatre as well? The condition of our stage is such, in my opinion, that nothing short of radical transformation will save it. It has lost its greatest power as an art form—the power to alter destinies, to affect men in a direct and meaningful way. Experimental research, therefore, has become as essential to its development as to the development of chemistry, biology, or medicine. Under an enlightened university administration, a theatre might be able not only to help preserve the past, but to make some experimental probes into the future as well.

My own estimate of the present condition of the American theatre is not quite so gloomy as Mr. Brustein's; nevertheless this seems to me an excellent statement of aims for a professional theatre in a university context. In view of Mr. Brustein's talk about "experimental research" with an eye toward the salvation of "our stage" at large, I am somewhat skeptical about his insistence, in a *New York Times* interview,† that the professional program "exists solely for the students"; it seems rather like insisting that a university's cyclotron exists solely for the students. But this is not to say that a university should not have a cyclotron.

* August 13, 1967.
† September 6, 1967.

THE
SUMMER
FESTIVALS

The Stratford National Theatre of Canada
(Stratford, Ontario)

It has been known for many years in the Old World that an interest in the more demanding forms of theatre is not necessarily confined to the months when oysters r in season, and that in fact people are willing to travel quite considerable distances for a chance to satisfy at the same time their cravings for greenery and dramatic art. Lately these facts have become common knowledge on this side of the Atlantic as well, and have led within the last two decades to the establishment, in various bosky environments, of a number of summer festival theatres, most of them devoted primarily to Shakespeare. The foremost of these, by a tremendous margin, is the Shakespearean Festival at Stratford, Ontario, now also known as the Stratford National Theatre of Canada.

This particular Stratford is an unlikely place for a festival that attracts an annual attendance of well over 300,000. It is located in the southernmost part of Canada, the part that sticks downward amid the Great Lakes, between Toronto and Detroit. Still, as a Canadian publication once remarked, "Stratford could not be described as the most accessible place in the world . . . It is not exactly on the main road from anywhere to anywhere."

The weary traveler, when at last he arrives in Stratford, finds quite an ordinary-looking town of some 23,000 souls, with a busy, pleasantly ugly little downtown surrounded by tree-lined streets of modest but comfortable-looking homes. I personally find Stratford's very mediocrity delightful; to me the place is ineffably peaceful, and my annual visit is about the best thing that happens to me all year. But in spite of the accident of its name, Stratford has no historic interest whatsoever, and its restaurants are, with few exceptions, awful. Aside from the festival itself, there is little for a visitor to do except paddle a canoe on the Avon River (locally pronounced "Avvn"), sit in the beautiful park along its banks, or swim in the Lion's Club pool. The surrounding countryside is cheerful and prosperous, well equipped with broad fields, big barns, and snug farmhouses; but when you've seen one of each, you've pretty well seen them all. Hundreds of thousands of people must, in their time, have wondered what such a festival was doing in such a place.

According to Tom Patterson, the local boy who founded the festival, he got the idea

> while lying on the banks of the River Avon listening to a band concert, and I thought if we couldn't have something better than this in a town by the name of Stratford, with the Avon River and the beautiful park system, swans floating along, there was something wrong with us. That was the sort of embryo of the plan . . .

This sounds pretty lame; and the reason it sounds lame is that the resources that entitle Stratford to its festival—the resources that in the final analysis make any theatre possible—are not material but human, and among the chief of Stratford's human resources are those of Mr. Patterson himself. He is a mild-mannered man, bespectacled, bow-tied, and bald, with an authentic and unspoiled Canadian accent; he looks like an associate professor, but the record indicates that his is the faith that moves mountains.

When he founded the festival, he had had no experience in the theatre whatsoever, and he was earning his living as associate editor of a Toronto periodical called *Civic Administration*. One day in 1951, while covering a convention of the Canadian Section of the American Waterworks Association, he ran into the mayor of Stratford. According to Mr. Patterson:

We were bragging about Stratford to the other people in the room, and I turned to him and said, "What about a Shakespeare Festival in Stratford?" and he said, "Fine, see what you can do."

So Mr. Patterson (then aged thirty-one) went to work, stirring up interest among Canadian cultural panjandrums in Toronto and elsewhere, and commuting to Stratford three times a week to use the names of the panjandrums to stir up interest at home. After a while, somebody suggested he get in touch with Tyrone Guthrie, so he telephoned Dr. Guthrie in Ireland (by now it was June of 1952). In a spirit of what-the-hell, Guthrie agreed to come to Stratford, meet Patterson and his committee, and give advice.

Guthrie writes in his autobiography about the results of the meeting:

> We agreed—and here my respect for the committee was great; and the more I think of it the greater it grows—that to present Shakespeare even adequately is a very, very expensive proposition; so expensive that there could be no hope of making ends meet in the first year, and comparatively slender hope that ends would ever meet. And still the committee was resolved to raise the needful funds and go forward.*

A thousand committees in a thousand small towns—and some large ones too—have been formed to Do Something to improve the cultural level of their communities. Where this group was distinctive was in being unwilling to settle for the little theatre or other small project suitable to their obscurity. Quixotically, they determined to have the best, no matter what it cost. And so, after many agonies and some prodigious feats of diligence and valor, they got it.

Guthrie agreed to stage the two plays that would comprise the festival's first season; Alec Guinness was engaged to star in them, and Tanya Moiseiwitsch to design them. Work was begun on a tent theatre to seat 1,500, beautifully located in a park overlooking the river. Meanwhile, fortified by Guthrie's assurances ("Shakespearean Theatre Here Not a Crazy Idea, Lions Told," headlined the local paper), the committee went to work to raise the neces-

* From *A Life in the Theatre*, p. 317, by Tyrone Guthrie, Copyright © 1959. Used by permission of McGraw-Hill Book Company.

sary $150,000. An amazing 50 per cent of this was found in Stratford itself (to date, the citizens have contributed an average of $22.50 *per capita*), but there were "several pretty terrible crises" (Patterson's phrase) when the money did not come in as fast as anticipated. Up until a few weeks before the opening, there was considerable doubt as to whether there would be a festival at all.

Finally, on July 13, 1953, the new tent theatre on the banks of the Avon was inaugurated on schedule with *Richard III*, Alec Guinness in the title role; the following night, *All's Well That Ends Well* entered the repertory, with Irene Worth as Helena. Brooks Atkinson of *The New York Times* and Walter Kerr of the *Herald Tribune* were there; they didn't like all they saw, but they were instrumental in giving the occasion the stamp of more than local importance. It was probably the first theatrical occasion in Canadian history to bear such a stamp.

During that first season, attendance ran to 98 per cent of capacity, and it was clear that the Stratford Shakespearean Festival was going to be a permanent institution. Today, the 1,500-seat tent theatre has given way to a permanent Festival Theatre that seats 2,258, and since 1956 the festival has used the 1,100-seat Avon Theatre, in downtown Stratford, as a second house; this gives it a far larger seating capacity than almost any resident professional theatre in the United States. That first six-week season of two plays has grown into an eighteen-week festival which in 1967 offered five plays, two operas, fourteen concerts, five exhibitions, and three seminars. Total season attendance has grown from 68,000 in 1953 to well over 320,000 in 1967. (The season now includes five weeks set aside for student performances, which attract 65,000 youngsters from Ontario, Quebec, Michigan, Ohio, and New York.) The box office takes in $1,300,000 a year. And the budget has grown from $150,000 to $1,800,000. The festival has sent productions to the Edinburgh Festival in Scotland, the Chichester Festival in England, and Expo 67; other Stratford productions have toured widely in Canada, the United States, and England. The Stratford production of *Oedipus Rex*, directed by Tyrone Guthrie, became a feature film, and several Stratford productions have been televised in Canada and the United States.

Basking in plaudits and popularity, the Stratford Shakespearean Festival has become one of the great theatrical success stories, and in this case the success has been entirely deserved. Stratford's distinction comes partly by virtue of its position as Canada's leading performing-arts institution, a source of cultural impetus for the whole Canadian nation, and partly by virtue of its standing as a theatre of international caliber, a monument to Tyrone Guthrie's brand of theatricality, and as such, an influence on the English-speaking theatrical world at large.

Tom Patterson performed the initial leap of faith by daring to believe that Stratford and its environs—in the absence of any living local theatrical tradition, in a country where an actor could hardly make a living outside of radio and television—could provide an audience for the plays of William Shakespeare. Patterson now thinks that most of the theatre's ills in the United States and Canada are due to overcentralization, and he has proved that decentralization is possible. For all its international réclame, the festival is solidly rooted in its environment: 71 per cent of its audience comes from the province of Ontario. This is an audience not just for stars, or for particular plays, or for productions that have received "rave notices"; it is an audience loyal (with occasional lapses) to the festival itself. In the 1963 season, for instance, the company had no stars; the plays were three of Shakespeare's least-known and least-loved, plus *Cyrano de Bergerac* for a bonbon; the critics were not particularly enthusiastic—and yet the estimated attendance, for 123 performances in a theatre larger than any of New York's legitimate houses, was 85 per cent of capacity.

Canadians come to Stratford to watch Canadians at work. Early on in their deliberations, Guthrie and Patterson and their colleagues decided that though they might use a few actors from Britain or elsewhere, including stars, yet, in Guthrie's words, "the project must be demonstrably a Canadian one, carried out not merely by Canadian initiative, and with Canadian finance but by Canadian actors."* Before the first season, Guthrie auditioned in Montreal, Ottawa, and Toronto, seeing 317 people in five days, and, with the exception of four British actors, he engaged an entirely Canadian company. (More British actors have joined over the years, but many of them have settled down and become

* *A Life in the Theatre*, p. 318.

Canadians.) Three actors from that first Stratford company appeared there again in 1967; one of them, Douglas Rain, has appeared there every season in between. Out of fifty-one principal actors in the 1967 aggregation, there were twelve veterans of five seasons or more; six of these were ten-year veterans. This is not only a Canadian company, but truly a *company* in the sense of a continuing body of actors, although it is only together for six months of every year. (Plans are now under way to provide the company with year-round employment.)

Guthrie's formula of a Canadian company, joined by a star or two, has served for most festival seasons. For six summers, even the star (Christopher Plummer) was a Canadian. From 1963—the year of my first visit to Stratford—until 1966, the festival got by without any stars at all. It could have used some. Many of Shakespeare's greatest plays are built around one or two great roles; many demand a heaven-storming tragedian who can take over the stage and magnetize an audience, who can make it clear instantaneously that he is made of different clay from ordinary mortals (if there is not a radical difference between Hamlet and even Horatio, why bother?), who can carry a whole play on his back. In other words, a *great* actor. This the festival has lacked. In 1963, for instance, it gave the title roles in Shakespeare's *Timon of Athens* and Rostand's *Cyrano de Bergerac* to a talented Canadian actor, John Colicos, who was not quite able to bring them off successfully.

I thought in 1963, when I made my first visit to Stratford, that the festival's success stemmed not from any special virtuosity on the part of particular performers, but from the vigor and imagination of the staging, and the soundness of the ensemble. The company struck me as solid all the way down—in itself an extraordinary achievement for a repertory company on this continent—but not inordinately brilliant. Since then the actors at Stratford have improved, or else I have mellowed. The company still lacks a great actor; even so it seems to me nowadays an absolutely superb ensemble, the cohesiveness of which does not obscure the rare distinction of many of its members. Before the festival, nobody knew how good Canadian acting was; now, it puts us to shame.

The festival's discovery of the possibilities of Canadian talent and Canadian audiences led to further attempts to make use of both these resources. "Theatre breeds theatre," as Patterson says.

He himself (along with Douglas Campbell, for several years a leading festival actor) founded the Canadian Players, a company that tramped the byways of Canada and the United States, taking professional theatre to places where there is usually none, even to Indian settlements in the far north. (The Canadian Players has recently been merged into a Toronto resident theatre.) In the wake of the Festival's success, other enthusiasts have set up theatres in Winnipeg (as noted), in Vancouver, and elsewhere. Patterson himself helped to start the Neptune Theatre in Halifax. He hopes that there will eventually be a chain of such theatres all across Canada, exchanging productions with one another.

To provide trained talent for Canadian theatre in the future, the indefatigable Mr. Patterson also helped to found the National Theatre School of Canada, which for several years spent its summer term in Stratford during the festival season. The school is co-lingual, as Canada is; its alternate title is the École National de Théâtre du Canada. As a Canadian theatre, Stratford recognizes a responsibility to French-speaking Canadians. French-Canadian actors have played the members of the French court in Shakespeare's history plays. For two seasons, the Théâtre du Nouveau Monde, a French-Canadian troupe from Montreal, presented Molière at the festival; its former director, Jean Gascon, has acted and directed at Stratford for several years, and in 1967 became the festival's executive artistic director.

Playwrights are always harder to find than actors, and none of any importance has as yet emerged from Canada. The festival is primarily a Shakespearean theatre, but it has presented three plays by Canadian playwrights so far (none inordinately successful), and expects to do more in the future.

All this is particularly meaningful for Canadians because, as the *Canadian Forum Weekly* observed in 1954, it happened in a country which "is noted for its lack of support for live theatre." Canada's cultural deficiencies, less apparent now, after Expo, but traditionally a sore spot, have been the subject for inquiry by a Royal Commission. ". . . in Canada," says the novelist Nicholas Monsarrat, a Canadian by choice, "any creative people—actors, writers, painters, musicians—are lumped together in the public mind as loose-living parasites who can't even add up a column of figures." After the first, triumphant Stratford season, when it was proposed that the City of Ottawa confer civic recognition, in the form of a signet ring, on a local actress who had appeared at Stratford, the proposal was opposed by Controller Paul Tardif on the ground that "it would detract from civic honors paid to Canadian amateur and professional athletes in the field of sports." When proponents of the actress remonstrated, Controller Tardif asked, "What championships has she won?"

If the festival's continued success did not convert many of those who held Controller Tardif's attitude, it provided a rallying point for those of the opposite persuasion, and enabled all those Canadians oppressed by a cultural inferiority complex to feel better. "Stratford has shown us—admittedly to our surprise—what we can do," said the London (Ontario) *Free Press.* A Toronto critic, no friend of the festival, grudgingly acknowledged "the national gratification" caused by its "continued popularity and esteem." His Excellency the Right Honourable Vincent Massey, then Governor-General of Canada, said when he laid the foundation stone of the festival's permanent theatre:

> This . . . is an event unique in our history. We are marking a great moment in the story of an enterprise which began as a local effort with unbelievable ambitions. We now see it as a national achievement winning incredible success.
>
> It has added lustre to the name of Canada abroad. Much more important, it has given to many Canadians a new and just sense of pride in themselves and in their land.

Even when much is discounted from this as official hyperbole, much remains. Though only a Canadian could be sure, there is evidence that the Stratford Shakespearean Festival marks a moment in the national self-consciousness of Canada, that it deserves the new title that designates it as Canada's national theatre.

As such, it is of interest to Americans as proof of the part that a theatre can play in national life; but the Canadian Stratford has more palpable, more directly theatrical claims on our attention. Sir Tyrone Guthrie has moved on from Stratford, but he has left a rich artistic legacy behind him. Asked what the festival owed to Guthrie, Tom Patterson replied, "Just about everything. . . . It was he who put the stamp of high standard on it from the beginning." By bringing to Stratford his immense resources of energy, influence, and imagination, Guthrie transformed the festival from a local to an international occasion.

The most material of his contributions is the magnificent stage which he created with his long-time colleague, the designer Tanya Moiseiwitsch. Michael Langham, the English director who succeeded Guthrie as artistic director at Stratford, observes that the theatre grew, as it were, from the stage outward; the change from tent to permanent, $2,150,000 Festival Theatre was basically a mere matter of putting a new "hat" over the central, essential, crucial stage; and the result, Mr. Langham says, is "The most exciting theatrical plant I've ever come across."

The festival stage is a very free adaptation of what we believe Elizabethan stages to have been like. From a façade that is an abstracted version of the Elizabethan "tiring house," with a balcony above a columned inner stage, it juts boldly into the auditorium, which is wrapped around it in a 220-degree arc. There is no proscenium arch to separate it from the audience; it can never be hidden behind a curtain; the sense of its presence dominates the auditorium at every moment. Neo-Elizabethan staging for Shakespeare is widely common nowadays, but something about the Stratford stage—its proportions, perhaps—makes it uniquely exciting, even during intermissions. And there is probably no other place in the world where they know so well how to use such a stage, how to take advantage of its special opportunities.

This stage is meant to be constantly seen and *felt* by the audience, not to be disguised and obliterated by scenery. For the most part there is no scenery at all; the ever-present stage is "dressed" by the actors in their splendid costumes, and by such props as they can bring on and off themselves. To take advantage of the fact that actors are more mobile than even the most elaborately mechanized sets, this flexible though unchanging stage has seven major acting levels, with nine major entrances and uncounted minor ones: toward, away from, above, under, and through the audience. Stage-waits are avoided; in Mr. Langham's 1963 production of *Troilus and Cressida*, for instance, the Greeks were onstage and doing before the Trojans had completed their exits—and on this stage such rapidity seemed perfectly natural. (It must have been the rule at Shakespeare's own theatre as well, where *Romeo and Juliet* was "the two-hours' traffic of our stage.")

At Stratford the setting is localized only insofar as the director feels the script demands it. As the characters come on, they bring their locale with them by words alone, or, if need be, by words combined with things. In the first scene in *Troilus and Cressida*, for instance, when Troilus said:

> Call here my varlet; I'll unarm again:
> Why should I war without the walls of Troy
> That find such cruel battle here within?

we knew that the bare stage was somewhere within the walls of Troy, which is all we needed to know. When Troilus left and Cressida came on, a rug, a pillow, a canopy, a seat, and a vessel of oil were brought on by servants, creating an atmosphere of luxurious femininity for her. When the props had made their point, they were taken off in mid-scene, except for the seat, which became a platform on which Cressida and Pandarus stood to watch the return of the Trojan soldiers. We could have assumed, had we wanted to, that the stage had represented first a street in Troy, then Cressida's boudoir, and then the roof of her house. But we didn't. The question of just exactly where we are is usually irrelevant to Shakespeare, and when we are not forced to consider it, it does not arise.

"This stage," as Michael Langham says, "will not be some literal, fixed location, but at any given moment will constitute the crucible in which the living elements of the play will interact." Of course, a neutral, nonlocalized stage can also be contrived behind a proscenium arch; but whereas a thrust stage like Stratford's encourages the director and the audience to regard it as a platform across which the action sweeps, bringing with it such minimal accouterments as it needs, the temptations of the picture-frame stage are all the other way.

There seems to be little chance that Stratford's example will lead to the supplanting of the proscenium altogether, and this is just as well. Plays not written to be staged in a neo-Elizabethan cockpit tend to suffer when dropped into one and deprived of the scenery against which they were intended to be seen. In Mr. Langham's production of *Cyrano de Bergerac*, for instance, the first act was highly bewildering because the audience never knew exactly where the actors were supposed to be, and such knowledge is essential for an understanding of the action. Moreover, only in proscenium staging can all parts of the audience see an actor's face simultaneously, and this is important because when an actor has his back to you, it becomes more difficult to understand what he is saying. (This is a problem which the festival is as yet a long way from solving.)

On the other hand, a thrust-stage auditorium brings more people closer to the stage: the Festival Theatre at Stratford has 2,258 seats, none of them more than sixty-five feet from the stage. And the fact remains that many of the greatest plays we have were written expressly for this sort of presentation.

In its brief history, the Stratford stage has already exerted a tremendous influence on theatre construction—that is, on the conditions under which people will see plays—all over the English-speaking world. Stratford, Connecticut, and Stratford, England, both of which started out with more or less conventional proscenium theatres, have both built forestages jutting out into the auditorium, in an attempt to come to some kind of compromise with thrust-staging. Two important new theatres, the Tyrone Guthrie Theatre in Minneapolis and the Chichester Festival Theatre in England, are explicitly patterned (with modifications, of course) after the one at Stratford, Ontario. (The work done in Ontario was, in fact, the inspiration for the entire Chichester project.) All over the United States, from Lincoln Center in New York to the Music Center in Los Angeles, resident companies have been building themselves thrust-stage theatres. The proscenium will not die out, but thanks to Guthrie's work at Stratford, the thrust stage—almost unknown twenty years ago—is now a widespread alternative.

On such a stage, one large, bold statement can make a tremendous impression. In the Langham-Moiseiwitsch *Cyrano*, for instance, a group of brown-clad nuns sat on the bare stage sewing at an enormous brown-and-tan tapestry. It did not tell the audience exactly where the action was supposed to be, but, economically yet surely and strongly, it helped to generate the desired sense of autumnal serenity. Such a stage lends itself to the virile theatricality that is Dr. Guthrie's trademark, and Mr. Langham's work at

Stratford is in the Guthrie tradition. In *Troilus and Cressida* (directed by Mr. Langham, designed by Desmond Heeley), Achilles, the selfish and sensual, appeared first in a huge red cloak that somehow managed to leave him half-naked; later, when finally aroused to fight, he was a stunning figure of vengeance in his bloody-red leather armor. His combat with Hector (arranged by Patrick Crean) was the most sensational stage-fight I have ever witnessed. And yet the sensationalism was not gratuitous: it helped to dramatize the opposition between chivalry and the naked exercise of power which is one of the important themes in the play.

In the final analysis, a Shakespearean theatre must be judged by its attitude toward its author. If this attitude is one of fidelity tempered by understanding, the result will probably be a well-selected group of actors, and a good use made of them. There may be defeats and even disasters, because in so perilous an undertaking as the production of Shakespeare's plays, the outcome must always be in doubt. But if the basic attitude is sound, then the successes will be the true expression of the theatre's nature and are likely to predominate in the long run; while if the attitude is frivolous, perverse, or indifferent, the successes will be flukes, and the failures typical. At Stratford, the basic attitude is sound.

Guthrie has always exercised to the full the director's right to interpret, to manipulate, to recreate the play for contemporary audiences. At his best, he can turn what is usually delivered as a mere purple patch into living drama. In his Stratford production of *The Merchant of Venice*, for instance, according to the festival's chronicler Robertson Davies:

> There was a splendour of danger about the trial, right until the moment of Portia's triumph, for in this production she did not arrive full of guileful certainty, and armed with a quibble by her cousin Bellario; she found her solution on the stage, before our eyes, and struck down her opponent almost on the spur of the moment . . .*

In such an interpretation, Portia has a reason for her "quality of mercy" speech. She is not merely playing cat-and-mouse with

* Robertson Davies *et al.*, *Thrice the Brinded Cat Hath Mewed* (Toronto, 1955).

Shylock; she is pleading desperately for Antonio's life, not knowing what she will do if the appeal fails.

Of course, an overcreative director can often do violence to a play; Dr. Guthrie himself has produced such controversial none-suches as a shy Petruchio. The imaginative liberty he has claimed can easily be turned into license by lesser directors. That is what happened in Jean Gascon's production of *The Comedy of Errors* at the 1963 festival. M. Gascon conceived of the play as a *commedia dell'arte* scenario. The action was held up for long passages of tedious byplay (authentically in the *commedia* tradition of pantomimic "*lazzi*," only not funny), and overwhelmed by crowds of extraneous zanies, interminably slapping their slapsticks (literally). God knows that *The Comedy of Errors*, as written, is a mechanical piece of journeywork, fit only to serve as a foundation for various sorts of theatricality (as in *The Boys from Syracuse*, the delightful musical adapted from it by George Abbott, Richard Rodgers, and Lorenz Hart). But when a play's director chooses not so much to interpret as to supersede it, he places himself under an obligation to improve upon it. This is impossible when attempted, as it often is, with such a script as *Twelfth Night*; it is relatively easy with *Comedy of Errors*, but M. Gascon was not able to do it by such expedients as having various characters spit on one another ten times during the course of a single short scene. Obedient, moreover, to his "concept" rather than to the needs of his script, he put all his male actors in masks: this is authentic *commedia dell'arte* practice, but the masks had the effect of totally depersonalizing the wearers—and the play needed all the personality that the actors could give it.

This kind of manhandling, however, is very far from being typical at Stratford. Michael Langham is that rarity among directors, a genuine admirer of Shakespeare, in both word and deed. He told me in 1963:

> I'm one of those people who believe that talking about [Shakespeare's] writing "for all time" is not just a platitude. . . . I really do believe that he was incredibly modern. . . . [He] created the cubism of the theatre, and now, over three hundred years since he lived, if we take what we regard as new in our theatre . . . we can find that all these are already contained in Shakespeare. . . .

Shakespeare wasn't just a dramatist who wrote farfetched plots and decorated them with genius. . . . he contrived, with a superb use of varying means, to create . . . a sense of totality of real life. . . .

Mr. Langham compared Shakespeare to Picasso, who came to feel that to paint people in profile or full face was "a sort of lie," and sensed that he could express a larger portion of the truth by painting both at once.

Shakespeare does the same thing; that's why I call it the cubism of the theatre. He can show not only what appears on the surface but what appears beneath the surface. This is the meaning of the striking metaphor and the purple passage . . .

The basis of the festival, he said,

is Shakespeare, and the interpretation of Shakespeare as a modern. . . . We're suddenly in the happy position of appreciating . . . his genius rather more fully than has been the case for about three hundred years, and if this is a theatre of today—and if it fails to be that it is doomed—then we have to set our sights on trying to unearth the truth of his works . . .

Shakespeare was ready to encompass, to embrace, the full span of man's experience and emotions . . . and if we're going to be a Shakespearean theatre of any significance, we have to aspire to embrace the same span, by doing all his works whether they are reputedly "popular," in quotes, or not.

In pursuance of this policy, Mr. Langham in 1963 directed two of the Bard's least popular works: *Troilus and Cressida* and *Timon of Athens*. In a disillusioned, anti-idealistic age such as ours, he felt, *Troilus* and *Timon* "seem strikingly attuned to the prevailing mood. Their content reveals the essence of contemporary life and thought with shattering point." His productions came near to justifying his faith in the plays.

Of *Troilus* he said, "I didn't want to do it other than honestly and simply," and honestly and simply he did it, with little obvious "interpretation." And yet, though the play is inconsistent and inconclusive to read, his direction, by scrupulously making the most of each scene, somehow mortared together the miscellaneous sharp fragments of love and betrayal, chivalry and cruelty, into a vivid and meaningful mosaic.

Timon was even a tougher problem, especially as Mr. Langham took it over from another director shortly before rehearsals began. It is a stark parable about a headlong lord whose life is one long orgy of compulsive giving, until he runs out of money; at that point, finding his friends unwilling to help him, he retires to a cave by the seashore, where he curses everything at very great length and then dies. There is also a fragmentary subplot about a discontented soldier named Alcibiades who leads a successful rebellion.

The plot of *Timon*, then, is both rudimentary and loose; the incidents are repetitive; the characters are flat. Nevertheless, Mr. Langham believed it to be the unfinished "scenario for a great work," and on this understanding he tried to supply what Shakespeare had left out, even to the point of putting in a whole new scene (almost entirely in pantomime) to provide some missing motivations.

To him, the play was a violent attack on materialism, the evisceration of a degenerate society. And he made it so for his audience. The script has less savor of particular time and place than any other play by Shakespeare. Timon is "of Athens" only because he is so in Shakespeare's source, and because "Athens" is as good an alias as any other for civilization at large. Therefore, of all Shakespeare's plays, *Timon* is probably the most amenable to production in modern dress. The dinner jackets and raincoats which Brian Jackson designed for this production were essentially no more impositions on the play than chitons or doublets would have been.

Mr. Langham expressed the fear that he would be accused of gimmickry in his innovations for *Timon*, and protested that they were "not there for jokes. They're there to reveal." And they did. Setting one scene just outside a concert hall, with a soprano shrilling offstage, and setting another in a massage parlor adjacent to a steam-bath—this was showy, it is true. But what it showed was the luxurious degeneracy of "Athenian" society—more vividly, for a modern audience, than the play could do otherwise. And the concept was carried through with great economy: the disciplining presence of Stratford's stage helped to keep the modern peculiarities from going too far.

After the intermission, the modernizations were, quite properly, less striking. Timon reappeared bearded and weatherbeaten, wearing rags that signified bare subsistence. When he needed to be, he was left austerely alone on the bare stage to curse as the script demands, without undue cleverness on the director's part. Since the last half of *Timon* thus rested, as Shakespeare demanded, on the shoulders of Timon himself, and since the actor in question (John Colicos) was not quite equal to the burden, the production as a whole could not be called a success. But in making it as exciting as it was, Mr. Langham performed a remarkable feat of devoted audacity.

For the 1964 season, the festival announced the beginning of a tremendous project: the production of Shakespeare's great double cycle of history plays, which trace the fortunes of the realm from the catastrophe of Richard II's deposition through bloody wars at home and abroad in the reigns of Henry IV, Henry V, and Henry VI, until order and peace are finally restored by the overthrow of Richard III by the Earl of Richmond, later Henry VII, the grandfather of Queen Elizabeth. *Richard II* was to open the 1964 season; the rest of the plays were to be mounted at a rate of two a year until the project was completed in 1967.

Richard II, directed by Stuart Burge, was an ensemble success, most notably in the quality of the verse-speaking. This is an early play of Shakespeare's, and its heavily accented verse cannot be left by the actors to take care of itself. At Stratford you could beat time to many speeches, but the meter never grew monotonous. The speaking was never merely "elocutionary"; rather, the verse became the wing on which the emotion soared.

This aural excellence—which was more than merely aural—was the greatest virtue of William Hutt's performance in the title role. Mr. Hutt gave a highly controlled performance, moving in its refusal to give way to emotion. But what is perversely magnificent in Richard is the voluptuous abandonment with which he wallows in grief; by his unwillingness to wallow, Mr. Hutt lost more than he gained. This detached Richard often knew his posturing for what it was, which helped Mr. Hutt to emphasize something not always noticed in the poet-king: a nice vein of sardonic comedy. But his self-knowledge detracted from the magnificence of many of Richard's gestures. The splendor to which he rose in the Deposition Scene, when for once he let loose, suggested that he might effectively have made more use of his trumpet-register. As Bolingbroke, Leo Ciceri trumpeted most rousingly, in a lower key; he vivified the great swathes of rhetoric in which the part abounds, and managed never to be less hard-nosed than this practical person needs to be. Why Mr. Ciceri has not been given more leading roles is Stratford's great mystery.

In the opinion of many people, *Richard II* was somewhat put in the shade by its companion in the repertory, Michael Langham's production of *King Lear*. The Canadian critics praised it fervently, in the true accents of men surprised by the intensity of their own emotion, and John Colicos, who played the title role, was given a standing ovation on opening night. But it seemed to me that the production fell far short of the script (not that *Lear* is by any means easy to realize onstage). Mr. Colicos' work was always professional; during the confrontation with Regan and Goneril at Gloucester's castle, he was remarkably lucid and touching, and he brought a rare and beautiful sweetness to his reconciliation with Cordelia, and to the consolations Lear offers her after they are taken prisoner. But though he seemed to age during the performance, he still remained rather young for Lear (his costumes were no help), and his majesty came and went. His curses were not magnificent; in the storm, though his emotion seemed real enough, it was general and vague; and he played his mad scene in a manner reminiscent of a superannuated Puck. The Canadian critics and the Stratford management seemed to think that Mr. Colicos was the kind of tremendous tragedian that the play—and the company—needed; but there were those who disagreed.

In 1964, the quadricentennial of Shakespeare's birth, Shakespearean manifestations lurked behind every bush. For this reason, perhaps, the Festival arranged a repertory in which *Richard II* and *King Lear* were balanced by Molière's *Le Bourgeois Gentilhomme* (in English) and William Wycherly's *The Country Wife*. I missed the latter; the former was chiefly notable for a brilliant performance by Douglas Rain as the eponymous bourgeois. With his small moustache and roly-poly body, he looked like those models who portray solid, middle-aged small businessmen in the advertisements in Canadian newspapers, and he had a gravelly voice and perfect small-town accent to match. His M. Jourdain was a charming, pop-eyed innocent, unpretentious in his very pretentiousness, who had made a lot of money and was having a marvelous time discovering what it would buy. The words and the clothes and all the details were seventeenth century, but without ever stepping out of context, Mr. Rain deftly let us know that Jourdain's attempt was thoroughly contemporary as well.

Without straining for it, the festival has found much that is contemporary in sixteenth- and seventeenth-century drama, but it has not, on the whole, had much to do with drama written in the twentieth century. The outstanding event of the 1965 season, however, was the North American première of a work written in the late 1920's: *The Rise and Fall of the City of Mahagonny* by Bertolt Brecht and Kurt Weill. Thirty-five years after its first production at Leipzig, *Mahagonny* was recognizable as a Weimar Republic period piece; nevertheless, it still seemed—and will seem tomorrow—as contemporary, as timeless, as a piece of Dead Sea fruit.

Brecht's Mahagonny is a mythical town on the coast of a mythical Florida, a shabby Never-Never-Land for grownups. The opera's story concerns a goodhearted lumberjack named Jim Mahoney, who turns up in Mahagonny with three of his buddies, looking for fun. But one lumberjack dies of gluttony, another in a crooked prize fight; Jim is betrayed by his remaining friend and by his girl Jenny, and he dies in the electric chair, guilty of Mahagonny's one capital crime: being without money.

As usual, Brecht is not primarily interested in his plot, nor yet in his characters. In this case they are merely the means of evoking Mahagonny itself, a multi-faceted metaphor for a civilization without solidarity or legitimate purpose, where the only rule is *sauve qui peut:*

> And if someone should kick, well, that's me, Sir,
> And if someone gets kicked it will be you.

Mahagonny is devoted to idleness ("Every week here will be seven days free from labor") and freedom ("Whatever you may want to do, There's nothing would prohibit you"). But in Mahagonny total freedom means total indulgence, an absolute abandonment to personal gratification: eating, fornicating, prize fighting, and drinking.

As Brecht portrays it, the life of pleasure lacks even the superficial appeal conventionally ascribed to it. From the first it is tawdry, and gradually it becomes grim. When God condemns everybody in Mahagonny to Hell, He is told that they are in Hell already. Here Brecht is echoing Shaw, who in *Man and Superman* defined Hell as "a place where you have nothing to do but amuse yourself." But in *Man and Superman* this idea remains one among many ideas, whereas in *Mahagonny* "amusing yourself"—the life of appetite—is the subject of the work.

> And appetite, an universal wolf . . .
> Must make perforce an universal prey,
> And last eat up himself.

Thus Shakespeare's Ulysses in *Troilus and Cressida*. But Ulysses was speaking conditionally, about what would happen *if*. Brecht believed that the process was already far advanced in the European bourgeois society he lived in; *Mahagonny* is the portrait of that society. According to Ulysses, appetite is unleashed by the abolition of "degree," of the system of power and subordination by which the world is ruled and anarchy prevented. Brecht, at this point in his career, did not consider the cause, nor did he propose a cure. At the end, the characters sing, "We can neither help ourselves nor you now," and walk offstage. *Mahagonny* is purely and simply the image of Brecht's despair.

As such, it might tend to seem somewhat repetitious, somewhat heavy-handed, especially in comparison with *The Threepenny Opera*, the other well-known Brecht-Weill collaboration. In *Threepenny*, Brecht is working with borrowed material, and the plot and characters are more than merely functional. *Threepenny*, moreover, is very funny in its sardonic way; *Mahagonny*, although bristling with ironies, provides very little to laugh at.

The variety and humanity that *Mahagonny* requires is provided by Kurt Weill's music. Much of it is merely atmospheric, harsh and relentless: underscoring, building up tension, keeping our nerves raw. But when Jim and Jenny sing their tender duet in the second act, a recurring theme in the orchestra suggests that perhaps love is possible even in Mahagonny. Brecht made his characters as vehicles for his own emotion; Weill's music, now and then, gives the characters emotions of their own. It is an odd sort of music; it reminded me of those "assemblages" which are put together out of assorted junk and fragments of anything that appeals to the artist. And yet, for all his eclecticism, Weill in his Brecht period had a pungent, poignant, highly personal style.

In the wrong hands, *Mahagonny* could be a bore; at Stratford it was fascinating. The production was done in English, not on the famous thrust stage but on the proscenium stage of the Avon Theatre downtown. Director Jean Gascon, designer Brian Jackson, and choreographer Alan Lund bodied forth Brecht's vision in a series of harsh, cogent, vivid images and actions. In the song about God's visit to Mahagonny, for instance, God stalked around on stilts, with an obviously fake beard and a pot for a hat, persecuted by a hideous green follow-spot. It was the very image of the modern dead God: pompous, impotent, and patently phony.

The performances were brash and broad, but never strident, never out of control. (Muriel Greenspon, a fat mezzo-soprano from the New York City Opera, played one of the founders of Mahagonny with tremendous aplomb; Thomas O'Leary, a tenor, was Jim, and Martha Schlamme was Jenny.) All the characters in *Mahagonny* spend much of their time speaking for the author directly to the audience, and the Stratford performers seemed as urgently involved with the author's emotions as with the emotions of their characters. Whether this had anything to do with the famous "alienation effect" I should hate to have to say, but it was an essential factor in the impact of this production.

Mahagonny (which has still never been seen in the United States) overshadowed all four of the 1965 offerings at the Festival Theatre. In John Hirsch's production of *The Cherry Orchard*, Douglas Campbell, William Hutt, and Frances Hyland were admirable as Lopahin, Gaev, and Varya, respectively, but whose idea was it to cast hearty, dumpy Kate Reid as Madame Ranevskaya, the exquisite last of a long line of aristocrats? There was also an indifferent *Julius Caesar,* and the history cycle was continued with good productions of both parts of *Henry IV,* directed by

Stuart Burge. The *Henries* featured Douglas Rain as a tough-minded Prince Hal, Tony van Bridge as a charming—sometimes too charming—Falstaff, Leo Ciceri as an imposing King Henry, William Hutt as a hilarious caricature of Justice Shallow, and Eric Christmas as a disgruntled, funny Bardolph—the last an amazingly creative performance in a dully written part.

The crown of the history cycle, in my eyes anyway, and the great event of the 1966 season, was John Hirsch's production of *Henry VI*, in John Barton's adaptation. The Barton version, made for the Royal Shakespeare Theatre at the English Stratford, condenses Shakespeare's *Henry VI* trilogy into two plays, which Mr. Barton calls *Henry VI* and *Edward IV*. The first of these was given at the Ontario Stratford in 1966, as a companion piece to *Henry V*; the second was planned for 1967, as a companion piece to *Richard III*, which concludes the cycle.

The *Henry VI* trilogy was probably Shakespeare's first work for the stage, and it has traditionally been dismissed as a piece of juvenile hack work. It does contain a good deal of blunt, splenetic language—"Presumptuous prelate!" "Saucy peer!"—from which I personally derive great pleasure, but which is difficult to take altogether seriously. But as edited by Mr. Barton and directed by Mr. Hirsch, without gimmickry or updating, it became a powerful and lurid picture of a world in chaos, startling in its contemporaneity.

In a program note, Mr. Hirsch quoted Yeats:

> Things fall apart; the centre cannot hold;
> Mere anarchy is loosed upon the world . . .
> The best lack all conviction, while the worst
> Are full of passionate intensity.

The twentieth-century poet has provided an exact description of this sixteenth-century play. Poor Henry VI, the weak son of a hero-father, is a good youth, but his goodness is no match for the passionate intensity of his self-seeking barons, each of them eager to chance the wreck of the kingdom in order to gain control of it. Henry lacks even enough conviction to save his most loyal servant, the good Duke Humphrey, from men who are the enemies of king as well as duke. And so the kingdom, the social structure, falls apart, and anarchy is loosed upon the world.

As a boy, Mr. Hirsch spent the years of World War II in the chaos of eastern Europe, barely surviving, and that perhaps gave him a special closeness to this material. He contrived vivid images of cruelty and violence, not with the nasty ingenuity of a Bond movie but in order to evoke a cruel and violent world. His production was unflinching, vigorous, swift, and extremely well acted.

There is always the danger, as with several of Shakespeare's histories, that this play will dissolve into a welter of more or less interchangeable mail-clad lords with geographical names, but at Stratford most of the characters in *Henry VI* were quite sharply individualized: bluff Duke Humphrey (Tony van Bridge), whose goodness is not weakness; tough, clever Suffolk (Leo Ciceri); the openly villainous Bishop of Winchester (Powys Thomas); York (Barry Mac Gregor), a surly boy, easily manipulated by insidious, subtle Warwick (William Hutt). Briain Petchey made an affecting King Henry—young, self-doubting, transparently eager to please; Frances Hyland, as Queen Margaret, was both attractive enough to make credible the young king's sudden infatuation, and strong enough for Margaret's bloody-minded plotting and hysterical grief. This is the play that contains Shakespeare's portrait of Joan of Arc as a screaming, cursing upstart whose power comes from witchcraft; Martha Henry played her with sympathy, but without whitewash.

Henry VI, with its unexpected pertinency and power, somewhat overshadowed Michael Langham's fine production of *Henry V*. Mr. Langham's program note suggests that he meant to show us the seamy side of war, instead of stressing the play's romantic, recruiting-poster aspects. And in fact his battle scenes, like the ones staged by Mr. Hirsch for *Henry VI*, made fighting look like the sweaty, ugly, agonizing business it is. But Mr. Langham presented Henry V as sincere in his belief that his war with France is just, and the seamier elements in play and production were not strong enough to overbear this view of the matter. It was thus essentially a conventional production, but admirable in its way, forthrightly staged and strongly acted. My only serious reservation was that Douglas Rain's personable and soldierly King Henry lacked the animal magnetism to make the most of his great speeches.

The two Henry plays were companioned by a lyrical, light-footed *Twelfth Night,* directed by David William, about which I had no serious reservations whatsoever. Mr. William displayed a lively comic imagination; he placed a swing in Olivia's garden, for instance, and had both Malvolio and Sir Andrew tangle hilariously with it, each in his own distinctive and characteristic fashion. He made clever fun of the love-stricken Orsino, but was never insensitive to the poetry of the play; and though a newcomer to Stratford, he used the thrust stage with authority and boldness.

While the three Shakespeare plays shared the main theatre, the festival presented a varied repertory on the proscenium stage of the Avon Theatre. Strindberg's *The Dance of Death* opened after I left town; so did *Rose Latulippe,* a new full-length ballet, based on a Quebec legend and performed by the Royal Winnipeg Ballet. The festival's production of Mozart's *Don Giovanni,* directed by Jean Gascon, had its shortcomings, but still made a good deal more sense dramatically than most productions of this difficult work. And, as it has not often done in the past, the festival also presented a new play, *The Last of the Tsars,* commissioned from Michael Bawtree at the last moment, after another new play about the Russian Revolution was tried out in Winnipeg and found wanting. It was good to see the festival putting its tremendous resources at the service of a new playwright, for a change. This was Mr. Bawtree's first full-length play, and as such it was a remarkable achievement: theatrical, witty, and full of ideas. But the language in which he writes about the Romanov glory is often hackneyed, and in spite of all his rhetoric he showed us an empire lost not through grand, splendid, outdated chivalry but through mere petty stupidity.

In 1967, the festival produced another new play at the Avon Theatre: *Colours in the Dark,* by the Canadian poet-playwright James Reaney. It was the third original work to be presented at Stratford in the fifteen years since the festival had been founded. Neither of the first two has ever been subsequently produced anywhere else; if the same fate befalls *Colours in the Dark,* it will be not so much a matter of the play's merits or lack of them, as of its peculiar suitability to Stratford. Mr. Reaney was born and raised on a farm only three miles away, and his play is a sort of collage of memories, anecdotes, and poems, based on the author's own life-journey, and extending out toward the universe. John Hirsch's lively and sure-handed staging featured extensive use of projections as background. The acting was simple, grave, and good. There were no roles in the customary sense; the performer with the most to do was Douglas Rain, a stubby, curly-headed fellow who has appeared at the Festival every season since it was founded. Few actors are so quietly, so unassumingly watchable as Mr. Rain. Even when (as often in this work) he seems to be doing nothing much of anything in particular, somehow he catches and holds the attention.

Three of the 1967 plays at the Festival Theatre were by Shakespeare; the fourth, a brilliant revival of *The Government Inspector* by Nikolai Gogol, was first staged by the festival for a transcontinental tour of Canada as part of the Centennial celebrations. (The previous season's *Twelfth Night* was its companion on the tour.) Since it concerns civic corruption and social pretension, there is no question as to the contemporary relevance of Gogol's satiric farce (written as long ago as 1835). Peter Raby, the festival's "dramaturge," adapted it into speakable and witty English; Michael Langham staged it boldly and broadly as a wild, harsh fantasia of greed, chicanery, hypocrisy, cruelty, vanity, self-delusion, and other little failings to which humanity is prone.

William Hutt was ineffably funny as Khlestakov, the insignificant young clerk who fetches up, dead broke, in a miserable provincial town, and is mistaken by the town's corrupt officials for a government inspector traveling incognito. Mr. Hutt's performance was the apotheosis of swish, and, under the circumstances, why not? Swish is, after all, an overelaborate assumption of elegance and refinement, and thus seems quite appropriate for a foolish young provincial who has gone to the big city and would love to be considered a man of fashion. At any rate, a line like "I just (pause) *wither* without sophisticated society" was to Mr. Hutt as honey is to a honeybear, and the actor licked it up with exquisite relish.

Gogol's play shows a fake butterfly alighting on a dunghill, and Mr. Langham surrounded his hero with a depthlessly sordid environment, populated by seedy grotesques. In a mordantly funny wordless scene, Khlestakov was triumphantly led through town, while a red carpet was spread in front of him and quickly rolled up behind so it could be spread in front again, and bed-ridden patients were slung ruthlessly out of the way so as not to interfere with the great man's inspection of the hospital. Mr. Langham's staging was full of ingenuity, and all the actors played right up to the hilt, and yet the director and the actors never seemed to be *making* the play funny; they seemed rather to be bringing out, in masterful fashion, the comedy that was in it all the time.

The season also included a production of *Richard III*, directed by John Hirsch: an entertaining show that went with a swing. Alan Bates' movie-star charm was used, not to whitewash Richard, but to make his success more plausible; here, for a change, was a Richard from whom somebody might conceivably buy a used car. Yet this *Richard III* was not what it might have been; it com-memorates an occasion when the festival's audience failed it. The production was originally planned to be done in repertory with *Edward IV*, as a climax to the great four-year history cycle. The two plays have a very close continuity: some half a dozen charac-ters survive from one into the other, including crookbacked Richard, and many events in the later play have roots in the earlier. But *Henry VI*, which precedes *Edward IV* in the cycle, and which I had so much admired in its Stratford production, had been generally condemned by the Toronto critics, and had been sparsely attended. As Jean Gascon, the festival's new artistic head, observed (in discussing the difficulty of selling *The Government Inspector*), "The people . . . are hoping to see the pageantry—the trumpets and the banners and the whole bit. It's very hard to break that pattern, but it must be done."

But M. Gascon also pointed out, "If you have one play here that doesn't work in a season, it means the whole financial situa-tion is in danger." *Henry VI* hadn't worked, and so *Edward IV* was scrapped. *Richard III* was left to stand by itself; this, of course, it is well able to do; but when, now, will we ever get a chance to see it in context?

Perhaps as a result of the scrapping of *Edward IV*, Mr. Hirsch's thoroughly competent staging of *Richard III* seemed for most of the evening to have no particular concept behind it, until, in the last act, Mr. Hirsch suddenly went off in a frenzy of half-cocked innovation. Richard for some reason *permitted* Richmond to kill him. A suicidal Crookback? Why? Richmond, moreover, was in this production not a radiant symbol of justice and order, but a snarling tough, in direct contradiction to the text. After three hours during which there was no indication that Mr. Hirsch had any strong feelings about the play one way or another, it suddenly seemed as if he had been reading Jan Kott when he should have been reading *Richard III*.

Edward *IV* was replaced in the schedule by *The Merry Wives of Windsor*, Shakespeare's most commercial script—written, presumably, to make a quick buck out of the continued popularity of Sir John Falstaff. Shakespeare wrote several plays that were worse in various ways, but none (except for *The Comedy of Errors*) more mechanical and less resonant. *Merry Wives* is not even a particularly good commercial piece; there are jokes in it that would make the author of *The Wayward Stork* ashamed. David William, the director, defended the play sturdily in a program note, but his production proved only that in the proper hands *The Merry Wives* can be hilarious. (Not, God knows, that I'm out to knock hilarity.) Tony van Bridge made a majestic, grandiloquent Falstaff; Zoe Caldwell as Mistress Page was a bouncing bourgeoise with a high opinion of her own dignity; Jean Gascon was the explosive Frenchman ("By gar!"), Dr. Caius; theirs were probably the funniest of many funny performances. Alan Bates as Ford, the neurotically jealous husband, managed by invisible means to abolish for the occasion his good looks and (which must have been harder) his celebrated charm; movie star though he is, he played this not-very-showy supporting role with self-denying conscientiousness.

Merry Wives, as might be expected, did very well at the box office, but the big popular hit of the festival was the season's final production, *Antony and Cleopatra*. This production was the focus of tremendous expectations. It was the only one of Shakespeare's major plays that had never been done at Stratford; it was the last production to be directed by Michael Langham before he retired as the festival's artistic director. (He is headed for La Jolla, California, to start a new theatre there.) And its leading roles were played by Christopher Plummer and Zoe Caldwell.

In the event, the production proved somewhat disappointing, for all its merits. Mr. Langham's staging used movie-style cuts and dissolves to get from scene to scene with cinematic speed. Costumes and props were austere, no mobs of extras were in evidence, yet the atmosphere of a luxurious, decadent court was created. The supporting cast was excellent, with William Hutt as a disgruntled Enobarbus and Kenneth Welsh as a chilly Caesar distinguishing themselves particularly.

Mr. Plummer was an expansive, magnanimous, virile Antony; it was easy to understand the loyalty with which his men served him. But though he played his scenes of suffering competently, some final dimension, some audacity, some kind of profoundest cutting loose was missing; this Antony was shaken, but not to his innermost depths.

Miss Caldwell's Cleopatra was a little, bouncy, redheaded woman, no competition for Elizabeth Taylor—but the converse is also true. Miss Caldwell has her own kinetic attractions, and her Cleopatra had plenty of exquisite arts with which to hold Antony. She began as a delightful, dangerous tiger-kitten, throwing all her energies tempestuously into every passing impulse: this was a Cleopatra who both could and would "hop forty paces through the public street," or tear the hair off a messenger who brought bad news, or keep Antony attendant on her whims when he should have been about affairs of state. Yet her intelligence shone through her self-indulgence in the form of irony, with which her words quivered and gleamed. The way she asked, on hearing of the death of Antony's wife, "*Can* Fulvia die?" was indescribable.

But Shakespeare's prescription demands "infinite variety," and this Miss Caldwell could not supply. She did not grow into the splendor of the final scenes. Insinuation became her better than grandiloquence. She continued to move as if she were about to climb a tree or beat the boys at softball. This is properly *one* of Cleopatra's modes, not her only one. A woman who wishes to die in her robes and crown would not wait till she puts them on to assume a noble bearing.

And so it seemed to me that this much-heralded production ran downhill after an excellent beginning. It was the old Stratford problem: even Mr. Plummer and Miss Caldwell could not supply the abiding lack of heaven-storming tragedians. But perhaps all I am saying is that this play demands great acting, which was not forthcoming. And have we ever a right to *expect* great acting? At any rate, this *Antony and Cleopatra* was an achievement of which no theatre would need to be ashamed.

When Mr. Langham left Stratford for La Jolla after thirteen years as artistic director, he was succeeded by Jean Gascon (as "executive artistic director") and John Hirsch (as "artistic director"), both of whom had been associated with the festival for several years. I had a talk with M. Gascon, and found him keenly aware of the dangers inherent in the festival's tremendous success. "There is a danger here of stagnation," he says. "It's probably the most important and organized company on the North American continent. But the danger of it is that it could become an institution. People get self-satisfied . . ."

In future seasons he plans to decrease the emphasis on Shakespeare, and to widen the repertory. Already he has invited a number of dramatists, both Canadian and foreign, to Stratford, with the hope that they will be tempted to write for the festival. He plans to have the company make films, and recordings, "and all sorts of things."

Within two years, the festival will finally become a year-round operation. It will make its winter home in the National Arts Center now being built in Ottawa, Canada's capital city. It will continue to play at Stratford for six months of the year; during the other six months, it will play in Ottawa and tour in Canada and abroad. The possibility of year-round employment will make it easier to attract and hold actors and staff; year-round operation will also provide more time and more scope for experiment.

Its summer season will continue to be called the Stratford Festival, but when performing outside of Stratford it will henceforth be known as the Stratford National Theatre of Canada.

M. Gascon is full of praise for what has been done at Stratford since its founding, but "if I was told tomorrow that I had to follow that line and stay there, I would just go away. I have to feel that there's development . . . and that will keep me alive as an artist—and the same for everybody here." As Canada's (and North America's) leading theatre comes, for the first time, under Canadian leadership, this kind of thinking is a good omen for the future.

The American Shakespeare Festival Theatre and Academy
(Stratford, Connecticut)

Stratford, Connecticut, is a pleasant small town just outside of Bridgeport, an hour and a half from New York by the Connecticut Turnpike or the New Haven Railroad. It is convenient to the prosperous suburbs of Fairfield County in Connecticut and Westchester County in New York State. On Elm Street in Stratford, amid green lawns overlooking the Housatonic River, the American Shakespeare Festival Theatre and Academy makes its home in a handsome, well-appointed 1,500-seat theatre. The ASFTA is a large-scale venture with an undisclosed but obviously lavish budget and an Equity company of forty-five (one of the biggest in the country). In 1967 it mounted four productions, in repertory, during a thirteen-week summer season; it played to 165,000 spectators, which is about 89 per cent of capacity. Before and after the regular season, there were twenty-three weeks of student performances, attended by nearly 200,000 students and their teachers, who came from as far away as Virginia. That makes a thirty-six-week season, and more than 350,000 spectators. Yet this comfortable, well-off, and highly popular institution, intended by its founder to "serve as a beacon from the past to the future, illuminating the eternal verities of truth, beauty, and poetic imagination,"* has a widespread and well-deserved reputation for genteel mediocrity.

Like the Repertory Theatre of Lincoln Center, the American Shakespeare Festival began as a gesture toward High Culture on the part of the theatrical Establishment. This festival, however, was the product of the generation previous to that of the original Lincoln Center duumvirate; it was the child of the old age of Lawrence Langner, who, nearly forty years earlier, had been a founder of the Theatre Guild. By the time the festival came into being, the Guild had declined from a true art theatre, with an acting company, a repertory of plays, and a permanent home, into an ordinary, commercial management—and not the least conservative and timorous of these. Whether the Shakespeare Festival,

---

* Lawrence Langner, *The Magic Curtain* (New York, 1951), p. 438.

which Langner hoped would "belong to the nation," was the offering of a subliminally uneasy conscience, or just a new repository for old, frustrated ambitions, who can say?

The theatre that Langner eventually built (after Katharine Cornell broke ground "with a ceremonial shovel," as a press handout put it), has a vague external resemblance to Shakespeare's Globe. Inside, however, in the words of the late Jack Landau, one of its ex-directors, it "was designed as a conventional nineteenth-century theatre, like any Broadway playhouse," complete with a picture-frame stage inside a proscenium. During the festival's first season, in 1955, *Julius Caesar* and *The Tempest* were produced in literal, heavily pictorial settings of the most old-fashioned sort; the action took place entirely behind the proscenium. Hollywood stars (Raymond Massey, Jack Palance) headed the heterogeneous, hastily assembled company; a number of talented younger actors (Christopher Plummer, Fritz Weaver) appeared with them. An English director named Denis Carey was imported to rehearse them, in a tremendous hurry, in a still-unfinished theatre. It is universally conceded that the results were a mess.

The following year, John Houseman (Orson Welles' old colleague at the Mercury Theatre, and the producer of the Hollywood *Julius Caesar*) was brought in to make a fresh start, with the assistance of a young director named Jack Landau. The first thing they did was to extend the forestage into the audience, producing a playing area that seems highly serviceable to me as a spectator, though several actors have told me that it is very difficult to play on. The two theatres of the Royal Shakespeare Company in Stratford-upon-Avon and London are proscenium houses similarly equipped with projecting forestages; people keep complaining that this sort of arrangement is an unwieldy compromise, but it has the advantage of allowing the director to decide, from moment to moment, whether his actors should be surrounded by scenery or by space.

The new directors opened their first season in June, 1956, with *King John* and *Measure for Measure*. Mr. Houseman wrote in *Theatre Arts Magazine:*

. . . we deliberately have chosen . . . two of the lesser known plays . . . We hope that each of them will have some of that quality of revelation that is shared by the actors and audiences during the performance of a new work—in this case two new works by the world's leading playwright.

This seems to show an agreeable audacity, an eagerness to offer audiences an adventure, instead of a humble willingness merely to gratify their preconceptions.

As if abashed by his own rashness, however, Mr. Houseman asked his audiences to fill out a questionnaire as to which plays *they* wanted to see at Stratford. The following year, armed with the results of this popularity poll, he announced—again in *Theatre Arts*—that he would present the play that "received 40 per cent more votes than its nearest competitor." This solicitude looks especially poor-spirited next to Michael Langham's statement that a theatre must "keep sticking its neck out, and doing what it believes. It must never attempt to woo popularity . . . We must have the guts to create fashion rather than follow it."

While Stratford, Ontario, under Langham's supervision, stuck its neck out, Houseman and Landau at Stratford, Connecticut, wooed popularity abjectly, with Hollywood stars and fancy production gimmicks. In order for a theatre to do what it believes, it must first believe in something, and it often seemed as if Houseman and Landau did not even believe in their playwright. Some of their work, especially in the tragedies, was merely dull; but a lot of it, especially Landau's, tended to justify the contention of Professor Alfred Harbage that "Modern production [of Shakespeare] is undertaken in the doubt that the plays still stand on their own merits, and is marred by a determined spirit of helpfulness." As a generalization, Professor Harbage's statement needs a good deal of qualification; things are not always so bad as that. But surely nothing but "a determined spirit of helpfulness" could have produced such anomalies as Stratford's Texas-style *Much Ado* (1957) or its Civil War *Troilus and Cressida* (1961).

But, as my father once asked, why shouldn't they serve Shakespeare with a little sour cream on the side? The answer is that in practice the sour cream is not just passively irrelevant; it actively mucks up the Shakespeare. And Shakespeare doesn't do the sour cream any good either. The people who came to see Katharine Hepburn in Landau's *Twelfth Night* (1960) would have seen more of her, and had a better time, had *The Philadelphia Story* been revived for her instead. And there was no question of anyone's coming to see Hepburn and staying to fall in love with *Twelfth Night*; Shakespeare's play was simply not there in any meaningful sense. As Viola, Miss Hepburn was almost ideally miscast. The role is all ardor, innocence, and youth; Miss Hepburn was all efficiency, astringency, and sophistication, and though she looked beautiful, she was obviously well past her girlhood. The famous Hepburn voice, so widely loved, so unmistakable and undisguisable, was death to the lyric poetry which is the life of the part. Viola is a plum; Miss Hepburn was a pineapple. And several other parts were similarly miscast, presumably to keep the leading lady in countenance.

The action was forced to take place in an English seaside resort in the nineteenth century; Orsino and his dependents were dressed up in sailors' uniforms out of *H. M. S. Pinafore*, and Malvolio was imprisoned in a striped bathing machine. It was very pretty, very chic. And the whole mythical way of life that Shakespeare created for his Illyria—with its Petrarchan love complaints, its jester, its restless ocean that washes up human driftwood—was overwhelmed, canceled, blotted out by all the sour cream. This was Shakespeare for people who hate Shakespeare.

Lawrence Langner had envisioned a company that would stay together all year round, occupying itself by touring the country when not at Stratford; but although *Much Ado*, *A Midsummer Night's Dream*, and *The Winter's Tale* were sent on the road, the touring idea never took root. In 1959, John Houseman resigned as artistic director after years of frustration in his attempt to put together a company and maintain it all year round. He left the reins to Jack Landau, who remained in charge through the 1961 season, when a new regime took over. The details of the transfer of power are not clear, but the precipitating factor seems to have been money: half a million dollars of it (about the cost of one big Broadway musical, but a lot of money for an art theatre), offered to Stratford in 1962 by the Ford Foundation, to finance a program for training American actors to perform the classics.

This might seem somewhat supererogatory; after all, the organization's name is the American Shakespeare Festival Theatre *and Academy*, and it had had some sort of program for training actors from the very beginning. For a time the academy program had run throughout the year, and had accepted students in New York who were not otherwise part of the festival. But this had not worked out, and the academy had dwindled to a few summer courses for the "apprentices" who had been engaged as extras.

Under the Ford grant—which was accepted, as half-million-dollar grants generally are—this apprentice program, though it continued, was overshadowed by a new training program for eighteen young actors, not neophytes but men and women already accomplished in their profession. These were paid a living wage while engaged in a full-time program of classes in acting, speaking, and body control. They began in October, 1962; in January, 1963, they were joined by eight more actors, somewhat older and with more experience. The two groups trained together until mid-March, when they began rehearsals as the 1963 Stratford company. Aside from extras, only two actors were brought in to appear with them: Morris Carnovsky (a Housatonic regular for many years) as Lear, and George Voskovec as Caesar in Shaw's *Caesar and Cleopatra*, the festival's first non-Shakespearian production. The directors of the training program, Allen Fletcher and Douglas Seale, directed the three Shakespearean plays presented (*Caesar* was directed by Ellis Rabb) and were generally in charge of the artistic end of the festival. The company opened at Stratford in May, 1963, and played there through the end of September. On November 1, classes began again, with few changes in personnel, and the cycle repeated itself. In the fall of 1964, a sizable group of actors had completed two full years of training and performing together. Langner's vision of a year-round company had been temporarily achieved, by means of training instead of touring.

More or less concurrently with the acceptance of the grant, Joseph Verner Reed, an aristocratic businessman who had produced on Broadway and served as special assistant to the American ambassador to France, took over as the festival's executive producer; he brought in Allen Fletcher and Douglas Seale. Mr. Fletcher (now artistic director of the Seattle Repertory Theatre) is an American who had worked at the San Diego Shakespeare Festival; Mr. Seale (now artistic director of Center Stage in Baltimore) is an Englishman who had worked at the Birmingham Repertory, the Old Vic, and the English and Canadian Stratfords.

The new regime was profoundly different from the old, which had sometimes seemed almost explicitly dedicated to bad work. Mr. Seale and Mr. Fletcher had their share of failures, but they were honorable failures: failures of skill only, not of will as well.

In 1963, the first season after the training program had begun, Mr. Seale's two productions were barely passable. The actors in his *Comedy of Errors* pushed self-defeatingly hard in their endeavors to wring every drop of comedy from a somewhat juiceless script. In *Henry V*, his leading actor, a slightly built and shy-looking youth, was like a man trying to play trumpet solos on the flute. Both productions suffered from execrable acting in certain small parts.

Mr. Fletcher's *King Lear*, on the other hand, was superb, strong both in verbal and emotional values, rhetoric and "guts." It was full of surprising revelations, but they were revelations of the play's greatness, not the director's cleverness. Goneril and Regan, for instance, were played from their own points of view, not from Lear's; he thinks they are monsters, but each of *them* presumably thinks herself a sensible, decent, much-put-upon woman. And so, instead of coming across as serious parodies of the Ugly Step-Sisters in *Cinderella*, they became comprehensible as people. When Lear cursed Goneril, she didn't just stand there projecting defiance as she waited for her cue; she was clearly suffering from the force of her father's hatred. This not only increased the effect that the curse had on the audience, but also provided a motive for Goneril's subsequent bitterness. Regan had a hard time getting into the swing of her nastiness; she was doing something she didn't like doing, but felt to be necessary. And then, slowly, she warmed to her task, and began to enjoy it, and we realized that these sisters were two quite different individuals, not just Big Poison and Little Poison.

Mr. Fletcher's unobtrusive skill was reflected in the entire absence of bad performances, and in the extraordinary number of admirable ones, of which Morris Carnovsky's magnificent Lear was the chief. From his first scene onward, trembling and mumbling and grunting, Mr. Carnovsky established his Lear as an old man no longer in full possession of his faculties; and yet this Lear never entirely lost his grandeur. Mr. Carnovsky did not alternate senility and strength, or pathos and majesty; he fused them. In the storm scenes, along with the director, the designers, and the composer, he was insufficient; but these scenes are notoriously too titanic for mortals, and ought to be acted by Michelangelo's Moses and staged by Almighty God. Everywhere else, he lived up to the famous exchange in which Kent says, "You have that in your countenance which I would fain call master"; "What's that?" asks Lear, and Kent replies, "Authority." Mr. Carnovsky has a splendid, deep voice, as everybody knows; it has sometimes happened that Mr. Carnovsky all too obviously knew it too. But this performance came from far deeper than the throat. His emotions were felt and expressed in every part of his body: his rages convulsed him, through and through, and at the end his grief melted him, through and through. (Mr. Carnovsky, incidentally, was a pillar of the Group Theatre, which incubated the Stanislavsky Method in the United States. His performance is conclusive evidence that the Method is not, as is often alleged, relevant only to modern psychological drama.)

It was in *Lear* that the company, halfway through its training program, revealed its quality. Patrick Hines was a Gloucester who, for once, did not seem to be merely Lear's understudy: foolish at first and fat throughout, he was able to make clear that his pathos was on a different plane from Lear's tragedy. Philip Bosco played Kent with humor, charm, abounding zest, and no hint of the sanctimoniousness that Kent can so easily fall into. Douglas Watson's Bastard was not a pasteboard, scowley-smiley villain, but a man who took spontaneous, keen delight in evil; he obscured the bitterness in the part, but his high spirits were infectious, and his rapport with the audience electric. Lester Rawlins played the Fool not as a slick professional jester, but as a true madman, nervous and stooped, his knuckles in his mouth, ever-ready to cringe from a blow; he got his laughs skillfully, and yet sometimes this Fool's riddling truths were appalling.

Mr. Fletcher's *Lear* was not only an artistic success but also a box-office sellout, two blessings that do not always light simultaneously on one production. Thus he was able to say, "We are now in a position where we can try, creatively and systematically, to build a company . . . so we don't have to rely on wildly going out and trying to find 'names' . . . The aim is to make the company the attraction at Stratford." For the 1964 season the festival announced that Mr. Bosco would appear as Benedick in *Much Ado about Nothing,* Mr. Watson would play Richard III, and Mr. Rawlins would tackle Hamlet.

Mr. Rawlins' Hamlet never made it to opening night. Joseph Verner Reed, the producer, didn't like his performance and fired him. Mr. Seale, who was directing *Hamlet,* either quit or was fired; Mr. Fletcher thus became sole artistic director, and served in that capacity for two seasons. Gradually, his directorial style became recognizable. His staging was a compromise between proscenium and open-stage technique. He used scenery (usually designed by Will Steven Armstrong), but sparingly: one or two large, emblematic, mood-evoking pieces at the rear of the stage, backed in turn by a sky drop or black drapes. The main acting area was essentially a bare platform, and there was no curtain. It was a sort of staging well adapted to the swift, fluid, uncluttered, nononsense work that Mr. Fletcher provided.

He seemed to be the most self-effacing of Shakespearean directors. His ideas for individual characters, individual scenes, were often original—and sometimes unfortunate—but it was usually hard to tell what he thought about a play as a whole. He seemed reluctant to impose a firm over-all concept on a production; instead, it seemed as if he gave each actor his head and encouraged him to do his utmost. His productions were almost never frivolous or perverse, but often they were uneven—varying widely in quality from moment to moment—and sometimes merely commonplace.

His *Much Ado about Nothing* had more personality than most of his productions; it was a broad, coarse piece of work that obscured the distinction between high comedy and low. Bernard Shaw pointed out years ago that Beatrice and Benedick, the rather self-consciously witty lovers in this play, are not really very witty at all. But this is beside the point; the audience enjoys their wit not for its quality as wit, but as the index of their folly. What can be more foolish, after all, than two merry chatterboxes whose very insults are a form of love-making—and who, for all their pride in their quick minds, have only the remotest idea of what is going on between them? And so—for a time—it worked to play Beatrice and Benedick as fools, busily earning their laughs with an assortment of outcries, chuckles, grimaces, and grins. Thanks to Mr. Fletcher's comic inventiveness, and the brio of Philip Bosco's Benedick, the first hour of the play was hilarious and charming.

But by nine o'clock we knew everything about these people that Mr. Fletcher would allow us to know. Shakespeare wrote them beautiful scenes in which their personalities open out like flowers, enabling the audience to realize that these rattlepates are capable of loyalty and dignity, that their love has a depth we would not have expected. But at Stratford, Beatrice ruined one such scene in an attempt to get cheap laughs by fake crying; Benedick destroyed another by a well-placed grunt; and so it went: nowhere. Meanwhile, the melodrama missed fire; Mr. Fletcher had been so careful to keep it from overbalancing the play that its central, sensational shock-effect was muted and damped. Only the low-comic simpletons, led by Rex Everhart's sturdy Dogberry, gave a reasonably complete account of their material.

The women in the cast ranged from dullish (Jacqueline Brookes as Beatrice) to downright annoying; the men were better. Mr. Bosco, who resembles John Gielgud in face and voice, but wisely does not press the matter, could probably do a good Benedick given wiser direction. But Mr. Fletcher did well by Frank G. Converse, who played Claudio with a delicate touch of parody as a not-too-bright Prince Charming. Nicholas Martin's Don John the Bastard was another deft parody, and another intelligent directorial conception: the Machiavellian villain as spoiled brat.

Mr. Fletcher's *Richard III* gave us another sort of Machiavel. Orthopedically strapped and booted, Douglas Watson as Richard clumped stiff-legged across the stage, but his voice was undisguised, and so, almost, from the waist up, was his body. This was a Richard hale, handsome, and hearty. Director and actor were presumably trying to avoid the shadow of Olivier's exquisite performance, but their success was paid for in several ways. The actor had to forego, for the most part, the creepy-nasty line-readings that usually make Richard such fun to listen to; but Mr. Watson was a pleasure even so, inexhaustible in zest and charm. A more serious effect was that, by being less a monster, Richard was less a man. Shakespeare wrote a character who hates himself for his disgusting body at least as much as anyone else can hate him, and who is driven by this hatred to revenge his deformities upon the world. But Mr. Watson's Richard was neither disgusting nor self-disgusted; thus motivation vanished, and we were left with a villain, period. Only when he broke down did he take on any dimension.

In an attempt, presumably, to overcome the play's repetitiveness, the breakdown began too early, and Mr. Watson played for a while directly against the text; near the end, however, there were some penetrating glimpses of a strong man falling apart—an aspect of the character not often dwelt upon so cogently.

After Mr. Seale left Stratford, Mr. Fletcher took over the direction of *Hamlet*; Tom Sawyer, who had been Mr. Rawlins' understudy, took over the title role. Mr. Sawyer was competent but colorless; so was the production. Like *Richard III*, *Hamlet* was typical of Mr. Fletcher's work in that there was very little to be said about the over-all approach, the directorial point of view, the "concept." This does not necessarily mean that the director has not done his job; it was true also of Mr. Fletcher's superb *Lear*. But his 1964 productions were certainly undistinguished.

The 1965 season, on the other hand, seemed to me probably the best in Stratford's history. Even the smallest roles were nearly always played with professional competence, presumably as a result of the training program. Leading actors who had been with the company for several years—Morris Carnovsky, Patrick Hines, Philip Bosco—were well cast and in good form; so were many of the new members and guest performers, notably Aline MacMahon and Ruby Dee. Mr. Fletcher directed three out of the season's four productions, and his hand was surer than it had usually been in the past.

As if to show that the festival now had a past it could be proud of, Mr. Fletcher revived his 1963 production of *King Lear*, with Morris Carnovsky once again in the title role. In 1963, however, not only had Mr. Carnovsky been magnificent, but half a dozen of the supporting actors had created faithful but fresh characterizations. Of those actors, only Patrick Hines remained. His fat, benevolent, easy-mark Gloucester was at least as good as ever; the new actors, on the other hand, were mostly satisfactory but stock. But Mr. Carnovsky's performance alone would have been enough to justify the revival.

Mr. Fletcher's *Romeo and Juliet* could have used some such justification; it was the weakest of the season's productions. And yet it was not bad, only uneven and uninspired. Maria Tucci, the Juliet, played the entire first half of the role on one note of tremulous ardor, with little playfulness and no exultation. This ardor of hers, moreover, was curiously unphysical; one might have wished, for the sake of this interesting actress, that the play had been about a girl who wanted to become a nun. On the other hand, Terence Scammell was an excellent Romeo: passionate, lyrical, and boyish, with a beautiful tenor voice that he used without self-indulgence.

The only production Mr. Fletcher did not direct that season was *The Taming of the Shrew*, and there was some question as to who *did* direct that one. The program read: "Original production concept by Don Driver, Directed by Joseph Anthony." Rumor had it that Mr. Driver went too far with his "production concept," which involved a troupe of strolling players, whose wagon becomes the setting for their play, and a lot of Spanishy accouterments. Mr. Anthony, it is said, was brought in to replace him and tone things down. At any rate, the strolling players, the wagon, and some Spanishy costumes and props, though still in evidence, were used somewhat sparingly, as if someone had recoiled at the last minute from the dangers of "Bright Idea" Shakespeare.

The directing, whoever did it, was tentative and inconsistent, quite undistinguished for farcical inventiveness. But the performance was easily, breezily good-natured, fast but not loud; nothing was forced, nobody worked too hard, there were no lapses of taste; and the performers were ingratiating and deft. John Cunningham was a conventionally swashbuckling, glossy Petruchio; Ruby Dee as Katherina was less bold, more subtle. The entire production—like the play itself—was easier to like than to admire.

Mr. Fletcher's excellent (and widely underestimated) *Coriolanus* provided a good balance for this amiable, trifling *Shrew*: for me at least, it vindicated an unpopular play that is traditionally easier to admire than to like. Hegel said that tragedy is the conflict of two rights; *Coriolanus* is the conflict of two wrongs. It suggests that neither democracy nor fascism is a viable form of government. The Roman populace is represented as ignorant, gullible, fickle, turbulent, and ungrateful; the martial hero whom they exile is "vengeance proud"—also foul-mouthed, unstable, and rash, true neither to his country nor himself. He is strong only in battle; otherwise he is abjectly at the disposal of his pride, of his anger, and of his formidable mother. He is not evil, but—far worse, for dramatic purposes—he runs the risk of being merely disagreeable.

It was the triumph of Philip Bosco's performance that in his hands Coriolanus was never disagreeable. Mr. Bosco simply cannot be unlikable on stage, which means, among other things, that he need never cheapen himself, or the character he plays, in order to be liked. It is true that Mr. Bosco, with his splendid Roman dignity and his urbane, stinging irony, did miss the character's sick intensity, the abandoned fury of his ragings. But to emphasize this side of Coriolanus would have been to risk forfeiting what is equally important: the element of greatness in the character, of which Mr. Bosco kept us always aware.

If the director did not try to expose and demean Coriolanus, did not make the play a tract against the Man on Horseback, he did not make it an anti-democratic pamphlet either. The mob might easily have been shown as not only turbulent but vicious. But Shakespeare's plebeians are not malicious, only misled, as this production's crisp and well-staged crowd scenes made clear. Mr. Fletcher even declined to make villains of the popular leaders, the Tribunes; one of them—as played strongly, finely, and without whitewash by Frederic Warriner—emerged as a worthy opponent of Coriolanus. On the patrician side again, Patrick Hines gave a funny, charming, touching performance—a subtle and lucid performance—as old Menenius. Mr. Fletcher, as is his custom, held the balance with scrupulous fairness. He showed us the best of all parties—not the only possible approach, but in this case the results justified it.

And then, of course, there was that remarkable creation, Coriolanus' mother Volumnia, in a deftly modulated performance by Aline MacMahon. This is the Age of Freud, and the evils and excesses of motherhood—from the Silver Cord, through Momism, to the formidable image of the Jewish Mother—are very much on the popular mind. We are therefore apt to see Volumnia somewhat differently from the way Mrs. Siddons played her, and of this Miss MacMahon was well aware. She was always believable as a Roman matron, never guilty of anachronism in speech or gesture, but she was not the old-fashioned with-your-shield-or-on-it sort of classical battle-ax either. As she tamed her son with a mother's ultimate weapon—guilt—she was reminiscent of all the Feiffer cartoons on the subject.

In playing the part as she did, Miss MacMahon was only bringing out what had been in the text all along. When Volumnia says to her son in a famous and climactic scene, ". . . thou shalt no sooner march to assault thy country than . . . to tread on thy mother's womb. . . . Thou hast never in thy life show'd thy dear mother any courtesy," what is she if not the precursor of the mother in *Bye Bye Birdie* who, when crossed, threatens to go home and stick her head in the oven? In Volumnia's scenes, as Miss MacMahon played them, I could see a little of why Shaw called *Coriolanus* Shakespeare's greatest comedy.

During that summer of 1965, it began to appear to me that after years of slow and sometimes painful effort, Mr. Fletcher's regime had finally begun to show results. In an article on that season, I wrote, "With its young and competent company, augmented by a few modestly cast guest performers; with its policy of sternly subordinating visual display to the purposes of the plays; with sometimes lusterless but generally creditable direction, the American Shakespeare Festival seems, in its eleventh year, to have finally found itself." Not long thereafter, the festival showed me what was what by firing Mr. Fletcher from his post as artistic director. No successor was appointed. For the last two years, the whole operation has been run by Joseph Verner Reed, who is not a theatre artist but a professional rich man. Under his leadership, or lack of it, Mr. Fletcher's work has largely been undone.

In 1966, Mr. Reed presented *Falstaff*, *Twelfth Night*, *Julius Caesar*, and T. S. Eliot's *Murder in the Cathedral*. All four were at least passable. The acting company was talented, and, on the whole, well schooled (though several actors had not mastered the pronunciation of the letter "s"); in all four productions there was only one really cloddish performance, and that in a very small part. The directors were all established professionals, and it seemed as if they had all approached their scripts with respect and affection. All that was missing was imagination, purpose, and passion.

Falstaff, directed by Joseph Anthony, turned out to be *Henry IV, Part II* with a couple of bits of Part I stuck in. Jerome Kilty, who played Falstaff, is a brilliant technician, and his depiction of age and obesity was impeccable. But what he lacked was crucial: Falstaff's marvelous impudence, and Falstaff's marvelous zest. John Cunningham was a personable Prince Hal, but he glossed over the character's ambiguities (just exactly what did he really think of Falstaff?), and he was defeated by his one emotional scene at his father's deathbed. *Twelfth Night*, directed by Frank Hauser, was similarly undistinguished.

No director for *Julius Caesar* was listed in the program; Allen Fletcher, who began it, was forced to leave for other commitments, whereupon Margaret Webster took over. (This switching directors in mid-stream seems to happen often at Stratford.) There was no sign in the production of discontinuity or cross-purposes. The acting was professional. The mob scenes and the battle scenes were not very convincing (they seldom are), but they were vigorous and not embarrassing. There was an occasional fine touch: the soldiers, for example, who stalked the streets, singly, silently, suggestively, in the scenes before the murder of Caesar. This is a small instance of the kind of theatrical imagination that this festival needs a great deal more of.

Murder in the Cathedral is a play I find peculiarly moving, and I found it so once again in the polished and reverent, but less than passionate, production that John Houseman (the festival's former artistic director) staged at Stratford. Joseph Wiseman's Becket was dignified, well spoken, gentle yet strong, and a little monotonous. There was no agony and no exultation in his performance, though the character has plenty of both. Not many actors could match Mr. Wiseman's air of lofty authority, but he sustained it so consistently, was so constantly and consciously superior to what was happening to him, that a hint of smugness crept in. His performance was a victory of elocution over emotion. The Chorus of Women of Canterbury was very strongly cast, with such mature and experienced actresses as Edith Meiser and Nancy Marchand, and it was often effective. This was probably the best production of the Stratford season; it was by no means a bad job, but it made rather a feeble best.

In 1967, Mr. Reed offered four productions, staged by four different directors: two solid old-timers of various vintages (Mr. Houseman and Jerome Kilty), a notorious chichi-merchant (Cyril Ritchard), and that year's hot young director (Michael Kahn). But one advantage of the festival's absolute eclecticism, its commitment to nothing except Shakespeare's name, is that some fine work now and then manages to get done.

The annual non-Shakespearean production was Anouilh's *Antigone*, a grave, intelligent, and yet impassioned meditation on the eternal struggle between freedom and order. The best single piece of acting to be found at Stratford that season was Maria Tucci's performance as Antigone; Miss Tucci had come a long way since

her nunlike Juliet. Delicate yet strong, her Antigone had depths of
sensibility apparent behind the Botticellian beauty of her face. She
was clearly marked out for tragedy from the moment she appeared,
and yet she was never pretentious or monotonous. Otherwise, this
Antigone was not a distinguished production. Morris Carnovsky
made a strong but ponderous Creon; constantly addressing Antigone as though she were a public meeting, he crushed much of the
irony, delicacy, and compassion out of his part. Jerome Kilty, the
director, decked the play in modern trappings—rock 'n' roll, mini-
skirts, pants-suits, a hand mike for Anouilh's one-man Chorus—but
they never seemed like anything but trappings.

The all-round best production of the season was once again
directed by John Houseman: a vigorous *Macbeth,* performed in a
cold, threatening, aluminum environment designed by Rouben
Ter-Arutunian (scenery) and Jennifer Tipton (lighting). When
King Duncan said, "This castle hath a pleasant seat," he was
obviously quoting Shakespeare instead of looking around him;
otherwise the problems of staging *Macbeth* were ingeniously and
conscientiously solved. John Colicos, the erstwhile tragic hero of
Stratford, Ontario, was a satisfactory Macbeth, and Carrie Nye
was a young, blonde, sinuous, bitchy Lady. (For a change, when
Lady Macbeth cried to the evil spirits, "Unsex me here," there was
something to unsex.) Mr. Houseman, his designers, and his actors
provided a cogent and skillful traversal of the play. Only later,
reading Herbert Blau, did I come upon words for what the
production seemed to me to lack: ". . . the subterranean life of
the plays (a *Macbeth,* for instance, clawing bloodily at 'the insane
root'), and instead of fidelity or capricious updating, an immediacy
of conception, by which I know that that world on the stage is
unavoidably mine."* But this (like most things that Mr. Blau
wants) is hard to find.

The festival's *Merchant of Venice* was remarkable in one respect. Michael Kahn, who directed, borrowed Tyrone Guthrie's
idea that Antonio, the Merchant himself, the man who risks losing
the famous pound of flesh, is deeply in love with his friend
Bassanio, in whose behalf he takes the risk. This may sound like
mere psychologizing, but in practice it makes excellent sense. It
turns Antonio, who in most productions is just a faceless necessity

---

* *The Impossible Theatre,* pp. 14–15.

of the plot, into a genuine and highly interesting character. It explains his mysterious sadness, his sense of himself as "a tainted wether of the flock." It lends poignancy to his willingness, at whatever risk to himself, to lend Bassanio money, though Bassanio has made it quite clear that he wants the money to go court a wife. Wisely, Mr. Kahn did not take the idea too far; the subsidiary Venetians discussed the matter in tones that dripped with unmistakable innuendo, but there was no pawing and no camping. The courage and magnanimity with which Antonio endures and abets what amounts to Bassanio's rejection of him give him considerable stature; as finely played by John Devlin, he rivaled Shylock in gravity and dignity.

In other respects, however, this *Merchant* was not up to much. Morris Carnovsky's Shylock was sustained by the actor's tremendous inborn dignity and strength, but it was a disappointment all the same. The ferocious irony in the part went for nothing; perhaps Mr. Carnovsky simply has no gift for irony. But one gift he does have is the power to thunder like Jove, and this he did not use. In the climactic scene after his daughter left him, he did not rage; he wept, damped down the scene with self-pity, and thus discouraged us from pitying him. Acting teachers tell you not to give rein to your sobs and tears, that it is much more effective to fight against them and barely manage to hold them in; they would seem to have a point. Barbara Baxley made a pretty, blond Portia, with an attractive shyness and a nice dry wit, but her thin, nasal voice set strict limits to what she could do with her part. Still another of the production's liabilities was that Mr. Kahn, desiring to show us that the Venetians were a giddy and superficial crowd, encouraged or at least permitted several of them to giggle and chuckle and frivol and revel with annoying insistence and lack of conviction. Notwithstanding all this, however, I enjoyed the trial scene enormously; I had not seen it for a long time, and had forgotten what a brilliant piece of dramatic craftsmanship it is.

Even more so than the trial scene from *Merchant*, "The most lamentable comedy, and most cruel death of Pyramus and Thisbe" from *A Midsummer Night's Dream* is an almost irresistible piece of writing for the stage, and in Cyril Ritchard's staging it was very funny. But on the whole this production of *Midsummer* was characterized by a disagreeably spurious chic. The court of Theseus was dressed in a sort of musical-comedy Empire style; the fairies pranced about in chiffon; the forest, hung with coldly glittering strips of plastic, looked like Tiffany's window. Mr. Ritchard turned the play into a star vehicle by doubling as Bottom and Oberon. His Bottom was comic enough, and his Oberon was not without dignity, but Mr. Ritchard has abused his considerable talents for so long that he is now the prisoner of his own persona and can do only superficial variations on his familiar routine. His production and both his performances had an air of campy meretriciousness about them.

Four plays then, four directors, four directions. This was a better season than many have been at Stratford, but once again there was a sense of aimlessness and discontinuity. Nothing, artistically speaking, leads to anything else at Stratford; nothing is being built. And meanwhile the plays themselves are not being grappled with on any very profound level. It appears that the real identity of the Connecticut Stratford is to have no identity, to be a large institution, conveniently located near a number of wealthy suburbs, with a big-name board of directors, an attractive and comfortable theatre, plenty of money, and only the vaguest idea of what it is trying to do.

The San Diego National Shakespeare Festival

When the California Pacific International Exposition opened in 1935 in San Diego's Balboa Park, one of its attractions was the Old Globe Theatre, which presented fifty-minute potted versions of various plays by Shakespeare. After the exposition closed, the San Diego Community Theatre was organized to occupy the Old Globe, and, with time out for the war, it has been offering its amateur productions there ever since. In 1949, the Old Globe began offering something new: a summer Shakespeare Festival doing full-length productions, using college students as actors. In 1954, a few professional actors were added to the festival company, and in 1959 it went Equity. Since then, the Old Globe has been offering amateur productions of this and that during the winter (everything from *The Boy Friend* to *Right You Are . . . If You Think You Are*), and a professional Shakespeare festival in the summer. As far as I know, it is the only such tandem amateur-professional arrangement in the country. The summer season has attracted professional directors of some considerable note, including Allen Fletcher (who staged thirteen productions at the Old Globe), William Ball, and Ellis Rabb.

The theatre has been somewhat remodeled since the exposition; nowadays the claim that it is a "replica of Shakespeare's original Globe Playhouse" is an impudent fraud. We don't know much about the Globe, but we do know that it was an open-air theatre, whereas the "replica" is roofed; Shakespeare's Globe had room for about 3,000 patrons, while San Diego's Globe seats 419; in the original Globe, the ground-floor area near the stage was for the groundlings to stand in, while in San Diego this area contains comfortable plush seats; in the original, the stage projected deep into the audience, which surrounded it on three sides, while in San Diego the stage projects hardly at all and functions pretty much as a proscenium stage with a small apron in front. (The permanent setting, with a balcony at the back, does have some vague relationship to what people think the Elizabethan stage might have looked like.) Still, the Old Globe somehow manages to be an excellent theatre: warm, intimate, full of atmosphere. It would be possible not to enjoy a play in it, but it would be harder than at most theatres. The festival uses a number of actors who have previously appeared at Stratford, Connecticut; according to Craig Noel, the Old Globe's managing director, "Mainly they come here because they like the theatre. They love the plant." I can believe him. Something in San Diego—something about the theatre, I think—seems to make actors look better there than they usually are at Stratford. (On the other hand, perhaps something at Stratford makes them look bad.)

I have seen *Twelfth Nights* that were both funnier and more lyrical than the one Edward Payson Call directed at San Diego in 1967, but Mr. Call's production was reasonably successful in both directions, and nicely balanced. The play began with soft music; then Feste, the jester, on the forestage, picked up his cap and bells and put them on. He blew the dust off his lute and began to strum, as other characters slowly awoke. They cleared away the cloths that covered the forestage, straightened the front curtain, and drew it back, revealing Orsino and his court in tableau. Clearly Mr. Call has a feeling for the play's magic; this production was very unlike the gimmicky Deep South *As You Like It* that he had staged at the Tyrone Guthrie Theatre the year before. Katherine Henryk was a pleasant, lyrical, boyish Viola, though she worked a trifle hard at being charming. Josef Sommer was good as an elaborately finicking Malvolio (though he had not impressed me in this part at Stratford). Some of the bit-players were inadequate, but on the whole this was a modest, simple, and charming *Twelfth Night*.

Its companion in the 1967 repertory (along with *Othello*, which opened after I left San Diego), was *All's Well That Ends Well*, one of Shakespeare's awkwardest plays. It concerns a girl named Helena, who tricks an unwilling young man into marriage by a highly unsavory combination of force and fraud. So far, so good; this might be an admirable basis for a somewhat sour comedy. But Shakespeare demands that we accept Helena, who acts like an unscrupulous, designing minx, as a saintly heroine, and poor Bertram, her prey, as a worthless, frivolous youth who is lucky that Helena is willing to look at him.

Malcolm Black's production, in spite of several uninteresting performances in important roles, made this uncomfortable script quite tolerable; I doubt if anybody could make it much more than that. Douglas Watson clowned vivaciously (with a not-unwelcome touch of Robert Newton's Pistol in Olivier's *Henry V* movie) as Parolles. With the help of a Cockney accent and a series of vaudeville bits, Anthony Zerbe as the jester Lavache succeeded in earning laughs with some of the most excruciating material in all of Shakespeare, and managed at the same time to suggest that what he was doing had something to do with the play. (Mr. Watson and Mr. Zerbe also played Othello and Iago, respectively, in the festival's third and final production.) And Jacqueline Brookes imbued Helena with such ardor, such candor, that she almost made me forget the nastiness of what she was doing.

Outside the theatre, on the "greensward," madrigalists and minstrels perform before the show. Little booths sell candy, "Shakespearean gifts," "Shakespearean Jewelry," "Olde Globe Enamels," and "English Tarts and Cakes." This self-consciously ye-olde atmosphere does not pervade the productions (if the two I saw can be taken as typical); still, one would not expect to see anything brilliantly iconoclastic or bruisingly contemporary or burningly relevant at the Old Globe. Within this limitation, however, and the further limitations imposed by the budget, the San Diego Festival seems to be doing unambitious and small-scale but quite professional and pleasant work. And somehow the whole of each production seems to be more than the sum of its parts.

The Shaw Festival (Niagara-on-the-Lake, Ontario)

Niagara-on-the-Lake is a serenely sleepy little town, located at the point where the Niagara River runs into Lake Ontario. It should on no account be confused with Niagara Falls (a much larger community a few miles away), because it is entirely uncorrupted by the vulgarities of the tourist trade and possesses not a single wax museum to bless itself with. What it does possess is, of all things, a Shaw Festival.

Located within easy reach of both Buffalo and Toronto, in the midst of a popular area for summer homes, Niagara is a sensible place for a summer theatre, and one was duly founded in 1962 by Brian Doherty, a local lawyer who had once written a successful Broadway play entitled *Father Malachy's Miracle*. "We agreed," says Mr. Doherty, "that it should be a festival, not the usual summer-stock operation, and, Stratford having appropriated William Shakespeare, we adopted Bernard Shaw . . ."

The festival now runs at very close to 100 per cent of capacity in its 375-seat theatre, and is planning a new theatre that will seat about 800. It has been the beneficiary of that historical irony whereby GBS, that sedulous iconoclast and radical, has become a favorite entertainer of the middle classes, beloved of the same nice, prosperous, middle-aged ladies and gents who, had they lived at the turn of the century, would have been scandalized by him. Recently, four of his plays were running at once in the West End of London, where Edwardian period pieces are cherished; *My Fair Lady* was a success on much the same terms.

But the plays have borne this ambiguous fate very well; if they can no longer scandalize, they can still stimulate as well as sparkle. And the festival seems disposed to deal with GBS in good faith. It has produced some of his tougher works (*Heartbreak House, John Bull's Other Island, Major Barbara*) as well as more pleasant ones (*You Never Can Tell, Pygmalion, Arms and the Man*). And though I cannot speak conclusively, having attended only two festival performances (one of a play not by Shaw), I have seen no sign of any inclination to go for the too-easy laugh. The festival authorities are obviously not averse to light entertainment, but neither are they under the widespread, but erroneous, impression that the plays have to be distorted in order to be entertaining at all.

This festival is in some respects quite a small-scale, even primitive operation. Its budget for a twelve-week season is a mere $98,000. Its auditorium is an unwieldy makeshift, set up in the town hall. (The projected new theatre is badly needed.) Its costume shop is located in the back of a dry-goods store down the street. And yet, in this cozily backward atmosphere, some excellent actors are doing excellent work. In 1966, Barry Morse and Zoe Caldwell were members of the company (Mr. Morse was also artistic director). The 1967 company included Douglas Rain, Martha Henry, and Kate Reid, all of whom have played leading Shakespearean roles at Stratford, Ontario, Hiram Sherman and Larry Gates from the United States, and Renée Asherson (Olivier's leading lady in the movie version of Henry V) from England.

The 1967 season began with a production of Arms and the Man that was strikingly superior to the successful production of the same play that appeared off Broadway at about the same time. It was directed by Edward Gilbert of the Manitoba Theatre Center in Winnipeg, and it featured Miss Henry as the romantic Bulgarian maiden, Mr. Rain as the hard-headed Swiss soldier who takes refuge in her room, and Paxton Whitehead, the festival's artistic director, as her Byronic fiancée. Mr. Whitehead was not handsome or dashing enough for his part, which really ought to be played by Errol Flynn, but Miss Henry, a fascinating girl with a husky voice, and Mr. Rain, an ordinary-looking, stocky, curly-haired man with a vein of puckishness, were very well cast and generally admirable. Sandy Webster, as Miss Henry's choleric father, distinguished himself particularly; all actors think they are funny when they shout, but Mr. Webster actually was.

The production suffered from various lacks and lapses. A character referred to as "middle-aged" didn't look it. An incapable bit-player made his two-minute appearance uncomfortable. The sets for the first two acts failed to convey the "half-rich Bulgarian, half-cheap Viennese" combination that the playwright specifies. But on the whole I have never seen Shavian comedy played with more conviction. The actors attended to their situations and their objectives, and did not worry too much about providing a constant supply of yocks. This course (like all courses) is a dangerous one for the untrained or untalented actor, but these were genuine professionals, and the performance built from a moderately amusing first act to a hilarious third. Far more reliably than God, GBS rewards those who trust in him.

Arms and the Man was succeeded by Somerset Maugham's *The Circle* (vintage 1921), perhaps the best comedy ever written about extra-marital relationships in an English country house. *The Circle* is a prime example of the kind of play that the Angry Revolution overthrew; its juvenile lead actually makes his entrance through the French windows, saying, "I say, what about this tennis?" A theatrical life dominated by this kind of play must have been just as stultifying as Kenneth Tynan says it was; still, the best work of Maugham or Coward can be very pleasant as a change of pace. *The Circle* is a gracefully lightweight piece, suave yet cozy, and beautifully constructed. It is well equipped with epigrams and repartee, and with amusing, deftly contrasted characters; it has a characteristically Maugham-esque flavor, cynical and romantic, world-weary and ardent all at once. It is still extremely funny, and, in the third act, gently touching. It is dated, of course, but this is all to the good; it stimulates reflection as to how mores have changed since the days when divorce led automatically to ostracism. GBS would probably have rejected it as frivolous and trivial, but by the same historical irony to which I have already referred, it now seems quite at home at a Shaw Festival. (How will Abe Burrows look at an Albee Festival in fifty years, I wonder?)

Paxton Whitehead, who directed, allowed some members of the cast to play very broadly indeed, but they did so, for the most part, on lines laid down by the author, and their extravagance only aided in realizing the original conception. The most extravagant of all was Kate Reid as Lady Kitty, the gushing, vain, frivolous old lady who has returned to visit the house from which she had run away, thirty years before, with her husband's best friend. From the moment of her first entrance, when she stopped to pose in the doorway, her arms outstretched and her mouth agape, Miss Reid had the play, the stage, and the audience in her pocket. She was so funny, so full of gusto, so completely in control, that I was hardly in a mood to complain that though the script calls for a garish, painted harridan of nearly sixty, Miss Reid refused to be bothered, and came on looking like herself, a rather blowzy broad of about forty. In every other respect, she was the absolutely ultimate Lady Kitty.

Some of the other roles in the play provided dangerous pitfalls, which were triumphantly avoided. Hiram Sherman as Lady Kitty's deserted husband, a self-described "downy old bird," was chipper and spry but never unpleasantly smug. As Lady Kitty's aged lover, Leslie Yeo was amusingly irascible, and as her son, Steven Sutherland was amusingly stuffy. All three unerringly found the comedy in their parts without ever exaggerating or becoming monotonous. (I hate to think what nuisances so many actors might have made of themselves in these roles.) Susan Ringwood as the young wife and Paul Collins as her prospective lover were attractive and sympathetic, but far better at making love than at making small talk. No matter; the others were more than funny enough.

The final play of the festival's season was *Major Barbara,* under Edward Gilbert's direction. After closing at Niagara in September, this production played an engagement at Expo 67, and then moved to Winnipeg to open the new season at the Manitoba Theatre Center. In its sixth season, people were beginning to notice the Shaw Festival.

Being a Shaw Festival, of course, imposes certain limitations. It commits you to a proscenium stage and limits the extent to which you can make experiments in stagecraft. It tends to saddle you, I would conjecture, with an audience not amenable to much experimentation. This Shaw Festival has no intention of limiting itself to Shaw exclusively, but it seems destined, whether by necessity or choice is unclear, to remain an exponent of drawing-room drama (not necessarily comedy only). This, of course, is the kind of drama against which theatre people have been reacting for many decades now. But it is, if you choose so to interpret it, the tradition of Ibsen and Chekhov as well as Shaw, Maugham, Noel Coward, and their less-considerable successors. Now that this tradition no longer exerts a stranglehold over the contemporary theatre, now that the denunciations of the well-made play and the proscenium stage have become clichés, perhaps it is due for reappraisal, or re-invigoration. (Is Ibsen still viable onstage? Pinero? How about Barker and Galsworthy? How do Anouilh's fantasies of life among the aristocracy compare to those of the English? Is Molière perhaps the father of them all? Do any American playwrights belong in this company?) There is plenty of work that a Shaw Festival could do. In a few years this one will have a big new theatre, which will enable it to play in repertory, to mount larger productions, and perhaps to take a few chances; at the same time, it will begin to run out of the obvious play-choices. It will be interesting to see what happens then.

The Ypsilanti Greek Theatre (*Ypsilanti, Michigan*)

In Ypsilanti, a small and undistinguished city near Detroit, some people seem to have taken note of what has been done at Stratford. A Mrs. Clara Owens decided that Ypsilanti ought to have a festival of its own, devoted primarily to Greek drama; and, like Stratford, Ypsilanti determined to have the best. The Ypsilanti Greek Theatre was launched with a budget of $800,000. The new organization hired as its artistic director Alexis Solomos, for fourteen years the artistic director of the National Theatre of Greece; it recruited a distinguished company headed by Dame Judith Anderson and Bert Lahr (unfortunately the two did not appear in the same play); and it spent $100,000 to convert a small baseball stadium into a reasonable facsimile of a classical Greek amphitheatre, with the traditional circular space marked out as the main playing area, and the traditional rectangular platform behind it. Finally, in June, 1966, it unveiled the two productions that comprised its first season: the *Oresteia* of Aeschylus and *The Birds* of Aristophanes, both directed by Mr. Solomos.

On Labor Day the new theatre closed its doors—probably forever. The public had reacted to the idea of Greek drama in Ypsilanti with massive indifference. The average attendance in the 1,920-seat theatre was less than 700 people a night. With so little money coming in at the box office, it became an open question every week as to whether the organization could meet its payroll. The season left a deficit of half a million dollars. After an unsuccessful attempt to raise new funds, the 1967 season was canceled, and nothing has been heard about 1968. As far as I know, nobody has officially announced that the Ypsilanti Greek Theatre is dead, but it certainly looks like it.

There are a number of probable reasons for this overwhelming lack of response. Greek drama has never been popular in the English-speaking countries, partly because we are unfamiliar with it in the theatre, partly for deeper reasons. Having been raised on Shakespeare, we love particularity in our dramas, details of character, quirkiness even, but the Greek plays are remorselessly general. We love swift action, but the Greek plays are stately and slow (being frequently brought to a dead halt by choruses with a fatal gift of platitude). The plays deal cogently with questions that are highly pertinent to our own lives, but the symbols and conventions by which they deal with them have had two thousand years in which to lose their ability to rouse our emotions. And, in addition to all this, there are the difficulties of translation, which Greek-speakers tell us are well-nigh insuperable.

Furthermore, when Greek drama is done in our theatre, it is seldom done well. It was certainly not done well at Ypsilanti. Mr. Solomos' two productions were interesting as curiosities (so *this* is the *Oresteia* . . .), but as aesthetic experiences they were less than overwhelming. It is true that Greek drama is fiercely difficult to do, especially for a new organization, and Ypsilanti deserved an A for effort and courage and enterprise and all that. But why should anybody have bothered to come there to see a couple of curiosities? Surely if the plays had been no more than that in the first place, they would never have survived. The *Oresteia* was by far the better of the two productions, but even so I was reminded of the dictum of that great critic, Christophero Sly: "This is a very excellent piece of work; would 'twere done." Mr. Solomos had condensed Richmond Lattimore's translation of the trilogy into a long evening's playing time; it was half over when Karen Ludwig as Electra recognized that Orestes was nearby, and I was touched by emotion for the first time.

Miss Ludwig is evidently very talented; she played Electra with plenty of strength and an appealing girlish awkwardness. Donald Davis made an imposing Agamemnon, and Richard Mangoode provided a welcome touch of ordinary humanity as a breezy Herald. Dame Judith Anderson, with her splendid bearing and her defiant air, appeared in all three parts of the trilogy as Clytemnestra, but her reputation led me to hope for a great explosion that somehow never came.

The Chorus of Elders in the *Agamemnon* was a bit of a

washout, since behind their beards the Elders were obviously very young; the female chorus in the other two parts of the trilogy was much better. (The Furies, however, could hardly have scared a child.) Helen McGehee, the choreographer, evidently felt more at ease with the women; Miss McGehee is a member of Martha Graham's company, and she made the Graham idiom seem appropriate to Aeschylus. Mr. Solomos' staging was dignified and formal, with no attempt to get the play even part way down from its pedestal. Fidelity to the text is an admirable thing in a director, but in this case, entirely unleavened by imagination, it failed to bring the play to life.

The Birds at Ypsilanti was even deader than the *Oresteia*. Aristophanes is the most topical of dramatists; were he writing today, his plays would be full of LBJ, the hippies, and Elizabeth Taylor. Mr. Solomos' efforts at topicality were few and feeble, and so were his attempts at slapstick; if the play meant anything to him at all, there was no trace of it in his direction. The scenery and costumes by Eldon Elder and the choreography by Gemze De Lappe were similarly unimaginative; much of the acting was merely annoying. Bert Lahr bravely gave his usual performance, but even he could not make much headway against so many obstacles. (William Arrowsmith's unidiomatic translation, full of painfully bad jokes, was another obstacle.) The play was short enough, and the whole experience was odd enough, so that the proceedings never became entirely boring; but that is the best I can say for it.

If the Ypsilanti Greek Theatre had survived, it would have been the only professional theatre ever to give sustained attention to the difficult question of how—and whether—Greek drama can make great theatre in English. The effect of its first and only season, however, was to suggest that perhaps W. H. Auden's view, that the Greek classics in English have more historical and anthropological than aesthetic interest, applies particularly to the theatre. It took Tyrone Guthrie's magnificent production in Minneapolis of *The House of Atreus*—an adaptation of the *Oresteia*—to counteract the effects of Ypsilanti and convince me that Aeschylus has a future on the English-speaking stage. I await with eagerness a director (Dr. Guthrie himself, perhaps?) who will do the same for Aristophanes.

13

POOR PEOPLE'S THEATRES (MORE OR LESS)

*

The New York Shakespeare Festival

It was obvious, when Joseph Papp was starting the New York Shakespeare Festival, that Mr. Papp was out of his mind. His formula was simple but revolutionary: a professional company giving outdoor performances of the plays of William Shakespeare to which the public is admitted *free of charge*. Shakespeare is an expensive author to produce; when you refuse, on principle, to charge admission, the whole thing becomes an economic nightmare. It is said that a certain foundation once refused to give Mr. Papp a grant on the incontrovertible ground that there was no prospect of his festival's ever becoming self-supporting. One New York critic publicly begged him to charge a small admission fee in order to stay alive.

But Mr. Papp, in addition to being a madman, is very smart (a good combination). He realized that free admission was the basis of his festival's identity, the justification for its existence, and he has stuck with it. As a result, his enterprise has prospered and become an empire, with an annual operating budget in the neighborhood of $1,770,000. Every summer, Mr. Papp mounts three productions in the festival's 2,236-seat outdoor theatre in Central Park, and one or two or three productions (depending on how much money is available), plus a children's show, that go on tour through the five boroughs, playing in parks and playgrounds. On dark nights in Central Park there are poetry readings and concerts, plus a two-week festival of dance concerts every year after the Shakespeare season is over. In the winter, Papp presents a season of plays (mostly non-Shakespearean) at his new indoor theatre on Astor Place, and sends a Shakespeare production on tour through the schools. The annual attendance for all these activities may go as high as half a million. Only at the new indoor theatre is an admission fee charged, and even here the price is kept down to $2.50 a ticket, which does not begin to meet production expenses.

Mr. Papp's work has had tremendous influence all over the country. Since he began his outdoor operations in 1956, other organizations have begun giving free outdoor performances in Brooklyn, Baltimore, Washington, D.C., Cleveland, Seattle, San Francisco, and Los Angeles. More recently, concerts of symphonic, operatic, popular and jazz music have been offered on the same basis, with tremendous success. It looks as if Mr. Papp's innovation has become a permanent part of American cultural life. One is reminded of the epigraph Moss Hart made up for one of his plays: "Mad, sire? Yes, sire, they are mad, but observe how they do light up the sky."

Joseph Papp himself is a short, dark, and handsome personage, with plenty of thick black hair; he was born in 1921, and looks younger than he is. He is fast-talking, hard-driving, busy, active, nervous: a born promoter, with the abilities—to persuade and to organize, to gamble and to persevere—that will sooner or later make a man a millionaire, unless he finds some other activity more interesting and more important than making money.

His way of speaking still shows traces of Williamsburg, the slum district in Brooklyn where he grew up. His father was a trunk-maker—"a workingman," Papp emphasizes; the family name was Papirofsky. The future impresario went to Eastern District High School, and then to work in a laundry, having no money to go to college. He worked at "about fifty different kinds of jobs, but mostly physical type of jobs," before enlisting in the Navy in 1941. Sometime during the war, he decided that theatre was his vocation, and after his discharge in 1946 he studied acting under the GI Bill of Rights. He appeared with the road company of *Death of a Salesman*, worked as a social director for a borscht-circuit hotel, and in 1951 joined CBS as a stage manager. These jobs he regarded as temporary expedients, ways "of keeping alive until I could have a permanent theatre."

Finally, in 1953, in a church on the Lower East Side, he established the Shakespearean Theatre Workshop, where actors in street clothes, with no scenery or props, performed Shakespeare and his contemporaries before small, invited audiences. Even then, the few critics who ventured so far south spoke of the workshop productions in terms of "freshness," an "American" approach, and freedom from hampering traditions—terms that were to become critics' clichés for talking about Papp's work.

Not far from the workshop's headquarters stood—and stands— the Grand Street Amphitheatre, an outdoor auditorium built by the WPA on a strip of parkland that runs alongside the East River. Here in the summer of 1956 the workshop produced *Julius Caesar* and *The Taming of the Shrew*, under the direction of a young man from Indiana named Stuart Vaughan. Brooks Atkinson came down to Grand Street, liked what he saw, and said so in the *Times*, which brought the enterprise to the attention of the public at large for the first time. The capacity of the church auditorium was no more than 200; that of the amphitheatre, 2,500. The group had broken through to its first mass audience. That initial outdoor season was a hand-to-mouth affair: everyone donated his services, and the total budget was about $750. The Parks Department lent the amphitheatre free of charge, and this was the beginning of the fruitful and portentous relationship between Papp's troupe and the often-reluctant government of the City of New York.

After another winter season at the church came the Summer of the Elizabethan Trailer-Truck. Constantly seeking a wider audience, Papp proposed a season of three productions, each of which would open in Central Park, play an outdoor engagement in each of the other boroughs, and end up at the Grand Street Amphitheatre. All this was to be done on a budget of $35,000; for the first time, the actors were to be paid. A second-hand truck was acquired, and fitted out with a peculiar structure that unfolded into a highly serviceable thirty-five-by-thirty-foot neo-Elizabethan stage. On moving day, it could be folded up again into the semblance of a truck; an ordinary truck-cab was hitched onto the front of it, and off the extraordinary vehicle went through streets and over bridges to the next borough.

The first production on the truck was *Romeo and Juliet*. The critics liked it, and the tour was a great success, attracting capacity audiences of over 2,000 people a night everywhere except—for some reason—the Bronx. But the truck was showing signs of drastic wear and tear, and so were the unpaid apprentices, some of them totally unskilled (myself being one), who spent their days caring for the truck and their nights walking on in the play, and then had to build and rehearse the next play in between times. And so the touring program was reluctantly abandoned, and the other two productions of the 1957 season stayed put in Central Park, where the company—by now a "festival" instead of merely a "workshop"—has spent its summers ever since.

During that summer of 1957 the city took another cautious step in the direction of partnership with the festival. The Department of Welfare owns, among the more incongruous of its goods and chattels, a small theatre within a welfare building far up Fifth Avenue at the edge of Spanish Harlem. Not much use had been made of this Heckscher Theatre for many years, and so it was turned over to Papp, who made it his new winter headquarters. There he put on commendable productions of *Richard III* and *As You Like It*—free, of course—for school groups in the afternoons and for the public in the evening. But something was missing: the crowds, the excitement, the whole *ambience* of the outdoors. It became clear that the festival's popularity, its very identity, was intimately bound up with the ease and festivity of outdoor theatre-going. And something else was missing: money, for the lack of which this first uptown winter season came to a premature end in February, 1958.

Papp had always, of necessity, run his company on a hand-to-mouth basis. On a somewhat more comfortable scale, he still does. After every performance, in the early days, he used to make a curtain speech appealing for funds. (Sometimes there would be cries of "Author!" as he came onstage, and he would smile, and begin by denying that he had written the play.) Had he waited to open each season until he had money in hand to pay for the end of it, there would have been no festival.

His plan for that abortive winter was to have the city pay half his costs. "Why shouldn't they do it?" he asked the New York *Post*, adding later in the *Tribune*, "I am trying to build our theatre on the bedrock of municipal and civic responsibility . . ." But Mayor Wagner insisted (in the *Post*) that the festival "simply is not an operation of government," and the city Board of Estimate refused the $40,000 Papp had asked for. He begged industriously, and several times the day was saved by last-minute contributions; but finally the winter season had to be cut short, and the festival's energies were focused on the scrounging of funds for the summer season of 1958, which duly took place.

The Papp strategy was now clear: he proposed to make the city government a silent partner in his enterprise, first by demonstrating that he both deserved and needed municipal subsidy, then by badgering and shaming the city fathers until he got it. The strategy failed in the winter of 1958; but in the long run it has succeeded. The New York Shakespeare Festival probably works more closely with the local municipality than does any theatre in the country. It operates in a theatre provided by the city and another which the city's Landmarks Commission helped it to obtain; its school-touring program is a cooperative venture with the city Board of Education; the city provides hundreds of thousands of dollars each year toward the festival's operating budget; and the mayor helps it to raise additional funds from private sources. And yet, having begun not as an arm of government but as an independent organization, it has never lost its independence.

Bureaucrats, however, can be dangerous colleagues, and Papp's insistence on his principles almost cost him the life of his festival in the Great Robert Moses Controversy (or the Great Joe Papp Controversy, as it is presumably known to Mr. Moses and his adherents).

Robert Moses, then the city's Commissioner of Parks, is well known as a public servant with his own ideas as to how the public should be served. He had always been very insistent that no admission fee should be charged for performances on Parks Department property, but on March 18, 1959, he suddenly declared that unless the festival began charging admission fees of $1 and $2 per person, and giving 10 per cent of the gross to the department, there would be no more Shakespeare in the park. The department's cut was to be used for "necessary improvements" to the festival site. "We can't maintain grass," Moses explained, "and serious erosion problems would soon face us unless the area is paved."

Papp said no.

Moses' henchman Stuart Constable clarified the department's position to a reporter from the *Tribune* (sounding rather like Soft-Hearted John in *Li'l Abner*):

> I know. We're the dirty dogs denying poor people of a little culture. But Joe Papp thinks that just because he's giving free performances of Shakespeare he can wear out Central Park to his heart's content.

Constable was quite right in his implied assessment of public opinion. Four New York newspapers came out editorially for free Shakespeare; Papp was also supported by Actors Equity, the minority leader of the New York City Council, the United Parents Association, and an *ad hoc* We Want Will Committee. Moses responded by circulating an unsigned letter attacking Papp for having refused, under the Fifth Amendment, to testify before the House Un-American Activities Committee. Even Mayor Wagner, who as usual stayed as vague as he could for as long as he could about the matter, was moved to express disapproval of the "technique" of anonymous letters. Moses' next public statement on the subject was that Papp's group would now not be allowed into the park under any circumstances.

Finally, the Appellate Division of the State Supreme Court ruled that the Commissioner had been "clearly arbitrary, capricious, and unreasonable." The city capitulated. Mayor Wagner raised $20,000 privately to tidy up the festival site, and on August 3 the 1959 festival season belatedly opened with *Julius Caesar*. Admission was free.

Generous in defeat, the Commissioner shortly thereafter asked the City Planning Commission to appropriate $250,000 of the city's money for a new, permanent, outdoor Shakespearean theatre in Central Park, to be custom-built for the festival. Bureaucratic wheels turn slowly, but on June 21, 1962 (after two days of delay on account of rain), a production of *The Merchant of Venice* finally inaugurated the Delacorte Theatre, as the festival's more stately mansion is called.

The great argument against government involvement with the arts is the danger that the government will end up dictating to the artists. In New York City, Robert Moses tried it, and Joseph Papp fought him and beat him, proving that though the danger is a real one, it can be overcome, and indicating that the rewards are worth the danger, at least sometimes. Nowadays it seems a long time since the mayor declared that the Shakespeare Festival "simply is not an operation of government."

Although Papp has been a pioneer in dragging the municipal government (kicking and screaming, at first) into an involvement with the performing arts, his greatest single achievement is his audience. The audience at his Delacorte Theatre in Central Park is still essentially a middle-class crowd and certainly must include many people who go to the Broadway theatres as well. But this audience is middle-class with a difference. Negroes, Puerto Ricans, and young people—three groups that earn less money than most New Yorkers, and who are glaringly under-represented in most New York theatre audiences—are often in evidence at Papp's Central Park productions. Especially young people; as Papp himself points out, one reason for his festival's popularity is that it provides a handy cheap date.

The Delacorte Theatre is a roofless, 2,236-seat structure, exquisitely located on the shore of a tiny lake, in the shadow of a miniature castle on a miniature crag. It is one of the best places in the city for looking at New Yorkers in their diversity; even the frequent foreigners add a characteristically New York note of cosmopolitanism. Every day during the twelve-week summer season, the crowds begin to gather late in the afternoon; by six o'clock there is usually a sprawl of people over the neighboring fields. At about six-thirty, with a great gathering up of blankets, the sprawl turns itself into a line, and the box office begins handing out free tickets for that night's performance. When the tickets are all gone, another sad little line forms to await possible cancellations. Meanwhile the ticket-holders disperse over the grass to lounge and picnic, returning in time for the performance at eight o'clock.

Listen to their conversations:

"Macbeth was a sniveling neurasthenic and a wife-leaner!"

"When I was taking zoology once I stole my frog out of the zoo lab."

"Let's go lie on the grass. I got a blanket and a deck of cards."

"Anybody want to play a game of geography?"

"I like a big stone in a little setting."

"So the king realizes, he finally comes back to his senses . . ."

A man in a beard and sandals walks by, and two cops on duty mumble "Beatnik!" and speculate as to the date of his last bath. But this is not, on the whole, a Villagey crowd; by and large it is remarkable for its wholesomeness.

A family from Long Island spreads out on its blanket: Mother reads the funnies, two daughters do their homework, and Father just relaxes. A Puerto Rican couple goes chatting by, and one daughter says to the other, "Hey, Jean, maybe they could do my Spanish for me."

At another blanket, three girls cluster around a braying portable radio; one reads a comic book, one *Mad*, and the third *Time*. At still another blanket, a girl lies basking between two men, flexing her bare toes complacently.

A young Negro woman, in slacks and matching blouse, offers her date a bite of popsicle. Two couples stand around the phone booth, chatting in French. An Orthodox Jewish boy goes by, in skullcap and bermuda shorts. A middle-aged couple sit on a pair of camp-stools, stolidly reading the *Times*.

Near the lake, a boy plays the recorder for his girl friend. A carefully dressed young man and his mother sit straight on a bench, eating Crackerjacks carefully. Another young man reads from *Tales from Shakespeare* to his girl friend, whose head is in his lap. A little Negro girl of about ten, in a pretty blue party dress, waits on the cancellation line with her mother. In front of them is a middle-aged musician (white) making notes in a score.

A young boy in chinos and a work shirt sits leaning against a tree, sketching. An Indian girl in a sari, a caste mark on her forehead and a long black braid swinging at her back, walks up and down hand-in-hand with an Indian man in a neat gray business suit. An old lady with a cane drops her Yiddish newspaper into a trash-can and hobbles into the theatre.

This is a new kind of audience. They feel different. "They haven't paid $9.90," as George C. Scott says; and perhaps as a result, there is no sign of the tetchy, overdressed, constipated air of the Broadway crowds. These people come in shorts, suits, dungarees, date dresses, whatever they're comfortable in. They are relaxed and expansive; they haven't come to discharge an obligation, they've come to spend an evening in the open air. And yet, once the play begins, by and large they give it the attention it deserves.

But this audience did not satisfy Mr. Papp. "There are still thousands of people in New York City," he told *The New York Times*, ". . . who cannot get to the Delacorte Theatre in Central Park on time because of working hours." The solution: to resume touring. It was during that one brief tour of *Romeo and Juliet* in 1957, before the festival settled down in Central Park, that it had attracted its most truly popular audience. It was in Brooklyn, on that tour, that one girl spectator nudged her neighbor during the balcony scene and said, "See, Dolores, she's just as flat-chested as you are!" And so in 1964 the festival expanded its operations to include a second company, which tours the five boroughs with its own portable 1,600-seat outdoor theatre, designed by Ming Cho Lee.

I used to catch up with the Mobile Theatre in a playground in Spanish Harlem; the audiences there seemed to be drawn almost entirely from the neighborhood, and they consisted mostly of small children. There were even a number of babes in arms. Most of the kids, and some of the adults, behaved as if they were at a ball game: sauntering in late, leaving early, wandering around the theatre, keeping up continuous conversations, occasionally shouting their opinions at the players. One little girl had a toy ray gun which she fired off noisily at intervals during the show. One performance in another part of Harlem had been bombed out by rock-throwers, but the audiences I was part of seemed to like what they were getting.

When Papp has the money, he puts on one production a year in Spanish, for the benefit of New York's newest minority group. At the performance I saw of *Romeo y Julieta*, the youngsters enjoyed the comedy, especially the bawdy passages, but they liked the fights best of all. When Mercutio fell to the ground and rolled over in his death throes, they laughed and shouted and clapped and cheered. Such a lively crowd makes empathy difficult, but after a while I realized that many people were sitting quietly and seemed to be listening attentively; the rest seemed to be enjoying the occasion and the spectacle, if not the play itself. Almost every scene in *Romeo* was applauded. A lot of ghetto children may grow up, if Papp's efforts prosper, far more familiar with Shakespeare than most of us above the poverty line.

Although, as Papp admits the "social impact" of his enterprise "has been greater than its artistic impact," yet in what time they can spare from fighting their various battles, he and his colleagues have been trying to create a style for playing Shakespeare that will make the most of the conditions under which they work. These conditions dictated an outdoor theatre as the cheapest way to get a couple of thousand people within reasonable proximity of a stage, and open-air staging introduces a number of factors beyond human power accurately to predict or completely to control. Unseasonable cold, the threat of rain, or airplanes overhead can make it difficult for an audience to concentrate. Lines can acquire new meanings: one night when the sky was threatening and thunder was in the air, the First Witch got a tremendous laugh with her opening line in *Macbeth*: "When shall we three meet again/ In thunder, lightning, or in rain?" Things can go wrong onstage: a high wind once blew over a standing torch, and Romeo and Paris had to rise from the dead to put it out, while Juliet, who had caught cold from lying so long on her bier in the night air, coughed gently in the background. Moreover, an unroofed theatre has an especially acute problem with acoustics. The Greeks and Romans built outdoor theatres far larger than the Delacorte, in which no mechanical amplification was necessary; modern technology seems to have lost the knack. The body mikes now used at the Delacorte are an improvement over the old stationary ones, but they still sound slightly mechanical at best.

And yet the open air has its advantages. When I played a peasant servant for the festival in 1957, I was able to gather fresh straw backstage every night to put in my hair. There is a feeling, in the open air, of improvisation-within-the-framework, of *bonhomie* in the audience, and amplitude in the production. It is a fresh sensation, and a stirring one, to see Macbeth's banners streaming in a real wind. And as Meyer Berger wrote in *The Times*:

When Caesar, richly gowned in royal purple, says, "But I am constant as the Northern Star, Of whose true-fixed and resting quality There is no fellow in the firmament," the Northern Star is truly where he points, a coruscating light in Gotham's roof.

Another constant of Central Park Shakespeare is the open stage, which has the audience fanned out around it on three sides. In the first Central Park season, a neo-Elizabethan stage was used: a permanent platform with an upper level at the back (useful for Juliet's balcony, the walls of a besieged city, and other elevated places); this stage never changed in its essentials, though it was repainted and somewhat redecorated for each production. More recently, Ming Cho Lee has been the festival's resident designer. He has usually used a unit set (often a variation on the neo-Elizabethan pattern) that changes little or not at all during a performance, but he has been able to do an entirely new set for each show. His work is handsome and simple; often his setting has been the best thing about a production. Now as in the past, the festival's settings are designed to make possible a rapid succession of scenes (as at Stratford, Ontario, and even, usually, nowadays, at Stratford, Connecticut), unpunctuated by the blackouts and stage-waits that hampered what might be called neo-Victorian Shakespeare, on which many of us were brought up.

The opportunities which this sort of scenery affords for head-long, vigorous, uncluttered action were seized enthusiastically by Stuart Vaughan, who directed most of the festival's productions from 1956 to 1959. Vaughan assumed a posture of rather self-conscious revolt against decorative and elocutionary Shakespeare. He published this credo in *Playbill* (the program-magazine distributed in the Broadway theatres):

I think our concept of what "style" and "poetry" are differs somewhat from the accepted "traditional" pattern. What passes on so many stages for the poetic and the subtle sounds to me very much like meaningless song and self-indulgent speechifying. What passes so frequently for "period movement" looks so often to me like posturing. Productions filled with this mouthing and posturing tend to be set and lit with all the inner elegance and beauty of a Lord and Taylor Christmas window . . .

[A character] does not speak in a Shakespeare play any differently than he does in life, because, as he is a character in a play, this *is* life to him . . . The actor must remember most of all that he must be inwardly and outwardly and impudently real . . .

The critical consensus about the festival's early work is summed up by what was said about the first Central Park season in—of all places—the London *Times:*

> The attack abounds in vitality and virility. This is not the Shakespeare of the academy but the Shakespeare whose plays had to compete with bearbaiting. If the poetry tends to be slighted, the sense of urgent dramatic action is not.

I was not entirely an objective observer in those days, having worked for the festival myself, but Vaughan's Central Park Shakespeare, as I remember it, was for the most part swift, intense, believable, and sexy, and it usually managed to avoid meretriciousness and superficiality. His stage-business had always plenty of zing, and was usually relevant to the play; in particular he was a master of low comedy, though he sometimes exercised this mastery in scenes where it was not needed. And he had a gift for discovering and letting loose actors—of whom George C. Scott and Colleen Dewhurst are deservedly the best known—who combined Shakespearean grandeur and passion with a willingness to work for $40 a week. The only important faculty in which Vaughan was occasionally deficient was restraint. (Oddly enough, some of his recent work with the repertory theatres of Seattle and New Orleans has seemed to suffer from too much restraint.)

Since Vaughan's departure, the festival's artistic policy has not changed very much, in outline; but its productions have seldom been very good. Papp himself has directed many of them, and his gifts as an impresario do not qualify him as an artist. As far back as 1958, he directed a depressingly heavy-handed *Twelfth Night,* in which every comic point was punched home and stomped on. The romantic leads seemed fundamentally out of sympathy with their material; the wistful poetry of the romantic main plot is lute music, and it did not work to try to strum it on a ukelele. This production gave me the impression that Mr. Papp does not care very much for poetry, and that if Shakespeare's plays had been written by Eugene O'Neill, he would really have been just as happy. His subsequent work has not tended to contradict this impression.

Papp is ever-conscious of his responsibilities toward an audience "composed of persons who insist that we serve them a style of Shakespeare they can relate to their contemporary experience . . . and will settle only for characters with whom they can identify." Perhaps with this in mind, he has often hired actors who were flatly unready to appear in Shakespeare, or at best, unready to play *these* parts in *these* plays. The hangdog, random, casual but uncertain way in which they stood and walked and talked—the way they talked, above all—kept bringing the action down to twentieth-century commonplace earth with a thud. The problem has been complicated by the fact that all of Papp's companies have always been sedulously integrated, and Negro performers, up to now, have had even less incentive than white ones to become proficient in Shakespearean acting. A melancholy feature of several festival productions has been some well-known and talented Negro actor looking bad in a role he wasn't ready for. But white as well as Negro actors have given terrible performances for the festival. There are plenty of good classical actors, of various colors, around for directors who know where to find them and how to use them. The last point is important; even when an actor is talented, well trained and well cast, bad direction can hinder him, as it has done more than once at the festival.

The problem is not just a matter of "verse-speaking"; the incongruity between the actor and the words he speaks goes far to destroy the very fabric of the play. In Papp's 1963 production of *Antony and Cleopatra*, for instance, the lush splendors of the "barge she sat in" speech were lost, because the actor playing Enobarbus couldn't speak it splendidly. But far worse, the whole play had its wings clipped by the miscasting, as Antony, of a tough-talking, hard-headed-looking little fellow who made the Roman hero into an American sergeant. The Cleopatra, on the other hand, was Colleen Dewhurst, who is probably as well equipped for the role as any actress in America. In her early scenes she played for comedy with just the right kind of extravagance; but though everybody knows that she is an actress of tremendous power, she just didn't have it for the final scenes. She and Papp, according to interviews they gave to the papers, decided that the *real* truth about Cleopatra was that she didn't love Antony at all; she just thought she did. This is an ingenious piece of psychological jiggery-pokery, and perhaps even a legitimate interpretation of the play, but it is not a theatrically viable idea. By stripping Cleopatra of her love for Antony, the director stripped the actress of the emotional resources which she needs in order to rise to the "immortal longings" of those last scenes.

Papp's work as a director has improved slowly over the years. Parts of his *Hamlet* (1964) were awkwardly staged; the end of the play scene, for instance, collapsed into confusion, with everyone rushing around madly. The actor originally scheduled to play Hamlet got sick, and Robert Burr, who had been understudying Richard Burton in the role on Broadway, substituted at the last minute. Mr. Burr is a highly competent classical actor, and he made a vigorous yet casual, unpompous, masculine Hamlet. But somehow his work was totally unexciting; something more than competence is needed to play Hamlet. Julie Harris was a good Ophelia, but Howard Da Silva played Claudius as a character out of Sholom Aleichem. The following summer, Papp undertook *Troilus and Cressida*. His production was entertaining enough; Richard Jordan, an excellent Shakespearean juvenile, was an appealingly vulnerable Troilus, and there were some funny caricatures and grotesques. But Shakespeare's savage anger was largely missing. The best thing about Papp's *King John* (1967) was Douglas Schmidt's set: a somber wooden tower like a siege engine, which was at once a beautiful object in itself, a cogent symbol for the grim, martial world of this play, and a highly serviceable environment for the action to take place against.

King John was decently acted all the way through; the clumsy novices who had been defacing the minor roles in these Central Park productions had gradually been growing less prominent, and by the time of *King John* they had disappeared altogether (permanently, one hopes). But this does not mean that *King John* was really well acted. Harris Yulin was polished but monotonous in the title role, and his death agonies were not very agonizing; as the sardonic and zestful Bastard Faulconbridge, the richest character in this uneven script, Robert Burr was once again highly competent, and once again totally lacking in charisma. The play is cumbersome and full of rant, and Papp's straightforward, routine direction was insufficient to pull it together.

Between 1961 and 1966, a good number of festival productions were directed by Gladys Vaughan (Stuart Vaughan's ex-wife), whose work was very much like Papp's: superficial and uninspired, with a number of absolute incompetents playing the smaller parts. In her production of *Othello* (1964), James Earl Jones's performance in the title role was widely praised, but I thought it ponderous, mouthy, and dead inside. Her *Coriolanus* (1965), with Robert Burr in the title role, was desperately dull.

The third director who has worked steadily for the festival over the past few years is Gerald Freedman, who was given the title of artistic director in 1967. Mr. Freedman's productions have been cast with well-trained actors, even in minor roles; and unlike his Central Park colleagues, he shows distinct signs of that special, nameless directorial quality that makes a stage come alive. In the first scene of his 1965 *As You Like It*, for instance, he had Orlando loading a hay-cart as he complained about his "servitude," which provided an intriguing event to watch, a nice rhythmic punctuation for the words, and—most important—substance and support for what was being said.

But somehow, in spite of Mr. Freedman's evident talents, something tends to keep his Shakespearean productions from ever being fully satisfying. In *As You Like It*, for instance, a young actor named Richard Jordan was a fine Orlando, but the production was disabled by a gawky, graceless young movie comedienne, brought in to play Rosalind, who seemed to be having pitiable difficulties simply in getting all those words out. In 1965, Mr. Freedman took on *Love's Labour's Lost*, an uneven, highly difficult early play. His production was slick but superficial; some of the low comedy came off well, but the high comedy—this play contains the first of Shakespeare's witty lovers—did not. Rae Allen as Rosaline was far too hard and blunt for the part, and Richard Jordan as Berowne rushed through his great speeches as if they were an embarrassment. Mr. Freedman's *Richard III* (1966) suffered from the fact that Joseph Bova, who played the title role, is an actor who cannot help coming across as a nice guy, which took the plausibility right out of the play. His *Comedy of Errors* (1967) was a competent job, fast, well acted, and full of bits. The audience loved it, but I find the play so intrinsically tedious that all Mr. Freedman's ingenuity and skill could not make it much more than tolerable for me.

Mr. Freedman's *Titus Andronicus*, which closed the 1967 festival season, was probably his most ambitious production to date, and it was much admired in certain quarters. Unfortunately, the performance I attended got rained out shortly after the heroine got raped, and so I can only discuss the first hour and a quarter of it with any authority. I have always been fond of bloody old *Titus*, perhaps because I played the Third Goth from the Left on the occasion of the play's New England première (which took place as late as 1957). But I got the impression that Mr. Freedman disliked *Titus* just as much as nearly everybody else does. This is the play with the famous stage direction, "Enter . . . Lavinia, ravished; her hands cut off and her tongue cut out"; connoisseurs, however, tend to prefer certain of its lesser-known stage directions, such as "Enter a Messenger, with two heads and a hand," or, "Re-enter Titus with a knife, and Lavinia with a basin." But Mr. Freedman's whole production seemed to have been planned to minimize the horrors, to prevent people from laughing at them by making it abundantly clear that nobody was trying to create any illusion of the real thing. Everything was elaborately stylized and ritualized, with much rhythmic knocking of spears on the ground to underscore speeches, and a lot of what the program called "Choreographic Movement by Joyce Trisler." Before Lavinia's rape, a lot of extras writhed on the ground and said "Oooo," after which they produced little stylized tree-branches and impersonated a forest. (Us Goths never had to do anything like that.) It looked rather as if Mr. Freedman had seen the Noh, or the Gagaku, or some equally recondite form of Oriental theatre, and then decided what the hell, nothing else is going to work, let's try it.

But the play is hard enough to follow at the best of times, with every man's hand seemingly raised against everyone else, and constant re-groupings of factions; Mr. Freedman's staging obscured the action to the point where even I, an old *Titus* hand, was hard put to figure out what was going on. The actors were all dressed in black and gray, and wore masks; several of them looked almost interchangeable, which did not in itself make for lucidity.

And the acting was bad. Sir Tyrone Guthrie's production of *The*

House of Atreus in Minneapolis has proved that the most stylized, ritualized acting can attain tremendous peaks of emotional intensity, but Mr. Freedman's players often seemed merely uninterested in what they were saying. They acted, for the most part, from the throat outward, and most of them did not even have pleasing voices.

The production had a certain degree of visual interest, however. Ming Cho Lee's setting was marmoreally impressive, and I was moderately intrigued by Lavinia's Dance of the Stumps, which took place immediately after she enters in the condition itemized by the famous stage direction—although the gauzy scarlet streamers that hung from her mouth and wrists to indicate missing members were borrowed from Peter Brook's production. It is possible, of course, that from nine fifteen on, everything about this *Titus* suddenly became marvelous, but somehow I doubt it. What I saw demonstrated that Mr. Freedman has imagination and courage, but it also demonstrated the recurring difficulty this talented director has in getting on Shakespeare's wave-length.

Guest directors are seldom invited to work at the Delacorte, but the best production I have seen there in recent years was staged by Michael Kahn, who to my knowledge never worked there before or since. His *Measure for Measure* (1966) was unevenly acted, in parts sloppily staged, and laughably overinfluenced by *Marat/Sade*, but he had a firm and accurate idea of what the play was about, and he made that idea live on the stage. Ming Cho Lee provided him with an excellent set: a dirty-white brick structure with empty windows and fire escapes, which told us right away that this was not going to be a pretty fairy-tale farce; nobody was playing games. "I have seen corruption boil and bubble/Till it o'errun the stew," says the Duke in the last act, and in this production the action took place in a sick body politic, suppurating with beggary, lechery, and cruelty. As Claudio was led struggling and stumbling to prison for getting his fiancée with child (a far smaller sin than one committed by the man who orders his execution), onlookers threw rotten fruit at him—and beggars scrambled to pick it up. Mr. Kahn's production marked the only time I had ever seen, at the Delacorte Theatre, real theatrical imagination functioning in harmony with the imagination of the playwright.

The work I have seen done by the festival's touring company

has been much like the work at the Delacorte, only worse (except, perhaps, for the Spanish-language *Romeo and Juliet,* which I am not altogether competent to judge). The first five-borough tour of the new Mobile Theatre, in 1964, offered an execrable *Midsummer Night's Dream,* directed by Jack Sydow. The following year, Mr. Papp himself directed a *Henry* V with Robert Hooks in the title role. In spite of some incongruities in his diction, Mr. Hooks was good in the first scene, which he played with surly kingliness; unfortunately he played all the other scenes the same way, reading the St. Crispin's Day speech, for instance, as if Crispin had been a personal enemy of his. Gladys Vaughan's 1966 *Macbeth* was so enthusiastically inadequate, so vigorously clumsy, that it took on a certain guileless charm. James Earl Jones as Macbeth stalked ponderously around the stage as if he didn't know what to do with his body, and rolled out the lines monotonously in his big, deep voice; from time to time, more or less at random, he made funny faces. In 1967 there was a dullish *Volpone;* George L. Sherman, the director, seemed to have no particular ideas about the play, except that he wanted it to be funny, which it wasn't very. Alexander Panas in the title role did a great many elaborate bits that seemed hardly worth the trouble; of Volpone the great sinner, the megalomaniacal Renaissance sensualist, there was little to be seen. The production's most notable performance was given by Roscoe Lee Browne, who played Mosca, Volpone's parasite, with a constant, sardonic suggestion that he had more in his head than he was quite willing to put into words. Having seen Mr. Hooks sulking his way through *Henry* V, and Mr. Jones bombinating his way through *Macbeth,* I was glad to be reminded by Mr. Browne's deft, gleaming subtlety that good Negro classical actors do exist.

It is admirable of Mr. Papp to refuse to condescend to his neighborhood audiences, and to insist on giving them Shakespeare and Ben Jonson instead of *Harvey* or *Mr. Roberts;* it is brave of him to schedule, in recent Central Park seasons, so many of Shakespeare's least popular plays. Papp has done more, perhaps, than any other single individual to widen the base of the American theatre audience; he has so spectacularly made two blades of grass grow where only one grew before, that it seems almost churlish to complain about the quality of the crop. It could be argued that since after all they're free, Papp's shows are bargains in any case. But a Shakespearean performance still costs three hours out of the life of every member of the audience, and this expenditure, even if there be no other, still demands compensation in the quality of the work. Furthermore, the quality of Papp's productions is such as to make it highly questionable how much of Shakespeare his audiences are actually getting. His work may well have put some people off Shakespeare forever; and if most people will accept the festival's work because they don't know any better, how are they going to learn?

Recently, the festival has begun a new project. Having acquired the old Astor Library, in downtown Manhattan between Greenwich Village and the Lower East Side, it is transforming this splendid hundred-year-old landmark (officially so designated by the City Landmarks Commission) into a "Public Theatre which will house two three-hundred-seat theatres, as well as a Children's Theatre, a Coffeehouse Theatre, a Chamber Recital Hall, a Children's Puppet Workshop, rehearsal halls, technical workshops, and administrative quarters for the Shakespeare Festival. All these changes are being accomplished without sacrificing the architectural integrity of the first free public library building in the City of New York." (I quote from a booklet published by the festival.) In the new building, Papp will charge an admission fee of $2.50 for every seat (scarcely a prohibitive sum), and will concentrate on contemporary plays.

The first of the Public Theatre's several auditoriums opened in October, 1967 with a phenomenon entitled *Hair*, and subtitled "An American Tribal Love-Rock Musical," which turned out to be exactly what it was. Its characters were all teenaged hippies, except for a couple of adults, designated "Mom" and "Dad," who served more or less the function of ducks in a shooting gallery. Since I had recently sat through a number of Broadway plays by middle-aged playwrights that fairly vibrated with mistrust, incomprehension, and dislike of the younger generation, I was glad to see a musical that was frankly—but not sententiously—pro-youth, and even pro-long-hair; unfortunately *Hair* turned out to have nothing new to say about youth or hippies or anything else. It tended to cop out in a number of directions; even before certain murders that took place only a few blocks from where *Hair* was playing, it was evident that hippies had a few other problems besides moldy-fig grownups, the draft, and unrequited love. (The plot of *Hair*, insofar as there is one, concerns a boy who digs a girl who doesn't dig him; she digs instead another boy who doesn't dig her.) But Galt MacDermot's score ("love-rock," as advertised), Gerald Freedman's fluid staging, and the irresistible high spirits of the performers, combined to make *Hair* a rousing entertainment. After its run at the Public Theatre, it was transferred to a large discothèque named Cheetah, where it flourishes as I write.

Mr. MacDermot also provided a rock score for the Public Theatre's second production: a studiously unconventional, rigorously random *Hamlet*, directed by Mr. Papp. The text was Shakespeare's, severely cut, much rearranged, and somewhat revised ("What do you read, my lord?" "*The New York Times*"). The staging was, to say the least, lively. In the middle of a scene between Polonius and Ophelia, Hamlet called "Intermission! House lights!" and came down the aisle handing out balloons and bags of peanuts; the nunnery scene followed, broken up into short passages which Hamlet addressed to various members of the audience, pausing in his denunciations to throw peanuts at Ophelia and Polonius. During the play scene, Hamlet ran around shooting home movies. Ophelia appeared for what used to be her mad scene in a cutaway, transparent tights, and a straw boater, and sang her songs into a hand mike. The implication of all this seemed to be that poor old *Hamlet* was finished, washed up, hopeless, viable only as a butt for mockery.

The most promising aspect of the production was the attempt to make the audience participate in the action—a way of creating meaning in the theatre that is just beginning to be explored. (Perhaps Mr. Papp has been reading Artaud, or perhaps he has merely been seeing the work of other directors who have been influenced by Artaud.) On the night I saw *Hamlet*, however, the spectators were embarrassed and unwilling to participate. During the recorder scene, for instance ("Will you play upon this pipe?"), Hamlet went about offering the recorder to members of the public, but found no takers. This, I think, was the result of a failure of nerve on the part of the actor, or perhaps the director; they left us in doubt as to what they wanted us to do, they failed to convince us that we were really expected to participate. Probably the root of the matter is that they did not want our participation badly enough. In the last scene, when the staging absolutely demanded that someone from the audience come on to the stage and join Hamlet in the variation of Russian roulette that Mr. Papp substituted for the duel, when the actor really needed to induce a spectator to participate, and was very clear as to what he wanted him to do, a participant was found without much difficulty. And this scene was the most exciting one in the production.

For most of the evening, however, the effect was as if a clever undergraduate had been given a large stage, some very capable actors, and a good deal of equipment to play around with. Some of it was very funny; some of it was tiresome. It was amusing, for instance, when Hamlet (personably played by Martin Sheen) began "To be or not to be" in a Speedy Gonzales accent; but by the time he finished the soliloquy, the joke had worn a bit thin.

What disturbed me about this uneven but interesting exercise in adolescent high jinks was the evidence that Mr. Papp took it seriously. He wrote in a program note:

> This production aims radioactive ididium 192 at the nineteenth-century HAMLET statue and by gamma ray shadowgraphing seeks to discover the veins of the living original, buried under accumulated layers of reverential varnish.
>
> Our method, or our madness, has been to concentrate on the outer truth of acting—an expression of the psychological truth which may turn out distorted or poetic. This essence, which in effect becomes a symbol of a reality, is left for the audience to interpret and recall in its own emotional memory.

I am not equipped to say exactly what is meant by all of this (is anybody?), but it seems to indicate that Mr. Papp doesn't know the difference between a legitimate production of Shakespeare's play and his own zany parody.

After *Hamlet* will come the world première of *Ergo* by Jakov Lind. According to Gerald Freedman, who will direct it:

> ERGO is a nightmare, an eruption, a sledge hammer, a vomit of anger and outrage. It is a darkly comic passageway into the murky depths of the most horrifying and unexpiable events that stained

forever middle-European life, culture and essence . . . ERGO is like a ganglion of Jakov Lind's traumatized childhood in Nazified Austria. . . . ERGO is a condemnation of all Western man.

Ergo will be followed by *The Memorandum,* an Ionesconian satire on Stalinism, de-Stalinization, and bureaucracy in general, by the Czechoslovakian playwright Vaclav Havel.

Mr. Papp never struck me as having much affinity with the Elizabethan past; maybe in his new premises, where he will concentrate on modern works (while continuing, of course, to produce free Shakespeare in the park in the summer), he will add a few artistic achievements to the tremendous, pioneering sociocultural contribution that is already to his credit.

The Free Southern Theatre (New Orleans)

For all its success in broadening the base of its audience, the New York Shakespeare Festival still plays mostly for the middle classes. Except for the Teatro Campesino, which plays for striking agricultural workers in California, the Free Southern Theatre is, as far as I know, the only theatre in this country that exists primarily to play for the genuine poor. Its audience is the black people of the South; its slogan is "Theatre for people who have no theatre." Its home base is New Orleans, but it spends most of the summer on tour, 4,500 miles through five states in the Deep South, playing in small towns like Bogalusa, Louisiana, Grenada, Mississippi, and Selma, Alabama. Lately it has begun to appear at Negro colleges. In 1967 it probably reached a total of about eight colleges plus fourteen towns, in addition to performances in and around New Orleans. Except at occasional fund-raising performances in the North, it never charges admission.

The FST is not a lavish operation; its annual budget is under $40,000. It travels in two small vans and a car, which carry sets, props, costumes, lighting equipment, and the six men and two women who make up the company. Two of the men are technicians; one confines himself to acting, as do the women; the rest have multiple functions. Robert Costley, the company manager (who is responsible for seeing that the group gets where it's going and does what it's meant to) also directs, acts, leads workshops, and answers correspondence from journalists. He is the only member of the troupe who is over forty; most of them are in their twenties. Except for one white actor, and a business manager who stays in New Orleans, the company is now all-Negro. The white actor, a young New Yorker named Murray Levy, defines the FST as "a black theatre in which whites work."

While on tour, the company members sleep in the homes of local FST sympathizers, and perform where they can, in churches, schools, union halls, cotton fields, bean fields, rice fields. They give two or three productions on successive nights; during the day they hold workshops in drama and creative writing. And then they move on to the next town.

It used to be a perilous business. In one town the sheriff arrested the entire company, let them go, and tipped off the Klan; the actors hid in the weeds as the Klansmen rode up and down looking for them. In Bogalusa and Jonesboro, Louisiana, armed members of the Deacons for Defense, a militant Negro organization, patrolled outside the hall, just in case. Lately there has been no trouble, and Mr. Costley does not expect any. Still, he packs a gun, just in case.

"Theatre for people who have no theatre." Granted, the black people of the South would have no theatre except for the FST, but they lack other things that are usually considered far more important. Why spend so much effort, in such primitive conditions, at a salary of $60 a week, to bring them theatre, of all things? For the same reason that impelled the juggler of Notre Dame, perhaps. How better can a man serve what he believes than by the use of such talent as he has? Theatre people will natually seek to serve through the theatre. (Not that Negro theatre people have such an abundance of competing opportunities.) In addition, according to Bob Costley, who played in *Blues for Mr. Charlie* on Broadway, there are tremendous satisfactions to be derived from playing before an "unsophisticated audience. . . . they tend to join right in: 'Amen,' 'Go on, darlin',' 'Tell it, honey.' It's this type of enthusiasm that the legitimate stage really lacks."

According to John O'Neal, one of the FST's founders, "we thought that if theatre means anything anywhere it should mean something here in the South too. . . . Theatre has taken the tone of the rest of our lives: meaningless, otherness, outsideness. The last *Dolce Vita*. Gil [Moses, the other founder] calls it the 'ice-cream parlor theatre'—a place you go to not even for dessert, just to do *something*. But the FST has to be bread—a bakery which makes something vitally needed. Theatre doesn't have to be entertainment. I don't know what it can be. We're young, naïve, probably stupid, but we're also arrogant and pretentious. So we're going to insist on doing something. Maybe we'll fall on our asses. But out of our involvement with these audiences—the audience *we have chosen*—meaning will come."*

This is vague enough, but it catches the character, the quality, the importance of the FST. Aesthetically speaking, some of its work is pretty poor—at least it was so at the time of my visit in the summer of 1967. The non-Equity company is inexperienced, and its work shows no particular imagination or intensity to make up for deficiencies in technique. Even by the low standards that prevail in the regional theatre, this is not really, at this point in its career, a fully professional group. But its productions are not genteely boring, as regional-theatre productions so often are, because this theatre is involved with its audience. Most of its productions deal with matters of immediate interest to the people it plays for. It is not hung up in an empty propitiation of the gods of Culture, as regional theatres so often seem to be; it is interested in setting up a dialogue with its audience, about matters of common concern. After every performance, the audience is invited to stay and talk over the play with the actors; these discussions are an integral part of the occasion. According to Bob Costley, the spectators in small towns find parallels between what happens onstage and what happens in their own lives. " 'I know a man just like so-and-so in the play. He lives over yonder. He has the same sort of outlook on me as that fella in the play has about the other fella.' " The FST really does succeed—as I am afraid very few regional theatres do—in helping people to look at their own lives. And most of its material, being close to its audience, is close to its actors as well, and does not make too great demands on their resources. These actors are ill-trained, but they *can* play contemporary American Negroes, and read contemporary American Negro poetry, tolerably well, and sometimes better than that.

* "Dialogue of the Free Southern Theatre," *Tulane Drama Review*, T28 (Summer, 1965), pp. 63, 67.

Gilbert Moses and John O'Neal started the FST in September, 1963; both had come south to work for the civil rights movement. In the summer of 1964 they took *In White America,* their first production, to "sixteen cities and towns, ranging in size from New Orleans to Mileston in Holmes County, Mississippi," according to Mr. Moses. "The Holmes County people came in from the farms to see us. We had to play in the afternoon because they wanted to get back home by dark." They brought the play up to date by the addition of some material on the murder of Chaney, Schwerner, and Goodman. "The amazing thing," said a member of the company, "was that this play gave people a frame of reference they'd never had before. They saw today's struggle as an *old* fight, and they recognized that people had been fighting much the same way, all over the country, for a long time: for *all the time.* They found the history they had always been denied."*

In November, 1964, the FST set out again with *Purlie Victorious,* by the Negro actor-author Ossie Davis, and *Waiting for Godot.* In Hattiesburg, Mississippi, they were greeted by a sign saying, "The Free Southern Theatre, the Theatre of Our Own Coming Back." *Waiting for Godot,* according to Bob Costley, was highly popular with FST audiences: "They dug it. They really dug it. Perhaps the sparseness of the set is akin to the sparseness of their lives." They identified intensely with Lucky, the slave. And the next year, people would ask, "Where's that play you do about the fellows waiting for God?"

The company described its 1965 productions as "plays about revolt—that sometimes bloody struggle to organize grievances for effective political change and action." The plays were *The Rifles of Senora Carrar* by Bertolt Brecht ("Not to fight for us, Teresa, doesn't mean he isn't fighting, it only means he's fighting on the other side"), and a revival of *In White America.* In 1966, the FST presented *Roots,* a new play by its co-founder Gilbert Moses, a double bill of *I Speak of Africa* by William Plomer and *Does Man Help Man?* by Brecht, and a program of Negro poetry and songs. The last of these was televised nationally on CBS.

In December of 1966, the company was awarded a grant of $62,500 from the Rockefeller Foundation, to be paid out over a three-year period. But in spite of this shot in the arm, 1967 seems

* *Ibid.,* pp. 63, 68.

to have been an off-year for the FST. The company was smaller than it had been, and confined itself to one-act productions. Company veterans felt that the one show that had been held over from last year had lost something since then.

I spent five days with the FST in July, 1967, while they were appearing at the Tuskegee Institute in Tuskegee, Alabama. Regular classes were not in session, but there was a "pre-freshman" program to help compensate for the deficiencies of southern Negro high schools by getting a group of youngsters ready for college. The FST was invited to help enrich the curriculum. The audience was composed of students and teachers; unfortunately, I never got to see the company play before farm people or ghetto inmates.

You get to Tuskegee down a road that runs past cornfields, cotton fields, and piney woods; the Greyhound bus is integrated. The institute looks like a college (which, of course, is what it is): it has a spacious campus with plenty of substantial buildings in 1920's Georgian style. One of these was the Dorothy Hall Guest House, maintained by the institute, where the company stayed, as did I. It was more comfortable than some Hiltons I know. On the dresser there was a sign: " 'No man who has the privilege of rendering service to his fellows ever makes a sacrifice.'—Booker T. Washington."

The company arrived on a Monday night, set up its equipment the next day, and on Tuesday evening gave its first performance: an "open rehearsal" of Ionesco's *The Lesson*. This turned out to be a dull, clumsy, spiritless walk-through, with both of the principals still on book. Perhaps it got better in the ensuing weeks (though I saw no signs that it would ever be good); but no company with even remotely professional standards would think for a moment of offering any audience such unfinished work. The actors weren't giving performances; they were merely giving cues.

Later on, I talked to the director, a young man named Thomas C. Dent. Mr. Dent considers himself primarily a writer; the FST, he says, "gives me a means of reaching an audience which I never had. . . . None of us can afford to be selfish and jump in the ivory towers of our art." He chose to do *The Lesson* because the company was playing at a lot of colleges, but also "to see how far we can go," and find out how abstract he could get in his own writing without losing his audience. Furthermore, he says, "My feeling is that *The Lesson*—though it wasn't written that way—is a racial play. It has a very applicable racial parallel: the condescension of the white person who in the end ends up destroying." In his production the Pupil was played by a Negro girl; the Professor, who eventually kills her, was played by a white man. "Surprisingly," adds Mr. Dent, "in our audience, not many people see it racially." This goes to show, perhaps, that there is a level of badness below which a production ceases to be stimulating—a lesson which all socially-committed theatres might take to heart.

Wednesday night the FST gave *Happy Ending*, by Douglas Turner Ward, before a nearly full house, with some additional spectators looking in through the windows. The play is by a modern American Negro playwright, and it is about modern American Negroes; it was within the capacities of the actors, and the audience was clearly finding it pertinent and close to home. It deals with a couple of Negro domestics who are bewailing the fact that their white employers are getting a divorce; Mr. Harrison has caught Mrs. Harrison in bed with his best friend. It turns out, however, that the two domestics had been stealing freely from the Harrisons for years, and are only unhappy because their supply of food, clothing, furniture, miscellaneous consumer goods, and money is being cut off. The happy ending of the title is brought about by a phone call saying that the Harrisons have decided to reconcile.

The discussion afterward got right to the basic question: how does the play relate to real life? "It was a very shocking thing to hear a black woman cry about a white marriage breaking up, but it was very well explained." (I gathered that without the economic motive it would be unconscionable Tom-ism for a Negro domestic to sympathize with her white employers.) "They were doing something that a great many people want to do. They were sucking the white man into his own trap." Nobody in the audience seemed to see anything wrong in stealing from rich white people.

One white man complained that the ending reduced the Negro characters to dependence on the whites, and that this was a bad thing. My first reaction was that he should have addressed his complaint to American society, not to the playwright; this is what *happens*, and the playwright who reports it is doing his job. But even aside from that, I think this man missed the point. What the play shows, in the first place, is that dependence is a two-way street. The Harrisons depend just as much on their domestics as the domestics depend upon them; and whereas the Harrisons depend on the energy and efficiency of Ellie and Vi, the servants depend on their employers only for money. Further than that, Ellie and Vi dramatize the rejection of Booker T. Washington's dictum that service is its own reward, by making sure that they are very well paid into the bargain. And what they take is more than material goods. They derive their *pride*, not from service as Booker T. recommended, but from deluding the white man, leading him by the nose, "sucking the white man into his own trap." By stealing they show—as many Negroes have been desperately impelled to show in this and other ways—that they were not the pawns of the white man, but independent, self-directed human beings.

The audience understood this, emotionally if not conceptually. The turning point of the play comes when Ellie reveals the truth about their relationship with the Harrisons:

VI. Who runs the Harrisons' house, Junie?

JUNIE. ??? . . . Ellie . . . I guess . . . ?

ELLIE. *From top to bottom.* I cook the food, scrub the floor, open the doors, serve the tables, answer the phones, dust the furniture, raise the children, lay out the clothes, greet the guests, fix the drinks and dump the garbage—all for bad pay as you said. . . . You right, Junie, money I git in my envelope ain't worth the time 'n' the headache. . . . *But—God Helps Those Who Help Themselves.* . . . I also ORDER the food, estimate the credit, PAY the bills and BALANCE the budget. Which means that each steak I order for them, befo' butcher carves cow, I done reserved TWO for myself. Miss Harrison wouldn't know how much steak cost and Mr. Harrison so loaded, he writes me a check wit'out even looking. . . . Every once in a full moon they git so goodhearted and tell me take some leftovers home, but by that time my freezer and pantry is already fuller than theirs. . . .*

At this point there was a tremendous burst of laughter and applause. The spectators were applauding not just Ellie, but themselves and their race and the fact that in the three-hundred-year struggle with the white man, against tremendous odds, they had quietly managed to win their share of victory, to find their own kind of dignity in unexpected places. Ellie's pride in her own capabilities was theirs, and the FST had given them a chance to come together and draw sustenance from it. This is one way the theatre can serve by affirming as well as attacking. (Most resident theatres, of course, fail to do much of either.)

One day I had lunch at the Guest House with one of the FST's technicians, a fervent Black Nationalist ("I dig Malcolm X") and a vigorous opponent of our policy in Vietnam. He was arguing furiously with a very ladylike Negro schoolteacher, who had come to Tuskegee for a seminar; she was defending our policy in Vietnam on the ground that there have always been wars, and hair-straightening on the grounds that everyone wants to look attractive. I asked him whether the FST was part of the Movement; he told me that the Movement was dead, and he didn't miss it. For him the important thing was not to look for acceptance from whites, but to develop black consciousness, black pride in being black; he was interested in the FST because it had the potentiality of being part of this. It is more than potentiality, I think.

Thursday night the company gave its "Evening of Afro-American Poetry and Prose" in the enormous Tuskegee gym, with five hundred youngsters, bussed in from twelve counties, in the balcony. Physically, the show consisted of three performers on stools: Bob Costley, Gary Bolling, and Cynthia MacPherson, all of whom read effectively. Sometimes Miss MacPherson sang, unaccompanied, ardently, in a deep, strong voice. The program consisted of forty minutes of short selections, mostly conventional agitprop, by Langston Hughes, Ted Joans, Julian Bond, Ossie Davis, and a number of others whose names were new to me. "America, I forgive you, I forgive you eating black children, I know your hunger." "I ain't killed no Vietnamese babies, or fourteen-year-olds in Mississippi." "It is time for rhinoceroses to roam the streets of Tuskegee—spreading joy." "She does not know her beauty. She thinks her brown body has no glory."

I had understood that the company had lost some of its militancy since the "Year of Revolt," when it had rejected *Happy*

Ending as being "too light." Bob Costley had told me, "We try to preach awakening and awareness rather than just preaching revolt. I don't think we're that powerful yet." Of course, the line is hard to draw. As one of the actresses said, "This theatre is geared specifically to show black people that they don't have to stand up for this *crap* any longer." Is that just "awakening and awareness," or is it "revolt" as well? At any rate, some of the "Afro-American Poetry and Prose" struck me as pretty strong stuff, especially a poem by David Henderson about the Harlem Riots with the refrain, "Keep on pushin'." The audience got the point. As somebody said during the discussion, "The only way we can get anything is through violence . . . this is what I got out of that."

The question of whether violence is a good idea for the Negro, or for the rest of us, is beside the point; the point is that the FST is dealing with questions that its audience finds important, that here at least art and life are not sealed off from one another. The art is not of the best—the FST has a long long way to grow—but at *this* time in *this* place it functions as more than a diversion, and this is not usually the case with the resident professional theatre. In the kind of theatrical culture I would like to see in this country, a couple of dozen theatres would be talking to their audiences with just as much immediacy and pertinence as the FST, and in terms far more subtle, complex, and profound; they would be bringing directly to bear on the experience of its audience the work of far better writers than Douglas Turner Ward and David Henderson. But right now that isn't happening. Until it does, the Free Southern Theatre has something to show the American theatre at large.

APPENDIXES

APPENDIX A

The Improvisational Cabaret Theatres

The ordinary resident professional theatre is an import agency: its primary purpose is to disseminate in Hartford, Memphis, or Seattle the international theatrical culture of New York, London, and Paris. There are, however, a few centers out there in the hinterlands where new original material is constantly being created. These institutions are resident and they are professional and they are theatres, but they are not resident professional theatres in the customary sense: they sell no subscription tickets, they conduct no fund drives, the Ford Foundation does nothing for them, they are not about to move into million-dollar buildings in civic arts centers downtown. Yet they have exported not only talented performers but whole productions, not only whole productions but a new—or at least a renewed—way of making theatre, to the metropolises. They are the improvisational theatres, the modern American exponents of the Aristophanic art of the satiric cabaret.

The Committee, which opened in San Francisco in 1963, has played an engagement on Broadway, covered the 1964 nominating conventions for National Educational Television, and even sent a company to colonize Los Angeles. The Premise (now deceased) which began in St. Louis, sent companies to Washington, New York, and London. (The London company got into trouble with the Lord Chamberlain, since improvised material obviously cannot be censored beforehand.) But the great fountainhead of the improvisational movement was the short-lived Compass Players company in Chicago. From it came Mike Nichols, Elaine May, and Shelley Berman; from its direct successor, the Second City—still flourishing in Chicago—came Barbara Harris, Alan Arkin, and several other remarkable performers now working in New York and elsewhere. Second City companies have appeared on Broadway, in a large New York cabaret (for three years), in London (twice), on television, and on tour all over the American map, while other Second City companies held the fort in Chicago.

Most of the evening at one of these improvisational cabaret shows is taken up by revue sketches, quite conventional in form. But instead of making a point in order to make you laugh, like the ordinary revue sketch, they tend to make you laugh in order to make a point. They are often rambling and overlong; sometimes they just do not come off; but on the whole they are distinguished for their intelligence and cogency, and for the quietness with which they are performed: no frenzied mugging, no fright-wigs, no funny hats. They are not rowdy and knockabout, nor are they chic and precious. The improvisational cabaret theatres have been largely responsible for an increased national interest in intelligent satire.

Paradoxically, perhaps, in view of their wide success, what distinguished the Second City and the Committee on their home grounds is that their work seems aimed at a very particular audience, an audience that shares the assumptions and predilections of the performer-creators. This kind of theatre is of, by, and for well-educated, urban young people, irreverent as a matter of course toward all authority, with no objections to what are still sometimes called obscenity and blasphemy (probably the only word that can still really shock them is "nigger"); people, finally, for whom leftist political assumptions are part of the air they breathe.

"But Job worshipped God," says a Second City performer, "with a fervor bordering upon stupidity." "There is a rumor," says a Committee member, "that J. Edgar Hoover is immortal." Both Second City and the Committee have had race-relations sketches in which white liberals were raked over the coals. The Second City sketch showed a couple of professed liberals driving through a Negro neighborhood in Chicago, and getting scared. "Black as a forest out there," says one. "You hear drums?" (Laughter: an audience laughing at itself.) At the Committee, a white girl and a Negro man shake hands. "It's just like on the Snick button," she says. Not a very funny joke to someone who has never seen a Snick button. (Since I saw this scene in 1966—how long ago that seems—it has, of course, taken on new dimensions of irony.) Both groups, again, have had sketches sympathetic to young men who don't want to be drafted. "Don't let 'em take your mind," says one draftee to another in the Second City sketch; it is something a lot of intelligent draftees, proud of their free-mindedness, must have thought as the Army tried to mold them into gung-ho soldiers.

The regular resident theatres are highly eclectic and this is a good thing in its way. But the result is a certain loss of personality. It is refreshing to discover theatres that (like the Berliner Ensemble, so they tell me) stand for one particular kind of theatre, one particular way of looking at life that they share with their audiences. At their best, the resident theatres deal, sometimes profoundly, with the important concerns of Western man; but too often their work seems to have very little relevance to the lives of their audiences. The improvisational theatres are seldom profound, but they deal particularly with the here and now, with what it is like to be a well-educated middle-class young man or woman living in Chicago or San Francisco at the time of the Great Society.

"Do you rememba," says a parody song-and-dance man at Second City, "when people who wore Levis—*worked?*" The Committee has a sketch about two housewives smoking marijuana (while doing their laundry, if I remember correctly). It is not a very funny sketch, but who else has even tried to reflect onstage the possibility of pot-smoking as part of respectable everyday life—a possibility that is just around the corner, especially in the San Francisco area. When Committee members ask the audience to suggest themes for improvisations, they get replies like "God is alive in Argentina," "Nietzsche is dead," "Pervert," "Vietnam," "The morning after LSD." Spectators and performers are on the same wave-length.

This, of course, has certain drawbacks, the main one being the danger of preaching to the converted. "We try not to go for the easy target," says Bernard Sahlins, one of Second City's producers. But when I was in Chicago in July of 1967, the show included no less than five sketches satirizing clergymen: not a very brave choice of targets for a thoroughly secularized audience. (On the other hand, when a touring Second City company hit Cincinnati recently, one of those sketches, about a TV faith-healer, had the audience almost up in arms.) Still, most of these sketches were pretty funny, and they provided the audience with the extremely pleasant sensation of having its convictions and assumptions reinforced. But isn't this exactly what the Broadway theatre is so bitterly attacked for doing? Perhaps those attacks are not altogether justified; perhaps reaffirmation of the group's convictions and assumptions is one of the important functions the theatre performs. After all, didn't the *Oresteia* do that for the Greeks? Perhaps it's all a question of how valid are the convictions and assumptions being reaffirmed, and with how much intelligence and artistry it is being done. Or perhaps the bitter attacks of the intellectuals against the Broadway theatre are in good part merely the result of alienated anti-bourgeois bigotry. Or perhaps—but I begin to digress.

At any rate, I like to go to the Second City because I feel there that I'm among like-minded people, which, I think, is an indication of its weakness, and at the same time of its strength. This is less true, for me personally, at the Committee, which seems to be somewhat more radical than either Second City or I am. But essentially the same situation prevails there too.

It might be asked at this point, what about the improvisation? Where does that come in? Do the actors make it all up as they go along? No. The material is invented by the performers, but most of what the audience sees at most performances has been conceived and developed in rehearsal, under the leadership of a director. It was improvised once, and perhaps it changes from show to show, but by the time you see it, it has usually been well rehearsed.

Some of it, indeed, may be made up on the spot. Before the intermission, the actors often solicit suggestions from the audience for topics to improvise on. The idea is that the actors will come back from the intermission with ideas for a handful of fire-new routines never tried before. It is a stunt, in a sense: the audience watches the improvising actors to see if they will make fools of themselves, as an audience in a circus watches a trapeze artist to see if he will fall. Can they *really* work up a sketch about Vietnam, perverts, or the death of God in ten minutes?

In many cases, of course, they don't have to. Tonight's audience is very unlikely to be the first ever to be interested in Vietnam, perverts, and the death of God. The company evidently makes sure to have something prepared on several popular topics. I have no doubt that material *is* frequently improvised before the audience's very eyes—I'm sure I've seen it on several occasions—but I also have no doubt that it often isn't. During one intermission at Second City, when the actors were supposed to be off cogitating furiously, I ran into one of them quite at his ease in the bar. I have no objection to this; theatre is the art of seeming, not of being. (To be is often the best way to seem— that is the basis of the Stanislavsky Method, and, in essential respects, of improvisational work as well—but it is not the only way.) And in any case the actors are required to think on their feet in order to get the audience to give them the suggestions they want, and in order, when necessary, to adapt prepared material to make it dovetail with the suggestions offered.

The Second City (Chicago)

The guru, more or less, of the improvisational movement (to the extent that it is a movement) is a stocky Chicagoan named Paul Sills.

Sills's mother, Viola Spolin, wrote the standard text on the subject, which is used in schools and colleges all over the country. Sills himself has founded four theatres, all of them in Chicago. The first of the four grew out of his work at the University of Chicago, and devoted itself to what are now the standard resident-theatre authors: Brecht, Shakespeare, Chekhov, Shaw. After twenty-five productions in two years this early venture closed down, and was succeeded in 1956 by the famous Compass, the first professional improvisational theatre in the country.

David Shepherd, Sills's partner in the Compass, wanted a working-class theatre, a theatre for Gary, Indiana, but Mr. Sills dismisses this as "sentimental." According to Sills, the Compass provided theatre that was "improvised from within the very middle of the community,"* but the community was Hyde Park, the University of Chicago neighborhood. Compass was "in the neighborhood, of the neighborhood, of the moment": a new two-hour show every week. But urban renewal pushed the Compass out of Hyde Park, and it moved to new quarters on the North Side. Here it lost its community roots: "More people from different sections were coming to see it, but fewer of them from each. It had no real base and so consequently it held because of its brilliance."† It grew, in other words, more proficient and less close to its sources: a familiar evolution in American life. It folded in 1956; three years later, Sills, Bernard Sahlins, and Howard Alk started Second City, "and it made it like crazy."

Having made it, Second City did not altogether confine itself to the production of revue sketches. In 1963 it presented, as the second half of its show in Chicago and then in New York, an absurdist one-act play: an ambitious, odd fantasia on psychological, political, and sexual themes. Obviously indebted to Jean Genet ("It is a reverse of Genet," says Sills, "a continuation of the dialogue from a different point of view"), it concerned two out-of-towners out on the town, who arrive at an odd sort of night club searching for a good old-fashioned dirty hot time. Instead of being regaled with a girlie show, however, they are made to act out various fantasies, until one of them finds his kicks in haranguing an imaginary mob (projections and sound effects) on behalf of a Cuban counterrevolution, and the other gets his from romancing Barbara Harris in the midst of what looked like a Salem cigarette advertisement. This extravaganza had its moments. Sometimes it even succeeded in what seemed to be its main purpose: to

---

* "The Celebratory Occasion," an interview with Paul Sills by Charles L. Mee, Jr., in the *Tulane Drama Review*, T22 (Winter, 1964), pp. 167–181. Unfootnoted quotations are, as usual, from personal interview or correspondence.

† "The Celebratory Occasion."

make the spectators ask themselves, "Is *this* what we really want? Is *this* the kind of fantasy-life we lead?" and forcing them to answer "Yes." But it was diffuse, it misused the freedom allowed by the absurdist convention, and ultimately it didn't come off.

In 1967, at Second City in Chicago, I saw a less ambitious, more successful effort: a sketch-situation developed far enough, and with enough delicacy and perception, to make it into a fine short play. It dealt with the efforts of a tense young man who lives on arty North Dearborn Street in Chicago to explain to his massively impermeable small-town family that he is a homosexual, that his roommate is not just his roommate. It was a very funny little play, with the laughs coming organically from the situation and the characters; the elements of caricature only served to emphasize how firmly rooted in reality the whole thing was.

Still, Second City remains essentially a purveyor of topical revue, and this does not satisfy Paul Sills. "Topical revue material," he says, "is nonsense."* And "Second City is a failure. . . . All these things are failures in terms of real organic theatre." But he feels that conventional resident theatres are worse failures: "No amount of pumping big civic repertory theatres into a town is going to make any difference in the cultural level of a town. . . . So-called intellectual theatre will not and cannot work."

"The Theatre," Sills says, "is out to confirm the fact that there is meaning in the world." But meaning to him is "not cognitive. It's not known in the head. It's known all through you. It's Jewish knowing. It's body knowing." The basis of his theatrical method, the primary means he uses to attain meaning, is play, is playing together, as children do in games. "Playing is a communion. . . . Play is freedom. Play is also mutual. You can't play alone." When preparing a show he gives his actors games and tries to get them to play instead of merely to "perform." "I fought my ass off to get them to see each other and play with each other onstage."

Sills believes in a theatre that is connected to the larger community, and yet is a community itself. The Compass and Second City broke through, he thinks, "because at a certain time they [the performers] were more interested in each other than they were in success. This is what it is to have a company . . . it's a brotherhood, a union, a guild." But professional actors are not noted for self-abnegation; they tend to resist playing together. And if they are talented, as many have been at Second City, the brotherhood tends to get broken up by offers from David Merrick or Hollywood. Sills maintains, moreover, that

* "The Celebratory Occasion."

"Culture is something that is created by the people themselves, not something they get fed in through the ear." This is essentially an indictment of the conventional theatre, but it may stand as an indictment of Second City too. And so, while continuing to do a show a year for Second City, Sills founded the Forty-Third Ward Game Theatre to make experiments in playing together with a group of amateurs from the neighborhood.

Over the years, Second City activities have ramified in many directions, under the leadership of Bernard Sahlins, Sheldon Patinkin, and Sills. (All three were born and brought up in Chicago, and went to the University of Chicago. Sahlins, born in 1922, is the oldest; he looks like a cheerful Bernard Malamud. Sills, stocky and ardent, earthy-looking but visionary-minded, was born in 1927. And Patinkin, portly and bearded, dates from 1935.) Their main commercial activity is of course the cabaret, which is run by Sahlins and Patinkin, with Sills as "artistic adviser." As commercial entrepreneurs, these gentlemen also send out touring companies to play road-show houses in large cities and concert dates in college towns. They also mount industrial shows and make industrial movies, and, in partnership with Bell and Howell and a distributor in California, are planning feature films, to be shot entirely in Chicago. (A couple of shorts made by Second City people are already extant.) The Second City Center for the Public Arts is run by Sahlins, Sills, and Patinkin as the umbrella for the non-profit Second City activities; these include the Game Theatre, which has a $34,000 grant from the Community Arts Foundation for "research on the application of theatre games in education and in the theatre." And then there is the Aardvark Cinemathèque, in which Second City has a one-third interest: a distributing company for experimental film-makers (especially those in Chicago), a sixteen millimeter movie house, and a film contest.

And finally there is the repertory company that occupies the Harper Theatre, in the Hyde Park neighborhood on the South Side, the University of Chicago district where Second City originally came from. This new project was begun as "an attempt to use what we've learned over the past ten years in this kind of work [cabaret], in doing plays." It opened in October, 1967, with Norman Mailer's *The Deer Park*, directed by Patinkin, with Sills in the leading role. Patinkin now considers *The Deer Park* a bad choice for a first play, since it tends to alienate people; the production closed almost instantly. The second play at the Harper was *The Cherry Orchard*, directed by Sills; it is still running as I write, and *The Glass Menagerie* is in rehearsal. Meanwhile, however, Sahlins and Patinkin have resigned from the repertory venture, leaving Sills and Byrne Piven in charge; according to Patinkin, its prospects are not bright.

The cabaret, however, continues to flourish. In the summer of 1967 it moved into new quarters in the heart of Old Town, Chicago's Greenwich Village; the move enabled it to more than double its capacity, from 140 to 290 seats. In the new premises as in the old, seating is at small tables and drinks are available. Bernard Sahlins says, "I think the Second City, the revue theatre, the popular theatre, has an on-going function. We're the inheritors of a three-thousand-year-old tradition. . . . We go on to other things because we need change of pace. However, we're always aware of this as the mother lode."

The Committee (San Francisco)

Alan Myerson, the director of the Committee in San Francisco, is a disciple, within limits, of Viola Spolin and Paul Sills. He was not always an improviser; at one time he was going to UCLA and planning to become a lawyer. Influenced, however, by his roommate, "a junkie who opened my eyes to a lot of stuff," he quit UCLA and went to New York to be a writer. After various vicissitudes he went to work for Second City, and at various times directed both the Chicago and the New York company. He quit Second City to go to the West Coast to meet his in-laws, and decided that San Francisco would be a good place for an improvisational cabaret theatre. The Committee opened in April, 1963, and has been going ever since.

Paul Sills of the Second City is interested in improvisation as an end in itself; for him, the medium seems to be the message. For Myerson and the Committee, however, the message is the message, at least part of the time. The Committee is more urgently interested in political satire than Second City is. "Our philosophic position politically," says Myerson,

> is that the society we live in stinks. And we are constantly frustrated by the jarring fact that commenting on the unhappiness that exists is not terribly relevant to any change. We have often performed for benefits of a political nature for groups like SNCC, CORE, the Vietnam Day Committee, and have often participated in their activities following our performances.

In 1965 the entire company joined a sit-in at the Federal Building in San Francisco to try to induce President Johnson to send troops to Selma, Alabama. More recently, the Committee busied itself collecting war toys to drop on the Pentagon. Myerson, like Paul Sills, wants to develop a group that will be part of a larger community; political activity, for the Committee, seems to be the central means to that end.

But Myerson's political commitment does not preclude a lively interest in the implications of improvisation as a theatrical form. Myerson puts down conventional theatre for lack of "penetration to the audience. . . . The audience is never permitted to make a choice." "The theatre," he says, "ought to be a gigantic discothèque at which everybody does some dancing at one time or another." He is interested in involving the audience, in making them *do* something, and within the Committee's cabaret-show framework, he has been conducting experiments toward that end.

On my second visit to San Francisco, in the spring of 1967, the revue was full of before-your-very-eyes improvisations based on suggestions from the audience; many of the resulting sketches were pretty poor. But I got the impression from Myerson that some rather more interesting things had been happening in my absence. Some nights, he said, an actor would come out and begin to discuss Vietnam with the audience. The actor would ask the hawks in the audience to holler, and then the doves, until the building rocked. Some nights the actors would sit down at the tables with the audience and talk with them about things both audience and actors found disturbing. Then, using material that came out of these discussions, they would improvise a "fear-guilt-and-impotence collage." Sometimes an actor would break character at a sensitive point and leave the stage saying, "I can't handle this; I can't take this," and the audience was left to wonder whether it was watching acting or an irruption of real life.

More recently, the Committee, like the Second City, has been interested in transcending the cabaret-show format altogether. In the spring of 1966, Myerson recruited an entirely new group to carry on the revue at Committee headquarters, allowing the old company (which had been at it, with a few changes of personnel, for three years) to turn its attention to a new project. For several months the members of the old company lived on unemployment checks and wrote plays. "We have regular irregular company meetings," Myerson reported, "in which anybody who wants to, reads whatever he thinks the rest of the group could be helpful with." The group provided applause, criticism, and sometimes "the actual improvisation of scenes from the scenario or from what the playwright-actor presents to us. The writer then takes any or all of this material and uses it . . . as he sees fit."

On April Fool's Day, 1967, the Committee opened its second theatre with a production of A *Fool's Play* by Larry Hankin, a member of the company. The play was set in an unnamed medieval country, where a play was being put on that the court jester had written. In the play-within-the-play, somebody was bring tried "for the crime of being guilty"; the trial was punctuated with fairy tales, vaudeville turns, pies in the face, and eight songs ranging from rock 'n' roll to mock-countertenor. The audience (seated at tables, as in the old theatre) was given fruit, flowers, and incense; "they could eat the fruit," says Myerson, "or they could throw the fruit." Actors wandered among them, commenting on the proceedings. According to Myerson, "Almost anybody under twenty-five who saw it loved it a lot," but it was not a popular success. I wish I could have seen it.

Three days after A *Fool's Play* opened, it was joined in repertory by the Committee's production of *Macbird*, which had some improvised material added to it. The show opened with actors circulating among the audience, armed with clipboards and questionnaires about current issues; the results of the poll were read out at intermission. *Macbird* was another box-office failure; when I got to San Francisco in June of 1967, the Committee's production of *America Hurrah* was playing previews at the new theatre. It struck me as a good piece of work, better, if anything, than the original Off-Broadway production; thanks, presumably, to their revue experience, the San Francisco actors were able to bring a bit more personality to their work, and stood out more clearly one from the other. This production was a success and ran until New Year's Eve.

Myerson insists, "I really don't want to be in the business of producing Off-Broadway hits." When I talked to him last spring, he had all sorts of plans (none definite) for his two theatres, between which, he anticipated, the Committee's actors would move freely as need arose. (The old theatre is still devoted to revue.) He was thinking about a new play by a member of the company, a one-man show by another, a production of *Slow Dance on the Killing Ground* by William Hanley, a new production of *Macbird*. He was preparing to start regular programs of theatre games. He was planning some improvisations to be done in various places in the outside world, not in the privacy of a theatre. And he was evolving a large opus of his own, to be called *The Meat Play*, which was intended to be "the story of the end result of paranoia." It was to deal, as I understood it, with a man who tries to get away from his identity; he turns into Albert Meat, and by the end of the play he is simply a hunk of meat. As Meat disintegrates, theatrical form would disintegrate as well. The stage would be in the center of the theatre; there would be four projectors, and each wall would be a screen. Fifty extras in uniform would be harassing the audience, while others "did nice things" to them. There would be a ballad singer, some readings from that day's newspaper, "tightly structured improvisational games," and a real butcher slicing a real side of beef while a trio, taking its rhythm from the butcher, "improvises meat music." Myerson expected, however, that it would take eight months to a year to put *The Meat Play* together, the major problem being "to get the actors and the technicians and me and the musicians so flowing together that when they decided to open like a flower they all open like a flower."

The leaders of the improvisational movement believe that improvisation can have profound and far-reaching effects on the theatre as a whole, and even on life beyond the theatre. Still, the fact remains that what the improvisational theatres have set before their audiences has mostly been revue material, not profoundly different in kind from what has been turned out in the past by sit-down writers. It has not always been first-rate revue material, either; improvisers often seem to find editing their work very difficult. Unless you want to count *America Hurrah*, which had its genesis in a New York improvisatory workshop called the Open Theatre, the improvisational movement has so far produced no single work of any great consequence. (And in the long run I have my doubts about *America Hurrah*.) But improvisation, as practiced by Viola Spolin, her son Paul Sills, and her other disciples, has had, and will continue to have, a significant influence on the theatre at large. "Our theatrical philosophy," Alan Myerson says, "probably depends on the whole concept of involvement: on the stage between the actors, off the stage in the audience, and direct confrontation between actors and audience." A number of signs—the resurgence of "happenings," for instance, and the tremendous success of *Marat/Sade*—indicate that we are ready and eager for a redefinition of the relationship between actors and audience. In this context, men like Sills and Myerson would seem to have a great deal to offer.

APPENDIX B

The American Place Theatre (New York City)

I was of two minds as to whether the American Place Theatre should be included in this book. It is often classified as an off-Broadway house. It has a permanent management and permanent premises, but no resident director and no permanent company. And since tickets are sold by subscription only, and only 5,500 subscriptions are available every season, it might be argued that the American Place is not a public theatre at all. Unlike most resident theatres, however, this theatre does stand for something in particular. Its official statement says:

> The American Place Theatre exists to foster good writing for the theatre. It hopes to accomplish this by providing a place, a staff, and a broad program of practical work to American writers of stature: our poets, novelists, and philosophers who wish to use the dramatic form, and to serious new playwrights.

The American Place presents only new American plays. *Variety** describes its procedure as follows: "Plays are given unstaged readings, then staged ones, which are paralleled by technical confabs designed to show the aspiring playwright what the theatre is and requires (as opposed to other writing disciplines). Most important, if the revised script merits a full-scale production, it gets it. An audience is guaranteed by subscription, and there is no commercial pressure." (Of course, if a script comes in that is ready for a public showing as it stands, it is given a full production without the intermediate steps.) By these means the American Place Theatre has perhaps done more for

* September 14, 1966.

371

American playwriting than any other single American theatre currently in existence. (This, however, is not in itself high praise.)

The American Place Theatre was founded in 1964 by the Reverend Sidney Lanier, at that time the minister of St. Clement's Church on West Forty-sixth Street. Mr. Lanier is still the president of the American Place; he has stepped down as minister, but the theatre still makes its home at St. Clement's. It has never had to worry too much about money; to date it has been allotted $992,000 in grants by the Ford and Rockefeller Foundations alone. It can afford to hire good directors and actors and it has generally done so; standards of production, in my experience, have been well above the resident-theatre norm.

Although it has eschewed big-name actors and directors, its authors comprise quite a stellar assemblage. Among them have been Robert Lowell, Paul Goodman, May Swenson, and Bruce Jay Friedman, who have received full productions, and George P. Elliott, John O. Killens, Philip Roth, and Robert Penn Warren, who have been working with the theatre *in camera*. "The selection of writers," says an American Place handout, "is not confined to any group, style, or point of view. The choice is eclectic, the primary factor being: is the voice worth hearing on the stage?" This would appear to be true; in the spring of 1967 the American Place produced *La Turista* by Sam Shepard, a twenty-three-year-old Artaudian wild man from the Café La Mama, and followed it with *Posterity for Sale* by Niccolò Tucci, who writes for the *New Yorker* and is nobody's wild man.

In spite of the care and expertise that seem to go into all the productions, I have spent some pretty dreary evenings at the American Place. That is only to be expected; there are just not many good new American plays to be had, and not all the money in the Ford Foundation's till will cure that condition very quickly, if ever. The wonder is that this theatre has done as well as it has. Its first production is probably still its most significant one: Robert Lowell's double bill of *My Kinsman, Major Molineux*, based on a story by Nathaniel Hawthorne, and—a more ambitious work—*Benito Cereno*, based on Herman Melville's novella. The two plays comprise two-thirds of a trilogy which Mr. Lowell has entitled *The Old Glory*. Robert Brustein, who praised this production as heralding a "renewal" of the American theatre, is better able than I to describe Mr. Lowell's plays:

The first and more difficult of the two plays is an eerie parable of the American Revolution, experienced, as in a nightmare, by a Deerfield youth and his twelve-year-old brother. Arriving in Boston, the "city of the dead," to seek their kinsman, Major Molineux (a "lobsterback" who symbolizes the British forces in continental America), the two innocents watch in astonished horror as the Revolution is born out of indecision, hatred, resentment, and self-interest. . . .

. . . Melville's story [*Benito Cereno*] concerns the shadow cast over a civilized mind by the primitive darkness: Lowell heightens this theme, examining along the way the ambiguous American attitude toward slavery and servitude. The plot concerns the visit of the Yankee merchant captain, Amasa Delano—a typically complacent, chauvinistic, wry, and generous American—to a mysterious slave ship anchored off South America, and captained by a noble Spaniard named Benito Cereno. The ship is a shambles, and the slaves are roaming freely about the deck. When Delano's curiosity and disapproval are aroused, Cereno—dogged and prompted always by his officious, unctuous, smiling slave, Babu—tells a halting, semi-hysterical story of calms, disease, and the loss of most of his crew. . . . A series of enigmatic rituals and ceremonies are enacted before [Delano] . . . and he begins to realize that, for all his belief in American ideals of freedom, in his heart he wants slaves. At last, he learns that Cereno is actually a prisoner on his own ship, which the revolting slaves have captured, murdering most of the crew. And when Babu unmasks himself as the leader of the rebels, forcing Delano's mate to kiss the lips of a ghastly skeleton and demanding that Delano sail the ship back to Africa, the Yankee shoots him down, crying "This is your future!" The final confrontation of Babu and Delano looks forward to the confrontation of black and white in modern America . . .*

I do not admire *Benito Cereno* as much as Mr. Brustein does (I find it somewhat uneconomical and finespun), but it is clearly a work of considerable stature. And though I only saw the American Place production, directed by Jonathan Miller, in its television version (on NET), I can testify that it was most beautifully acted by Lester Rawlins as Delano, Frank Langella as Cereno, and Roscoe Lee Browne as Babu.

After its American Place engagement, *The Old Glory* had a short run at a regular Off-Broadway house; but financially the most successful American Place production to date has been *Hogan's Goat*, by a Harvard professor and poet named William Alfred, which ran off-Broadway for a year and a half. *Hogan's Goat* was a real oddity: an

* *Seasons of Discontent*, pp. 256–258.

attempt to write a full-fledged blank verse tragedy about politics among the Brooklyn Irish in 1890 or thereabouts. It did not come off; the hero, who was supposed to be tragic, was merely annoying in his arrogant egotism. But the old-fashioned plot-twists were so ingenious, and the Brooklyn Irish local color so irresistibly lively, that the play was entertaining all the same. The American Place may have done other plays as good as these; my travels have prevented me from seeing more than a fraction of its work. But, in any case, two such plays as this in only three seasons comprise an accomplishment of some significance. And the full achievement of the American Place will not be seen until the *next* play by each of its writers is produced; only this will show how much they have been stimulated, and how much they have learned.

APPENDIX C

The Negro Ensemble Company (New York City)

A couple of years ago, a pair of short plays by Douglas Turner Ward, entitled *Happy Ending* and *Day of Absence*, had a successful run off-Broadway. They were produced by Robert Hooks, who had not then become a television star; Mr. Hooks and Mr. Ward both appeared in the all-Negro cast. Out of this production grew, with the help of a $434,000 grant from the Ford Foundation, a new resident professional theatre and school called the Negro Ensemble Company. Mr. Ward is its "Artistic Director," Mr. Hooks its "Executive Director"; its "Administrative Director" is Gerald S. Krone (a white man) who managed the production of *Happy Ending* and *Day of Absence*. Six members of its acting company were in *Day of Absence*, in addition to Mr. Ward and Mr. Hooks. And the Negro Ensemble Company has its headquarters at the Saint Mark's Playhouse on Second Avenue, where *Happy Ending* and *Day of Absence* were presented.

The new organization offers training in acting, dance, voice, theatre crafts, and theatre administration to about a hundred and eighty students; programs for playwrights and directors are in the process of formation. The professional acting company numbers thirteen, all Negro, all on one-year contracts; its first season, offering a series of four plays to the general public both Negro and white, began officially on January 2, 1968.

The company's first production was the American première of *Song of the Lusitanian Bogey* by Peter Weiss, the German-Swedish dramatist who wrote the *Marat/Sade*. The bogey in question turned out to be a huge monster made out of junk, representing the evils of colonialism; the play, which I saw at a preview, turned out to be a repetitive, simplistic, and tedious piece of expressionistic agitprop.

There is no plot, only a collage of short scenes depicting various forms of colonial exploitation in the Portuguese colonies of Angola and Mozambique, replete with all the abundant clichés that the subject affords. Much of it is couched in execrable verse: "On every hand their rich complex traditions/Were wiped out by invading penal expeditions," "Here is the reason, and it is stark,/Why the African continent is labelled 'dark,' " and—my favorite—"After all, a crucifix/ Without this he would be nix." The prose is better, being merely undistinguished: "Deceived, exploited, hungering, by your labor you have laid the foundation for Europe's wealth," "Fourteen hours a day I worked on the cotton plantation," "I must go home now, one of my children is sick." Lee Baxandall was the translator; I am not equipped to say exactly how the credit should be apportioned between him and Herr Weiss, but clearly there is plenty for both.

Michael A. Schultz's staging, with dance direction by Louis Johnson, was vigorous, inventive, apposite, and fluid. Coleridge-Taylor Perkinson provided an eclectic jazz score, played by an onstage four-man band; much of the text was sung, which helped markedly in easing the tedium. The actors appeared to be a capable group, though one or two of them could use a good deal of work on their diction. (I see no reason why a Negro company should not perform in Negro dialect, but on some happier occasion than this, I might perhaps want to be able to make out all the words.)

Given some more interesting material to work on, the Negro Ensemble Company may turn out to have a significant contribution to make to the theatrical scene at large; it can hardly help but have a more clearly-defined identity than most American theatre companies. The other productions it has announced for its first season are *Summer of the Seventeenth Doll* (Ray Lawler's Australian play about migratory sugar-cane-cutters, slightly adapted), *Kongi's Harvest* by the Nigerian playwright Wole Soyinka, and *Daddy Goodness*, adapted by Richard Wright from a French play by Louis Sapin. It strikes me as a sensible policy for the Negro Ensemble Company to use material by white authors that it finds relevant, or can make relevant, to Negro concerns; and to present three American premières in the course of a four-play inaugural season would seem to reflect a commendable willingness to take chances.

INDEX

INDEX

(Play titles are listed under their authors' names; musical comedies and reviews are listed under their titles. See the Table of Contents for theatres.)